# A VIEW OF
## VICTORIAN LITERATURE

# A VIEW OF VICTORIAN LITERATURE

*by*

Geoffrey Tillotson

CLARENDON PRESS · OXFORD

*Oxford University Press, Walton Street, Oxford* OX2 6DP

OXFORD  LONDON  GLASGOW  NEW YORK
TORONTO  MELBOURNE  WELLINGTON  CAPE TOWN
IBADAN  NAIROBI  DAR ES SALAAM  LUSAKA  KUALA LUMPUR
SINGAPORE  JAKARTA  HONG KONG  TOKYO
DELHI  BOMBAY  CALCUTTA  MADRAS  KARACHI

© *Oxford University Press 1978*

**British Library Cataloguing in Publication Data**

Tillotson, Geoffrey
  A view of Victorian literature.
  1. English literature—19th century—History
  and criticism
  I. Title
  820'.9'008    PR461    77–30178

ISBN 0–19–812044–3

*Filmset and printed Offset Litho in Great Britain by
Cox & Wyman Ltd, London, Fakenham and Reading*

# PREFACE

WHEN Geoffrey Tillotson died in October 1969 he left unpublished a substantial work on Victorian literature. This book represents it as faithfully as is compatible with the need for abridgement and minor revision, and its separation from the series for which it was originally designed.

It had been planned as the first of two volumes on the mid-nineteenth century (1832–80) in the Oxford History of English Literature, and early in 1969 had been submitted, partly in draft form, to the general editors. The manuscript included (1) a very long introduction appropriate to both volumes, (2) nine chapters, sometimes interconnected but each centred on a major author, (3) bibliographies.[1] Since the Press and editors had only recently consented to two volumes instead of one, the exact line of division was not yet finally decided; the work as submitted was much too long for a single volume; and other questions of revision needed to be considered. But when, in April, Geoffrey Tillotson had unexpectedly to undergo a severe operation, all discussion was by mutual agreement deferred in the expectation of his recovery; an expectation not groundless, but unfulfilled.

In 1970 the Delegates of the Press reached the inescapable conclusion that the work, too incomplete for the series, yet with too clearly defined an approach to be completed by any other hand, could no longer form part of the Oxford History. But they wished it to appear as an independent book, and asked me to revise and prepare it for publication. This I undertook to do, sustained by long

[1] These were subsequently passed to other O.H.E.L. editors.

familiarity with the work through most of its phases, and by the author's often expressed assumption, while his writing was in progress, that we would revise it together before publication. Though I had read several of the chapters in some form, I had not seen the whole manuscript in its latest state until the Press returned it to me. There were incidental problems, partly unforeseen: the inclusion of very long quoted passages from which the most relevant extracts had not yet been selected; a few gaps, where an unspecified quotation was to be 'supplied later'; and a frequent absence of references (which the rules of the Oxford History exclude) for short quotations and allusions, sometimes remote. This part of the revision merely took time, and was in other ways rewarding. Decisions and procedures of abridgement and compression were more exacting, and shadowed with regret for parts which had to be left out so as to bring the whole within reasonable compass. It has seemed preferable sometimes to sacrifice a whole section (such as the account of travel-literature) and preserve unity and continuity elsewhere; and one of the nine 'author' chapters I eventually decided to omit. The voice of Newman is often heard in other parts of the book, and the chapter on him would, I believe, have been recast if the author had lived to read the twelve volumes of letters and diaries published since 1968.

Chapters on all the other single authors intended for the first volume are here, and everything in their text is Geoffrey Tillotson's writing, except for linking sentences supplied to fill gaps caused by occasional omission and rearrangement. Though all have been shortened, the loss is nowhere substantial. Of the Introduction, much more had to be omitted. Some of its material belonged rather to the plan of an Oxford History: along with facts and dates defining the limits of the period, there were, for example, accounts of methods of publication; of the reading public and its distinction of class, education, age and sex; of the

importance of women writers; and of what he liked to
call 'the melting-pot' of ideas. Much of this material is
available elsewhere, though here given an individual
treatment and unusual illustration. (The regard paid to
women, he noted, was 'neatly evinced' when John Stuart
Mill, revising in 1850 his 1843 *System of Logic*, added 'and
Mary' to the typical 'John, Peter, George').

The Introduction is represented first by a selection (pp.
1–22), and then, more extensively, by what is now Chapter 1 ('Earnestness'). This chapter, while particularly
relevant to the first half of the period, includes ideas and
illustrations central to his 'view' of the whole mid-
century.

The authors chosen for this volume belong to the 'first
generation' of Victorian writers; all, except Carlyle, were
born in the remarkable decade 1809–18. If dates of publication had been taken as the dividing line, one would
have expected to find Clough and Arnold among them;
but their influence was rightly seen as greatest in the latter
half of the period. Where an author's work extended into
the 1880s (as with Trollope, Tennyson, and Browning)
this is not excluded; but it may be worth noting that the
completed *Idylls of the King* would have figured in the
second volume along with Victorian 'medievalism' and
in relation to Rossetti and Morris. Generally, there is less
of a chronological approach than might be expected in a
literary history. This was not from disregard: 'a sequence
of dates', the author wrote in an omitted passage of his
Introduction, 'forms the background of all human
studies', and he was justified in claiming to have become
'intimately aware of chronology—of this half century as
comprising five decades, fifty distinct years with twelve
months in each'. Behind this book and its predecessors
lies what he called 'a long historical enquiry', evident in
his range of reference, and in his understanding of the
past, including earlier centuries. At the heart of his
approach is the distinction he made when writing of

Walter Pater, whose work he admired, but whose interest in the past, he said, was

> less that of a scholar trying to understand it than of an aesthete rifling it for his own purposes... I myself have tried to see the object not—as Arnold and Pater counselled—as in itself it really is, but as in itself it really was.

Much had been done towards the second volume, but only a few chapters drafted. For some, including Arnold and Pater, the loss is partly compensated by Geoffrey Tillotson's previously published essays and articles; and two long reviews at least indicate the line he would have taken on Swinburne. A greater loss is his chapter on Ruskin—as can be imagined by the students in his graduate seminars in the early 1960s, and by me, from many conversations and the vivid memory of the last summer of his life. At that time, he turned from the earlier and hitherto best-loved works on art and landscape, to read the whole of *Fors Clavigera* and to re-read *The Crown of Wild Olive*, which he now saw as the core and culmination of Ruskin's message to his own time and ours.

All parts of the present book are published for the first time. The chapter on Thackeray repeats nothing from the author's full-length study first published in 1954; but it is affected by his work on the *Critical Heritage* volume of 1967—as is the Charlotte Brontë chapter by his posthumously published introduction to *Villette* for the American Riverside series. An unpublished introduction to *Esmond* is printed as an Appendix; marginal notes on the typescript show that it was originally meant to be 'used' in the Thackeray chapter, which as it stands includes little on this novel.

Throughout, the footnotes are mostly my additions; the great majority are such references as I thought necessary; others contain matter summarized from what was once in the text, and a very few are 'editorial'. In a few places (as on pp. 217, 374) it seemed right to supplement the text by a reference to later-published work. But obviously there is not, and ought not to be, any attempt to bring the book as a whole up to date. None of it was written later than the winter of 1968–9. It remains Geoffrey Tillotson's book.

He left no complete record of the obligations he had incurred during many years' work. But I have no doubt that he wished to put in the forefront his thanks to the young scholars who were in turn his research assistants at Birkbeck College: Carol Landon, Michael Slater, Anthony Burton, and Brian Jenkins, of whom he wrote, 'they have worked as hard and devotedly as the earnest Victorians themselves'. To Birkbeck College in the University of London he owed much gratitude: to successive Masters, colleagues within and outside the Department of English, librarians and secretaries, and most of all, to his undergraduate and graduate students through twenty-four years. Next to his writing, and apart from family and friends, his deepest attachment was to Birkbeck. For my own part, I am grateful to the College for its generous provision of time and space when I was sorting and transferring papers and books in 1970, and to Brian Jenkins for his continued assistance. Thanks are also due to many libraries, especially the Library of the British Museum, the University of London, and the London Library.

Certain chapters were read in an earlier form by our friends W. J. Bate and Gordon Haight, and by the late Bonamy Dobree in his capacity as general editor. I wish also to thank Professor Norman Davis, the other general editor, for the time and care he gave to reading the manuscript in 1969; the Oxford University Press, for advice and encouragement; and above all, the adviser who read the entire work in both its original and present form and to whose discerning and constructive comments I am much indebted. The typing of a complicated manuscript was undertaken by Nina Burgis, who also helped with the finding and checking of references. Finally, I would record my gratitude to three of our oldest friends: Harold Jenkins, Mary Lascelles, and James Sutherland.

KATHLEEN TILLOTSON

*December 1976*

# CONTENTS

# INTRODUCTION

THE NINETEENTH seems to have been the first century that saw itself as having a number. 'The nineteenth century (I believe that's the phrase)', says Vivian Grey's father in Disraeli's novel.[1] Constantly used in a variety of tones ('this nineteenth century of ours', even 'this so-called nineteenth century'), it had become by 1877 the title of a periodical, and in the writings of Ruskin a term of abuse.

Carlyle was right when he asserted in 1831 that 'Never since the beginning of Time was there ... so intensely self-conscious a society'.[2] Moreover, never had there been an age more given to looking back, and therefore more conscious of change. Writers great and small paused, on occasion, to describe the present, and often to compare it with a remembered past: the past of a generation before, or a decade, or of only a year or two. Each of their remarks represents a fragment of literary history; pieced together and annotated, they would make a lively account of the period, and might surprise readers versed in the textbooks.

Here, first, is a selection of contemporary observations bearing on the state of poetry in 1840–70.

In 1841 a writer in *Tait's Magazine* noted how 'spasmodic in their affections' were the British nation: this

---

[1] *Vivian Grey* (1826), Ch. ix. Tennyson in 1846 described some comments on Scripture as 'very clever and full of a noble 19th century-ism (if you will admit such a word)' (Letter to Mary Howitt; *Alfred Lord Tennyson, a Memoir by his Son*, 1897, I. 238).
[2] 'Characteristics', *Edinburgh Review* (Dec. 1831).

winter a 'strenuous determination to be funny' was 'manifested on all sides by the literary world', whereas yesterday they were weeping over Byron.

Henry Taylor in 1843 contrasted the 'nascent poetical spirit of the last few years' with that of twenty years ago; in place of 'sentimental passion' there were now 'higher moods and worthier endeavours', but a tendency to 'obscurity, subtlety, and forced thinking'.[1]

A new edition of Campbell's *Specimens of the British Poets* in 1842 occasioned a comparison, in the March number of *Fraser's Magazine,* with the state of poetry on the first appearance of this collection in 1820, when Byron was 'lord of the ascendant': now 'the spell is broken, though its influence is not departed'. Wordsworth, then 'lost in the greater light of Byron', is 'now rapidly ascending the scale, and cannot advance much higher. Extensive popularity he can never obtain...' No younger poet is mentioned (Tennyson's two volumes had yet to appear) and 'many years must elapse before another such compilation can present similar attractions'. Looking back at this period from 1855 Patmore (reviewing *Maud* in the *Edinburgh Review*), remarked that Tennyson had made his reputation 'after the singular lull in the groves of Parnassus' which succeeded the first twenty years of the century.

In 1853 Charles Kingsley made an unexpected contrast between the 'new poetry' of the day and the further past:

What! Do you wish, asks some one, a little contemptuously, to measure the great growing nineteenth century by the thumb-rule of Alexander Pope? No. But to measure the men who write in the nineteenth century by a man who wrote in the eighteenth; to measure their advantages with his: and then, if possible, to make them ashamed of their unmanliness.

What is wanting is courage, faith, and common sense; and in expression, terseness and clearness. Kingsley

[1] *Quarterly Review* (May 1843).

commends to the young poets of the fifties as models two more recent examples, Hood's 'Song of the Shirt' and 'Bridge of Sighs': there they will find

no taint of this new poetic diction into which we have now fallen, after all our abuse of the far more manly and sincere 'poetic diction' of the eighteenth century; ... no loitering by the way to argue and moralise, and grumble at Providence, and show off the author's own genius and sensibility; [but] two real works of art, earnest, melodious, self-forgetful, knowing clearly what they want to say, and saying it in the shortest, the simplest, the calmest, the most finished words.[1]

In 1858 an *Edinburgh* reviewer noted the present taste for 'a calm and subdued expression ... familiar emotions, the drama of domestic life' in contrast with the poetry of twenty-five years ago, 'appealing violently to the imagination or the passions'.

The *Westminster*, reviewing the first instalment of *The Ring and the Book* in 1869, recalled hearing in 1860 'a well-known author and editor'[2] declare that he had never read a word of Browning, 'And the declaration struck nobody present as at all surprising. The exception, then, was to have read him'; now, it would be a confession of ignorance. 'But the British public at large still know no more about Mr. Browning than they did about Mill before he became member for Westminster. "The Ring and the Book" will, however, we venture to say, introduce Mr. Browning to the British public.'

In 1870 *Blackwood's Magazine* remarked that 'a generation ago ... poetry on the secondary level was ... discountenanced by all the world'; they had 'leisure enough only for the best'. Yet, what to this reviewer is

---

[1] 'Alexander Smith and Alexander Pope', *Fraser's Magazine* (Oct. 1853); collected in *Literary and General Essays* (1880).
[2] Possibly Froude, who edited *Fraser's* in the sixties, and in 1862 told a contributor that 'he knew very little of Browning' (W. H. Dunn, *James Anthony Froude*, 1963, p. 327).

'simply unintelligible', Mr. Rossetti's poems have reached a third edition in a month or two. This change 'puzzles the critic, who has been accustomed to say, and to hear it said, that the present age is not an age for poetry'.

But it was generally thought to be an age for the novel—'the form', it was predicted in 1849, 'in which much of the poetry of a coming time will be written'.[1] Two instances from the year 1855 point to the changed expectations that readers now brought to the novel: the first from *The Times* review of *The Newcomes*,[2] distinguishing the society depicted in the modern novel from that of Fielding and Richardson:

Society now-a-days is more large and complex, and includes a greater variety of elements. It is no longer exclusively fashionable, but political, religious, mercantile, professional, literary, artistic, and with an outlying fringe of a Bohemian tendency which carries it to the verge of pure undisciplined nature. As these various circles combine and intersect, the ideas and sentiments derived from their different centres act and react upon each other. Our social, like our solar system admits of remote influences which require an enlarged survey ... The old novel is no more adequate to present a picture of life now-a-days than the old orrery to show us our planetary relations.

Emily Winkworth in a letter of the same year thought *Westward Ho!* 'glorious'—but 'the tale is too outward to suit one's modern taste;—no, not too outward; it can't have *too much* on that side, but it has too little of the inward. And though every one else since Walter Scott may push the latter too far and be morbid, still it *is* worth its true weight for all that.'[3]

Such readers had been well prepared by Thackeray and Charlotte Brontë for the coming of George Eliot.

[1] *Prospective Review* (1849), p. 37.
[2] 29 Aug. 1855; probably by Samuel Lucas.
[3] *Memorials of Two Sisters*, ed. M. J. Shaen (1908), pp. 128–9.

Looking into people brought an increased sense for both novelists and poets of the complexity of human minds and morals. Carlyle, like Pope, felt 'the strong antipathy of good to bad', and mocked at those who 'mashed up Right and Wrong into a kind of patent treacle'.[1] But the plain and ancient fact that the people labelled bad are always partly good, and not wholly responsible for their badness, was now kept well in view; to Browning's Bishop Blougram malefactors were seen no longer as types but mixed individuals; there were 'a thousand diamond weights between'. Wordsworth had already held up Rob Roy, the arch-despoiler, as a popular hero; Trollope created in Mr. Scarborough a sort of Rob Roy contemptuous of lawyers, primogeniture, entails, and the law itself—even the law of marriage. He is not condemned by Trollope, who allows Mr. Merton's posthumous appraisal to rest as the last word:

'The poor old boy has gone at last, and in spite of all his faults I feel as though I had lost an old friend. To me he has been most kind, and did I not know of all his sins I should say that he had been always loyal and always charitable. . . . One cannot make an apology for him without being ready to throw all truth and all morality to the dogs. But if you can imagine for yourself a state of things in which neither truth nor morality shall be thought essential, then old Mr. Scarborough would be your hero. He was the bravest man I ever knew. He was ready to look all opposition in the face, and prepared to bear it down. And whatever he did he did with the view of accomplishing what he thought to be right for other people.'[2]

Heredity and circumstance were given more weight in extenuation of faults; also the relation of body and mind. Thackeray in his review of Fielding, noting his 'very loose morals' in his youth, says 'A number of errors must be attributed to his excessive and boisterous health'.[3]

[1] See p. 59.
[2] *Mr. Scarborough's Family* (1883), Ch. lviii.
[3] *The Times* (2 Sept. 1840).

Trabb's boy in *Great Expectations* guides Pip's rescuers to where Orlick holds him captive, but would have been disappointed if he had known that Pip was thereby saved from being thrown into the lime kiln. 'Not that Trapp's boy was of a malignant nature, but that he had too much spare vivacity, and that it was in his constitution to want variety and excitement at anybody's expense.'[1] Environment is blamed for at least some of Adolphus Crosbie's perfidy:

Crosbie, as soon as he was alone in his chamber, sat himself down in his arm-chair, and went to work striving to make up his mind as to his future conduct. ... The atmosphere of Courcy Castle had been at work upon him for the last week past. And every word that he had heard, and every word that he had spoken, had tended to destroy all that was good and true within him, and to foster all that was selfish and false.[2]

What cannot be excused can still be explained; but as a character says in the pointedly entitled *Can You Forgive Her?* 'There are things which happen in a day which it would take a lifetime to explain'.[3] Addressing his readers in *Castle Richmond*, Trollope wonders how he can 'succeed in exciting their sympathy' for the Molletts (the blackmailing ex-husband of Lady Fitzgerald and his wife). 'And yet why not? If we are to sympathise only with the good, or worse still, only with the graceful, how little will there be in our character that is better than terrestrial? The Molletts also were human, and had strings to their hearts.'[4]

Indeed we are much beholden to mid-century novelists for the humanizing of morality.

Much was said of the questioning attitude of the time

---

[1] Ch. liii.
[2] *The Small House at Allington*, Ch. xxiii.
[3] Ch. xxxvi.                    [4] Ch. xxiii.

and the need for fresh thinking on every subject. Carlyle's 'Characteristics' might again serve as a text:

Our whole relations to the Universe and to our fellow-man have become an Inquiry, a Doubt; nothing will go of its own accord, and do its function quietly; but all things must be probed into, the whole working of man's world be anatomically studied.[1]

The process was continuous and accumulative, so that W. Y. Sellar, reviewing the *Poems and Prose Remains* of Arthur Hugh Clough in 1869 and noting the 'tentative and gradual process' by which these had been published since his death, saw him as

in a very literal sense before his age. His point of view and habit of mind are less singular in England in the year 1869 than they were in 1859, and much less than they were in 1849. We are growing year by year more introspective and self-conscious ... more unreserved and unveiled in our expressions ... more sceptical in the proper sense of the word, losing faith and confidence ... gaining in impartiality and comprehensiveness of sympathy. In each of these respects, Clough, if he were still alive would find himself gradually more and more at home in a changing world.[2]

The kind of attitude Sellar had in mind is represented by Arnold's second Oxford lecture *On Translating Homer* (1861), where he sets up as an ideal for English literature what has long been the main effort of French and German—'a *critical* effort; the endeavour, in all branches of knowledge—theology, philosophy, history, art, science—to see the object as in itself it really is', and by his Preface to *Essays in Criticism* (1865). Here Arnold disclaims the wish 'to dispute on behalf of any opinion, even [his] own, very obstinately', believing that

[1] 'Inquirer' was a common pseudonym, and the *Inquirer* a title used by periodicals.
[2] *Westminster Review* (Oct. 1869).

To try and approach Truth on one side after another, not to strive or cry, not to persist in pressing forward, on any one side, with violence and self-will,—it is only thus, it seems to me, that mortals may hope to gain any vision of the mysterious Goddess, whom we shall never see except in outline, but only thus even in outline.[1]

Or, as he wrote ten years after Sellar's summary: 'There is not a creed which is not shaken, not an accredited dogma which is not shown to be questionable, not a received tradition which does not threaten to dissolve.'[2] But if Arnold at this date responded cheerfully (even jauntily) and thought this imminent dissolution made poetry 'an ever surer and surer stay', he had as a young man felt the challenges as keenly as any one, and showed it with overwhelming poignancy in such poems as 'Dover Beach'.

Not only creeds and dogmas were shaken and threatening to dissolve; the spirit of questioning had effects on the form of literature, as literature consists of what had previously been called 'kinds'. The situation was not quite so simple as Kingsley suggested when he said that a 'poetry of doubt' could 'never possess clear and sound form'; that 'the highest forms of verse', such as 'tragedy, epic, the ballad' required 'a groundwork of consistent self-coherent belief'.[3] But it was felt that, when so much was new, literary forms should be new also; whereas it had been often assumed that a number of fixed forms existed to be filled repeatedly, writers now preferred the content of a work to will, as it were, a form appropriate to it and

[1] Also in 1865, Catherine Winkworth wrote of 'the extreme liberal party within the Church' and their 'determination . . . to follow Truth *wherever* she may lead them. But the difficulty is that Truth does not seem to lead them anywhere in particular' (*Memorials of Two Sisters*, p. 239).
[2] Preface to *The Hundred Greatest Men* (1879); repeated in 'The Study of Poetry' (1880).
[3] 'Alexander Smith and Alexander Pope'.

to it alone. After Coleridge, the analogy was often drawn between a literary work and a plant grown out of the individual seed in accordance with its individual conditions—the writer, we may suppose, acting as the discreet gardener. The Spasmodic poets—'Festus' Bailey, Alexander Smith, and Sydney Dobell—had taken the new principle so much to heart that they had almost banished the gardener. Thomas McNicoll described Smith's *Life-Drama* and Dobell's *Balder* as 'having the length of an epic, the form of a drama, and the nature of a rhapsody';[1] and the 'modern critic' sternly admonished by Arnold in his 1853 Preface held that 'perhaps the highest thing' that could be attempted in poetry was 'a true allegory of the state of one's own mind in a representative history'.[2] Others too saw the new freedom as leading too easily to mere vagrancy and fragmentariness. Lewes (speaking of prose as well as verse) complained in 1845 that 'crudeness is avowed as if it were a merit . . . the author seems to pique himself on his dashing off-hand carelessness, and christens his work "Sketches of Philosophy;" "Hints to Chemists;" or "Poetical Fragments"'.[3] In Masson's 1860 article on 'Three Vices of Current Literature', the first was the 'slipshod';[4] Arnold in the 'Epilogue to Lessing's Laocoon' spoke of 'our day of haste, half-work, and disarray'; Swinburne, turning temporarily against Browning in the early sixties, attacked him as representing 'the Chaotic School';[5] Tennyson saw in Mrs. Browning's *Aurora Leigh*, as in Dobell's *Balder*, the 'organizable lymph' of poetry rather

---

[1] *Essays on English Literature* (1861), p. 184 (from *London Quarterly Review*, 1854).
[2] *North British Review*, Aug. 1853 (Arnold believed the writer was J. M. Ludlow).
[3] *Hood's Magazine* (Apr. 1845).
[4] *Macmillan's Magazine* (May 1860).
[5] In an essay first published in *New Writings of Swinburne*, ed. C. Y. Lang (Syracuse, 1964).

than 'compacted and vertebrate poems'.[1] All these poet–
critics had some right to criticize, being themselves both
formalists and adventurers; and by 1870 two great long
poems of the age, *The Ring and the Book* and *Idylls of the
King*, had justified their 'appropriate form'.

Carlyle, writing to William Allingham with advice on
his proposed studies in history, emphasized the need of
finding a centre:

the subject growing more luminous at every step, you will see
more and more where the real centre of it lies for you, and how
you are to strive towards that. For every subject, and History
above all others, has what we call a different 'centre' for every
different man; and it is of great importance that every man
should candidly listen to the monitions of his own mind in
regard to what *is* really interesting and nutritive to him as an
individual, and *try* all foreign monitions, with patience, with
modesty yet with courage, and silently reject them if they do
not fit with this.[2]

One such 'centre' in the 'history' of the mid–century is
the new conception of the man of letters.

In his fifth lecture on *Heroes and Hero-Worship* (1840)
Carlyle introduced 'the Hero as Man of Letters' as a new
and 'very singular phenomenon', in contrast to other
forms of heroism which 'belong to the old ages'. He is
'our most important modern person'; and this lecture
accordingly is concerned with the recent past, the present, and the possible future. Here, on the authority of
Fichte[3]—whose creed in so many ways he had made his
own—Carlyle proclaims 'Men of Letters as a perpetual

[1] F. T. Palgrave, in *Tennyson, a Memoir*, II. 506.
[2] *Letters to William Allingham* (1911), p. 131 (letter of 4 Sept. 1850).
[3] In *Das Wesen des Gelehrten* (1805); compare Carlyle's much earlier and
more straightforwardly descriptive account in 'The State of German
Literature', *Edinburgh Review* (Oct. 1827).

Priesthood' of the 'Divine Idea of the World': 'In the true Literary Man there is thus ever, acknowledged or not by the world, a sacredness; he is the light of the world; the world's Priest;—guiding it, like a sacred Pillar of Fire, in its dark pilgrimage through the waste of Time.' As elsewhere in Carlyle's writings, the divine and heroic are expressed in images of fire and lightning: 'the Great Man was always as lightning out of Heaven; the rest of men waited for him like fuel, and then they too would flame;'[1] he is concerned always to emphasize the enkindling, illuminating effect.

But such sacred fire belongs only to 'the *true* Literary Man' discriminated 'with sharp zeal' by Fichte, and still more sharply by Carlyle, from 'multitudes of the false unheroic'. In this lecture he had no perfect example to put forward; from what would have been his 'chosen specimen', Goethe, he was debarred, in addressing a general audience in 1840, by their ignorance of his work. His imperfect examples, Johnson and Burns (and, more doubtfully, Rousseau), are shown as struggling 'in far inferior circumstances' to Goethe's, but with the heroic virtue of sincerity; not 'words and formulas', but 'truths and facts'; 'wild, wrestling naked with the truth of things'. (Sympathy here verges unconsciously on self-portraiture; to our eyes it is Carlyle himself in 1840 who is the modern 'hero'—his name from this time 'running like wildfire through the British Islands'.[2])

One element in the 'circumstances' that trammel the hero as man of letters Carlyle saw as 'the wild welter of a chaos that is called Literary Life'; in suggesting the need for some 'Organisation of Men of Letters', he raised issues which were much discussed in the following

[1] End of Lecture II, 'The Hero as Prophet'. In the opening lectures, using the same image, he attacked the prevailing belief that the Time 'called forth' the Great Man, as if the sticks made the fire.

[2] David Masson, *Carlyle Personally and in his Writings* (1885), p. 67; see also p. 83, and much other evidence.

decade. His later public utterances were mainly minatory and destructive; 'Maecenas Twiddledee' was unfit to recognize the 'Man of Genius' and confused the God-inspired with the counterfeit, 'Valetism' with 'Heroism'.[1] (In practice, as always, his actions were more positive, as in helping to obtain a Civil List pension for Tennyson in 1845.) But what he counted on most and continued to urge was the recognition of genius for what it was:

Genius, Poet: do we know what these words mean? An inspired Soul once more vouchsafed us, direct from Nature's own great fire-heart, to see the Truth, and speak it, and do it; Nature's own sacred voice heard once more athwart the dreary boundless element of hearsaying and canting of twaddle and poltroonery . . .[2]

Although misplaced and false 'hero-worship' and an excessive concern with 'the coming poet' were common enough in the mid-century[3] there was no lack of such recognition of the inspiring power of genius; of Rousseau, in whom Carlyle had seen 'a spark of heavenly fire' along with much weakness, George Eliot wrote in 1849 (in almost Carlylean terms) that she might be persuaded that Rousseau's 'views of life, religion, and government' were erroneous, but

[1] *Past and Present* (1843), IV. vii, 'The Gifted'.
[2] Ibid. II. ix; the outburst is again occasioned by the inadequate recognition of Burns.
[3] Especially by reviewers of the Spasmodics, and by Alexander Smith himself in *A Life-Drama* (1853), II. ix (the passage referred to in Matthew Arnold's 1853 Preface as 'the mere delirium of vanity'). George Gilfillan avowed himself 'a "Hero-worshipper"'—'even now, there are many heroes' (*A Gallery of Literary Portraits*, 1845, Preface) and discovered all too many. He recalled that in 1835 he had written, 'The age is now awake. The slightest symptoms of original power are now recognised', and continued, 'No mean place among our rising poets must be allowed to J. Stanyan Bigg' (*A Third Gallery of Portraits*, 1855, p. 170). 'Scarce a week elapses without a shout being raised at the birth of a thin octavo', as Aytoun wrote in *Blackwood's* (Mar. 1854), attacking Gilfillan and anticipating his own lethal burlesque (Sept. 1854) '*Firmilian*, by T. Percy Jones'.

it would not be less true that Rousseau's genius has sent that electric thrill through my intellectual and moral frame which has awakened me to new perceptions ... the rushing mighty wind of his inspiration has so quickened my faculties that I have been able to shape more definitely for myself ideas which had previously dwelt as dim 'ahnungen' in my soul.[1]

That its inspiring power was independent of views and opinions was often said: the same distinction was drawn by Hopkins in retort against R. W. Dixon's slighting reference to Carlyle: 'I hate his principles, I burn most that he worships and worship most that he burns ... but the force of his genius seems to me gigantic.'[2]

For Carlyle the writings of genius were a means for getting at the genius himself, at the man. Burns to him is 'a great Original Man', recognized by all who met him: 'waiters and ostlers at inns would get out of bed, and come crowding to hear this man speak! Waiters and ostlers:—they too were men, and here was a man!'[3] This held latent dangers from which Carlyle might be immune, but weaker minds were easily led by literary hero-worship and the cult of genius to cant—for example, to the 'self-glorifying' on inadequate grounds which Kingsley called 'Authotheism'.[4] Bulwer Lytton's 18-year-old hero, Ernest Maltravers, 'a Man of Genius', demonstrates it chiefly by standing apart 'with folded arms and thoughtful countenance' and apostrophizing Art and Nature—pretensions punctured by Thackeray when he observed that Clive Newcome's 'genius' was 'not gloomy, solitary, gigantic, shining alone like a light-house',[5] and perhaps by Dickens in *Nicholas Nickleby*, where Miss Knag's brother, a reader of fashionable

---

[1] *The George Eliot Letters*, ed. G. S. Haight (1954, 1955), I. 277.
[2] *The Correspondence of Gerard Manley Hopkins and Richard Watson Dixon*, ed. C. C. Abbott (rev. edn. 1955), p. 59.
[3] 'The Hero as Man of Letters'.
[4] 'Alexander Smith and Alexander Pope'.
[5] *The Newcomes*, Ch. xxxiv.

novels, 'took to scorning everything, and became a genius'. Kingsley's Major Campbell would not acknowledge genius 'where there is no steadiness of character'[1] and the chaplain in 'George de Barnewell' (Thackeray's burlesque of Bulwer's *Eugene Aram*) says that 'Homicide is not permitted even to the most amiable Genius'.[2]

Carlylean hero-worship, when directed at the living, had other excesses. Thackeray in 1840 found Paris 'deluged with a host of gods': 'Monsieur de Balzac feels himself to be inspired; Victor Hugo is a god; Madame Sand is a god; that tawdry man of genius, Jules Janin, ... has divine intimations ... you may fancy what a religion that must be which has such high priests.'[3]

The last thing Thackeray himself wanted was to join the pantheon; he knew that men cannot afford to be confused with gods. Perhaps he also foresaw the dangers, to the undiscriminating, of Carlyle's emphasis on 'the Great Man' as 'the indispensable saviour of his epoch' and 'Men of Letters' as 'a perpetual Priesthood'.[4] In his own lectures, a decade later, Thackeray may have intended a mild corrective, by choosing, among men of letters in the eighteenth century, 'Humourists' rather than 'Heroes', and by indulging in such side-glances as 'I cannot afford to make a hero of Harry Fielding'. Carlyle, who heard some of the lectures in 1851, is reported[5] to have said after a conversation with Thackeray on Swift that he wished he 'could persuade Thackeray that the test of greatness in a man is not whether he would like to meet him at a

[1] *Two Years Ago*, Ch. xv.
[2] *Punch's Prize Novelists* (Apr. 1847).
[3] *The Paris Sketch Book*, 'Madame Sand and the New Apocalypse'.
[4] *Heroes*, I and VI; and cf. 'The State of German Literature'. Froude's 'hero', Markham Sutherland, quotes Carlyle and longs to be an author: 'to make my thoughts the law of other minds!—to form a link, however humble, a real living link, in the electric chain which conducts the light of the ages!' (*The Nemesis of Faith*, 1849, Letter vi.)
[5] By G. S. Venables, 'Carlyle's Life in London', *Fortnightly Review*, xxxvi (Nov. 1884).

tea-party'—which may be a fair comment on Thackeray's occasional tone, but not on his purport, which has
still much in common with Carlyle's. His 'humourists'
are 'week-day preachers'; and at one point he says, 'He
who reads these noble records of a past age, salutes and
reverences the great spirits who adorn it'.[1] Like Carlyle
on Burns and Johnson, Thackeray concerns himself with
'the men and . . . their lives, rather than . . . their books'.
   Thackeray's 'counsel', delivered modestly but
weightily, was that we should 'learn to admire rightly';[2]
*rightly*, and not with the cant that he detected in 'Madame
Sand and the New Apocalypse'. 'Worship of genius',
'worshipper of genius', phrases common in the mid-
century, would be uncongenial to him outside burlesque;
also to Carlyle, who would surely have deprecated the
use of *Heroes* for advertisement purposes in the
announcement, in 1846, by the free-thinking publisher
John Chapman, of a new work in his 'Catholic Series',
translated from the German of Carl Ullmann:[3]

*The Worship of Genius*. Being an Examination of the Doctrine
announced by D. F. Strauss, viz. 'That to our Age of Religious
Disorganization nothing is left but a Worship of Genius; that
is, a Reverence for those great Spirits who create Epochs in the
Progress of the Human Race, and in whom, taken collectively,
the Godlike manifests itself to us most fully,' and thus having
reference to the views unfolded in the work entitled, *Heroes and
Hero-Worship, by Thomas Carlyle*.

   Elizabeth Barrett in her letters of the 1840s often
referred to herself (and seriously) as 'a worshipper of
genius', exemplifying it particularly in her references to
Tennyson; and this is the appellation bestowed by
George Henry Lewes on Alexander Main, one of the

---

[1] Lectures I and IV.
[2] Lecture IV.
[3] *Der Cultus des Genius* (1840); the quotation is from Strauss's article of
1838 (which originated the phrase), but Ullmann's purpose is rather to
correct the excesses of Strauss's followers.

many worshippers of George Eliot and the selector of *Wise, Witty, and Tender Sayings* from her works. Such worship was often very fervent, and George Eliot received much quasi-ecclesiastical homage, from strangers as well as disciples.[1] She was also regarded as a more than 'week-day' preacher. Mrs. Cowper-Temple confessed to having copied passages from *Romola* into her New Testament, and John Blackwood, staying at home from evening church to read proof of *Middlemarch*, told its author that 'Dorothea is better than any sermon ever preached by man'.[2] More orthodoxly, *In Memoriam* was used as a source of texts for sermons; and the personal 'worship' of Tennyson is equally well documented.

Even before the 1840s the 'lionizing' of authors in private gatherings had gone to great lengths. Harriet Martineau, in an article in the *Westminster Review* of 1839, 'Literary Lions',[3] referred to scenes that show, if it were needed, how much topical truth underlies Dickens's Mrs. Leo Hunter. She allowed that at public assemblies like the British Association 'the popular veneration for intellectual achievement' might be acceptable, but saw 'the sordid characteristics of the modern system' in parties in private houses: drawing obviously on the many occasions on which she had been decoyed as lioness:

All the books of the house are lying about,—all the gentry in the neighbourhood are collected; the young men peep and stare from the corners of the room; the young ladies crowd together, even sitting five upon three chairs, to avoid the risk of being addressed by the stranger. The lady of the house devotes herself to 'drawing out' the guest, asks for her opinion

---

[1] There are many instances in *George Eliot Letters*, v–vii, and K. W. Mackenzie, *Edith Simcox and George Eliot*.

[2] *George Eliot Letters*, v. 276, 307; cf. vi. 198, 227.

[3] She reprinted most of it in her *Autobiography* (1877) (beginning of Sect. II).

of this, that, and the other book, and intercedes for her young friends, trembling on their three chairs, that each may be favoured with 'just one line for her album.' The children are kept in the nursery, as being unworthy the notice of a literary person, or brought up severally into the presence, 'that they may have it to say all their lives that they had been introduced,' &c., &c. Some youth in a corner is meantime sketching the guest, and another is noting what she says,—probably something about the black and green tea, or the state of the roads, or the age of the moon. Such a scene, very common now in English country houses, must present an unfavourable picture of our manners to strangers from another country or another age.

By various means, many great writers had become more personally accessible to their admirers. Whereas Dr. Johnson had complained that the Scriblerus Club had cut itself off from the rest of mankind as something superior, Carlyle, in his essay on Burns, had, in contrast, noted that 'Our chief literary men ... no longer live among us like a French colony'. Their very voices could be heard, and after hearing could 'haunt [the] memory still'.[1] Both as host and guest, Tennyson would read *Maud*—his most frequent choice—and other poems, and lived long enough to record his Wellington Ode on phonographic cylinders. For Dickens—born to act as well as to write—private readings to chosen groups of friends in the forties led first to public readings for charity, and then, for the last twelve years of his life, the famous reading tours in Britain and America, increasing the cash returns from the worship he was evoking as an author, finding what he placed 'above all other considerations', a fuller expression of the 'personal affection' between himself and his audience.[2] Authors were also in demand as after-dinner speakers, and here too Dickens excelled: Edmund Yates thought him 'by far the best ... I

---

[1] Arnold, 'Emerson' (*Discourses in America*, 1884).
[2] *Letters to Angela Burdett Coutts*, ed. Edgar Johnson (1953), p. 364.

have ever heard'[1] and Trollope despaired of giving 'any idea' of the 'general charm' of his manner.[2]

The main outlet for 'authotheism', however, was that of the lecture or course of lectures. In the seventeenth and eighteenth centuries most lectures were hardly distinguishable from sermons; by the nineteenth they had been extended into the secular field, notably by Hazlitt, who learnt the art on his feet (from disastrous beginnings), and Coleridge. Carlyle followed, driven in the first place by financial necessity, with courses of lectures in four consecutive London seasons.[3] 'Nothing that he has ever tried', his wife wrote at the end of the first series, 'seems to me to have carried more conviction to the public heart that he is a real man of genius';[4] and when, twenty-six years later, he was once more prevailed upon to address an audience in his Rectorial Address at Edinburgh, the personal impression he made was equally strong: Alexander Smith recalled the eager anticipations of many fellow Scotsmen, and his own sense of fulfilment in seeing at last one whose work he had long admired: 'When I saw him for the first time with the eye of flesh stand up amongst us the other day, and heard him speak kindly, brotherly, affectionate words ... I am not ashamed to confess that I felt moved towards him as I do not think, in any possible combination of circumstances, I could have felt moved towards any other living man.'[5]

In 1850 Newman's lectures on *Certain Difficulties felt by Anglicans* were attended by many besides those on the

---

[1] *Recollections and Experiences* (1884), II. III.

[2] *Macmillan's Magazine* (July 1870). Both are quoted, with many other tributes, in K. J. Fielding's edition of *The Speeches of Charles Dickens* (1960).

[3] On German Literature (1837); On the History of Literature (1838); On the Revolutions of Modern Europe (1839); On Heroes, Hero-Worship, and the Heroic in History (1840). The last alone were 'written out' and published the same year; but a version of the second course was published in 1892 from 'full reports' (of all but one) by T. C. Anstey.

[4] J. A. Froude, *Carlyle's Life in London* (1884), I. 105 (30 May 1837).

[5] 'Mr. Carlyle at Edinburgh', *Last Leaves* (1868), p. III.

verge of following him; Charlotte Brontë was among them, and R. H. Hutton, who wrote

I shall never forget the impression which his voice and manner, which opened upon me for the first time in these lectures, made on me. Never did a voice seem better adapted to persuade without irritating ... its simplicity, and frankness, and freedom from the half-smothered notes which express indirect purpose, was as remarkable as its sweetness, its freshness and its gentle distinctness.[1]

Still more famous are Newman's lectures 'On Catholicism in England' in Birmingham in 1851, and his university lectures in Dublin. Among other lecturers were Thackeray and Arnold, in America (where the worship of men of genius was even more zealous and personal curiosity more irrepressible) as well as in England; and all these lectures in their revised and published form still carry something, enforced by many eye-witness accounts, of the writer's voice, manner, and presence. Most of the lecturers themselves had doubts of one kind or another about the efficacy—and the dignity—of lecturing; Carlyle was thankful to abandon what he called 'a mixture of prophecy and play-acting', and of few, perhaps, could it be said as of William Morris that even before he began to speak 'he seemed in a remarkable way to open his whole being to the audience' and 'expressed what was in his mind as exactly as words could do', without the 'over-emphasis and hyperbole' of Carlyle and Ruskin.[2] Of all lecturers Ruskin (from 1853) was the most prolific, professionally and otherwise, and much sought after; and if he fell below one young lady's preconception of a literary genius for his lack of the requisite 'dark hair, pale face, and massive marble brow',[3] most

---

[1] *Cardinal Newman* (1891), pp. 207–8.
[2] Bruce Glasier, *William Morris* (1921), pp. 22, 156.
[3] *Works*, ed. E. T. Cook and A. Wedderburn (1903–12), XII. xxxi; from a newspaper report of the *Edinburgh Lectures on Architecture* (1853).

were captivated both by his manner and his message.
Michael Sadler recalled his 'entrancing' voice and his
half-humorous delivery of violent expressions, 'the very
passages that the critic who never heard Ruskin would
quote as proofs of his over-vehemence in denunciation'.[1]
But by 1874 Ruskin had become suspicious of the
public's addiction to lectures:

Everybody wants to *hear*—nobody to read—nobody to think;
to be excited for an hour—and, if possible, amused; to get the
knowledge it has cost a man half his life to gather, first
sweetened up to make it palatable, and then kneaded into the
smallest possible pills—and to swallow it homoeopathically
and be wise—this is the passionate desire and hope of the
multitude of the day. It is not to be done. A living comment
quietly given to a class on a book they are earnestly reading—this kind of lecture is eternally necessary and wholesome; your modern fire-worky, smooth-downy-curry-and-
strawberry-ice-and milk-punch-altogether lecture is an
entirely pestilent and abominable vanity; and the miserable
death of poor Dickens, when he might have been writing
blessed books till he was eighty, but for the pestiferous
demands of the mob, is a very solemn warning to us all, if we
would take it.[2]

Apart from public occasions such as readings,
speeches, and lectures, there were the private ones,
informal or semi-formal, in the authors' own homes
and more or less on their own terms: in the thirties,
Coleridge's Thursday evenings 'on the brow of Highgate
hill', in the sixties, George Eliot's Sunday afternoons at
the Priory, and for some thirty years, the less regular and
more numerous evenings at Cheyne Row, where many
were magnetized by Carlyle's talk. Of this especially
there is abundant and vivid record, sometimes adding
another dimension to the voice we seem to hear so clearly

[1] *Sir Michael Sadler, a Memoir by his Son* (1949), pp. 32–3 (Sadler's recollections of 1882).
[2] 26 May 1874, to Mr. Chapman of the Glasgow Athenaeum Committee,
declining an invitation; *Works*, xxxiv, 517.

in his writings: as Arnold said of one of his *Examiner* articles, 'it is in the style and feeling that the beloved man appears'.[1] He was the more lovable when met in person partly because he was less unremittingly earnest. In his life of Froude, Herbert Paul noticed a shortcoming that was perhaps inevitable:

One thing Froude did not give, and perhaps no biographer could. Carlyle was essentially a humourist ... [In his] most lurid denunciations of all and sundry, he would give a peculiar and most significant chuckle which cannot be put into print. It was a warning not to take him literally, which has too often passed unheeded ... No man loved laughter more, or could excite more uproarious merriment in others. I remember a sober Scotsman, by no means addicted to frivolous merriment, telling me that he had come out of Carlyle's house in physical pain from continuous laughter.[2]

For Thackeray, the testimonies of friends asserted his lovableness and his large-heartedness, against those who saw him as a cynical writer; John Blackwood missed, in the articles on him after his death, 'any real picture of the man with his fun and mixture of bitterness with warm good feeling' and recalled how when he 'spoke with real feeling of men and things that he liked, the breadth and force of his character came out';[3] Dr. John Brown found him 'so much greater, so much nobler than his works, great and noble as they are'.[4] As a formula of praise this is not uncommon in the nineteenth century: to Coventry Patmore, as to others, Clough's character had 'a consequence beyond that of his writings with all who knew him though ever so slightly; and the halo of this sanctity

---

[1] 8 Mar. 1848 (*The Correspondence of Arthur Hugh Clough*, ed. F. L. Mulhauser, 1957).

[2] *Life of Froude* (1905), p. 425.

[3] Mrs. Gerald Porter, *Annals of a Publishing House John Blackwood The Third Volume of William Blackwood and his Sons* (1898), p. 99.

[4] 'Death of Mr. Thackeray', *Scotsman* (25 Dec. 1864); partly reprinted in *John Leech and Other Papers* (1882), pp. 179–87.

hangs, through the report of his friends, about all that he has done, and renders cold criticism of it almost impossible'.[1]

The words, and the sentiment, recall once again Carlyle's seminal essay on Burns:

Criticism, it is sometimes thought, should be a cold business; we are not so sure of this; but at all events, our concern with Burns is not exclusively that of critics. True and genial as his poetry must appear, it is not chiefly as a poet, but as a man, that he interests and affects us ... we see in him a freer, purer development of whatever is noblest in ourselves; his life is a rich lesson to us, and we mourn his death as that of a benefactor who loved and taught us.

Far from being 'a cold business', much of the criticism written in the nineteenth century is warmed by sympathy and admiration, whether at first or second hand, for the man as well as the writings; and recognition of the 'spark of heavenly fire' is attested by the use of such terms (unusual in our own day) as 'benefactor', 'sanctity', and 'noble'. Such recognition, as we have seen, often transcended differences of opinion, however extreme: there is ample evidence of what George Eliot found in Carlyle's *Life of Sterling*, of which she said: 'Above all, we are gladdened by a perception of the affinity that exists between noble souls, in spite of diversity in ideas.'[2] One source of that affinity was the 'earnestness' which is the subject of the next chapter.

---

[1] *Principle in Art* (1889), p. 120.
[2] *Westminster Review* (Jan. 1852).

# 1. 'EARNESTNESS'

[In 1877] a clergyman of advanced years ...
remarked [to Herbert Spencer] on the great
change which had taken place in men's minds
during his life. He said that, whereas in his
early days indifference was the rule, nowadays
everybody is in earnest about something or
other. The contrast struck me as one of great
significance.
(Herbert Spencer, *Autobiography*, 1904,
II. 306)

'You are so dreadfully in earnest!' he [Jeffrey]
said to me, once or oftener.
(Carlyle, 'Lord Jeffrey' in *Reminiscences*,
1881; recalling the year 1831)

[When Ernest Pontifex was born in 1834] the
word 'earnest' was just beginning to come into
fashion.
(Samuel Butler, *The Way of all Flesh*,
begun 1873, Ch. xviii)

Be earnest, earnest, earnest; mad if thou wilt;
Do what thou dost as if the stake were heaven.
(Charles Kingsley, *The Saint's Tragedy*,
1848, II. ix)

TOWARDS THE end of the nineteenth century Frederic
Harrison, then in his sixties, wrote that 'this rich, many-
sided, strenuous literature, which will place the name of
Victoria higher than that of Elizabeth in the history of our
language, would form a splendid study hereafter for one

of our descendants who was equal to the task of treating our Victorian literature as a whole.'[1] The epithet 'strenuous' is apt. Trollope's notion of 'human bliss' was having 'twelve hours of work with only six hours in which to do it'.[2] Huxley said that if he had not been a man he would have preferred to have been a tug. Newman thought that 'one gains nothing by sitting still. I am sure the Apostles did not sit still: and agitation is the order of the day.'[3] When he reached the age of 37 Ruskin calculated that he could hope for 11,795 more spells of twenty-four hours, and started counting them down one by one in his diary.[4] He took 'To-day' as the motto for his seal. By 1840 Mill saw one rule of life as 'eternally binding', and 'independent of all varieties of creeds': 'try thyself unweariedly till thou findest the highest thing thou art capable of doing, faculties & outward circumstances being both duly considered—and then DO IT.'[5]

The sense of mission, of being born to have a big effect on one's fellows, was strong. Fitzjames Stephen, reviewing *Tom Brown's Schooldays* in the *Edinburgh Review* (Jan. 1858), held that the word 'earnest' had been brought in by Dr. Arnold 'and his admirers', who had substituted it for 'serious' (perhaps because of the Evangelicals' use of that word); earnestness was seriousness in action.

With all this in the smoky air, when, as Mill noted in his *Autobiography* (1873), 'dissatisfaction with life and the world' was 'felt more or less in the present state of society and intellect by every discerning and highly conscientious mind',[6] Charles Kingsley for one remembered Nero, the arch-aesthete: 'As for a ballad... there is no use

---

[1] *Studies in Early Victorian Literature* (1895), p. 17.

[2] *Orley Farm*, Ch. xlix; see below, pp. 269–70.

[3] Letter of 31 Aug. 1833; *Letters and Correspondence of John Henry Newman*, ed. Anne Mozley (1891), I. 449.

[4] *The Diaries of John Ruskin*, ed. Joan Evans and J. H. Whitehouse (1958), p. 519 (7 Sept. 1856).

[5] *The Earlier Letters of John Stuart Mill*, ed. Francis E. Mineka (1963), pp. 426–7.

[6] p. 74.

fiddling while Rome is burning'.[1] Poets now felt unable to proceed as Goethe and Keats had done. Mill, writing to Sterling in 1840, regretfully saw what was being sacrificed, and how inevitably: 'What you say about the absence of a disinterested & heroic pursuit of Art as the greatest want of England at present, has often struck me, but I suspect it will not be otherwise until our social struggles are over. Art needs earnest but quiet times—in ours I am afraid Art itself to be powerful must be polemical—Carlylean not Goethian . . .'[2] Goethe had counselled the poet to do as he himself had done, and tear himself to pieces. Only so could the poet produce great lyrics and great narratives. This course, however, now seemed too self-indulgent, and the former conception of the artist too remote. Arnold, for one, expressly rejected Goethe's recommendation, as no longer binding. And Clough, for another; Sellar applauded his choice not to become a full-time writer, but saw what it cost him: 'His sense of the duty and necessity of taking his own share, and more than his own share, of practical work, may have been a safer guide for him to follow than the impulses of his poetic and speculative faculty. But freedom and leisure would have given him a better chance of becoming a great poet.'[3] Harriet Martineau may also be regarded as one who in less pressing times would have written more novels than *Deerbrook*, and so have been even more securely placed among writers just less than great. Instead she wrote what the times seemed most in need of. And that the same cruel choice was still inescapable for at least certain writers later in the century, by which time the condition of England was somewhat easier, there is testimony from that hard-working and gifted reformer,

[1] Letter to Thomas Hughes, 12 Dec. 1854. But he went on with *Westward Ho!*: 'a sanguinary book, but perhaps containing doctrine profitable for these times'.

[2] *Earlier Letters*, p. 446.

[3] *North British Review* (Nov. 1862).

Edith Simcox, in her *Natural Law, An Essay in Ethics* (1877):[1]

We are not blind to the sublimity of mathematical truth, or callous to the emotions vibrating in the voice of poetic passion, only while men and women are starving round us in brutal misery, or battening in brutal ease, the problem and the poem seem far away from half our life, and we become unwilling accomplices in the indifference of our age to some of the noblest works of man. We are called away from the peaceful life of intellectual perception, and many of us are fain to turn reformers in despair, not because we have the reformer's talent or the reformer's taste, but because the world needs so much reform.

For all the cry of 'art for art's sake' raised from the sixties onwards, the contrast between the two halves of our period on this score shows rather a difference of degree than of kind. Whereas the social conditions of the thirties and forties wrung the consciences of all men who were worth the name, those of the later decades wrung the consciences only of those who wanted the affairs of working men and women to improve still further.

The easing of the social tension did enable certain writers to retreat, more or less, from what may be called the 'newspaper' world. Rossetti was one of them. He had been the moving spirit in the Pre-Raphaelite Brotherhood, founded in that year of revolution, 1848. Some of the Pre-Raphaelite pictures, particularly Ford Madox Brown's 'Work', had carried political implications, while according with the aims they had drawn up in their short-lived periodical the *Germ*—aims that were more vividly expressed for them in 1853 by Reade, who, in his first novel, *Christie Johnstone*, made his artist exclaim: 'With these little swords [brushes] we'll fight for nature-light, truth-light, and sun-light, against a world in arms, no, worse, in swaddling clothes.'[2] Even when Rossetti's

---

[1] p. 331.                    [2] Ch. vi.

earnestness for the reform of painting cooled off, he still
had it ascribed to him. In the first number of *Macmillan's
Magazine* in 1859, F. D. Maurice championed the Pre-
Raphaelites against the charges of Kingsley: 'I know
nothing of art; but I find too much conscientiousness and
earnestness among those of my friends who are called
Pre-Raphaelites, ever to look down upon them as he
does.'[1] Benjamin Webb in the same year spoke of the
'growing sense ... of the importance of the true mission
of art [which] we owe to the so-called Pre-Raffaellites'.[2]
Rossetti himself had always disclaimed a concern with
politics, and by the sixties, at least, his very gait had
become an insult to Carlyle: Allingham recorded that
'[He] walks very characteristically, with a peculiar loung-
ing gait, often trailing the point of his umbrella on the
ground ... Then suddenly he will fling himself down
somewhere and refuse to stir an inch further. His favourite attitude—on his back, one knee raised, hands behind
head. On a sofa he often, too, curls himself up like a
cat ...'[3]

Rossetti apart, there seems no loss of earnestness in the
second half of the period, even if some of it promoted the
cause of 'art for art's sake'. What was over from that went
straight into political and social writings, as we have seen.
Ruskin became more politically earnest as he increasingly
mixed economics with art. His writings, unlike Carlyle's,
addressed workers as well as discussed them—it was a
great honour done them when a writer, whose sentences
waved gloriously as banners, put them in the centre of his
prose. And they and he together were honoured when in
1854 the Working Men's College marked its inau-
guration by reprinting a chapter of *Stones of Venice*, which
they re-entitled *On the Nature of Gothic Architecture: and
herein of the True Functions of the Workman in Art*, and

[1] I. 119.
[2] *Bentley's Quarterly Review*, I. 169.
[3] *William Allingham, A Diary* (1907), p. 162.

giving a copy of it to each of the 400 people who came
along: a chapter that Morris, who thought it 'one of the
very few necessary and inevitable utterances of the century',[1] himself reprinted as one of the earliest books
issued from the Kelmscott press. Now that the workers
were no longer starving, they were being encouraged by
both Ruskin and Morris to be not only human beings but
artists. Ruskin was seconded by Morris, who contrived
to serve two masters, the political, in its completest sense,
and the poetical. Arnold's career repeated Ruskin's,
*mutatis mutandis*: it started with thoughtful poems and
ended with books on politics and religion. His earnest
prose sought to help forward the education in sweetness
and light both of the middle class, which was his first
concern, and of the poorer class, whom he met as school
inspector. 'Service' was his watchword. It might be said
to have been Pater's also, for at bottom he too had a
mission. And though he spoke to the few in the first
place, he could count on the few as now the more numerous because of the prior labours of Ruskin and Arnold. If
he seemed to be advertising an ivory tower he kept it well
thronged with visitors. That there was nothing political
about him simply meant that he saw the chance of building on the results of politics that had done much to make
the middle class what it now was. Those younger men,
Swinburne, J. A. Symonds, and Richard Burton were
earnest, if mainly in iconoclasm. When in 1867 Swinburne was contemplating 'a sort of étude à la Balzac *plus*
the poetry', which was to become *Lesbia Brandon*, he
added, 'I flatter myself [it] will be more offensive and
objectionable to Britannia than anything I have yet
done'.[2]

Meanwhile a quieter crusade was proceeding. Charles
Reade, for all his noisy power, appealed to the same quiet

[1] Preface to 1892 edn.
[2] *The Swinburne Letters*, ed. C. Y. Lang (1959–62), I. 224 (letter to Richard
Burton, 11 Jan. 1867).

principle as George Eliot did—he spoke of an author 'seiz[ing the reader's] sympathies by the wonderful power of fiction—touch[ing] his conscience through his heart'. And there is the case of Hopkins, who acted according to the principle put forcefully in a letter of Newman, discussing one of his fellow Oratorians who not only wanted to write a book on Plain Chant, but to argue that it was predestinated: 'He must not be a *literary* man ... We must have no literary selfishnesses and jealousies among us. I own I am hard hearted towards the mere literary *ethos* for there is nothing I despise and detest more. He is only half a man if he can't put his book into the fire when told by authority.'[1] Writing what poetry he felt he had permission to write, Hopkins was earnest towards his God rather than towards the printing-press—unlike Newman, who felt free to accommodate both purposes. Nor, reverting to Pater, need we take too seriously the cry of 'art for art's sake'. Art was still for men's sake.

When authors were being encouraged to think twice before writing, and when they did write, to write about matters of public moment, there was a danger that poems and novels that ignored those matters might be mis-judged—that is, judged according to criteria they were never meant to satisfy. In their earnestness Carlyle and Newman sometimes ranked literature as a whole with Nero's fiddling. Being, ironically, great writers, what they said, therefore, was at variance with what they wrote on cooler occasions, and with the implications of how they wrote even when inflamed. In his 'Tamworth Reading Room'[2] Newman rounded on Brougham for recommending novels and poems as agents of moral

[1] J. H. Newman, *Letters and Diaries*, ed. C. S. Dessain (1961–77), XII. 311 (letter of 27 Oct. 1848).
[2] Letters to *The Times* (Feb. 1841); collected in *Discussions and Arguments* (1872).

improvement, instead of going to the root of the matter and either making people Christians, or holding Christians to their obligations. Brougham had nothing to offer, he alleged, except a 'philosophy of expedients'. No one knew better than Newman that expedients must be resorted to by any reformer; we find him fully admitting their inevitability in the Preface to the 1877 edition of the *Via Media*. If Brougham resorted to expedients in recommending pure literature, so did Carlyle and Newman in decrying it. Both of them sometimes spoke as if Shakespeare's plays had no right to exist, while, at other times, themselves writing literary criticism of the first rank. At one juncture literature was slighted, at another honoured. When Newman spoke of 'mere' literature, he was not always at leisure to specify the host of glorious exceptions. At one time he sighed for '*quiet* times' so as to think more truly and so write better, at another declared that the greatest literature has always sprung from the heat and hubbub of its age. In the *Tamworth Reading Room*, again, he spoke of 'the small beer of literature and science', without recalling either what literature includes, or that science was proving no pleasant drink for him and many others. Both he and Carlyle at times spoke of poems and novels as variants of street brawling while being aware in their bones that they were produced by the sublimest of arts. They designed pamphlets as firebrands, but attended fastidiously to their shaping and colouring as if they were Gothic statuary or Grecian urns. What George Eliot admired most in Carlyle was the artist; and almost from the start Lockhart, a most unanglican Scot, considered Newman the greatest of contemporary writers. However pressing they found the 'bad days', they did not let their badness interfere with their aim at literary perfection, and Carlyle in particular produced some works that were unrelated to the times, apart from asides and implications. Although Newman protested his hard-heartedness towards the mere literary ethos, some of his ferocity of tone was due to his feeling tempted to be soft-hearted—'My great fault', he confessed in 1843, 'is doing things in a mere literary way from the love of the work, without the thought of God's glory'.[1] He vouchsafed his writings a supererogatory elegance, as Carlyle did a supererogatory gloriousness.

Whatever their own practice, however, they felt it expedient to dissuade those of their juniors who had literary gifts from exercising them, if any other course were open. Hard times existed first of all for men of action. 'Man', declared Carlyle, 'is created to fight'.[2] 'Life', declared Newman, 'is for action'.[3] Let there be as little writing as possible, and let the writing that was done contribute to militant action—that was their message at its baldest.

In delivering it each of them had much the look of being an 'Athanasius contra mundum'. The mundus, it was plain, was immovably in possession, and among other things held fast to the right to read about man, not as if he were brand new in the nineteenth century, but as he had always been, and as he still was when not heated by the hottest breath of the *Zeitgeist*—a creature mainly concerned with the irreducible cares and pleasures of morning, noon, and night. Carlyle and Newman fully saw that this was so. In his essay on Burns, where he was urging poets to rediscover the eternal topics of poetry in the men around them, Carlyle reminded them that 'Man's life and nature is, as it was, and as it will ever be'.[4] A reminder of Newman was to the same effect: 'Man's duty, perfection, happiness, have always been one and the same. He is not a different being now from what he ever was; he has always been commanded the same duties.'[5] That was said in the course of a parochial sermon to

[1] *Correspondence ... with Keble* (1917), p. 245.
[2] *Past and Present*, III. x.
[3] 'The Tamworth Reading Room', Letter vi.
[4] *Edinburgh Review* (Dec. 1828).
[5] *Parochial Sermons*, III (1835), 193–4.

Anglicans, but applied also to others, the non-church-going included.

But people insisted, in this age as in others, on being entertained, the contemporary dramatic pieces, the vast comic literature, the sensation novels—and indeed the great novels themselves—providing amply for that, and sometimes providing for it in conscious opposition or supplementation of what was being urged by Carlyle and Newman. In 1837 Dickens, as editor of *Bentley's Miscellany*, spoke of his 'sincere anxiety for the amusement and light-heartedness of the community'. As Mr. Sleary, the circus proprietor, said in *Hard Times*, 'People mutht be amuthed'. In 1844 the prospectus for *Hood's Magazine and Comic Miscellany* announced that its mood would be light-hearted, and that such earnest matters as 'panaceas for agricultural distress' would be ignored. The mid-century reader was not going to be bludgeoned into forgetting what the great literature of the world had been about. Its perennial matter had been jealously prized in the former century—a century when Dr. Johnson could say that most authors had been content to rearrange the human matter set out in Homer's epics, and as a matter for literature relegated affairs of state to a position inferior to that of personal relations:

> How small of all that human hearts endure,
> That part which laws or kings can cause or cure.

In the new century likewise the claims of this age-old literary matter had been powerfully asserted, for poetry by Shelley in his *Defence*, and for novels by Jane Austen, glossing the apologetic 'only a novel' with: 'only some work in which the greatest powers of the mind are displayed, in which the most thorough knowledge of human nature, the happiest delineation of its varieties, the liveliest effusions of wit and humour are conveyed to the world in the best chosen language'.[1] The same

[1] *Northanger Abbey*, Ch. ix.

Johnsonian wisdom was comfortingly repeated later in the century. In his essay on Dobell, Alexander Smith, sounder as a critic than in his practice as a Spasmodic poet, spoke a timely word:

It is astonishing when one reflects on it, to what few and simple root-ideas the entire poetry of the world may be traced. I am, I was, I love, I hate, I suffer, I am glad, I must die—these lie at the bottom of all song. After the death of Abel the first family had pretty nearly gone the round of all possible experiences. In the primordial elements of human experience there is nothing trite—except to the trite; the only fruitful originality comes out of an entire and noble apprehension of those primordial elements, and the man who can to that noble apprehension give musical utterance is a poet, and a sufficiently original one, too, for all purposes.[1]

Bishop Stubbs, in his 1878 lecture 'Learning and Literature at the Court of Henry II', said that even after all the discoveries of the nineteenth century human life was not changed, not 'essentially' at least,

by railways, or excise, or newspapers, or even by the property tax: the people before the flood ate and drank, married and were given in marriage, planted and builded; still Jacob finds his Rachel at the well, and David and Jonathan make their covenant together, and David mourns for Absalom. Natural selection, and the survival of the fittest, have not done away with sin and sorrow, and, whatever evolution may have done in the producing of new [human] types, those new types have not swept away the old. To go beyond and behind the ancients, what else do we find in Egypt, Babylon and Nineveh, in Japan, and in the China of immemorial sameness?[2]

Arnold summed up the traditional matter of literature in the phrase 'primary human emotions', matter that still asked of writers as good a deal as they could manage.

In the mid-century, more than at some other times, such things needed to be repeated if only because great

[1] *Last Leaves*, pp. 176–7.
[2] *Seventeen Lectures . . . at Oxford . . . 1867–1884* (1886), p. 117.

writers of the age immediately preceding had sometimes ignored the principle they stated. At any time literature that is popular expresses and represents the primary human emotions, but not always worthily. In the early years of the nineteenth century those emotions had sometimes been insulted even by authors like Scott and Byron. When Bagehot in 1864 reviewed *Enoch Arden* and Browning's *Dramatis Personae* in an essay entitled 'Wordsworth, Tennyson and Browning; or, Pure, Ornate, and Grotesque Art in English Poetry', he charged Thomas Moore, author of *Irish Melodies* and *Lalla Rookh*, with having debased the public taste: his verses 'fixed upon the minds of a whole generation ... engraved in popular memory and tradition, a vague conviction that poetry is but one of the many *amusements* of the light classes, for the lighter hours of all classes'. The reason for that was not that Moore, or Scott in his poems and Byron in his eastern tales and even *Childe Harold*, had not concerned themselves with the primary matter of literature, but that they had said so little about it that was worthy, was on a par with what Scott said of it in his novels, and Byron in *Don Juan*, and Wordsworth and Jane Austen all the time. Let the new age do better, if it could. Bagehot saw a great need for it: 'The mere notion, the bare idea, that poetry is a deep thing, a teaching thing, the most surely and wisely elevating of human things, is even now to the coarse public mind nearly unknown.' And if this was true of poetry, it was true also of stories. In claiming 'depth' for great poetry he was doing no more than Carlyle had done, and in claiming that poetry was 'a teaching thing' he was recommending it especially to writers of the time, so many of whom were professionally (whether paid or not) concerned with education, and in claiming that it elevated the mind he was supporting the doctrine that ascribed nobility to man.

Some part of the greatness of mid-century literature is that the writers of it responded to the old matter as their well-schooled readers expected them to, and gave it of their best. At bottom the literature they produced is like that of the cooler eighteenth century, and of all other centuries, whatever their temperature, in being firmly founded in the heart of man, that heart that cannot but be 'conservative' about such matters, even though political opinions under economic or perhaps psychological stress become 'liberal' or 'radical'—to use the terms that were now coming into use.

Nevertheless, even writers who in a quieter age would have written nothing but pure literature, as Gray had done and Sterne (apart from his sermons) and Goldsmith (when not doing hack-work), felt that now they must do more, writing even an occasional pamphlet, but, if not that, working some of the *Zeitgeist* into their otherwise 'pure' poems and novels.

To begin with, while they treated the old matter of literature with reverence, they treated it more 'wildly', as they put it, than any earlier writers. It may be that wildness always characterizes the stuff of great literature during its prior existence in the mind of the writer, the difference between one written instance of it and another being due to the degree of tranquillity imposed on its expression. In some ages, however, a writer feels more encouragement towards quietening it down than in others. Though Pope planned more than one substantial poem, each of which was to have been 'a very wild thing', he did not write them. We know that anything written by Pope would have had primary human nature at its centre. The wildness he had in mind was therefore wildness in the expression. It is mainly in its expression that the literature of one age differs from that of another, as *Guesses at Truth* suggested: 'Every age has a language of its own; and the difference in the words is oftentimes far greater than the difference in the thoughts. The main employment of authors, in their collective capacity, is to translate the discoveries of other ages into the language of their own.'[1] The new age used wild language to match its own wild discoveries, and the same linguistic wildness was applied also to its rediscovery of matter as old as the hills. Pater spoke in 1886 of 'the wild mixture of poetry and prose, in our wild nineteenth century'. He instanced the writings of Carlyle and Dickens—and those of their many followers—and Chesterton spoke of 'the wild comedy of "Pickwick" and the wild tragedy of "Oliver Twist"'. Few writers escaped wildness altogether, even when dealing with matter that had remained constant from Homer's time, let alone the matter that was new.

To satisfy the times writers avoided as much as possible what might look studied and 'literary' in the bad sense. For that reason Hopkins rejected archaisms almost totally—their use, at least noticeably, 'destroys earnest'.[2] The use of dialect in poems and novels was a way of flourishing the good news that the appearance of sophistication had been avoided. In his lecture on preaching Newman put 'diction, elocution, rhetorical power' in their place:

Does the commander of a besieging force dream of holiday displays, reviews, mock engagements, feats of strength, or trials of skill, such as would be graceful and suitable on a parade ground when a foreigner of rank was to be received and *fêted*; or does he aim at one and one thing only, viz., to take the strong place? Display dissipates the energy, which for the object in view needs to be concentrated and condensed.[3]

With that we may compare Browning in *Men and Women*:

> Grand rough old Martin Luther
>    Bloomed fables—flowers on furze,
> The better the uncouther:
>    Do roses stick like burrs?

[1] [J. C. and A. W. Hare], *Guesses at Truth*, 2nd edn. (1838), p. 192. (The authors later changed 'discoveries' to 'thoughts'.)

[2] *Letters to Robert Bridges*, ed. C. C. Abbott (rev. edn. 1955), p. 218.

[3] Delivered 1855; included in *The Idea of a University* (1873)

Arnold as a young man meditating poetry saw how differently a poet should now proceed even from Keats's way:

And had Shakespeare and Milton lived in the atmosphere of modern feeling, had they had the multitude of new thoughts and feelings to deal with a modern has, I think it likely the style of each would have been far less *curious* and exquisite. For in a *man* style is the saying in the best way *what you have to say*. The *what you have to say* depends on your age. In the 17th century it was *a smaller harvest than now*, and sooner to be reaped: and therefore to its reaper was left time to show it more finely and more curiously. Still more was this the case in the ancient world. The poet's matter being *the hitherto experience of the world, and his own*, increases with every century.[1]

As we should expect, Carlyle grasped the nettle firmly, his practice corroborating his claim that if a writer has achieved a meaning that is 'genuine', 'deep', and 'noble', most of the expression will have been achieved with it: 'the proper form for embodying [the meaning], the form best suited to the subject and the author will gather round it almost of its own accord'. Even though much is to be read into that 'almost', his advice freed the writer, and especially the poet, from seeing form as existing in the abstract. In a letter to Sterling of 4 June 1835 Carlyle declared that form could not now be other than an extemporization, even in its minute particulars (Sterling had been reading *Sartor* and taking exception to its diction): 'Know thy thought, *believe* it,' Carlyle urged, 'front Heaven and Earth with it,—in whatever *words* Natural Art have made readiest for thee! If one has thoughts not hitherto uttered in English books, I see nothing for it but that you must use words not found there, must *make* words,—with moderation and discretion of course.'[2] (He

[1] *Correspondence of Clough*, p. 65.
[2] *Letters to Mill, Sterling, and Browning*, ed. A. Carlyle (1923), pp. 191-2.

proceeds, however, to bow to Sterling's objection to the new word 'talented'.) The sort of way Carlyle saw contemporary form soon reached New England, where the *Dial* in 1839 greeted Bailey's *Festus* as if it were a new thing among vegetables, a thing not so much written as a part of God's inkless universe: 'We know of no book in our time so subordinated to nature. Do not consider it as a book or as a work of art at all, but as a leaf out of the book of life. With all its faults, it answers to the call of the age for a *sincere* book.' Even the slovenliness that Bagehot thought inevitable in writings designed for the periodicals was preferable to a too visible art. In the *North American Review* for 1853 Clough noted that 'poems after classical models, poems from Oriental sources, and the like, have undoubtedly a great literary value. Yet there is no question, it is plain and patent enough, that people much prefer Vanity Fair and Bleak House.' So much for so-called 'literary value'. Carlyle thought imitation the 'deadliest of poeticalisms', not recalling how, in quieter times, imitation had released the creative powers of Dryden, Pope, and Johnson. David Masson, two years earlier than Clough, in his joint review of *David Copperfield* and *Pendennis* in the *North British Review*, had rejected the same or a similar criterion: 'The modern epic, the modern Elizabethan play, the modern historical painting, have an academical, imitative look, which stamps their producers as scholars ...' The cult of poetry that is 'difficult' or made to look so was also in accordance with this avoidance of seeming to write without earnestness—the difficult poetry of Browning, the Spasmodics, Hopkins, and Meredith carried the welcome marks of application. Browning in his 'difficult' poetry took the other course of admitting patches of careless expression that suggested the haste of the runner who bears a message. Clough had mentioned novels. Many of them were trivial and foolish, but the rest, of which he gave two supreme examples, were, as Masson recognized in that same review of another couple of masterpieces, what the earnest age was looking for:

The manner in which both Thackeray and Dickens people their canvass, the cloud of persons who are watching the action of the story, touching it at detached points, or merely subjected to the observation of the actors, and the way in which that cloud resolves itself into touches, each quivering with its own distinctive individual life, characterize very peculiarly the genius of both authors. It is this wonderful affluence of creative powers which will give them a place in the motley history of modern imaginative literature above that of many producers of more complete works of art [he has been inveighing against periodical publication as making for piecemeal writing that achieved no final unity]. [They show] how plainly their works bear the marks of an unquiet and chaotic time ...

Prose ran least risk of looking 'literary', especially prose published in the reviews. Carlyle made his opinions brilliantly clear in his life of Sterling, reproducing a letter of his of the late thirties:

Why *sing* your bits of thoughts, if you *can* contrive to speak them? By your thought, not by your mode of delivering it, you must live or die. ... And the Age itself, does it not, beyond most ages, demand and require clear speech; an Age incapable of being sung to, in any but a trivial manner, till these convulsive agonies and wild revolutionary overturnings readjust themselves? Intelligible word of command, not musical psalmody and fiddling, is possible in this fell storm of battle. Beyond all ages, our Age admonishes whatsoever thinking or writing man it has: O, speak to me some wise intelligible speech; your wise meaning in the shortest and clearest way; behold I am dying for want of wise meaning, and insight into the devouring fact: speak, if you have any wisdom! As to song so-called, and your fiddling talent,—even if you have one, much more if you have none,—we will talk of that a couple of centuries hence, when things are calmer again. Homer shall be thrice welcome; but only when Troy is *taken*: alas, while the siege lasts, and battle's fury rages everywhere, what can I do

with the Homer? I want Achilles and Odysseus, and am
enraged to see them trying to be Homers![1]

In accordance with this view, Arnold, late in the fifties,
like Ruskin before him, veered from verse to prose in an
attempt to gain the ear of the times, as Carlyle had gained
it. Metre, however much it tries to free itself from the
smell of effort and midnight oil, had come to seem in-
appropriate; Arnold's free verse, which he imported from
Germany, was designed to ingratiate itself by seeming
half-way to prose. The main reason for Hopkins's invention of a partly new basis for English metre was to prove
that metre was as earnest a medium as prose if it avoided
the flow of blameless iambs that might suggest a schoolboy's entry in a magazine contest. Wordsworth's description of the poet as 'a man speaking to men' was almost
literally interpreted by those many writers in metre who
avoided anything that sounded songlike and so suggested
singing robes. But it was for prose writers that 'speaking'
shook off most of its metaphor. For they often tried to
remove the aesthetic distance between the page and its
reader, and became present to him as a physical voice.
Authors leaned out of their books in earnest monologue
or would-be dialogue. At the end of his *Essay on
Development*, cutting off the text with rows of dots,
Newman added his pleading personal postscript. In
'Jesuitism' Carlyle gives us a characteristically physical
paragraph:

Prim friend with the black serge gown, with the rosary,
scapulary, and I know not what other spiritual block-
and-tackle,—scowl not on me. If in thy poor heart, under its
rosaries, there dwell any human piety, awestruck reverence
towards the Supreme Maker, devout compassion towards this
poor Earth and her sons,—scowl not anathema on me, listen to
me; for I swear thou art my brother, in spite of rosaries and
scapularies; and recognise thee, though thou canst not me; and

---

[1] *Life of Sterling* (1851), III. I.

with love and pity know thee for a brother, though enchanted into the condition of a spiritual mummy. Hapless creature, curse me not; listen to me, and consider;—perhaps even thou wilt escape from mummyhood, and become once more a living soul!

'Listen to me'—that form of words had also been used by Newman in an early sermon. Thackeray, who cultivated the art of man-to-man commentary, will pause to ask the reader to 'Lay down this book, and think', and Mrs. Gaskell, who is dove and eagle by turns, can cry in *Mary Barton*: 'Oh! Orestes! you would have made a very tolerable Christian of the nineteenth century!'[1] Mid-century prose of thinking is sometimes as wild as the Spasmodic poetry. The calm of Ruskin's, which exists plentifully, seems as miraculous as a rainbow supervening on storm. For the expression of effects of shifting light in the skies he did manage to allow syntax to survive, but again it was by a narrow margin. Queen Victoria, who, after her fashion, exemplified the earnestness of the age, used underlining furiously as correspondent and diarist. In published writings the armoury of the printing-house was called in. Abnormal type and type in abnormal sizes were resorted to. Ruskin used 'bold' type and even, in later editions, sporadic red type—he did publicly what the aged Horace Walpole had done in letters, writing 'in red ink as only suitable to such deeds' as the French Revolution. Much italic bespatters verse as well as prose, and Carlyle went further, and italicized a word in part.[2] Carlyle, Bulwer Lytton, Disraeli, Dickens, and Charlotte Brontë emphasized words by the trick of initial capitals. Sometimes phrases or whole sentences received the emphasis of being printed in capitals. They improved on Mrs. Stowe, whom Reade, in the middle of one of his novels, commended for writing books 'in red ink and with the biceps muscle'. Reade himself used type in

[1] Ch. xviii.
[2] See p. 103.

eccentric ways, including multiplied marks of exclamation, and for a less sportive purpose than Sterne's. His tone, like Charlotte Brontë's, is constantly urgent, and not only when he is haranguing the reader (its role in the narrative part of their novels is a much subtler matter for the critic than its role in a letter, essay, or passages of comment in a novel). The hammering style of declamation on platform or stage was imitated for their earnest purposes. Earnestness can be read in the titles of books—*Yeast, Put Yourself in His Place, Fors Clavigera*—and in the text itself by banner-like phrases in capitals.

The published voice of the earnest mid-century is sometimes strident. Even Newman's could come near stridency. He cynically remarked in reply to critics that if he had written calmly in his contest with Kingsley no one would have believed he was in earnest. On a much earlier occasion he had said: 'The age is so very sluggish, that it will not hear you unless you bawl—you must first tread on its toes, and then apologise.'[1] Carlyle originated this stridency. His first writings—for the *Edinburgh Review*—were almost indistinguishable in point of staid tone from those that surrounded them (no doubt that is why they were acceptable from a novice), but for *Sartor Resartus* he adopted a percussive tone deliberately, his aim being to win attention, which he successfully did after the lapse of a decade. Dickens, Ruskin, Charlotte Brontë, Kingsley, Reade, even Trollope and Henry Kingsley, take up his tone, and there is much of it in Hopkins's verse.

The art of using the sort of tone practised by Reade—it has its art like any other—was well in train by the time the Crimean War prompted further urgent use of it. The third volume of *Modern Painters* appeared in 1856, towards the end of the war, and is frankly sub-titled 'Of

---

[1] In 1837; quoted by William Robbins, *The Newman Brothers* (1966), p. 72, probably from an unpublished letter.

Many Things', which signified that no interesting matter arising would be excluded by anything so pedantic as literary form. After many 'things' arising of an aesthetic sort comes the final 'thing' very much otherwise: 'I cannot close this volume without alluding briefly to a subject of different interest from any that have occupied us in its pages. For it may, perhaps, seem to a general reader heartless and vain to enter zealously into questions about our arts and pleasures, in a time of so great public anxiety as this.' And so to the argument that the war is a good thing for England at that point of our history. The tone of the writing may be gathered from the second of his seven ensuing paragraphs:

But I ask *their* witness, to whom the war has changed the aspect of the earth, and imagery of heaven, whose hopes it has cut off like a spider's web, whose treasure it has placed, in a moment, under the seals of clay. Those who can never more see sunrise, nor watch the climbing light gild the Eastern clouds, without thinking what graves it has gilded, first, far down behind the dark earth-line,—who never more shall see the crocus bloom in spring, without thinking what dust it is that feeds the wild flowers of Balaclava. Ask *their* witness, and see if they will not reply that it is well with them and with theirs; that they would have it no otherwise; would not, if they might, receive back their gifts of love and life, nor take again the purple of their blood out of the cross on the breastplate of England. Ask them: and though they should answer only with a sob, listen if it does not gather upon their lips into the sound of the old Seyton war-cry—'Set on.'

At least authors could avoid continuing to write in certain kinds now suspect, though sometimes favoured by their younger selves. We have seen that Clough thought the age slighted poems after classical models and from oriental sources (which carried with them the obligation of certain forms); and Carlyle sneered at 'songs by persons of quality'. Much writing in such forms had been done during the eighteenth and early nineteenth centuries, writings that prompted Words-worth to mock those who 'converse with us as gravely about a *taste* for Poetry, as they express it, as if it were a thing as indifferent as a taste for Rope-dancing, or Fron-tiniac or Sherry'. In Newman's collected poems we pass suddenly from verses that could be read out at a party—verses sub-titled 'For an Album'—to the fierce poems first contributed to the earnest *British Magazine*, before being collected in the *Lyra Apostolica* of 1836, all of them written when he had come to see that the metre that had amused him as a youth could be made to work as 'an effective quasi-political engine'. ('Do not stirring times', he asks, 'bring out poets? Do they not give opportunity for the rhetoric of poetry, and the persuasion?')[1] The change in the *Zeitgeist* was plain when it was thought worth while to remark that Arthur Hallam, the earnest Apostle who died in 1833, was no good at elegant verses.[2] So far did the pendulum swing back that in 1871 Andrew Lang complained that Clough's poems were 'poetry about the Thirty-nine Articles'.[3]

It might be expected that such earnestness would choose the medium of formal satire; but this fell into disuse, at least with writers of standing—partly from doubts of the right of one man to condemn another at a time when moral and intellectual canons were generally questioned, and partly from the feelings that satire is too 'literary' a form to be taken seriously: towards the end of his political series *Who's to Blame?*, published during the Crimean War, Newman pronounces the caution, 'Let no man call this satire, for it is most seriously said'. There was also some mistrust of allegory, and of irony when

[1] Letter of 1 Dec. 1832; *Letters*, ed. Mozley, I. 281.
[2] Editor's Preface to *Remains . . . of Arthur Henry Hallam* (1834), pp. ix–x.
[3] To the question what subjects he thought suitable, his reply was 'Apple-blossom' (E. M. Sellar, *Recollections and Impressions*, 1907, pp. 24–5).

sustained throughout an argument or fiction; the one masterpiece is *The Fair Haven* (1873), Samuel Butler's pretended defence of miracles, with a constructional ingenuity worthy of Swift.

But humbler forms were promoted, notably the ballad. Wordsworth had seen what strength of thinking it could carry, and passed the knowledge on to Tennyson, Kingsley, and Matthew Arnold. And comic ballads and parodies (the most favoured form of 'imitation') were often topical and hard-hitting, an effective kind of journalism.

Other humble forms were those that carried controversy. Arnold spoke of the 'controversial life we all lead'. Pamphlet and controversial letter to the Press brought the great and lesser writers to the condition of fighters, which condition both Carlyle and Newman saw as proper to man. Newman quoted Juvenal's 'Facit indignatio versus', adding: 'I do not feel this in the case of verse; I do, in the case of prose'.[1]

The plainest writing for the times was in such forms. Earnest writers sent letters to newspapers—a collection of them would impress like a bonfire with fireworks. The parson in Reade's *It is Never Too Late to Mend* threatens to go over the heads of the Civil Service and write both to the Press and the Queen—'That Lady has a character; one of its strong, unmistakeable feature is a real, tender, active humanity.' Poems could be 'effective ... engines' even if '*quasi*-political', but Thackeray (and others) could be wholly and directly political. He marked the occasion in 1843 when Lord Lowther, the Postmaster-General, accepted the tender of a Scottish firm to make mail-coaches for Ireland by describing in powerful doggerel for the Dublin *Nation* an imaginary but all too likely scene in the family of an Irish coach-builder now thrown out of work:

[1] Letter to W. G. Ward, 15 Mar. 1862.

He turns from their prattle as angry as may be,
  'O daddy, I'm hungry,' says each little brat;
And yonder sits mammy, and nurses the baby,
  Thinking how long there'll be dinner for that.

For daddy and children, for babby and mammy,
  No work and no hope, Oh, the prospect is fine!
But I fancy I'm hearing your lordship cry—'Dammee,
  Suppose they *do* starve, it's no business of mine.'

This was the year that Hood wrote his 'Song of the Shirt' and Elizabeth Barrett her 'Cry of the children', written after reading the official report on the employment of children in mines and factories, a set of verses ending:

'How long,' they say, 'how long, O cruel nation,
  Will you stand, to move the world, on a child's heart,—
Stifle down with a mailed heel its palpitation,
  And tread onward to your throne amid the mart?
Our blood splashes upward, O gold-heaper,
  And your purple shows your path!
But the child's sob in the silence curses deeper
  Than the strong man in his wrath.'

and the year that Dickens, 'perfectly stricken down with the Blue Book you have sent me', wrote *A Christmas Carol*.


The most lasting products of this need to strike hard and produce political results are those achieved by novelists. Novels had been used for practical ends in the late eighteenth century—Mrs. Inchbald's *Simple Story*, Godwin's *Caleb Williams*, Bage's *Hermsprong* all belong to the 1790s. When defending the novel form Jane Austen had claimed it as the repository of the highest powers of a writer, powers that in earlier times had produced epics and tragedies. Half a century later, in *Bentley's Quarterly Review* for 1859, Anne Mozley concentrated on a novel's effect on its reader. While being 'amused' by it, as all novel readers insist on being, not only do 'we expect to have our feelings roused, our taste cultivated', but also, in these bad days, 'our social conscience refined and quickened'. And she adds: 'To these requirements, even to the last, all must subscribe'. By that time there had been many novels that hoped to refine and quicken a reader's conscience. In 1850 a reviewer could note that 'books of fiction are all now connected in some way with the condition of society', and six years later a letter to *The Times* from Sidney Godolphin Osborne, the well-known clergyman and philanthropist, noted (in the course of his argument for the reinstating of Sunday band-playing in the Parks) that not only the philanthropists but the novelists 'have left no one feature of [the] condition [of the 'working-classes in our great towns'] unmasked'. It is not the concern of a critic and even a historian of literature to recount the fortunes of literature in producing a practical effect on the life of the time, though it is amusing to recall that *Nicholas Nickleby* led to a closing-down and bankruptcy of schools in Yorkshire, and that after the emergence of Bumble in the course of the serial publication of *Oliver Twist* there were lectures in Chelsea rebutting the implied charges against parochial maladministration.[1] To Dickens's credit, one must pause to modify the widely held view that as a novelist-reformer he was often beating at an open door. Fitzjames Stephen described him as 'get[ting] his first notions of an abuse from the discussions that accompany its removal',[2] a view later supported by Humphry House. It was unlikely that anybody in that widely earnest age could claim to be the first mover towards a particular reform, and Dickens no doubt usually joined his earnest and far-carrying voice to that of others, but it is also true that most of the doors on which he beat his tattoo were fast shut indeed. The

[1] *Morning Chronicle* (2 Sept. 1837).
[2] *Edinburgh Review* (July 1857).

evils of the workhouse system survived into the twentieth century, and even some of the wicked imbecilities of the Court of Chancery.

We are concerned with these many 'purpose' novels, which had at least the immediate effect of powerful letters to *The Times*, because they are also novels in their own right. Sometimes a purpose spoils the art of a novel. Elizabeth Barrett Browning, even with *Mary Barton* before her, could hold that 'these class-books must always be defective as works of art',[1] and T. A. Trollope, writing of his mother's *Life and Adventures of Michael Armstrong, the Factory Boy*, which, appearing in 1840, was early in the newly opened field, remarked: 'it never became one of the more popular among my mother's novels, sharing, I suppose, the fate of most novels written for some purpose other than that of amusing their readers. Novel readers are exceedingly quick to smell the rhubarb under the jam in the dose offered to them, and set themselves against the undesired preachment.'[2] A purpose novel might offend by the obtrusiveness of its purpose. Anthony Trollope later withdrew from *The Three Clerks* the chapter discussing Civil Service reform; Reade was to be more circumspect—he placed in an appendix to *Put Yourself in his Place* his discussion on strikes. Again, a purpose novel might falsify the impression of 'truth' in the sense advocated by Thackeray. Mrs. Henry Wood's first novel, *Danesbury House*, the winning entry in a competition devised by a society advocating teetotalism, appropriately to that end, ascribed the disasters overtaking its personages solely to alcohol. She was unnecessarily limited as a psychologist because of her terms of reference. Better novelists saw to it that their works were not damaged as novels by what was practical in their purpose. Their principles when writing them were clearly enunciated by Thackeray in the reviews he

[1] *Letters of Elizabeth Barrett Browning*, I. 472.
[2] *What I Remember* (1887), II. 7–8.

contributed anonymously to the *Morning Chronicle* in
1844–5—reviews of Disraeli's *Coningsby* and *Sybil*,
Lever's *St. Patrick's Eve*, and some of the 'Christmas
Books' of the latter year. He disliked public purpose in
novels because for him it lay wholly outside the field
proper for a novelist: 'Morals and manners we believe to
be the novelist's best themes; and hence prefer romances
which do not treat of algebra, religion, political
economy, or other abstract science.'[1] But it is because the
better purpose novelists give first attention to 'morals
and manners' that they produce literature. When it comes
to their purpose they avoid 'abstract science' in favour of
concrete examples in which its principles are embodied,
and the concrete examples must be persons complete as
human beings. Such a novel, complete as a human document even if it is also a social document, is *Bleak House*,
which is a multi-purpose novel. Dickens's grand social
object, of attacking the law's delays especially as they
exist in the Court of Chancery, leads him to achieve a
theme to which all the action and characters are related.
With this main purpose, however, he interweaves
subordinate ones, such as that of ridiculing misguided
philanthropists in the persons of Mrs. Jellyby and Mrs.
Pardiggle, the dangerous and shocking condition of
metropolitan graveyards, and in Guster, Mrs. Snagsby's
servant, the results of parochial baby-farming. These
objects of public purpose are shepherded into the plot,
and not by means that seem improbable in the general
multitudinousness of a novel by Dickens. Esther, a ward
in Chancery, is made to go and stay at Mrs. Jellyby's. Jo,
the crossing-sweeper, whom the philanthropists ignore,
lives in a slum which is Chancery property, being be-
friended by a poor law-writer, 'Nemo', who turns out to
be Esther's father. Later Jo becomes a vital witness in the
hunt for Lady Dedlock. Being in the plot, none of these

---

[1] 13 May 1845; *Contributions to the Morning Chronicle*, ed. G. N. Ray (1955),
pp. 77–8.

personages exists solely to point a moral. Guster, for instance, is not simply a hard-done-by orphan but a pungent individual. For a purpose novelist setting out to satirize the legal system it would have been enough to create a set of indistinguishably devious lawyers. But Dickens creates individuals—the sinister courtly Tulkinghorn, 'an oyster of the old school whom nobody could open', 'Conversation' Kenge, the funereal and 'respectable' Mr. Vholes—but one cannot characterize such complex people in an epithet or two. It is the same with the philanthropists—Mrs. Pardiggle, with her knack of seeming to be able, when entering a room, to upset small pieces of furniture at a great distance, is overpoweringly an individual. Even in so purposeful a novel as *Hard Times* Dickens does not let his literary sense be drowned by his social purpose. It may be that Mr. Bounderby is too near to caricature for the taste of certain critics, but Mr. Gradgrind is indubitably a suffering human being as well as a representative of utilitarian philosophy: witness his bewildered distress when his daughter flies to him as a refuge from the hateful marriage in which he has involved her (again the imagery has a Carlylean ring):

'. . . I only entreat you to believe, my favourite child, that I have meant to do right.'
He said it earnestly, and to do him justice he had. In gauging fathomless deeps with his little mean excise-rod, and in staggering over the universe with his rusty stiff-legged compasses, he had meant to do great things. Within the limits of his short tether he had tumbled about, annihilating the flowers of existence with greater singleness of purpose than many of the blatant personages whose company he kept.[1]

In her hard-hitting review of Reade's *It is Never Too Late to Mend,* George Eliot honoured his power. Without doubt he is the most powerful of purpose novelists because he can dwell on the abuses, so inexhaustibly, so

[1] Bk. III, Ch. i.

fiercely, so grippingly. Indeed the grip comes near to torture, as near as it can without annihilating the 'psychical distance' that must continue to exist between the reader and page if the reader is to continue to read. If Reade got a part, and sometimes a great part, of his material from print—blue-books and newspapers—he took only such as were gifts for a novelist, exposing madhouses, strikes, and prison discipline. He digested his material, and re-imagined it. He used many means to bring his point to bear on the reader. His novels both show and say. The 'show' part is technically strong; Reade narrates in a violent fashion but with control, making a use of the 'sensational' that is legitimate: the reader is, as it were, whipped along his course. The 'saying' part is divided between the personages and the narrator. The personages discuss the abuse, Reade being represented by him who has right on his side, and that side having a great deal to be said for it. Even in semi-delirium, the prison chaplain conducts a lucid debate with an imaginary opponent on the advantages of a parole system over the ticket-of-leave.[1] And Reade also frequently backs up his narrative—which stands on its own feet as firm as a war-horse—with earnest and indeed urgent harangues in his own authorial person: here is an instance concerning the brutalities of prison discipline:

Were you ever seized at night with a violent cramp? ... Imagine now the severest cramp you ever felt artificially prolonged for hours and hours. Imagine yourself cramped in a vice, no part of you moveable a hair's breadth, except your hair and your eyelids. Imagine the fierce cramp growing and growing, and rising like a tide of agony higher and higher above nature's endurance, and you will cease to wonder that a man always sunk under Hawes's man-press.[2]

These purpose novels of Reade's, appearing when there was coming to be a fashion for 'sensation' novels,

[1] *It is Never too Late to Mend*, Ch. xviii.    [2] Ibid.

authenticate the form in advance. No mid-century novelist is more sensational in the literal sense of affecting the
reader physically—with sick horror or chilled spine—and
yet there is nothing in *It is Never Too Late to Mend* and *Put
Yourself in his Place*, or nothing that matters, to offend
against possibility or probability, in the way there is
much to offend against these respectable sisters in the
sensation novels of Miss Braddon or Mrs. Wood. He
does not take a humdrum theme and stick horrors on to
it, but takes the horrific as his theme.

We cannot say that for Dickens a practical purpose
either helped or hindered his art as a novelist. Disraeli's
*Sybil* is, however, a botched book showing an author
mistaking his powers because of his practical purpose.
Disraeli's literary powers were best employed in writing
high social comedy, and he would have been happier, as a
purely literary genius, if he had lived in, say, the Edwar-
dian era, and written Ada Leverson's sort of novels. His
literary talent, however, was overmastered by his genius
for public affairs; he is more remarkable as a politician
than as an author. There are chapters in *Sybil* that call out
his powers congenially because they exhibit satirical
specimens of the upper of the 'Two Nations', the rich,
many of whom, existing in the nineteenth century, could
not but be politically active, and who encouraged the
activities of hangers-on like Tadpole and Taper, who live
for the business of party. Disraeli's purpose in writing the
novel, as also in *Coningsby* and *Tancred*, however, was an
electioneering purpose: he wished to air his 'Young England' views, which provided for a return to the supposed
felicities of the Middle Ages; and this political purpose
entailed an exhibition of the other of the two nations.
Turning to exhibit the poor, however, he does not fare so
well. He needed as a novelist to go more deeply into them
than into the rich, who can exist for a reader happily
enough even if exhibited merely as glittering surfaces—
a high degree of civilization is itself interesting and

adequate material for the satirist. For the depiction of the poor we need some power that can penetrate deeper into their nature. This power, which was conspicuously Mrs. Gaskell's, Disraeli lacked. He can give a picture of the stricken miners and factory-workers which is brilliant as a piece of political showmanship. But that is not enough for a novel. Thackeray, reviewing *Sybil* in the *Morning Chronicle*, shrewdly suggested that the pictures of Wodgate might 'send travellers, in quest of sensations, to Wales or Lancashire this summer, in place of the Alps or Baden'. When his miners and factory-workers, male and female, speak vividly, it is as if they know they are going to be quoted in blue-books. They are providing politicians with ammunition, with something effective to say in a speech. They do not talk as Mrs. Gaskell and Dickens make their poor people talk, with speech arising out of flesh and blood.

The story is a mere piece of theatricality. Sybil, the daughter of a Chartist leader, is all grace and charm and refinement, and therefore offends against the novelists' principle of 'truth'. As a novel *Sybil* has a spine of tinsel. The love between Sybil and Egremont is that of personages in an operetta, though they have talks about politics that would be interesting on an electioneering platform. Disraeli's purpose certainly helped him to get more readers. It was as much educational as party-political. It helped open people's eyes to the horrors of the big towns. And since blue-book material is always interesting, it has won him indulgent readers in our time also.

Because of the practical purpose of much mid-century literature Arnold felt called upon to restate the prime principle of criticism, 'disinterestedness', which Carlyle had found it expedient to ignore. If Carlyle had been born a generation later, when conditions were easier, he would not have misjudged the writing of Keats and Lamb. Arnold saw that earnest readers were liable to ask only a single question of a work of literature—did it advance their cause? He insisted that a piece of literature must not be judged by its worth in the field of practice, unless by good management its worth for the aesthetic sense was assured. That Pater made such a fuss of his 'aesthetic criticism' is an index of his need to remove obstacles. Swinburne was soon to write of Wilkie Collins's *Miss or Mrs?*, a purpose novel designed to aid the reform of the marriage laws:

> What brought good Wilkie's genius nigh perdition?
> Some demon whispered—'Wilkie! have a mission'.[1]

Heads of a requisite coolness had not been wanting throughout the mid-century. Of some heads no calm whatever could be expected—of Kingsley's, or Reade's, in particular. But those of other earnest writers found stillness within their power. Thackeray, perhaps with Charlotte Brontë in mind, declared that 'Art ought not to be a fever';[2] Lewes called Thackeray 'the quietest perhaps of all contemporary writers'.[3] Pater said of Newman that he had 'dealt with all the perturbing influences of our century in a manner as classical, as idiomatic, as earnest and elegant, as Steele's'.[4] Mrs. Gaskell's 'Cousin Phillis' is as calm as a reflection in a mirror. Tennyson and Arnold give us passages in which calm—the calm of despair—is profound. H. G. Wells recalled his master Huxley as 'deliberate, balanced, never losing his head in any rashness of assertion, never winning a point in the game by any trick, implacably fair, inflexibly discreet', and believed that the world would remember him as 'a calm voice asking questions'.[5] They had all felt the tumult of the times but had the power to stand back from it. They achieved the calm that, in Wordsworth's words, subsists at the heart of endless agitation.

[1] *Fortnightly Review* (Nov. 1889).     [2] *The Newcomes*, Ch. xxii.
[3] *Morning Chronicle* (6 Mar. 1848).
[4] *Guardian* (17 Feb. 1886; collected in *Essays from* The Guardian, 1901, p. 16).
[5] Not traced.

# 2. CARLYLE

AMONG THE 'wild' prose-writers,[1] poetical and farouche
as an Old Testament prophet, stood Carlyle. His writing
inaugurated and spanned the great middle decades of the
century—work of his, including the *Reminiscences*, was
still coming out posthumously in the 1880s. He also
dominated the age, an unusual achievement for a writer
whose stated topic was often history more or less ancient.
He devoted something like two decades to writing his
*The French Revolution: A History*, his *Oliver Cromwell's
Letters and Speeches: with Elucidations*, and his *History of
Friedrich II of Prussia, called Frederick the Great* in its six big
volumes. It was from the past, again, both remote and
more recent, that *On Heroes, Hero-Worship, and the Heroic
in History* drew its giant examples; its chapter on
Mahomet stimulated if it did not create the interest in
'comparative' religion, which is at least partly a historical
interest. Finally, many of his *Critical and Miscellaneous
Essays*, which fill six volumes in the collected edition of
1869, are on past men and things, and his interpretation
of Abbot Samson in *Past and Present* is one of the finest
as well as one of the first documents in the great
nineteenth-century recovery of the Middle Ages. Looked
at from the other side, it is equally surprising that the
historian of Cromwell and the rest was also the up-
to-the-minute commentator on affairs, the author of
*Chartism*, the strictly contemporary half of *Past and Present*, the *Life of Sterling*—a tract for the times as well as a
biography for all time—and *Latter-Day Pamphlets*. Along
with these go the many writings on the literature and

[1] See p. 36.

philosophy of Germany that virtually introduced that
large, wild, and lively literature to England. It might also
seem surprising that Carlyle cared so much for a present
which he never ceased to stigmatize in phrases like 'these
our afflicted times', 'this dislocated time', 'these anarchic
times', 'these quite unmusical days', 'the most distracted
and divided age', 'our poor Nineteenth Century', 'our
poor, jarring, self-listening Time', 'this sad age of cob-
webs,    worn-out    symbolism,    reminiscences    and
simulacra', 'these unspeakable days'—or more simply, in
the phrase Arnold borrowed for his well-known sonnet,
'these bad days'.[1] But for reasons that will become clearer
later on, it was just because the age was all he said it was
that he could not forsake it. As he said of London, 'Deep
in your soul you take up your protest against it, defy it,
and even despise it; but need not divide yourself from it
for that.'[2] The key to his interests stares at us from the title
of his *Past and Present*.

He dominated the mid-century because, whatever his
topic, his eye was on the present, wholly or partly. It had
been Hazlitt's view, and it became Dr. Arnold's and
Carlyle's, that the moral justification for learning about
the past lay in its relevance to the problematical present.
The historian of Cromwell and the rest went so far as to
say that a past century was 'worthless except precisely in
so far as it can be made the nineteenth'.[3] That doctrine
might seem the scholar's defence against the charge that
the present was one of the things he conveniently
ignored. It would be inconceivable, however, for these
men to have contemplated escape, and Carlyle for one
voiced his contempt for the 'reading-corps, who read
merely to escape from themselves'.[4] Newman might

---

[1] *Past and Present*, I. 6; other examples also from *Past and Present*, *Life of
Sterling*, 'Goethe's Works', 'Corn-Law Rhymes', and 'Diderot'.

[2] *Correspondence of Carlyle and Emerson* (1883), I. 92.

[3] Ibid. II. 10.

[4] 'Dr. Francia' (1843; *Critical and Miscellaneous Essays*, VI).

sigh for an age more closely wrapped in superstition, or Morris and Arnold (in some of their moods), hanker after an age supposedly of Christian faith, or supposedly merrily free from the painful drudgery of clattering weaving-sheds, but a wish to avoid the present, or to pretend to, was not among the weaknesses of any of them, any more than of Hazlitt, Dr. Arnold, or Carlyle. 'I do believe for one thing', Carlyle said, 'a man has no right to say to his own generation, turning quite away from it, "Be damned." '[1] His first concern was with his living fellows: 'My heart is sick and sore in behalf of my own poor generation'.[2]

He remained faithful to his age, both for its own sake and because he was unusually gifted to deal with it. In two comparatively early essays, 'Signs of the Times' (1829) and 'Characteristics' (1831), he gave of set purpose a completer account of the present than that given by any other great writer of whatever period. Because of those essays, and the knowledge and insight they represented, he was the spokesman of what Hazlitt called the spirit of the age, a quantity vague but palpable which Carlyle preferred to call the *Zeitgeist*, and which was much discussed, Buckle summarizing it as the 'pressure of surrounding opinions'. It was an idea of his (out of which Browning's Blougram made a page of vivid argument) that what men say in any one age is the voice of that age and of no other, and that the form taken by the public life of men not hereditarily bound to manual tasks (and many even of these were now doing new tasks) is the form imposed by the age. Blougram said he would have been a Christian in the sixteenth century, an unbeliever 'of course' in the late eighteenth century, and in the nineteenth a man hesitating before a choice. Carlyle was engaged in modifying the *Zeitgeist* as much as in responding to it, as were all his fellow writers.

[1] *Carlyle and Emerson*, II. 12.
[2] Ibid. II. 10.

Even Carlyle did not voice that spirit completely. For all its amplitude and up-to-dateness his philosophy had omissions and parochial corners. In particular it misjudged the discoveries of mid-nineteenth-century scientists;[1] this disqualified him from participating in the geological controversy which was upsetting people's trust in Genesis as a historical record, and later from considering what Huxley called the question of questions for the nineteenth century—'man's place in nature'. Nor did he join his middle-class contemporaries in poring over the appearance of rocks and stones and trees, of clouds and waves, an occupation that accounted for perhaps a quarter of the matter of mid-nineteenth-century-literature. He did encourage his fellows to 'see', and to see for themselves; but to see what was being seen by him, not by the young Ruskin. Then again, Carlyle missed the first firm moves towards the emancipation of women, to which his disciple, John Stuart Mill, was so much alive—the world of Carlyle's writings is totally, aggressively, and indeed Nordically and primitively a male world. In addition, he lagged behind his age in some of the 'moral sensibility' claimed for it by David Masson, who noted also its inevitable lack of 'moral vigour'. For he had too plain, perhaps because too Scottish, an idea of moral right and wrong, and some of his menacing confidence is due to that plainness:

Tolerance and a rose-water world is the evil symptom of the time we are living in: it was just like it before the French Revolution, when universal brotherhood, tolerance and twaddle were preached in all the market places; so they had to go through their revolution with one hundred and fifty a day butchered—the gutters thick with blood, and the skins tanned

[1] His own extensive scientific studies belonged to the 1820s (when he attained some eminence in mathematics), but his mistrust of the 'Mechanical' spirit is evident at least from 1829 ('Signs of the Times') and his hostility to Darwinian theory is notorious. But Tyndall was impressed by his grasp of scientific principles: see, e.g., 'Personal Recollections of Thomas Carlyle', *Fortnightly Review*, 1890, collected in *New Fragments* (1892).

into leather: and so it will be here unless a righteous intolerance of the Devil should awake in time.[1]

He did not benefit enough from the completer investigation of human character and personality, and the part played in their formation by heredity and environment, which during the eighteenth century and later were showing how rough and hasty were the verdicts usually passed on them by moralists. He deprecated what he alleged of the prison reformers—this 'indiscriminate mashing up of Right and Wrong into a patent treacle'[2] —and accused Monckton Milnes of being 'perpetual president of the Heaven and Hell Amalgamation Society'; but Milnes may have been more aware than he of the newly discovered reasons for doubting the old confidence in these things. He was sometimes more ready with his pity for wrongdoers than with his wish to explore why wrong was done. In saying this I speak of him rather as an abstract thinker than as a historian; when he came to consider individual men, he was ready to temper his blacks and whites. Finally, he always underrated the good that French literature had to offer England, seeing in it little more than 'wretched mockeries about marriage' and 'canine libertinage' and writing on one occasion: 'The French literature of G. Sand & Co., which many people told me was a new-birth, I found to be a detestable putrefaction—new life of nothing but maggots and blue-bottles.'[3] He even jibed at the French as 'ever-talking, ever gesticulating', forgetting for a moment that the words described himself.

Why he is chargeable with these insufficiencies invites speculation, which anyone interested can supply for himself in the way fashionable at the moment. Something

[1] Quoted without source in Walter Lewin, *Thomas Carlyle, Table Talk* (1890), p. 54.

[2] 'Model Prisons' in *Latter-Day Pamphlets* (1850).

[3] Letter to John Forster, *c.* 1844, MS. Victoria and Albert Museum.

must be put down to his own personality—for
instance, that he admired the clear-cut because he shared
the large quantity of chaos he noted in Tennyson and
Thackeray—and something to the date of his birth and
the circumstances of his family. In his 1832 review of
Ebenezer Elliott's *Corn-Law Rhymes* he rightly saw that
there were certain advantages for a would-be writer starting from the lowest class in having to carve out his way to
the top, but the labour was too much for a self-taught
Elliott, and might also have proved too much for the son
of a Scottish peasant. Though his parents were all that he
described them to be—indeed, he called himself his
father's second volume—they could not imagine a higher
destiny for him than that of the ministry. Then again, his
birth in 1795, and his early hardship, may have decisively
limited as well as helped to sharpen his wide-ranging
sense of the times. Certainly the position of science rela-
tive to the position of traditional thought was stronger in
1850 than it had been in 1820.

Furthermore, if Carlyle cannot be said to be up to date
at all points, he also cannot be said to be wholly sound in
what he did try to master. As Robert Buchanan said,
'Carlyle—a poet in his savage way—has driven some
new and splendid truths (and as many errors) into the
heart of the people.'[1] 'Dubious metal', existing in his
ideas along with 'abundance of gold' has been found, in
particular by economists. And his recommendation of
hero-worship had its dangers.

Limitations and dubious things apart, in the thirties
and forties he was abreast of his age as no other writer
was, and if by the sixties his comments began to seem a
little old-fashioned and *entêté*, he was still dealing with
burning questions. He was the first writer to give his
readers the sense of living in a new era, in what could
really be called the nineteenth century. His immediate
predecessor of similar kind and stature, Dr. Johnson,

[1] *Master-Spirits* (1873), p. 108.

seemed to exist on a further shore. Perennially interesting, Johnson's writings lack the modern furniture of
Carlyle's. They are typified by the *Rambler* and Carlyle's
by the *Edinburgh Review* of the 1830s. It was because
Carlyle sensed the new importance of the periodical
Press, from newspaper to review, that he was so well
informed about what their many columns were discussing—and even advertising. His head had a thousand
ideas in it on a wider range of topics than had ever come
men's way—topics as far apart as the nature of genius and
Puseyism, as contemporary affairs in Paraguay and the
British Parliament, as theories about dandies and Land,
Labour, and Capital, as Sanitary Reform and the 'aristocracy of talent', as State education and the 'cash-nexus',
the census, and the ballot. He was the first great writer to
star his pages with remarks that shocked both by their
novelty and by the significance claimed for them, such
as this from 'Signs of the Times' in 1829: 'Has any man,
or any society of men, a truth to speak, a piece of spiritual
work to do; they can nowise proceed at once and with the
mere natural organs, but must first call a public meeting,
appoint committees, issue prospectuses, eat a public
dinner.' Carlyle's description in 1827 of one of his
German heroes, Jean Paul Richter, even more closely fits
himself: 'a man understanding the nineteenth century and
living in the midst of it'. He had made the powerful effort
to take his place in world history—world history, for he
saw that 'Steam and iron are making all the Planet into
one Village'.[1]

Eight years after 'Characteristics', his friend John
Sterling wrote a mammoth survey of his writings in
the *Westminster Review* for October 1839. It was described
by John Stuart Mill, the editor, as 'this attempt . . .
(we believe the first attempt yet made) at a calm
and comprehensive estimate of a man, for whom our

[1] *Carlyle and Emerson*, I. 207.

admiration has already been unreservedly expressed, and whose genius and worth have shed some rays of brightness on our own pages . . .' Carlyle took it as the clearest sign that he had arrived: 'The first generous human recognition, expressed with heroic emphasis and clear conviction amid its fiery exaggeration, that one's own poor battle in this world is not quite a mad and futile, that it is perhaps a worthy and manful one, which will come to something yet: this fact is a memorable one in every history.'[1]

How much of his work was already accomplished, there were *Sartor Resartus*, the *History of the French Revolution*, and four volumes of *Critical and Miscellaneous Essays*, all of which Sterling was reviewing, to show. His arrival was through a jungle of achievement. As a recent student of *Sartor Resartus* has said:

It is a case of several apprenticeships. As journalist Carlyle ends his apprenticeship only with the publication of his Schiller biography in 1825. As a translator . . . with the translation of *Wilhelm Meister* in 1824–25. As a literary critic . . . with the writing of *German Romance* in 1826. As an essayist [he] has surely arrived with the 1827 *Edinburgh Review* essay on Jean Paul. As a novelist [he] had to write 'Illudo Chartis' and 'Wotton Reinfred' before his apprenticeship ends with *Sartor Resartus* in 1830–1831.[2]

With all that behind him he migrated to London from Scotland in 1833.

That migration had unusual significance. It was at the hub of things that, like Johnson, Lamb, and Dickens, he ought to have been born. For his ruling passion was for man, as completely as it had been that of his great eighteenth-century predecessors—in France as well as England—man individual and aggregated, English and European, man in America, black and white, man as he stretched from 'your Luther, your Knox, your Anselm,

[1] *Life of Sterling*, III. i.
[2] G. B. Tennyson, *Sartor called Resartus* (Princeton, 1964), p. 25.

Becket, Abbot Samson, Samuel Johnson', Cromwell, and Frederick to the Negroes and the 'successful skilful workers some two millions, it is now counted, [who] sit in Workhouses, Poor-law Prisons; or have "out-door relief" flung over the wall to them,—the workhouse Bastille being filled to bursting,'[1] and 'multiform ragged louts, runaway apprentices, starved weavers, thievish valets; an entirely broken population, tending towards the treadmill'. And the mass of men now, as he informed England, included Germans, who once again claimed the attention they had had in Luther's day. Like his great predecessors he achieved some of those discoveries about men in general that delighted Johnson by coming home to the business and bosoms of everybody. To the instances scattered over this present chapter I add one more, because it is irresistible: 'The whole world seems against you; but it is not so: other men who knock against you are simply thinking of themselves, not of you at all.'[1] Mankind, and individual men, are universal in his forty volumes. And for all the bluster of his masculinity, his passion for them is maternal in its warmth and solicitude. It was men he was looking for when he played the historian, one of the reasons why he was a historian at all being that men were the prime glory of the universe, and that heartening records of them were plentiful. He saw history as the 'essence of innumerable biographies'. The past is whirling smoke, and the historian's main task that of peering into it for human faces. As Augustine Birrell said:

Imaginary joys and sorrows may extort from [Carlyle] nothing but grunts and snorts; but let him only worry out for himself, from that great dust-heap called 'history', some undoubted fact of human and tender interest, and, however small it may be, relating possibly to some one hardly known,

[1] *Past and Present*, I. 1.
[2] From a conversation of 1859; *Anne Gilchrist, her Life and Writings*, ed. H H. Gilchrist (1887), p. 74.

and playing but a small part in the events he is recording, and he will wax amazingly sentimental, and perhaps shed as many real tears as Sterne or Dickens do sham ones over their figments.[1]

This is how Jocelin of Brakelond appears to him in *Past and Present*: 'a veritable Monk of Bury St. Edmunds is worth attending to, if by chance made visible and audible. Here he is; and in his hand a magical speculum, much gone to rust indeed, yet in fragments still clear; wherein the marvellous image of his existence does still shadow itself, though fitfully, and as with an intermittent light!' And King John:

As through a glass darkly, we with our own eyes and appliances, intensely looking, discern at most: A blustering, dissipated human figure, with a kind of blackguard quality air, in cramoisy velvet, or other uncertain texture, uncertain cut, with much plumage and fringing; amid numerous other human figures of the like; riding abroad with hawks; talking noisy nonsense;—tearing out the bowels of St. Edmundsbury Convent (its larders namely and cellars) in the most ruinous way, by living at rack and manger there.[2]

Any human face that emerges from the murk of the past is welcome.

Men, again, are his first concern as a literary critic. Like Johnson he could say strong and subtle things about literature as it lies on the page, but, like him again, he preferred to see it as the evidence of personal character. He introduced the climax of one of his greatest essays with 'But to leave the mere literary character of Burns ...', and even if 'mere' still meant 'pure' for him, the assumption is that he is moving from the writings to their climax in the man. In speaking of a lack in Coleridge he showed what he himself possessed: he found him deficient in 'sympathy for concrete human things either

[1] *Obiter Dicta* (1884).
[2] *Past and Present*, II. I.

on the sunny or the stormy side'.[1] The word 'concrete' is
important. He never neglected the flesh and blood of his
subjects. He could not write about dead men till he had
acquired the power to imagine their living faces. (If portraits survived, he pasted them on a screen.[2]) He paid his
compliments to any writer who had achieved a human
portrait, especially one from life. For instance, the
traveller-historians on whom he had to rely for his knowledge of Dr. Francia of Paraguay were deplorably
vague—they seldom deigned to give a date—but he
warmed to them when for one blessed moment they
achieved a 'remarkable visuality': 'through a pair of clear
human eyes, you look face to face on the very figure of
the man'. If he did not encourage word-painting of nature
(which he called 'view-hunting') he excelled in the
word-painting of men. As a describer of them he shared
Dickens's ferocity of vision. His paintings are rather
sketchings, and this because he is intent on catching truth
in all its liveliness. He has been called the Rembrandt of
such things, but though that comparison indicates the
colours he liked, it belies the fiery hit-or-miss earnestness
of his method. The well-known description of Coleridge
in the *Life of Sterling* is an extended example; a briefer one,
that of Dickens in 1840:

He is a fine little fellow—Boz, I think, clear, blue, intelligent
eyes, eyebrows that he arches amazingly, large, protrusive,
rather loose mouth, a face of most extreme mobility, which he
shuttles about,—eyebrows, eyes, mouth and all,—in a very
singular manner while speaking. Surmount this with a loose
coil of common-coloured hair, and set it on a small compact
figure, very small, and dressed a la D'Orsay rather than well
—this is Pickwick. For the rest, a quiet, shrewd-looking little
fellow, who seems to guess pretty well what he is and what
others are.[3]

[1] *Life of Sterling*, i. 8.
[2] Sir Charles Gavan Duffy, *Conversations with Carlyle* (1892), p. 92.
[3] *Carlyle's Life in London*, i. 177-8.

Still more flashingly vivid is this of the American, Daniel Webster, with the added echo of his speech:

a grim, tall, broad-bottomed, yellow-skinned man, with brows like precipitous cliffs, and huge, black, dull, wearied, yet unweariable-looking eyes under them; amorphous projecting nose, and the angriest shut mouth I have anywhere seen. A droop on the sides of the upper lip is quite mastiff-like—magnificent to look upon; it is so quiet withal. I guess I should like ill to be that man's nigger. However, he is a right clever man in his way, and has a husky sort of fun in him too.[1]

Indeed the readiest proof of his genius lies in these portrait-sketches: Trelawny 'a huge black-whiskered, beetle-browed column of a man'; Babbage 'with his frog mouth and viper eyes'; Milnes 'a pretty little robin-redbreast of a man'.[2]

Whatever the text of any of his works, the topic is man, and to Carlyle may be ascribed the strength of the biographical in the literary criticism of later nineteenth-century critics such as Arnold and Pater. Because that prime interest was strong, it prompted in him a great originality—that of 'honour[ing human] greatness in all kinds'—or at least all masculine kinds. For him as for Johnson genius was a 'general capacity of mind', which in any one instance might fulfil itself in one or more of a hundred directions: 'I have no notion of a truly great man who could not be *all* sorts of great men'.[3] It was not a thing limited to expression in words, notes, or paint. But whereas a Johnson would honour genius in a man as far off from a poet as a lawyer, general, or statesman, Carlyle rejoiced that England, 'this favoured England', 'was not only to have had her Shakespeares, Bacons, Sidneys, but

---

[1] Ibid. I. 164.
[2] *New Letters*, ed. A. Carlyle (1904), I. 14; *Life in London*, I. 171; *Carlyle and Emerson*, I. 302.
[3] *Heroes and Hero-Worship* ('The Hero as Poet').

to have her Watts, Arkwrights, Brindleys'.[1] Mill, writing of Bentham, had seen 'his lot [as] cast in a generation of the leanest and barrenest men whom Europe had yet produced'. But because it had bred the first of the great engineers, inventors, and industrialists, Carlyle was ready to remove, at least temporarily, the stigma he himself had laid on the eighteenth century; he pauses to note that it is a 'calumniated' century,[2] as if it had not been calumniated most by himself. In *Past and Present* he quietly bracketed Arkwright's name with Goethe's.[3] He admired poems that began, or might have, with 'Arma virumque cano', but saw that in their modern equivalents the arms ought rather to be of the Ebenezer Elliott kind: 'Not "Arms and the Man"; "Tools and the Man", that were now our Epic'[4]—'an infinitely wider Epic' because of iron and steam. It was as much Carlyle as the engineers themselves who inspired Samuel Smiles to his greatest work, *The Lives of the Engineers*, and on the title-page of his *Industrial Biography: Iron Workers and Tool Makers* of 1863 Carlyle is quoted. Carlyle's admiration for the Arkwrights made him a sound philosopher at a time when the worst-off among his beloved fellow men were smashing the machines in their practical despair. In fastening on machines' importance he was much ahead of William Morris—of Morris the theorist at least, for the designs of Morris the craftsman presupposed their aid, and put them to excellent use. Machines being beneficial to man, it was a double outrage when they were used not to help the men who manned them so much as to fill the too ample and too often buttoned-up pockets of their owners.

The condition of the poor, now so much more hard at work, was the crying shame of the time. The seriousness of the 'condition-of-England question' was seen and

[1] *Chartism*, Ch. viii.
[2] Ibid.       [3] IV. 8.
[4] *Past and Present*, IV. 1; cf. 'Corn-Law Rhymes'.

understood by Carlyle, who awakened the conscience of the upper classes in language of the utmost urgency. The most important practical task he set for himself was to do what he could to help. His final greatness as a man is that the philosopher, the historian, the explorer of German literature, the writer of the introspective *Sartor Resartus*, the wielder of fiery poetry and turbulent musical speech, could also see that what he called 'the condition-of-England question' was paramount for the thirties and forties. Harriet Martineau in her *Autobiography* discerned the true Carlyle, beginning with the description of his appearance and behaviour:

... [his] rugged face, steeped in genius ... I have seen [his] face under all aspects, from the deepest gloom to the most reckless or most genial mirth; and it seemed to me that each mood would make a totally different portrait. The sympathetic is by far the finest, in my eyes. His excess of sympathy has been, I believe, the master pain of his life. He does not know what to do with it, and with its bitterness, seeing that human life is full of pain to those who look out for it: and the savageness which has come to be a main characteristic of this singular man is, in my opinion, a mere expression of his intolerable sympathy with the suffering. He cannot express his love and pity in natural acts, like other people; and it shows itself too often in unnatural speech. But to those who understand his eyes, his shy manner, his changing colour, his sigh, and the constitutional *pudeur* which renders him silent about every thing that he feels the most deeply, his wild speech and abrupt manner are perfectly intelligible.[1]

The pain and the warmth of his sympathy are clear in such a passage as this:

In 1755 Merthyr Tydvil was a mountain hamlet of five or six houses, stagnant and silent as it had been ever since Tydvil, the king's or laird's daughter was martyred here, say 1300 years before. About that time a certain Mr. Bacon, a cunning Yorkshireman, passing that way, discovered that there was iron in

[1] pp. 287–8.

the ground—iron and coal. He took a 99 years' lease in consequence, and—in brief, there are now about 50,000 grimy mortals, black and clammy with soot and sweat, screwing out a livelihood for themselves in that spot of the Taff valley. Such a set of unguided, hard-worked, fierce, and miserable looking sons of Adam I never saw before. Ah me! it is like a vision of hell, and will never leave me, that of these poor creatures broiling, all in sweat and dirt, amid their furnaces, pits and rolling mills. For here is absolutely no aristocracy or guiding class; nothing but one or two huge iron-masters.[1]

The composite genesis of *Past and Present* lay in outraged sympathy. He said of it: 'A most questionable, red-hot, indignant thing, for my heart is sick to look at the things now going on in this England; and the two millions of men sitting in poor-law bastilles seem to ask of every English soul, "Hast thou no word to say for us?" '[2] 'Pity' is one of the words that recur most often in his writings. His sympathy is dependent on his seeing, and he has the double credit for seeing that suffering was there to be seen, and for not forgetting it. At bottom there was the difference that, unlike most of his fellow writers, he had experienced for himself grinding poverty and the hunger that goes with it, and further, that unlike some writers who have risen in the social scale, he retained his sympathies with his former equals. He knew, as few of his fellow authors did, that if hunger could be prevented it ought to be. He would talk of souls with the best, but he differed from Newman in thinking that bodies came first.

But though there was all this sensitiveness to what was painful in man and in his heavy condition there was at least an equal response to what was glorious in him, however rarely it sparked or blazed. To the Swiftian readiness to wince he added what we might call the Michelangelesque admiration for the physical and moral greatness of man at his best. He admired more of man

---

[1] *Carlyle's Life in London*, II. 51–2; letter of [Aug.] 1850.
[2] *New Letters*, I. 281.

than Newman did. Newman counted manliness as the
power to master yourself. Carlyle honoured also the
physical animal for which mastery was mainly due. He
was partly responsible for the manliness of Browning's
mature poetry, and for the idea of the muscular Christian,
Tennyson's 'great broad-shouldered genial Englishman
... / Fair-haired and redder than a windy morn', which
Charles Kingsley typified; and for what Henry James
called the 'noble school of fiction', of which the novels of
Charles Reade and Henry Kingsley are the splendid rep-
resentatives. Because of all this we are sorry for Carlyle
when he reaches that point in his vast biography at which
he has to record and weigh Frederick's flight from the battle
of Mollwitz, which unexpectedly ended in a big victory.
That was a bad moment for Frederick, which his biographer might have admitted to. Instead he praised him by
special pleading. Seeking men great enough to worship, he
wished to worship them whole, and he found enough of
them to form an impressive band. To admit weakness in
Frederick was like alleging it of the Godhead.

Any account of Carlyle must place his socio-political
writings in the foreground. What he had to say on that
crucial topic first becomes unmistakable in 'Characteristics':

How much among us might be likened to a whited sepulchre;
outwardly all pomp and strength; but inwardly full of horror
and despair and dead-men's bones! Iron highways, with their
wains fire-winged, are uniting all ends of the firm Land; quays
and moles, with their innumerable stately fleets, tame the
Ocean into our pliant bearer of burdens; Labour's thousand
arms, of sinew and of metal, all-conquering everywhere, from
the tops of the mountain down to the depths of the mine and
the caverns of the sea, ply unweariedly for the service of man:
yet man remains unserved. He has subdued this Planet, his
habitation and inheritance; yet reaps no profit from the
victory.

He saw deeply enough to see, as Darwin was to, that man is a struggler. For him the struggle for social betterment is 'the one true war'.[1] It was a war that was being fought not only by the various parcels of the middle class that Thackeray was soon to delineate in his *Book of Snobs*, but by the lowest also, and by them for the first of all principles—that a man has the right to eat if food is available. The peace it aimed at was the peace supervening on work that has earned a satisfying meal. More than even that blessing might transpire if food was shared out first. In the end all men might have come to see that '"we are members one of another" and "none liveth to himself", that riches are a trust, and power a ministry, and the State for all its children a family and a school'.[2] It was well if this long struggle now once again beginning from the very bottom, being a struggle for physical survival, proceeded without bloodshed, and the hope that it might do so lay in achieving a just estimate of work. The master, he insisted, must come to see that work bestows a dignity on the doer, and honour him accordingly. After all, the masters he was addressing, the factory masters, had not long attained that other dignity, the dignity of washed hands. Because of their presence in the factory they visibly shared in the work that is 'the grandest of human interests'. 'All work,' insisted Carlyle, 'even cotton-spinning, is noble'.[3] He wanted to help build up respect on both sides. Each side must respect the manhood of the other, the men respecting masters, who see that more is at issue than cash ('Love of men cannot be bought by cash-payment'), and the masters the men, who have responded to Carlyle's call: 'But it is to you, ye Workers, who do already work, and are as grown men, noble and honourable in a sort, that the whole world calls for new work

[1] *Past and Present*, IV. 4.
[2] A. M. D. Hughes's summary in his edition of *Past and Present* (1918), p. lxxx.
[3] *Past and Present*, III. 4.

and nobleness.'[1] He expected his book to reach the workers, but it was addressed first to the middle class. And
because the rest needed instructing in the facts, he made
his books as much paintings as arguments. The title of the
first chapter of his *Chartism* in 1840 was addressed to the
intellect, 'Condition-of-England Question', and its first
sentence, if arresting, was quietly so: 'A feeling very
generally exists that the condition and disposition of the
Working Classes is a rather ominous matter at present;
that something ought to be said, something ought to be
done, in regard to it.' But thereupon followed a discourse
as graphic as anything of Swift's. Carlyle subjects that
condition to analysis, but his main point is such as could
be made by anybody. For he asks men to use their physical eyes, not in reading learned articles complete with
their statistics (he quotes the 'witty statesman' who had
said 'you might prove anything by figures', which neatly
shows us how modern is the nineteenth-century treatment of such matter), but in looking at 'the concrete
phenomena' and 'for himself'. 'Eyesight' is 'the best evidence'. He asks his reader to notice 'with his own eyes'
the condition of the workers. He had already seen that
'two Sects ... extend through the entire structure of
Society ... two contradictory, uncommunicating
masses'[2]—which may well have inspired Tennyson's
lines, 'These two parties still divide the world, Of those
that want and those that have' in 'Walking to the Mail',
and the more famous 'Two Nations' of Disraeli's *Sybil*.
When for his part he describes their condition, he enters
into it as a novelist would, and so vivid is the account of
their plight—as it had been in a flash or two in 'Characteristics'—that it was almost enough to read Carlyle. The
'feelings' that John Sterling in 1840 saw to be so important a part of Carlyle are high, but for all their fire there is
an adventurous and decisive intellect at work among the

[1] Ibid. IV. 4, 8.
[2] *Sartor Resartus* (1838), III. 10.

difficult materials. He speaks the language not only of a Jeremiah, but also of an Adam Smith, and is a student of the professional 'political economy' he despised. All this speech was carried on with even more magnificent feeling in *Past and Present*, which followed three years later. His fanfare rang out clear in that work:

It is of importance that this grand reformation were begun; that Corn-Law Debatings and other jargon, little less than delirious in such a time, had fled far away, and left us room to begin! For the evil has grown practical, extremely conspicuous; if it be not seen and provided for, the blindest fool will have to feel it ere long. There is much that can wait; but there is something also that cannot wait. With millions of eager Working Men imprisoned in 'Impossibility' and Poor-Law Bastilles, it is time that some means of dealing with them were trying to become 'possible'! Of the Government of England, of all articulate-speaking functionaries, real and imaginary Aristocracies, of me and of thee, it is imperatively demanded, 'How do you mean to manage these men? Where are they to find a supportable existence? What is to become of them,—and of you!'[1]

It was sometimes objected that there was more fanfare to Carlyle than concrete proposals. Douglas Jerrold spoke of him as one beating a drum under your window, but having nowhere particular to lead you to when you fell in behind him. Matthew Arnold charged him with carrying coals to Newcastle, because the English were already earnest enough. Of these criticisms the first overlooks the uses of a drum when it is the rousing of interest that is in question, and the second was directed by one whose historical sense was weak, and from the eighties, a time that was more settled partly at least because of Carlyle's timely intervention. All told, enough middle-class people took notice of him to help prevent that bloody revolution that was so sharp a fear in the first decades of the mid-century. Carlyle had done what he

[1] *Past and Present*, IV. I.

could for those of his fellows who at that time and to his way of thinking needed it most. He was at his best in a protracted emergency, and the state of the country in the early 1840s is the emergency that brought his practical powers to their height in *Past and Present*.

Trying to help the condition of England, Carlyle was no firebrand for all his imprecations and exclamations. What could be done should be done by legislation, if at all possible. He praised Elliott because of his concern with politics as a thing to discuss in poetry: 'He has turned, as all thinkers up to a very high and rare order in these days must do, into Politics ...' Carlyle's politics, though aiming at radical change, were aristocratic, heroic and in *Latter-Day Pamphlets*, *Shooting Niagara*, and also in *Frederick*, he made onslaughts on the idea of democracy. His love of man often took the form of explosive contempt. He greeted the census of 1841 with 'Twenty-seven millions, mostly fools'.[1] His sense of the complexities of most electoral issues led him to ridicule the principle of 'one man one vote', and late in life he appended a dash after repeating the catchword 'Manhood Suffrage', following it with 'Horsehood, Doghood ditto, not yet treated of'.[2] His regard for negroes was that of a century earlier. He saw them as grinning, nimble, useful animals, and expressed his scorn for their mental powers in the title of an essay he published in *Fraser's* of 1849, and later reprinted as a pamphlet 'The Nigger Question'. He also aroused fury in 1866 when he justified the brutal treatment meted out to them by Governor Eyre when they rioted in Jamaica.

His contempt for them, however, and for men paler of skin and nearer home, was provisional. He was waiting,

---

[1] 'Stump-orator', p. 45 (*Latter-Day Pamphlets*), and earlier; cf. *Past and Present*, I. 2.

[2] 'Shooting Niagara, and After', *Macmillan's Magazine* (Aug. 1867).

impatiently, for them to fulfil their destiny. He knew
only too well how far in the future lay the fulfilment of
any rosy hope for them. Man could be expected to do so
little for himself: 'Man, all men seem radically dumb;
jabbering mere jargons and noises from the teeth outwards; the inner meaning of them,—of them and of me,
poor devils,—remaining shut, buried for ever.'[1] Was
there ever a more accurate account? And yet he believed it
to be incomplete. He claimed, for instance, that 'No man
at bottom means injustice; it is always for some obscure
distorted image of a right that he contends.' And so he
accepted the old theological idea that a 'divine spark' lay
'slumbering' in man. He even allowed something good in
movements and sects he deplored, movements and sects
being composed of human beings. After his remark
about men's love of light, he continued:

A deep feeling of the eternal nature of Justice looks out among
us everywhere,—even through the dull eyes of Exeter Hall; an
unspeakable religiousness struggles, in the most helpless manner, to speak itself, in Puseyisms and the like. Of our Cant, all
condemnable, how much is not condemnable without pity;
we had almost said without respect! the *in*articulate worth and
truth that is in England goes down yet to the Foundations.[2]

Firmly holding on to this view, he could ask in *Past and
Present*, excitedly, 'Is not every man, God be thanked, a
potential hero?'[3] *Past and Present* and the rest were
designed to help to fan the divine spark into a glow. That
germ of good was a 'talent' universally possessed, and the
problem for every man was simply, and therefore in the
end hopefully, 'How unfold one's little bit of talent; and
live and not lie sleeping, while it is called Today'.[4] Carlyle's history books were as much as anything examples
of heroes for the not yet heroic to imitate. Indeed his

[1] *Carlyle and Emerson*, II. 111.
[2] *Past and Present*, IV. 8.   [3] III. 12.
[4] *Life of Sterling*, II. 3.

adoption, in the teeth of common sense, of the idea that might is right—or rather, in its final form, that right in the end accumulates power to overthrow might exercised for evil ends—is solely for the sake of helping fools not to destroy themselves. The foolish hurl around edged tools, and of all things must be helped not to. He had a horror of power being given to those who had not yet become men. He thought he knew the way to help them: 'Fraternity, liberty, etc., I want to explain, is not the remedy at all; but true *government* by the wise, true, and noble-minded, of the foolish, perverse and dark, with or *against* their consent; which I discern to be the eternal law of the world, and a rugged and severe but most blessed law, terribly forgotten in the universal twaddle, insincerity, and cowardly sloth of these latter times.'[1] And the wise, the true, and noble-minded was sometimes blessedly found in one man, the hero, the leader. Men need a leader because they need a disciplinarian. Indeed his hero is something of a drill-sergeant. Carlyle advocated drill on a large scale and warms to Frederick's practice of it. His comment on Mill's *Liberty* could not be more dismissive: '[it] appears to me the most exhaustive statement of precisely what I feel to be untrue on that subject'.[2] His ideal hero, however, unlike the drill-sergeant, exists for the sake of the private. Accordingly the belief that might is right is rather a hope and a prayer than an idea, a prayer to the strong man to arise and take on heroic benevolence. Acton was to see the drawbacks: 'Power tends to corrupt and absolute power corrupts absolutely', and he may have been helped by Carlyle's opposed view to see this. But Carlyle knew enough history and psychology to be aware that his heroes were chosen for his purposes. They are the proof of his concern for the weak.

The same sort of explanation accounts for his constant

---

[1] *Life in London*, I. 431; letter of 24 Mar. 1848.
[2] Quoted without source in Lewin, *Carlyle, Table Talk*, p. 30; cf. *New Letters*, I. 196.

cry for sincerity from authors. It was a beseeching of them to be so excellent as men that their readers could be edified by a direct expression of that excellence. He did not want sincerity from weaklings. And the explanation is the same for his cry for earnestness. As George Gilfillan pointed out, the worth of earnestness depends on the end it is serving.[1] Carlyle's encouragement of it paid men the compliment of assuming their ends to be good. He was so rapt by his love of goodness that he supposed that others were so too, or if not yet, would become so. Against all doubts he foresaw a human happiness distantly in store, hardly the brimming sort the Utilitarians advertised in their famous shibboleth 'the greatest happiness of the greatest number', but a grim painful happiness that has already been the blessed lot of the few who have become public-spirited heroes. It is strange that he was often thought a pessimist when he believed that 'Men love not darkness, they do love light',[2] and he had borrowed the old idea of the divine spark simply for the purpose of remaining where he wanted to be, and thought he had warrant in wanting to be, on this side pessimism. Introducing a collection of his sayings, Walter Lewin said truly:

On the whole it was not safe to go to Carlyle, nor is it safe to read his books, hoping to be soothed and made satisfied. His purpose seems to be to make one dissatisfied. But, even so, his method is energising. He says in effect, not 'You are "incompetent,"' but 'Are you not ashamed that you did not do better?' For he is in no wise a prophet of despair but of new and strenuous endeavour.

To his passion for man we can also ascribe his neglect of the important discoveries of the scientists. 'The Everlasting No' in *Sartor Resartus* shows him horrified by the

[1] *A Gallery of Literary Portraits* (1845), p. 137.
[2] *Past and Present*, iv. 8; and cf. i. 6.

French materialists of the eighteenth century, who maintained that man is a bag of matter. And Carlyle himself sometimes subscribed to the doctrines of materialism—in such remarks as 'The actual well seen *is* the ideal. The *actual*, what really is and exists: the past, the present, the future no less, do all lie there';[1] or, gloriously, 'Thy daily life is girt with Wonder, and based on Wonder, and thy very blankets and breeches are miracles'.[2]

But if Carlyle neglected the scientists he did not neglect the material universe—or his version of it. Neglect of that was unthinkable if only because of the poet in him—some of his finest writing comes in his phrases describing darkness and fire, and the 'sea of stars'. And there was more to it than a source of imagery, for, even more than heroes and men of genius did, it provided him with a substitute for a personal God. Newman, unlike Carlyle, found the 'supernatural' to be a person, a 'luminously self-evident being', and on one occasion composed what in the seventeenth century would have been called a 'character' of Him. Carlyle, however, preferred to the term 'God' such terms as the 'Eternal Heavens', the 'Eternal Verities'. Sensitive to the *Zeitgeist*, he saw that a personal God was now outmoded. Much of Him had already disappeared for the English Deists of the eighteenth century, and He had disappeared still more wholly for the German poets and philosophers—it was these men, not the theologians, who were for him the 'true sovereign souls' of German literature. He acknowledged a particular debt to Fichte, who had sought to discover the 'secret of the universe' by peering at it as a poet might. Fichte confronted the universe as it appeared to his body, mind, and spirit—or at least to that part of the mind that does not acknowledge the utility or wisdom of using telescopes or scientific experiments. He had thought that the universe would yield men more as they confronted it as primitive man

---

[1] *Carlyle and Emerson*, I. 314; cf. *Sartor Resartus*, II. 9.
[2] *Sartor Resartus*, III. 9.

might have. Carlyle's indirect debt to the scientists, how-ever, could not but be heavy because it was they who had carried on the primitive tradition of gazing hard at the spacious firmament on high, rather than consulting Holy Writ about its nature.

The universe was necessary to him on another, related count. Man, as he saw, was a worshipping animal, and so had to find some object for his worship. Many of those who had worshipped the God of their fathers had now lost Him. For such the Church offered no hope because it persisted in clinging to its bundle of what Carlyle called 'Hebrew ol' clo'es', and flapping its 'enormous bat-wings'. Recounting the story of Sterling's novel *Arthur Coningsby*, in which the desperate hero solves his intel-lectual problems by taking orders, Carlyle comments, before going into the matter at length, 'Such could by no means seem to me the true or tenable solution',[1] as Arnold was to say of Newman's, which he found 'frankly impossible'. Appealing over the head of any Church to the 'earnest sky', Carlyle invented, in his late essay 'Jesuit-ism', a New Englander, Gathercole, allowing him the last word to explain the discredit now fallen on the Churches:

Alas, if its [the Christian Church's] roots are now dead, and it have lost hold of the firm earth, or clear belief of man-kind,—what, great as it is, can by possibility become of it? Shaken to and fro, in Jesuitisms, Gorham Controversies, and the storms of inevitable Fate, it must sway hither and thither; nod ever farther from the perpendicular; nod at last too far; and,—sweeping the Eternal Heavens clear of its old brown foliage and multitudinous rooks'-nests,—come to the ground with much confused crashing, and *disclose* the diurnal and nocturnal Upper Lights again! The dead world-tree will have declared itself dead. It will lie there an imbroglio of torn boughs and ruined fragments, of bewildered splittings and wide-spread shivers: out of which the poor inhabitants must make what they can?[2]

[1] *Life of Sterling*, i. 15.
[2] *Latter-Day Pamphlets*.

Among the 'ol' clo'es', however, were certain things Carlyle thought still useful. Just as he had borrowed the universe from the scientists, he borrowed for the benefit of that universe the morality ascribed to God by the Church; he endowed it with the justice that the Jews had introduced into the world's idea of God. The only reason why he could make this transference was the specious reason that the universe obeyed what the scientists called 'laws'. By a stretch of terms this could be called 'justice', a word which men apply to something they have set up among themselves, having made for themselves a morality which the stars know nothing about. Carlyle therefore wanted to have it both ways. Peering into the universe, he was peering into it for something human in it, for what helped his humanist programme. He saw it as just, because in 'these bad days' there was a deficiency of justice among men. His procedure was exactly what Wordsworth had ascribed to the poet, who, 'pleased with his own passions and volitions [is] delight[ed] to contemplate similar volitions and passions as manifested in the goings-on of the Universe, and habitually impelled to create them where he does not find them'. If this is the procedure expected of the poet, it is not the procedure that the scientist and philosopher hopes he is himself following! Carlyle wanted to find corroboration of his religion in the heavens because the heavens were in fashion, but wanted that religion to be indistinguishable from what he could have derived from human society. As he drew it for his reasons, the universe was a standing criticism of their shortcomings. It was as much a Carlylean hero as it was a machine. It worked without pause—Carlyle was fond of Goethe's motto 'ohne Hast, aber ohne Rast'. He declared that God, as if adding to the Commandments, had said 'Idleness shall not be',[1] a commandment aimed at the too-leisured rich. (In 'Corn-Law Rhymes' he went deeper and, remembering

[1] *Past and Present*, IV. 6.

that all men were strugglers, found that this new divine injunction was indeed being obeyed universally, but though no man idled, not all were busy doing good—the so-called 'idle' were working all right, but for the Devil; and again the universe was to hand with its reproof: the work being done by the universe is the work of God.) Moreover, it did its 'duty' silently, and silent work was to be recommended to man, whose noisy words were so often foolish and whose cries an unmanly whine.

Something else ecclesiastical existed that was not outmoded: the office of the priest. 'All religion', Carlyle said, 'issues in due Practical Hero-worship'.[1] His plea at the end of *Past and Present* is a plea for a man, a man with a 'living voice', and poets and writers of great literature generally are precisely that. Again Carlyle is indebted to Fichte, as he acknowledged in 'Jesuitism'; 'The Poet in the Fine Arts, especially the Poet in Speech, what Fichte calls the "Scholar" or the "Literary Man", is defined by Fichte as the "Priest" of these Modern Epochs—all the Priest they have.' Accordingly Carlyle called Schiller a priest, as Arnold did Wordsworth, and to Fichte and Carlyle may be traced the common nineteenth-century idea that what men had looked for and found in Christianity was now increasingly to be found in so-called profane literature, especially in poetry. Even as early as 'Characteristics' Carlyle had written: 'Literature is but a branch of Religion, and always participates in its character: however, in our time, it is the only branch that still shows any greenness; and, as some think, must one day become the main stem.' Of all religious men Carlyle was the most frankly secular. His religion did not cut him off from men, for all men are religious, almost simply because they are alive: 'A man's "religion" consists not of the many things he is in doubt of or tries to believe, but of the few things he is assured of, and has no need of effort for believing.'[2] Or, again, he equated 'faith', the word and

___

[1] Ibid. IV. 15.     [2] 'Jesuitism'.

thing that exercised Newman so long and painfully, with a 'notion of this Universe'. All men, having a notion of that, have a faith. 'The fearful unbelief', he said 'is unbelief in yourself'.

The universe helped Carlyle to add bugles to his orchestra. With it at call he was not at too great a disadvantage beside the prophets of the Old Testament, who could call on God confidently, as on a father. Like any of them, he could thunder: 'Sooty Manchester,—it too is built on the infinite Abysses; overspanned by the skyey Firmaments ...'[1] Industrialists in Lancashire could be counted on to attend to words like those. They proceeded as from a pulpit in a Dissenting chapel.

Having gazed for help at the stars he finally circled back to man. What he found in them he found nearer home: 'What this Universe is, what the Laws of God are, the Life of every man will a little teach it you; the Life of All Men and of All Things, only this could wholly teach it you,—and you are to be open to learn.'[2] Man, the worshipping animal, worships something in himself, even if what is within has a counterpart in the universe at large. Most nineteenth-century authors, equally secular, find in themselves, as he did, what God it is they do find. And perhaps, like him again, they confirm the discovery by peering earnestly into the sea of stars.

In 1851 in his *Life of Sterling* Carlyle noted that Coleridge 'had, especially among young inquiring men, a higher than literary, a kind of prophetic or magician character ...' By this date his description also fitted himself, and better than Coleridge; by 1859 F. D. Maurice did not 'know many men of this day' who were not 'under obligations' to him. It was also from among the young and inquiring that, as Mill noted in his *Autobiography*, Carlyle's disciples were drawn. He meant less

---

[1] *Past and Present*, III. 15.     [2] 'Jesuitism'.

to his coevals and seniors, many of whom he ridiculed: whereas John Stuart, the son, found him an opener-up of new worlds despite 'a form and vesture less suited than any other to give them access to a mind trained as mine had been', his father, twenty odd years older than Carlyle, found in him nothing but 'insane rhapsody'. James Mill, therefore, confessed himself behind the times.

For the young, in the forties and later, Carlyle was the tangible equivalent of the *Zeitgeist*—tangible and inviting, unlike the exploratory Coleridge, who had done nothing to attract followers. Carlyle beat a drum below your window, and the effect of it on other minor writers may be instanced in Ebenezer Jones, as reported by his brother in the memoir introducing the 1879 reprint of *Studies in Sensation and Event*: 'Whole passages from Carlyle were got by heart among us, and recited'. To him all the younger writers who were not to remain minor responded. Even Newman approached the brink of the whirlpool, though, being only six years Carlyle's junior, his footing remained firm: as late as 1840, when he was 39, he described Carlyle as 'a man of first-rate ability, I suppose, and quite fascinating as a writer', and continued: 'His book on the "French Revolution' is most taking (to me). I had hoped he might have come round right, for it was easy to see he was not a believer; but they say he has settled the wrong way. His view is that Christianity has good in it, or is good *as far as it goes*, which, when applied to Scripture, is, or course, a picking and choosing of its contents.'[1] The pervasiveness of his influence was well expressed by George Eliot, writing anonymously in the *Leader*, in 1855:

It is an idle question to ask whether his books will be read a century hence: if they were all burnt as the grandest of Suttees on his funeral pile, it would be only like cutting down an oak after its acorns have sown a forest. For there is hardly a

[1] *Letters*, ed. Anne Mozley, II. 300.

superior or active mind of this generation that has not
been modified by Carlyle's writings; there has hardly been
an English book written for the last ten or twelve years that
would not have been different if Carlyle had not lived.[1]

He affected his followers as people, and, oddly for a
writer, made them see the writing of literature as not
necessarily the most honourable of occupations. Choice
of profession was open to at least those of them whose
genius was 'a general capacity of mind' rather than
the particular sort that confined them—as it did
Tennyson—to writing, and even writing in one kind.
When choice was available, the deciding motives, as
always, must have been mixed. Among them, inevitably,
was the financial; most mid-century writers needed or
wanted to earn more money than could normally be
expected from writing poetry or even novels. Clough
and Arnold are ready instances of men whose genius,
being of the general sort, gave them a choice, and who
may well have been guided by Carlyle in choosing to
write in what leisure was left over from teaching and the
inspecting of schools. If Carlyle was not often named as
influencing choice decisively, he encouraged them to the
sort of choice they made, sometimes by word of mouth
as well as pen. It is true that writers in earlier ages had
taken up professions additional to that of writing, but
professional work was now busier and more in the public
eye, observed and criticized by newspapers.

Disraeli the novelist had Carlyle's implicit approval for
his brilliant career in politics, small as was Carlyle's
respect for an institution he nicknamed the 'National
Palaver'. The Carlylean blessing fell on many
others—Arnold the inspector of schools, Trollope the
civil servant, Charles Kingsley the popular priest and
campaigner for sanitary reform. And those for whom

[1] 27 Oct. reviewing Thomas Ballantyne's *Passages Selected from the Writings of Carlyle*.

literature could be made to pay well enough often par-
ticipated in the running of organized charities, in good
works that were public, and not, as for their eighteenth-
century predecessors, private. If a man could not act,
Carlyle advised him to preserve a manly silence so as at
least not to intrude on the work being done by others, and
add to the 'universal twaddle, insincerity, and sloth of
these latter times'. People were quick to joke about his
failure to follow his own advice. He shared in the joke,
taking little satisfaction from his authorship. The main
pleasure his books gave him was the relief of having them
off his hands. But though books were inferior to manly
deeds, he had made them come as near to manly deeds as
possible. What he found lacking in Coleridge, Byron, and
most of his seniors and coevals was not found lacking in
him. Even if he did not invariably instruct those who by
the time they read him had got knowledge elsewhere, he
provided the will to go and get more, and to get it from
trustworthy sources. Sterling described himself as a 'pen-
sive' reader of Carlyle, and George Eliot saw his function
to be not so much that of teacher as of purveyor of
inspiration. He also deflected writers from assuming that
their office was to lackey the aristocracy. He encouraged
them to turn frankly to their middle-class fellows, and to
find in newspaper matter as much material as the satirists
of the preceding century had found there.

On some authors Carlyle's praise of German 'transcendentalism' coupled with what was transcendental in
his own writings had a bad effect—inevitably, since what
is cloudy, or if clear is overweeningly and pre-
sumptuously so, is not the best matter for literature, as
Froude came to see: 'At any rate,' he said in preferring to
write history rather than fiction, 'one has substantive
stuff between one's fingers to be moulding at, and not
those slime and sea-sand ladders to the moon "opinion".'[1] Even Tennyson and Arnold, not to mention

[1] Letter to Clough, 22 Nov. 1853 (Herbert Paul, *Life of Froude*, 1905, p. 66).

Browning, needed, when thinking, a firmer, more re-
straining hand than Carlyle's—they would have bene-
fited from the ideal that Clough set for himself. The
worst offenders, however, were the Spasmodics, who
were ambitious to plumb the universe to its depths. If
Carlyle had once sharply reminded people of the difference between navigating the globe and the Isle of
Dogs, he was the first to recommend the latter trip to
those who lacked the mind, heart, and skill of a Drake. It
was true that he could be cloudy with the best of them,
but also true that, unlike them, he had an abundance of
common sense. It was this abundance of concrete soundness in him that did so much to help mid-century literature to its feet. Carlyle was a bad influence only on
writers who had a yellow streak in them. All the greatest
writers responded properly to his grand injunction—'To
the Poet as to every other [man and writer], I say first of
all See!'[1] For 'see' was used, first and foremost, in its
straightforward sense, which applied to the bodily eyes,
even if its secondary sense was almost as important—the
sense denoting the mental act of interconnecting and
ordering all that had been experienced with the bodily
eyes. Browning showed a poet relying on eyesight in the
first part of his 'How it Strikes a Contemporary':

> He stood and watched the cobbler at his trade,
> The man who slices lemons into drink,
> The coffee-roaster's brazier, and the boys
> That volunteer to help him turn its winch.
> He glanced o'er books on stalls with half an eye,
> And fly-leaf ballads on the vendor's string,
> And broad-edge bold-print posters by the wall.
> He took such cognisance of men and things,
> If any beat a horse, you felt he saw;
> If any cursed a woman, he took note ...

Carlyle wrote to him saying, 'That old "corregidor" is a

[1] *Heroes and Hero-Worship* ('The Hero as Poet').

diamond',[1] and in praising *Men and Women* as a whole he complimented Browning on his 'pair of eyes'.[2] 'It is hard to say', he remarked on another occasion, 'what one might *not* learn by keeping one's eyes well open'.[3] He was himself as close an observer of men and things as were the great novelists, whom he recommended, if they insisted on writing fiction, to take 'truth' as their topic—that is, concrete typical human stuff undergoing the experiences that normally come its way. This meant that he had no sympathy with the 'idealist' school of fiction then in fashion, the airy falsities of Bulwer Lytton and others. He would have applauded the procedure of his admirer, Thackeray, who did not start to write till he heard his personages talking together. He chose to write on the author of *Corn-Law Rhymes*, because he 'can handle both pen and hammer like a man'. If one had to confine oneself to the pen, then what one wrote of would be the better for being, as Froude put it, 'substantive'—solid as matter struck by the hammer. Biography was respectably substantial, being a species of history. And it followed that novels might also be in proportion as they aspired to be history and biography. Some of the great mid-century novelists took Carlyle's advice literally, and practised actual reporting. Henry Kingsley worked on a Glasgow newspaper. He had read and marked this passage from Carlyle's essay on Francia:

Francia, Dictator of Paraguay, is, at present, to the European mind, little other than a chimera; at best, the statement of a puzzle, to which the solution is still to seek. As the Paraguenos, though not a literary people, can many of them spell and write, and are not without a discriminating sense of true and untrue,

---

[1] A. Carlyle, 'Correspondence between Carlyle and Browning', *Cornhill Magazine*, xxxviii (May 1915); and see C. R. Sanders, 'Some lost and unpublished Carlyle–Browning correspondence', *Journal of English and Germanic Philology*, lxii (Apr. 1963).
[2] *Letters to Mill, Sterling, and Browning*, p. 298; letter of 25 Apr. 1856.
[3] Not traced.

why should not some real *Life of Francia*, from those parts, be still possible! If a writer of genius arise there, he is hereby invited to the enterprise. Surely in all places your writing genius ought to rejoice over an acting genius, when he falls-in with such; and say to himself: 'Here or nowhere is the thing for me to write of! Why do I keep pen-and-ink at all, if not to apprise men of this singular acting genius, and the like of him? My fine-arts and aesthetics, my epics, literatures, poetics, if I will think of it, do all at bottom mean either that or else nothing whatever!'

And he responded with one of his finest pieces, a piece strikingly Carlylean, 'Eyre's March', which recounted the heroic ride of Eyre across Australia, written by one who had lived there for two years: Kingsley writes such Carlylese as the following:

So in camp he remained for six weeks, his horses improving day by day. Baxter, the self-devoted hero, was a somewhat diligent and unromantic hero, and all this time worked like a galley-slave. A strange fellow, this quiet Baxter. He could make shoes among other things, could shoe the horses, make pack-saddles, do a hundred and fifty things; all of which he did with steady, quiet diligence these lonely six weeks, as if a little voice was ever singing in his ear, 'The night cometh in which no man can work.' I confess that I should have liked to know that man Baxter, but that is impossible; one can only say that once there was a very noble person whom men called so, and that not ten educated persons living ever heard of his name.

Writing novels, authors tended to draw on their own experience, now more fully assured of its high credentials—even the mid-century habit of writing of an earlier generation was often because knowledge and understanding of what was available to youthful years seemed most substantial. Novels about the present and its troubles might, like *Hard Times*, be dedicated to Carlyle, or, like *Beauchamp's Career*, be expressly inspired by him. When the novels were of the 'historical' sort, the Scott standard of 'truth' was maintained as far as possible.

Thackeray, Kingsley, George Eliot, Reade, and Pater, aware of the advantage of bodily sight, laboured over books, places, and pictures in an effort to get it at second hand from sources as reliable as possible. They tried to make their fictions as accurate as Carlyle's own histories. Samuel Laing was right when in *Modern Science and Modern Thought* (1885) he claimed that Carlyle 'changed the face of fiction' and even of other more concrete things as well:

The whole literature of fiction has been transformed. The fashionable novel, with its dandified coxcomb heroes and simpering fine lady heroines, has been superseded by works like those of Dickens, Thackeray, Trollope, and George Eliot, which satirise folly and pretension however highly placed, and aim at honest, earnest, simple and sincere ideals of true men and women ... There is vastly more real equality and real fraternity among men, and every one recognises, in theory at any rate, the dignity of honest labour, whether of hand or head ... For these results, which have now become almost commonplaces, those who derived them in their youth direct from works like 'Sartor Resartus' can best judge to what an extent modern thought has been indebted to Carlyle.[1]

If an author reported on books rather than things, reported as a reviewer, he might well ask if the specimen before him was in accord with Carlylean principles. Absence of Carlylean 'purpose' in a novel was often counted as a drawback. Reviewing *Pendennis* and *David Copperfield* in the *North British Review* of 1851, Masson saw Thackeray as no reformer, but 'far gone in a kind of grim, courteous *pococurantism*'.

Finally, there was Carlyle's general preference for prose over verse; his advice to Sterling was always 'steady against Poetry',[2] and Browning's 'Transcendentalism' ('Stop playing, Poet! May a brother

---

[1] p. 240.
[2] *Life of Sterling*, III. 1; cf. *Letters to Mill, Sterling and Browning*, pp. 237, 240; *Carlyle and Emerson*, II. 49.

speak?') is perhaps his comment on a passage in 'The Hero as Poet': 'What we want to get at is the *thought* the man had, if he had any: why should he twist it into jingle, if he *could* speak it out plainly? It is only when the heart of him is rapt into true passion of melody, and the very tones of him ... become musical by the greatness, depth and music of his thoughts, that we can give him right to rhyme and sing.' But many poets as well as other writers responded, as Matthew Arnold did, to the poet in Carlyle, to his 'surpassingly powerful qualities of expression'.[1]

Each writer's general debt to Carlyle coexisted with authorial borrowings still more tangible. Indeed, unless we have prior knowledge of his writings, we find ourselves crediting his successors with novelty—felicitous or odd—that really belonged to him. Two of his books were found particularly educative in this way—*Heroes* and *Past and Present*. Mill's idea for *On Liberty* was inspired by the latter, even if he inverted what he found, and George Eliot, Ruskin, and Morris found their social philosophy already at least indicated there. It was Ruskin who was conspicuously proud to acknowledge his debts, and the passage in which that acknowledgement is dwelt on may be quoted both for its own sake and for its bearing on the indebtedness of other writers. It occurs in the essay 'Plagiarism', which provides one of the appendixes of *Modern Painters*, III:

I owe ... most of all, perhaps, to Carlyle, whom I read so constantly, that, without wilfully setting myself to imitate him, I find myself perpetually falling into his modes of expression, and saying many things in a 'quite other,' and, I hope, stronger, way, than I should have adopted some years ago ... It would be both foolish and wrong to struggle to cast off influences of this kind; for they consist mainly in a real and healthy help;—the master, in writing as in painting, showing certain methods of language which it would be ridiculous, and

---

[1] See 'Emerson', in *Discourses in America* (1885).

even affected, not to employ, when once shown; just as it would have been ridiculous in Bonifazio to refuse to employ Titian's way of laying on colours, if he felt it the best, because he had not himself discovered it. There is all the difference in the world between this receiving of guidance, or allowing of influence, and wilful imitation, much more, plagiarism; nay, the guidance may even innocently reach into local tones of thought, and must do so to some extent; so that I find Carlyle's stronger thinking colouring mine continually; and should be very sorry if I did not; otherwise I should have read him to little purpose. But what I have of my own is still all there, and I believe, better brought out, by far, than it would have been otherwise.

Ruskin acknowledged debts general and particular; such debts, especially to *Past and Present*, were also incurred by Browning, Dickens, and Arnold, from whom a few illustrations are selected.

We have seen that a salient passage in 'Bishop Blougram's Apology' was inspired by Carlyle.[1] So also was the climax of one of the passages that are most splendid:

> Just when we are safest, there's a sunset-touch,
> A fancy from a flower-bell, some one's death,
> A chorus-ending from Euripides,—
> And that's enough for fifty hopes and fears
> As old and new at once as Nature's self,
> To rap and knock and enter in our soul,
> Take hands and dance there, a fantastic ring,
> Round the ancient idol, on his base again,—
> The grand Perhaps!

Plainly this looks back to Carlyle's 'we quietly believe this Universe to be intrinsically a great unintelligible PERHAPS'.[2]

Dickens admired Carlyle idolatrously, especially his *French Revolution*. It would be a mistake to underrate the

---

[1] See p. 57.
[2] *Past and Present*, III. 1; and cf. 'Burns'—'his religion is ... "a great PERHAPS"'.

intelligence that exists in, as well as behind, his early work, existing as plainly as the high spirits and the immediate results of using the senses. In the later work, however, the intellect is spreading itself more widely and deeply, and the impetus to do so was at least partly due to Carlyle, who provided a sort of university education for him, and sharpened his social conscience, which had already implied its existence in the account of the Fleet Prison in *Pickwick Papers*. Carlyle showed up the abuses of the law in *Past and Present*, not only in the aside, 'From the time of Cain's slaying Abel by swift head-breakage, to this time of killing your man in Chancery by inches...' (where 'man', as always in Carlyle, is a word of prime force), but also in the extended indictment towards the close of the work:

The man in horsehair wig advances, promising that he will get me 'justice': he takes me into Chancery Law Courts, into decades, half-centuries of hubbub, of distracted jargon; and does *get* me—disappointment, almost desperation; and one refuge: that of dismissing him and his 'justice' altogether out of my head. For I have work to do; I cannot spend my decades in mere arguing with other men about the exact wages of my work: I will work cheerfully with no wages, sooner than with a ten-years gangrene or Chancery Lawsuit in my heart![1]

Passages such as these surely contributed to the placing of Chancery delays at the centre of *Bleak House*, Dickens transforming 'your man' into the ward Richard Carstone, and recording the 'inches' of his decline. Also at the centre of *Bleak House*—much is clustered at that point as well as spreading to the circumference—is the poor crossing-sweeper. When Jo dies of fever and starvation Dickens breaks out into cries of outraged disgust. In *Past and Present* Carlyle had made similar invocations and petitions, for instance: 'May it please your Serene Highnesses, your Majesties, Lordships and Law-wardships, the proper Epic of this world is not now 'Arms and the

[1] *Past and Present*, II. 17; IV. 3.

Man;' how much less 'Shirt-frills and the Man:' no, it is now 'Tools and the Man:' that, henceforth to all time is now our Epic;—and you, first of all others, I think, were wise to take note of that!'[1] Both Carlyle and Dickens are big enough, deeply moved enough, and courageous enough to stand 'Athanasii contra mundum'.

The strength of Dickens's allegiance to Carlyle is remarkable because of the oppugnancy of their temperaments as men and authors, and the philosophies that come of them.[2] David Masson, in his review of *Pendennis* and *David Copperfield* (May 1851), characterized Dickens's general philosophy by an implied contrast with that of Carlyle:

Kindliness is the first principle of Mr. Dickens's philosophy. the sum and substance of his moral system. He does not, of course, exclude such things as pain and indignation from his catalogue of legitimate existence ... still, in what may be called his speculative ethics, kindliness has the foremost place. ... In short, in his antipathy to Puritanism, Mr. Dickens seems to have adopted a principle closely resembling that which pervades the ethical part of Unitarianism, the essence of which is, that it places a facile disposition at the centre of the universe. Now, without here offering any speculative or spiritual discussion ... we may venture to say, that any man or artist who shall enter upon his sphere of activity, without in some way or other realizing and holding fast those truths which Puritanism sets such store by, and which it has embodied, according to its own grand phraseology, in the words sin, wrath, and justice, must necessarily take but half the facts of the world along with him, and go through his task too lightly and nimbly. To express our meaning in one word, such a man will miss out that great and noble element in all that is human—the element of *difficulty*.

[1] Ibid., III. 12.
[2] 'His theory of life was entirely wrong. He thought man ought to be buttered up, and the world made soft and accommodating for them, and all sorts of fellows have turkey for their Christmas' (Duffy, *Conversations with Carlyle*, p. 75).

What Carlyle and Dickens agreed on existed at a level lower than cheerfulness and gloom of mind. They agreed that men should not be treated like animals, or rather worse than animals, that at least they should be fed and kept alive. Those things secured, Carlyle offered them work in grim earnest and whatever grim pleasures come of that, while Dickens offered them, first and perhaps last, as much cheerfulness as possible with firelight brightening the festival cups. Dickens wanted to multiply the Bob Cratchits of the world. He did not greatly care for heroes.

As important for Dickens as Carlyle's ideas and energy of social purpose were his ways of ordering and presenting his matter. It is a comment on Carlyle that a great novelist and a special sort of poetic novelist could learn so much from one who was mainly historian and 'philosopher'—in other words, that Dickens could reread the *French Revolution* '500 times'. He was as much interested by the artist in Carlyle as by everything else. It was Carlyle's methods of unifying and at the same time enriching descriptions or paragraphs of thinking by means of repetitions and the protracted working-out of a metaphor that helped Dickens to his own similar methods. Carlyle's are well indicated by a New Englander, Margaret Fuller, who recorded her meeting with him:

I admire his Scotch, his way of singing his great full sentences, so that each one was like the stanza of a narrative ballad . . . He sings, rather than talks. He pours upon you a kind of satirical, heroical, critical poem, with regular cadences, and generally, near the beginning, hits upon some singular epithet, which serves as a *refrain* when his song is full, or which as with a knitting needle, he catches up the stitches, if he had chanced, now and then, to let fall a row.[1]

The same description could be applied to many passages

---

[1] Margaret Fuller Ossoli, *Memoirs* (1853), II. 184 f., 189 f.

in *Bleak House*: this paragraph too is a 'satirical, heroical, critical poem':

Jo is brought in. He is not one of Mrs. Pardiggle's Tockahoopo Indians; he is not one of Mrs. Jellyby's lambs, being wholly unconnected with Borrioboola-Gha; he is not softened by distance and unfamiliarity; he is not a genuine foreign-grown savage; he is the ordinary home-made article. Dirty, ugly, disagreeable to all the senses, in body a common creature of the common streets, only in soul a heathen. Homely filth begrimes him, homely parasites devour him, homely sores are in him, homely rags are on him: native ignorance, the growth of English soil and climate, sinks his immortal nature lower than the beasts that perish. Stand forth, Jo, in uncompromising colors! From the sole of thy foot to the crown of thy head, there is nothing interesting about thee.

And we need only recall that 'Gathercole' paragraph quoted above[1] to see how Dickensian Carlyle's enriching unifications are. Like Pope, Carlyle and Dickens prefer external nature as it is broken up into images, and thoroughly mixed up with their ideas about man, when it helps them to brand those ideas on to the mind. The richness of texture in the later novels of Dickens is a further enrichment of the sort of prose texture Carlyle had invented.

To read Carlyle word by word and idea by idea is to shrink one's conception of the originality of Arnold. Indeed the danger is to shrink it too far, and so to underrate the greatness of those best poems of Arnold that precisely are the best because most indebted to Carlyle. In those weighty yet half-conversational lyrics Arnold calls for Carlylean courage and grimness in the struggle and reduces the hot-headed expectation of happiness. That famous line:

> Who saw life steadily and saw it whole,

is a succinct testimony to what Arnold owed to him, as

[1] See p. 79.

also to the Newman of the Anglican sermons—the line might have been written by either of them, thought and words together. That other most famous fragment:

> Wandering between two worlds, one dead
> The other powerless to be born,

owes nothing to Newman, but everything except metre to Carlyle, who had said the same thing with the same imagery many times.[1] Arnold sees the stars as Carlyle did, and allots them the same role of instructing mankind:

> Yes, while on earth a thousand discords ring,
> Man's senseless uproar mingling with his toil,
> Still do thy sleepless ministers move on,
> Their glorious tasks in silence perfecting:
> Still working, blaming still our vain turmoil;
> Labourers that shall not fail when man is gone.

That sonnet is early work. But one of the great poems is deep in Carlyle's debt, in the same way as some of Clough's are: 'The Buried Life'. In *Past and Present* we get

Blessed is he who has found his work; let him ask no other blessedness. He has a work, a life-purpose; he has found it, and will follow it! How, as a free-flowing channel, dug and torn by noble force through the sour mud-swamp of one's existence, like an ever-deepening river there, it runs and flows;—draining off the sour festering water, gradually from the root of the remotest grass-blade; making, instead of pestilential swamp, a green fruitful meadow with its clear-flowing stream.[2]

Sometimes, as in other writers, what seems odd in Arnold is explained by reference to Carlyle. The theme of Arnold's poem 'Yes, in the sea of life enisl'd' must have been suggested partly at least by the following outburst in *Past and Present*:

Isolation is the sum-total of wretchedness to man. To be cut off, to be left solitary: to have a world alien, not your world; all

[1] e.g. in 'Signs of the Times' and 'Characteristics'.
[2] III. 11.

a hostile camp for you; not a home at all, of hearts and faces who are yours, whose you are! It is the frightfullest enchantment; too truly a work of the Evil One. To have neither superior, nor inferior, nor equal, united manlike to you. Without father, without child, without brother. Man knows no sadder destiny. 'How is each of us,' exclaims Jean Paul, 'so lonely in the wide bosom of the All!' Encased each as in his transparent 'ice-palace'; our brother visible in his, making signals and gesticulations to us;—visible, but forever unattainable: on his bosom we shall never rest, nor he on ours. It was not a God that did this; no![1]

This passage also explains what strikes one as odd in Arnold, the line:

> A God, a God, their severance rul'd.

People have argued that when in 'The Scholar Gipsy' Arnold speaks of one who 'takes dejectedly His seat upon the intellectual throne', he had Carlyle in mind (though Arnold said later it was Goethe). Carlyle had used the same image in the *Life of Sterling*: 'Goethe ... was in the throne of Sterling's intellectual world'.[2]

Arnold spoke of himself as his 'papa's continuation', but could have bracketed Carlyle with Dr. Arnold. His religious views were built on Carlyle's. Many of his political views also come from the same source—particularly the dislike of 'doing as one likes', which was Carlyle's phrase before it became a chapter-heading in *Culture and Anarchy*. Finally, Arnold, who knew his Greek and Roman classics well, was unusual in also knowing his modern European classics, and his encouragement to make that addition was largely Carlyle's doing, to whose influence we must regretfully assign, among many honours, the Nordic 'Balder Dead'.[3]

Carlyle's influence affected other writers who repudiated much of his thinking, such as Gerard Manley

[1] IV. 4.    [2] II. 3.
[3] See *Heroes and Hero-Worship* ('The Hero as Divinity').

Hopkins: 'I do not like his pampered and affected style, I hate his principles'.[1] But some features of that style found their response: among the Carlylean phrases that surely inspired Hopkins are 'intricate the outrage', 'stalking with a downlook', 'a sharp sunglance', and sentences like 'Frondent trees parasol the streets', and 'the Sun's first level light-volley shears away sleep from living creatures everywhere'.[2]

The age being everything Carlyle said it was, the inherited way of writing English, especially English prose, did not now satisfy everybody. Hopkins, whose own prose, when not descriptive, was 'golden' rather than 'wild', believed nevertheless that 'a perfect style must be of its age'. By 'perfect' he meant fitting the thought as skin does the hand (to use Carlyle's image), however much the hand had become misshapen and scarred by the pioneer labour the age was now demanding of its heroic thinkers. The inherited way of writing prose seemed to some not to suit the new things the age was asking to have expressed. Coleridge had seen the prose of Gibbon as positively falsifying: he dismissed it as not being one in which it was possible to tell the truth— meaning the truth as the nineteenth century had come to see it.

What was to be rejected from the inherited prose was vaguely thought of as the 'Addisonian'. Johnson had advised the young prose-writer to give his days and nights to the study of Addison, but already in the eighteenth century the Addisonian was being superseded by an ampler music. Prose quite un-Addisonian was written by Sterne and Burke. Moreover, some of the

---

*espondence with R. W. Dixon*, p. 59; and see ibid., 75: 'I always him morally an impostor ... And his style has imposture and in it. But I find it difficult to think there is imposture in his genius

m 'Dr. Francia'.

novelists had represented crises of the emotions so faithfully as to write for the occasion prose that was vividly
chaotic. Even in the eighteenth century the Addisonian
had been slighted by implication when the English language itself was blamed for deficiencies that had been
designed by Addison as polite avoidances. Even Johnson
had desiderated more literary ways of expressing emotion—perhaps he overlooked the ways being found by
the novelists, whom he did not fully recognize as literary.
In the following century deficiency was frequently
charged against English, for one reason or another. In
*The Gay Science* of 1866, for instance, a work energetically discussing literary principles, E. S. Dallas saw
English as 'inadequate to express the various content of
the word *pleasure*', and James Martineau, Harriet's
much-thinking brother, held that it was thanks to
Tennyson, and him alone, that it was not inferior to
German in one important department:

Have you not often found that our very language seems incapable of holding the delicate tracings and true colouring of
German sentiment, so that the thought which has impressed
you disappears in the attempt to transmit it to another? Yet
Tennyson's 'In Memoriam' shows that this is an illusion; and
that there is no light or shade of consciousness that may not
paint itself faithfully and transparently with materials purely
English.[1]

But this sort of competence Tennyson had achieved in
verse, and his achievement was accordingly not so generally useful. Even Newman, who found the English of
Addison plastic enough for all his many subtle purposes,
deprecated the pompous expressions of at least the
inferior among those nineteenth-century writers who
were still clinging to the obvious things in Addison: as
editor of a periodical he advised a would-be contributor
not to begin his essay with 'Of all the virtues that adorn

[1] *Correspondence of Clough*, pp. 291–2.

the human breast . . .' Again, Arnold, who like Newman remained faithful to what still survived of Addisonian prose, departed from it at least as far as to admit some of Carlyle's mannerisms: he took over some of his diction and his way of inverting prose-order elaborately.

Some of the defaulters from the Addisonian were led to reconsider the merits of a way of writing that the eighteenth century had rejected—that of the earlier, unreformed seventeenth. Whately, later to write a book on logic (to which his pupil Newman contributed) and a book on rhetoric, recognized the advantages of the prose of Hooker, Bacon, and Hobbes: 'What our language has gained in elegance it has lost in force', he declared, adding that 'one of the chief corruptors was Addison'. Clough, desiderating forcefulness, regretted the current neglect of the racy idiom that had characterized seventeenth-century prose as a whole. And, more prominently still, a revival of the prose of the earlier seventeenth century was the ambition of De Quincey. In a lecture on Dryden, however, Clough showed just why the imputed helpfulness of the earlier, unreformed seventeenth-century style was illusory: at bottom it was the prose of men who had learned to arrange their thinking according to the Latin manner, which had been superseded.

Carlyle himself described the present state of prose, both as to vocabulary and syntax, in a letter to Sterling of 4 June 1835: 'Do you reckon this really a time for Purism of Style; . . . I do not: with whole ragged battalions of Scott's-Novel Scotch, with Irish, German, French and even Newspaper Cockney . . . storming in on us, and the whole structure of our Johnsonian English breaking up from its foundations—revolution *there* is as visible as anywhere else.'[1] And at the very end of our period there was Pater's endorsement: 'The ever-increasing intellectual burden of our age is hardly likely to adjust itself to the exquisite, but perhaps too delicate and limited,

[1] *Letters to Mill, Sterling, and Browning*, p. 192.

literary instruments of the age of Queen Anne.'[1] He saw the need for a prose 'rich, intense, exceptional', such as Carlyle's had inaugurated.

Early in the mid–century it became known that Carlyle had found the new style. By 1841 *Fraser's*, which had serialized *Sartor Resartus* in 1833–4, was referring to 'Carlylism' as a manner of writing, and by 1858 at least came the inevitable term 'Carlylese'. For its historical purposes Carlylese was so well suited that most authors of the time incorporated much or little of it into the prose they themselves were writing.

Carlyle did not write Carlylese from the start, though there are signs of it in early letters.[2] His earliest practice had been to accept the minimum change from the English of the eighteenth century. His first articles in the *Edinburgh Review* were written like anybody else's—as far as that was possible; no doubt they would not otherwise have been accepted for publication. And the prose into which early in his career he had translated *Wilhelm Meister* was to win pointed praise from Arnold: 'Never was Carlyle's prose so beautiful and pure', the implication being that elsewhere it was grotesque and impure, though Arnold himself in his youthful letters to Clough had revelled in imitating it.

By 'pure' Arnold meant 'clear' as well as free from idiosyncrasies. We should misjudge Carlyle fatally, how-ever, if we thought that in avoiding the Addisonian spinet-music he wanted to avoid the Addisonian clarity. After receiving a copy of *Sordello* he wrote to Browning encouraging him to go on fighting in order to 'unfold' difficult meaning into 'articulate clearness'. He may have thought that Addison's voyage was rather to Ramsgate and the Isle of Dogs than round the globe (to use the brilliant distinction which closes his essay on Burns) and

[1] *Guardian* (17 Feb. 1886; *Essays from* The Guardian, p. 14).
[2] A. Macmechan (ed. *Sartor Resartus*, 1898) aptly cites a passage in a letter of 1815 from *Early Letters*, ed. C. E. Norton (1886), p. 2.

as Arnold noted, it is 'easy to express oneself well, if one will be content with not expressing much, with expressing only trite ideas'—though Addison's achievement of elegance had been no easy one in his own day. In times now more difficult the task that Carlyle set himself was proportionately more difficult than Addison's, but he aimed no less at giving a clear account of it. If he did not always achieve it, clarity was his aim. 'Clear' is a constantly recurring adjective. The grotesque, he knew, need not be less clear, less pure, than the beautiful.

Even though Carlylese had been prepared for in the eighteenth century by the elaborateness of Burke and the abruptness of Sterne and Macpherson, inspiration was to be drawn from German literature, in particular that of Jean Paul Richter. This sort of German seconded something more important still—the language of 'the old farmhouse at Annandale'[1]—for the unacademical Scots are conscious artists in the use of language that is energetically expressive: here, for instance, is a scrap of Scots as reported by P. P. Alexander in his Memoir of Alexander Smith: 'it's no *my* kind o' poetry. Jist a blatter o' braw words, to my mind, an' bit whirly-whas, they ca' *eemages*!'[2] Carlyle acknowledged the source from which he had drawn most deeply when he described the prose of his *French Revolution* as 'plain Scotch-English',[3] and when in *Past and Present* he described a characteristic phrase as 'in Scottish dialect'.[4]

I have said that Carlyle wanted his sense to come through clearly. That desideratum, however, scarcely prepares us for his recommending not only clarity but transparency: the young must learn 'to be intelligible and transparent, no notice *taken* of your "style"'.[5] Notice of it when it was, and is, Carlyle's is inescapable. A mere glance at the page discovers exclamations, capitals, italics,

---

[1] *Life in London*, I. 40.
[2] *Last Leaves*, p. xix.
[3] *Carlyle and Emerson*, I. 103.
[4] III. 4.
[5] 'Edward Irving', in *Reminiscences*.

the very 'style' of his advice being noticeable in the italics of '*taken*'. Sterling remarked that a letter of Carlyle's had 'the writer's signature in every word as well as at the end'.[1]

Some of Carlyle's italics are more striking still by being confined to a part of a word, as in '*in*visible' and 'mis*seen*'. These words, being negatives, introduce the consideration of something deep in his mind—his inability, when thinking, to state a positive without also stating its negative, as if by mirror-image. We cannot but link this idiosyncrasy to the sharp division he insisted on seeing between right and wrong, and seek to explain it as a means of keeping up his faith in a dichotomy that the times were more and more inclined to question. In *Past and Present* he writes that 'In wondrous Dualism, then as now, lived nations of breathing men; alternating, in all ways, between Light and Dark; between Joy and Sorrow, between rest and toil,—between hope, hope reaching high as Heaven, and fear deep as very Hell.'[2] On another occasion he remarked that 'all things have two faces, a light one and a dark'.[3] Availing himself of the permissive genius of the language, he expressed the antithesis he embodies in almost all his sentences by exploiting the various ways of forming negatives. He will sometimes reserve his negative, as if leading the reader up the garden path deliberately: 'The sum of it, visible in every street market-place, senate-house, circulating-library, cathedral, cotton-mill, and union-workhouse, fills one *not* with a comic feeling!'[4] Not content with doubling the number of adjectives by supplying them all with an 'un-', he will sometimes add that prefix to a noun; we find 'Laws' and 'Unlaws', 'workers' and 'unworkers'. After Carlyle the practice was further extended. Arnold, who had borrowed from the Germans the word *Geist*, capped it in *Friendship's Garland* with '*Ungeist*'; both these words

---

[1] *Life of Sterling*, II. 4.      [2] *Past and Present*, II. I.
[3] Ibid., II. 4.      [4] Ibid., III. 4.

were taken up by the newspapers. The historian Stubbs could count on the right sort of laugh when he referred in a lecture of 1877 to his 'friends' and 'unfriends' (Carlyle had used the word, a Scotticism, in *Past and Present*), partly because of Freeman's liking for such forms.

There are more oddities to note in Carlyle's diction—things like 'hebetude and cecity', 'indolences and esuriences'[1] (ink-horn terms with a vengeance!); long-discarded forms like 'beautifuller' and 'beautifullest', and, more oddly, 'doabler' and 'fataler'; Teutonic compounds (like the 'snow-and-rosebloom maiden' which Sterling found 'uncouth', or the 'love-deeps' that made Swinburne shudder); and the 'choking double-words' that Thackeray objected to in his *Times* review of the *French Revolution*.

All this cumbrousness and chokingness was earnestly devised, and was doubly ensured by frequent inversions. The rearranging of the straightforward word-order of a sizeable clause has the effect that going upstairs would have if we were to find the steps in the wrong order—as 'A cheap worship in Paraguay, according to the humour of the people, Francia left ...' (Among his disciples we must number Mrs. Micawber: 'Talent, Mr. Micawber has; capital, Mr. Micawber has not'.) Also frequent are contortions such as those Swinburne mocked at in a letter: 'but from a quite other orifice (to speak in Carlylese)'. Sometimes to start a sentence Carlyle piled up adjectives like a bulging cumulus cloud: e.g. 'Grand, surely, harmoniously built together, far-seeing, wise and true'.

All these characteristics of Carlyle's expression were so noticeable that it became a minor occupation of literary criticism to describe his explosiveness. George Eliot remarked that he hurled his 'verbal missiles' as Milton's angels hurled rocks, and Meredith independently hit on the same image.[2] Carlyle was seen by some as the first and

[1] *Life of Sterling*, I. 8.                    [2] See p. 109.

largest of the Spasmodics (a term he himself used to characterize Byron) and accordingly was attacked along with them in Aytoun's *Firmilian* for 'dislocating language'. Harriet Martineau called him, in 1855, 'the greatest mannerist of the age', which term Carlyle had pinned on Richter. Sometimes he deserved the implied disparagement: he sometimes employed his tricks from habit. But usually his manner is another name for the style that is the man, and the man has too much life in him to have adopted anything so habitually constricting as a manner. His sentences are usually the form that his particular sense of his matter fulfilled itself in. He himself described them in one of his favourite three-deckers as 'piebald, entangled, hyper-metaphorical'.[1] His wording springs directly out of the Carlylean matter, and is not imposed on it by one who has turned away to dip into somebody else's chest of drawers for it. It was, in his own phrase, a 'skin' rather than a 'coat'.[2]

Pervasive in the great writings of the mid-century are prominent items of Carlyle's diction, words he had made specially his own—'earnest', 'sincere', 'silent', 'deep', 'intense', 'clear', 'needful', 'struggle', 'energy', 'lie' (the noun), 'indispensable', 'impossible'. His disciples liked to borrow both his leading ideas and the words they had first been expressed in. Indeed when we are struck with the oddity of a word in the mid-century literature, a knowledge of his writings sometimes explains why it was not odd to the writer or his well-informed first reader. In Browning's 'Misconceptions' the familiar diction is sharply arrested by the word 'dalmatic' (a rich garment), which was less odd for Browning because Carlyle had used it in *Past and Present*. Another odd expression of Browning's—'extinguish the man'—is explained by the phrase being Carlyle's. Arnold's 'ground-tone' in the Obermann poems and his

[1] *Sartor Resartus*, III. 12.
[2] *Letters to Mill, Sterling, and Browning*, p. 203.

'brother-world' recalled Carlyle's use of them in 'Corn-Law Rhymes' and *Past and Present*; his 'far-shining' in 'Rugby Chapel' is in the *Life of Sterling*. Pater was beholden to him for the word (and the idea, paradoxically) that makes his essay 'Style' most memorable—Carlyle had happily promoted the term 'surplusage' from legal usage, using it in 'The Hero as Poet': 'The gifted man is he who *sees* the essential point, and leaves all the rest aside as surplusage.' The opening line of Hardy's 'Convergence of the Twain' is a quotation from Carlyle's *Life of Sterling:*[1]

> In a solitude of the sea

—a neat instance of how the poetical mind creates new language as it expresses its thought. That same *Life* speaks of 'God's earnest sky', which reappears in Hopkins's journal. And it was because all mid-century writers read Carlyle as he ought to be read, that is, slowly and savouringly, as poetry, that they borrowed his individual words gratefully for their own purposes.

In offering his summary Sterling described Carlyle's writings as the 'representation of a pure and lofty mind—and one original, if only in this, that his doctrine is but the dogmatic form of his whole feelings and character.' Sterling does not follow up his discovery and make it bear on Carlyle's worth as a thinker. It was a discovery of the time, however, that the truth a man aimed at is inevitably at the mercy of his powers of seeing—or thinking or hoping or believing or fancying he is seeing it. St. Augustine had said that no one speaks of 'my' or 'thy' truth, but only of 'the' truth. It now seemed, however, suitable to speak of truth more limitedly, except where truth of facts was concerned—or rather of the plainest aspects of facts, such as the rough groupability claimed by their having been given names. Darwin did not claim

[1] I. 14.

for evolution more than was implied in his repeated possessive adjective, 'my theory'. Carlyle's 'truth' was based on what he saw for himself; that did not detract, however, from its interest for his fellow men, Carlyle having so remarkable a pair of eyes. Like the rest of his fellow writers, including Newman, he was more interesting as a writer than as a purveyor of what he claimed as truth, and one of his main merits lay in inspiring others to see as much as he had done in things in general. After reading and marking him they turned away to exercise their own powers as he had done his, and so reap all the many satisfactions of doing so. It was as much personality—the word was new early in our period—as anything else that drew their attention to him. We know from the accounts of innumerable friends of his, of which Harriet Martineau's is a brilliant example, how pungent was the impact of his physical presence. Friends noted particularly the way his earnest speech was punctuated with guffaws,[1] suggesting that his earnestness was to be taken for what it was worth, being only that of Carlyle, a man poised, like sooty Manchester, over the infinite abysses. The result was that when he held the pen, all this combined sighing and groaning, this earnestness and guffawing was transferred from his tobacco-laden armchair to the pages of his strong, clear, closely held-in handwriting, and so to those of print, in what Meredith called 'his fine grisly laughter'.[2] Part of his authorial personality is the combination of gloom and humour—humour as Thackeray defined it: 'humour is wit and love ... the best humour is that which contains

---

[1] See esp. David Masson, *Edinburgh Sketches and Memories* (1892), p. 332: 'those who have never heard Carlyle's laugh, or known how frequently it would interrupt the gathered tempests of his verbal rage and dissipate them in sudden sunburst, can have no idea of his prodigious wealth in this faculty ... I have heard the echoes of Sloane Street ring with his great laugh many and many a night ...'
[2] *Letters of George Meredith*, ed. C. L. Cline (1970), I. 327.

most humanity'.[1] Carlyle had said this too in 1827: 'The essence of humour is sensibility; warm, tender fellow-feeling with all forms of existence ... True humour springs not more from the head than from the heart; it is not contempt, its essence is love . . .'[2]

A striking instance of such humour closes 'Jesuitism', the last of the *Latter-Day Pamphlets:*

Well; rejoice in your upholsteries and cookeries, then, if so be they will make you 'happy.' Let the varieties of them be continual and innumerable. In all things let perpetual change, if that is a perpetual blessing to you, be your portion instead of mine; incur that Prophet's curse, and in all things in this sublunary world 'make yourselves like unto a wheel.' Mount into your railways; whirl from place to place, at the rate of fifty, or if you like of five hundred miles an hour: you cannot escape from that inexorable all-encircling ocean-moan of ennui. No: if you would mount to the stars, and do yacht-voyages under the belts of Jupiter, or stalk deer on the ring of Saturn, it would still begirdle you. You cannot escape from it, you can but change your place in it, without solacement except one moment's. That prophetic Sermon from the Deeps will continue with you, till you wisely interpret it and do it, or else till the Crack of Doom swallows it and you. *Adieu: Au Revoir.*

At that last phrase we laugh, but in the mystified way we should if the baton flew out of the hand of the maestro as he finished conducting a symphony. If the essay as a whole is quintessentially Carlyle as a thinker, its conclusion, the effect of which defies analysis, is quintessentially Carlyle as a person. And this is the person who, for much of the time, was writing that solemn thing, history! A final glance at his way of writing it may serve to summarize his literary genius.

Carlyle helped to inaugurate the golden age of our historians, all of whom, except him, treat their august subject with suitable stateliness. Splendidly readable as

---

[1] 'On Charity and Humour' (1852).       [2] 'Jean Paul Frederick Richter'.

they were—one of them, as every schoolboy knows, rivalled a novelist for readability—all but Carlyle achieved this excellence without relaxing their gravity. But Carlyle's dignity has to fend for itself while he exhibits a personality compounded of mind, feelings, and indeed body. No writer except the avowed comedians dared treat the past so familiarly. Carlyle is as free with it as if he were a showman dealing with puppets in the way Thackeray represented the novelist. He shows us his honesty in admitting ignorance where it exists, but he admits it cheerfully, as Johnson did over the Dictionary, so that emotion is involved. Over his indestructible and sacrosanct material—so sacrosanct that unlike some of his contemporaries he was at pains to transcribe his documents accurately—he poured the lava of his spleen or veneration. The very style in which he writes of it is at worst that of a bully and at best that of a benevolent despot, both of which roles we respect and even love (to Matthew Arnold he was 'the beloved man') for their blend of weary cantankerousness and hard-won and be-grudged good humour, and for the sparks of poetry that assert themselves in every paragraph—poetry as genial as Shakespeare's or Dickens's. Landor, who thought the *French Revolution* 'wicked', wore out one of its three volumes 'in tossing it on the floor at startling passages'. Meredith called him 'the greatest of the Britons of his time—and after the British fashion of not coming near to perfection, Titanic, not Olympian: a heaver of rocks, not a shaper. But if he did no perfect work, he had lightning's power to strike out marvellous pictures and reach to the inmost of man with a phrase.'[1]

To his secondary material Carlyle accords a tolerance more or less contemptuous. 'In these confused Prussian History-Books', he writes in *Frederick*, 'opulent in nugatory pedantisms and learned marine-stores, all that is human remains distressingly obscure to us.' And a few

[1] *Letters*, II. 661.

pages earlier two of the obscure creatures have received this characteristic dismissal:

[Schulenberg] is nephew of George I's lean Mistress: who also is a Schulenberg originally, and conspicuous not for sol-diering. Lean mistress we say; not the Fat one, or cataract of tallow, with eyebrows like a cartwheel, and dim coaly disks for eyes, who is George I's half-sister, probably not his mis-tress at all; and who now, as Countess of Darlington so-called, sits at Isleworth with good fat pensions, and a tame raven come-of-will, probably the *soul* of George I in some form. Not this one, we say:—but the thread-paper Duchess of Kendal, actual Ex-mistress; who tore her hair on the road when apoplexy overtook poor George, and who now attends chapel diligently, poor old anatomy or lean human nailrod. For the sake of the English reader searching into what is called 'History', I, with indignation, endeavour to distinguish these two beings once again: that each may be each, till both are happily forgotten to all eternity. It was the latter, lean maypole or nailrod one, that was Aunt of Schulenburg, who now presides at Cöpernick.

The negotiations by which Wilhelmina was to have become Princess of Wales, and Friedrich marry an English princess, are represented as carried on in the language of birds, a passage ending with 'And indeed we will here leave off, and shut down this magazine of rubbish; right glad to wash ourselves wholly from it (in three waters) for evermore.'

The past is a smoke and 'endless clouds of ever-whirling idle dust'. In his profound early essay 'On History'[1] he rejected the 'philosophical' history that was already being begun in England by Milman and which was soon to be aflame in Buckle: how is a historian, being a finite human being, to hope to grasp a coherence in 'the current of human affairs' which is 'intricate, perplexed, unfathomable' with its 'thousand-fold blending move-ments'? History may have been described as 'Philosophy

[1] *Fraser's Magazine* (Nov. 1830).

teaching by Experience', but 'so imperfect is that same Experience, by which Philosophy is to teach. Nay, even with regard to those occurrences which do stand recorded, which, at their origin have seemed worthy of record, and the summary of which constitutes what we now call History, is not our understanding of them altogether incomplete; is it even possible to represent them as they were?'

No complete representation, let alone understanding, was possible. And so meanwhile there was ample room and justification for the deep-fetched sighs of the elegiac and the epic poet, the guffaws, chuckles, and musical outpourings of this most unusual historian.

# 3. DICKENS

THE MID-CENTURY produced a bigger quantity of fiction, good or great, than the eighteenth or the early nineteenth centuries, splendid as theirs had been. Accordingly it had, and has, more to say to mankind. Of all the literary forms, that of fictitious narrative has the closest connection with people at their most 'normal'—by that clumsy term I mean people who sustain a balance, however precarious, between the self and others. We can learn something about novels in general by looking at ourselves, who are either normal or enviously knowledgeable about what it must be like to enjoy that blessing. And we are more like novelists than most of us are aware, because we not only experience life as it comes, but imagine bits of it beforehand or re-enact, for ourselves or for friends, bits of it retrospectively. Writers of novels differ from the rest of us in encouraging this shadow-life to spread into courses of action that may have no concern with themselves. That difference—in the quality of the shadow-life of the mind—marks them off from their fellows, even from those of their fellows who are lyric poets, whose shadow-life more wholly concerns themselves. Differences also exist among the novelists. Some of them resemble the lyric poets in clinging to the self as much as possible. They do imagine people in action, but the imagined persons turn out to be as like themselves as possible. Virginia Woolf was such a novelist; it might be that little of her mind would have been lost if she had rearranged her novels as a vast autobiography. Other novelists are most concerned with one other person in addition to themselves. They bring more than that one into their fictions, but the strength of their imagination is directed into the soul-and-body mate they have created for themselves: Charlotte Brontë would be an instance. Others seem to forget self almost entirely, and create a field full of folk, each of whom they understand as if from the inside outwards. Among many other mid-century novelists, Dickens is an instance of this third kind.

Certain mid-century novelists counselled aspirants not to begin writing their novels too early. 'Take my advice,' wrote Meredith to the 29-year-old Robert Louis Stevenson, 'defer ambition and let all go easy with you until you count forty;—then lash out from full stores.'[1] And in the same year, 1879, George Eliot, whose own *Scenes of Clerical Life* had not been written until she was nearing the advised degree of ripeness, noted that 'at the age of twenty only a rare genius could produce anything really valuable in the form of fiction'.[2]

The complete and shining exception, however, was Dickens. In 1833, when he was 21, his eyes were 'dimmed with joy and pride' on finding in the December number of the *Monthly Magazine* his first story, 'A Dinner at Poplar Walk' (later called 'Mr. Minns and His Cousin'), exhibited 'in all the glory of print'. That story begins with a description already characteristic, if crude:

Mr. Minns was a bachelor of *about* forty, as he said—of about eight and forty, as his friends said. He was always exceedingly clean, precise, and *tidy*, perhaps somewhat priggish, and the most 'retiring man in the world.' He usually wore a brown frock-coat without a wrinkle, light inexplicables without a spot, a neat neckerchief with a remarkably neat tie, and boots without a fault; moreover, he always carried a brown silk umbrella with an ivory handle. He was a clerk in Somerset House, or, as he said, he held 'a responsible situation under Government.'

[1] *Letters*, II. 569.
[2] *George Eliot Letters*, VII. 178.

Thereafter appeared the various tales and sketches collected early in 1836 as the first series of *Sketches by Boz*.
They were widely noticed; the *Court Magazine and
Monthly Critic* in April 1837 had a review of a special kind,
'Some Notes on Arch Waggery in General and on Boz
in Particular'. Their effect was recalled in what may be
the first substantial and worthy piece of Dickens
criticism—the article by George Henry Lewes, himself
only 20. It appeared in the *National Magazine and Monthly
Critic* for December 1837, and dealt with the *Sketches*,
*Pickwick Papers*, and the eight of the twenty-four
instalments of *Oliver Twist* that had so far appeared in
*Bentley's Miscellany*. By that date Lewes could already
award superlatives:

'Boz' has perhaps a wider popularity than any man has enjoyed
for many years. Not alone are his delightful works confined to
the young and old, the grave and gay, the witty, the intellectual, the moralist, and the thoughtless of both sexes in the
reading circles, from the peer and judge to the merchant's
clerk; but even the common people, both in town and country,
are equally intense in their admiration. Frequently have we
seen the butcher-boy, with his tray on his shoulder, reading
with the greatest avidity the last '*Pickwick*;' the footman,
(whose fopperies are so inimitably laid bare,) the maid-
servant, the chimney-sweep, all classes, in fact, read '*Boz*.' ...
He chose, perhaps, the worst possible medium for making his
*entrée*—the columns of a newspaper! Yet such was the delicacy
of touch, the fineness of observation, and the original, quiet
humour of these papers, that he was induced to collect and
publish them in two volumes. When the '*Sketches*' came out,
'Have you read Boz?' was the eternal question. ... Byron used
to say, that he awoke one morning and found himself celebrated: Boz may say the same; for never was a more rapid,
more deserved a reputation made.

This universal conquest was inevitable, especially after
*Pickwick*; but it was inevitably easy only because his
originality was the sort that built plainly on that of others.

However topless his towers, their foundations were reassuringly familiar. As far as obvious things went, he was no innovator. The context into which he burst was well put by a contemporary, Mrs. Margaret Baron-Wilson, in 1839. After tracing the supersession of Monk Lewis's type of novel by the Waverley novels, she remarked the 'short-lived popularity' of the novel of fashionable life, and the reaction against it by Theodore Hook and Bulwer:

a famous wit undertook to explore 'the remote regions of Russell Square,' and an equally famous, but somewhat affected legislator, dived into the recesses of St. Giles's. Descriptions of tenth-rate dinner parties took the place of minute details of fashionable *ennui-ism*; and pictures of the lowest of low life were conveyed to the higher classes, by the aid of the slang dictionary. To these has succeeded a far better order of things in this particular department of fiction. A genius has lately sprung up who, steering midway between the inanities of high life and the vulgar depth of its antipodes, is producing, with astonishing celerity, a class of novels whose only model is nature. The mantle of the novelist has alighted upon Dickens, and a bold manly tone of sentiment, an unequalled perception of the peculiarities of human character, besides powers of unexampled truthfulness in description, were never combined in any one writer, to render him better entitled to wear it.[1]

The effect of Dickens's first writings on his first readers was also remembered by the obituarist in the *Illustrated London News* (17 June 1870) as

a reaction, about thirty-four years ago, as many of us can well remember, against the high-flown affectation of classic and aristocratic elegance which pervaded the romances of Sir Edward Bulwer Lytton. Just when Ernest Maltravers had posed himself in a sublime attitude of transcendental nobility, Mr. Pickwick, of Goswell Street, in his gaiters and spectacles, with Sam Weller at his heels toddled forward and took possession of the stage.

[1] *Life and Correspondence of M. G. Lewis* (1839), I. 177–8.

Early reviewers saw Dickens as reverting to an older tradition, and were reminded of Fielding and especially of Smollett. We know that for him, as for David Copperfield, these were a refuge and inspiration in childhood: 'Roderick Random, Peregrine Pickle, Humphrey Clinker, Tom Jones, The Vicar of Wakefield, Don Quixote, Gil Blas, and Robinson Crusoe, came out, a glorious host, to keep me company'—along with certain European and Eastern classics—*Don Quixote, Gil Blas*, and *The Arabian Nights*, and (an item from the golden age of literary forgeries) the young James Ridley's *Tales of the Genii* (1764). Furthermore, in 'Lying Awake',[1] he recorded his reading, also as a small boy, of some of the American classics. One of them was by 'that delightful writer', Washington Irving, though his influence on Dickens can be overstated by those who do not allow for the influence on both of Lamb. In the same essay Dickens quoted Benjamin Franklin's 'paper on the art of procuring pleasant dreams', the quotation, seven lines long, being introduced with 'I often used to read that paper when I was a very small boy, and ... I recollect everything I read then, as perfectly as I forget everything I read now ...' Along with these classics he absorbed the eighteenth-century periodical essays, which are usually half 'character' and sometimes half story, and eighteenth-century comedies and farces.

Some of his early writings could have appeared half a century before they did without striking readers as premature: many of their details recall Addison, Pope, and Swift. It was Smollett, however, who contributed most, both to the fantasy life of the young David and to Dickens's education as a writer of stories: but as the *Athenaeum* approvingly noted, it was Smollett 'without his coarseness'. In that more squeamish age—for by the thirties prohibitions, which had been edging in during the late eighteenth century, were now gathering

[1] *Household Words* (30 Oct. 1852).

force—Dickens could not salt his stories with his own version of Smollett's coarseness. That could find straight expression only in the letters to men friends. What 'coarseness' could be attempted in the novels had to struggle between the lines, as in some of the equivocal but innocent escapades of Mr. Pickwick; or in one of the Weller episodes in *Master Humphrey's Clock*:

'It's in wain to deny it mum,' said Mr. Weller, 'this here is a boy arter his grandfather's own heart, and beats out all the boys as ever wos or will be. Though at the same time mum,' added Mr. Weller trying to look gravely down upon his favourite, 'it was wery wrong on him to want to—over all the posts as we come along, and wery cruel on him to force poor grandfather to lift him cross-legged over every vun of 'em. He wouldn't pass vun single blessed post mum, and at the top o' the lane there's seven-and-forty on 'em all in a row and wery close together.'

It is a pity that the palette of Dickens lacked some of the colours that Chaucer, Shakespeare, and Pope had used brilliantly and even exquisitely. Their omission apart, Dickens showed himself as a glorification of Smollett, narrating action in Smollett's rattling many-claused prose, though proceeding differently in dialogue and description.

It requires an effort of the historical imagination to picture how the novel form was thought of in Dickens's early days, and indeed later. In the *Prelude* Wordsworth called a novel 'a work of humour', and it is as humorists that Dickens and Thackeray both speak of themselves, Thackeray referring to his novels as 'comic books' in which pathos should only be occasional.[1] Perhaps the term lingered longer because Dickens was inimitable as a funny writer, Forster claiming, rightly, that comedy lay at the heart of his genius: his 'mighty creative imagination', said the obituary already quoted, was at its best in comic, not pathetic, passages, or in those 'meant to be

[1] *Letters and Private Papers*, ed. G. N. Ray (1945), II. 424–5.

terribly grand'; and Arthur Helps recalled him as 'both witty and humorous, a combination rarely met with'.[1] We must go deeper than Trollope, who in his *Auto-biography* held that *Pickwick Papers* would not endure as *Jane Eyre* and *Adam Bede* would, though he admits that (a generation later) it is still very much alive. Fielding had offered his *Joseph Andrews* as a 'comic epic in prose', meaning comic in the old sense, applicable rather to the comedies of Jonson than of Shakespeare. The comic for Jonson, as for Fielding, included what provoked the con-demnatory social laugh (the satirical) and what in the nineteenth century was called the 'horse' laugh (the far-cical): whereas for Shakespeare the comic also provoked the sympathetic laugh (humorous rather than satirical humour being nicely hit off by Thackeray, when he saw it as the produce of wit and love).[2] Dickens grew up in the midst of comic writing mainly restricted to the Jonsonian. It abounded in the naval and Irish novels then in fashion, and at its raciest in the comic drawings of Cruikshank. Thackeray's long essay on him, in the *Westminster* for June 1840, celebrated a career as illustrator that had begun early in the century. Cruikshank's draw-ings, of which Dickens had the benefit for his *Sketches* and his second novel, were mainly satirical and farcical. Where not, they were grim, or fantastic in a new way that Dickens may have had in mind when he spoke of his 'creative pencil'.[3] That the Jonsonian comic was supreme in Dickens's early days is suggested by the titles of some of the books Cruikshank illustrated: Pierce Egan's *Life in London; or the Day and Night Scenes of Jerry Hawthorn, Esq. and his Elegant Friend Corinthian Tom, accompanied by Bob Logic, the Oxonian, in their Rambles and Sprees through the*

[1] 'In Memoriam', *Macmillan's Magazine* (July 1870), 236.
[2] 'Charity and Humor' (1852).
[3] There are good examples in William Clarke's *Three Courses and a Dessert* (1830), such as the trio of lemons, well described by Blanchard Jerrold: 'Remaining lemons that you might squeeze, they are [still three] convivial fellows in close confabulation' (*Life of George Cruikshank*, 1882, I. 190).

*Metropolis* (1821); William Hone's *A Slap at Slop and the Bridge Street Gang* (1822); John Wight's *Mornings at Bow Street* (1824); and Lamb's *Satan in Search of a Wife* (1831). All told, Cruikshank's drawings pre-create some large part of at least the appearance of the comic world of Dickens's early novels, as they do that of the comic worlds of Edward Lear and Lewis Carroll. For them as for Dickens the comic included the humorous.

Dickens's writings entertained an audience that was to encourage comic writing for a long time. An article on Douglas Jerrold in the *British Quarterly Review* for August 1849 shows the comic as still supreme:

The immense and increasing number of our comic writers is a curious sign of the times. There appears to be something in the air of London that especially favours this kind of growth. Whether it be that the number of odd actual sights to be seen in London, queer faces, quaint street-groups, amusing incidents, and so on, necessarily beget a comic mode of thinking among the inhabitants, as might be inferred from the circumstance that the best practitioners of London wit are the cabmen, the omnibus-drivers, and such as, like them, combine learned leisure with peculiar facilities for observation ... Certain ... it is, that all native London talent, if left to itself, runs to wit. To describe Beaks, Peelers, Jews, kitchen areas, garrets in Fleet-street, fat city gentlemen, and young good-hearted rascals who get into scrapes, is the pre-established vocation of the London literary aspirant. .... [He] concocts jokes, meditates a farce to be produced at one of the theatres, or writes a novel in which the hero, Jack Smith, or Bob Webster, goes through the proper amount of funny experience before he is married. Happy the young author who, like Dickens, is saved from the wretchedness of this element by the real genius that he brings into it.[1]

The sum of all this popular 'literature' reminds us that Dickens's novels were rooted in common life, as were Shakespeare's plays. Writing in 1889, G. S. Merriam saw this as a source of his power:

[1] pp. 195–6.

Dickens belongs to the common people. He stands among the rising forces. That middle and lower class of England which the fastidious observer finds so dreary and Philistine, Dickens reveals as palpitating with human interests, with tragedy and comedy. He is as strenuous a champion of the poor as Victor Hugo. ... He is a man of the common people too in that he lives far more by feeling than by reason. He not seldom falls into exaggeration, for the sake of immediate effect, unrestrained by that accuracy of sight and speech which is the austere virtue of the intellect.[1]

The first and last thing, therefore, to say of Dickens is that he was born and fated to contribute to this 'odd', 'queer', 'quaint' comic literature, and to do by means of rarest genius what others were doing by means of something less.

*Sketches by Boz* bore the sub-title 'Illustrations of Everyday Life and Everyday People', and that this commonplace topic was metropolitan was taken for granted: at this date a provincial scene had to be signalized in title or sub-title—as *Our Village*, or 'A Tale of Manchester life'. The reviewers of the *Sketches* praised them for the right reasons—as Forster recalled: 'The *Sketches* were much more talked about than the first two or three numbers of *Pickwick*.' The main reason was their

unusually truthful observation of a sort of life between the middle class and the low, which, having few attractions for bookish observers, was quite unhacknied ground. It had otherwise also the very special merit of being in no respect bookish or commonplace in its descriptions of the old city with which its writer was so familiar. It was a picture of every-day London at its best and worst, in its humours and enjoyments as well as its sufferings and sins, pervaded everywhere ... with the absolute reality of the things depicted.[2]

[1] *The Story of William and Lucy Smith* (1889), pp. 662–3.
[2] *The Life of Charles Dickens*, ed. J. W. T. Ley, I. v. 76–7; compare the reviews cited in John Butt and Kathleen Tillotson, *Dickens at Work* (1957), pp. 36–7.

Right to the end of his life the favourite milieu of his novels was London. In the end, little of it remained unrepresented: the high and mighty in Belgravia had by then been added to the 'everyday' in the more ancient and now fallen purlieus.

Writing of the unfashionable City and what surrounded it, and in the early work writing of it mainly comically, he was stamped as vulgar for certain readers—such as Lockhart, who thought *Pickwick* 'damned low', or, initially, Sydney Smith who said he held out successfully up to *Nicholas Nickleby*; Spedding in 1843 thought that as a man of 'desultory' education 'whose studies have lain almost exclusively among the odd characters in the odd corners of London', Dickens was hardly qualified as an impartial observer of American society. By the forties the upper middle class had so far proceeded in refinement that not only Fielding and Smollett but Jane Austen were regarded as coarse. For all his care not to offend the squeamish openly, Dickens seemed to such people as grossly vulgar as Cruikshank did. His love of human oddity jarred, particularly at a time when '... ground in yonder social mill / We rub each others' angles down, / And merge ... in form and gloss / The picturesque of man and man'.[1] In this human picturesque, now confining itself more and more to the lower ranks of society, Dickens revelled, and let it be seen that he was revelling. Accordingly, his audience was, first and foremost, lower middle class. Its members assured the huge sales of his shilling parts—the copy that Lewes saw in the hands of the butcher's boy must have been borrowed, passed on, or worse. His vulgarity was no vulgarity to the lower middle class, and, like Charlie Chaplin's in the early twentieth century, it tested the competence of his first critics, many of whom stood higher on the social scale, by showing whether or not they scented his true Shakespearian worth.

[1] Tennyson, *In Memoriam*, 88.

For David Copperfield books, like the magic bottles in *The Arabian Nights*, emitted living creatures, the heroes of eighteenth-century novels providing him with a 'glorious host' of companions in his solitude. He would not have got the same help from poetry; for a novelist people are what charity was for St. Paul, everything else taking second place at best. This was put with authority and power by Gissing, writing of *Pickwick*:

Among the various endowments essential to a novelist of the first rank, the most important is that which at once declares itself to critical and uncritical reader alike; the power of creating persons. . . . Were it only by the figures of Sam and Tony Weller, Dickens would in this book have proved himself a born master in the art of fiction. Let this ever be kept in view when his standing in literature is debated. That his creations (here, at all events) are more or less ignoble, and represent an unlovely world, is nothing to the point; the same kind of power went to the shaping of Mr. Pickwick's man-servant as to the bodying forth of Mercutio—power which, in its infinite manifestations, we indicate by the one word genius.[1]

The proposal of Chapman and Hall that he should provide adventures for the 'Nimrod Club', which the popular Seymour would illustrate, suited him well as far as the club went. The only thing that did not suit him was the Nimrod part, which required the expert knowledge of a Surtees, whose Jorrocks papers had already figured in the *New Sporting Magazine* from 1831 to 1834, and which were to be collected four years later in *Jorrocks' Jaunts and Jollities, or the Hunting, Shooting, Racing, Driving, Sailing, Eating, Eccentric and Extravagant Exploits of that Renowned Sporting Citizen, Mr. John Jorrocks of St. Botolph Lane and Great Coram Street*; with illustrations by Phiz. As men participate in jaunts and jollities, eat, are eccentric and

[1] *Charles Dickens* (1898), p. 47.

extravagant, Dickens was ready to honour them with invented exploits by the score. But he clung to that classification 'citizen' and such places as St. Botolph Lane and Great Coram Street, bargaining with the publishers to be allowed greater latitude than a Surtees would have wanted. 'My views being deferred to, I thought of Mr. Pickwick', was his account of the genesis of what, to his surprise, turned out to be his first novel, as great a piece of literature as any that were to follow, exhibiting, as Gissing put it, 'exuberance of animation [and] joyous exercise of happiest faculties'.[1] His account was of a human birth in the heart of London. The second chapter begins with Mr. Pickwick throwing up his window that fair morning, and alertly finding that 'Goswell-street was at his feet, Goswell-street was at his right hand—as far as the eye could reach, Goswell-street extended on his left; and the opposite side of Goswell-street was over the way'—words that bestowed a subtle individual life on him, and a life in London. It is true that Dickens's idea of Pickwick changed into something more normally or fully human as he provided him with Sam Weller for squire, and true also that there was a more protracted and composite genesis for some at least of the more fully integrated later novels (*Great Expectations*, for example, sprang not from a single character, but a 'grotesque tragi-comic conception'[2]), but vivid persons remained his primary concern.

'Exuberance of animation ... joyous exercise of happiest faculties'; 'As the distinctive note of Thackeray is truth, so that of Dickens is ardor. He is brimful of emotion and energy ... His genius has a richness, an elation, a satisfaction, like Nature's own'[3]; 'When he read,

---

[1] *The Immortal Dickens* (1925), p. 17.
[2] Letter to Forster, 4 Oct. 1860; Forster, IX. III.
[3] Merriam, op. cit. p. 662.

or when he spoke, the whole man read or spoke'.[1] These
are typical testimonies, to the work and the man,
confirmed by early sketches, caricatures, and portraits.
This energy and exuberance showed themselves in his
passion for acting (and later, in the public readings from
his works) which also reflects the dramatic quality of his
imagination—sometimes regarded as exaggeration. But
as he said in the Preface to *Chuzzlewit*, 'What is exaggeration to one class of minds and perceptions, is plain
truth to another'.

We may recall Addison: 'Words, when well chosen,
have so great a Force in them, that a Description often
gives us more lively Ideas than the Sight of Things themselves.'[2] Dickens had a power, beyond most writers, of so
describing a common thing that we seem to be looking at
it again with opened eyes: as, a 'brass toasting-fork hanging in its usual nook, and spreading its four idle fingers
out as if it wanted to be measured for a glove';[3] or a boat's
figurehead as having 'a firm formality of bosom and her
knobby eyes staring two inches out of her head'.[4] Such
examples may be regarded as 'plain truth', though rarely
observed. But what of old Weller, who, describing the
discomforts he had arranged for Mr. Stiggins, the
bibulous 'Shepherd', laughs in a crescendo that cul-
minates in 'a rapture of winks'? Are these the winks that a
particular Cockney coachman can produce on a special
occasion, and of which Dickens had seen samples and
accurately remembered at his desk? Or are they human
winks gilded with heavenly alchemy? Are Dickens's
descriptions no more than a silent criticism of the inade-
quacy of the seeing and observing done by most of us,
and no more than an indication that Dickens's bodily
apparatus was a more efficient one than our own? Or did

---

[1] Arthur Helps, 'In Memoriam', 239.
[2] *Spectator*, No. 416.
[3] *The Chimes*, 4th Quarter.
[4] *Great Expectations*, Ch. liv.

his superiority lie in what the mind added to the report supplied to it by the bodily apparatus? That his visual powers were unusually active is testified by many; Helps was reminded of 'those modern magicians whose wondrous skill has been attained by their being taught from their infancy to see more things in less time than other men. Indeed, I have said to myself, when I have been with him, he sees and observes nine facts for any two that I see and observe.' There is no way of telling for certain whether, as well as seeing 'more things in less time' than the ordinary man, Dickens also saw further into each: but as we shall see, even his factual descriptions usually include something for which the bodily scene could have supplied no more than the materials—the means of comparing one thing with another.

Critics have given much consideration to the relation of Dickens's creatures to human beings, some seeing them as fairy creatures, who might well step over into Lewis Carroll's Wonderland, others claiming them for Thackerayan beings, inevitably coloured by the Dickensian magic, but still frankly recognizable as people we might meet. Certain of them plainly are that. For instance, the novels in the first person have Thackerayan heroes—David Copperfield and Pip. With them go Esther Summerson, by means of whose diary record *Bleak House* is in part a first-person novel, and those persons who at some point recount their history—as Miss Wade does in her written narrative 'The History of a Self-Tormentor' in *Little Dorrit*—or, outside the novels, Mrs. Lirriper. Otherwise, one can say as a generalization that any person not mainly comic, wildly eccentric, or hideous-minded is passably a human being as Thackeray's personages all are.

There is something tactless, however, about the whole inquiry, since Dickens's aim was not usually the transference, so to speak, of actual people into his fiction. His novels have often more in common with allegories such as *The Pilgrim's Progress*, and satiric comedies such as Jonson's, than with Thackeray's. Like them he gives us human nature generously, but not necessarily through the medium of human individuals.

It could never be said of Dickens as of Scott that

You can hardly read any novel of [his] and not become better aware what public and political issues mean ... The boldness and freshness of the present are carried back into the past, and you see Papists and Puritans, Cavaliers and Roundheads, Jews, Jacobites, and free booters, preachers, schoolmasters, mercenary soldiers, gipsies and beggars, all living the sort of life which the reader feels that in their circumstances and under the same conditions of time and place and parentage, he might have lived too.[1]

Contrast this framework, held in place by a giant intellect, with the framework of Dickens's account of the world of public affairs. This power of comprehension Dickens does not have; and yet his world is as complete as Scott's, the difference being that instead of holding the whole thing with the cool strength of an Atlas, he sallies into what of it he needs for the moment—a 'Circumlocution Office', a work-house, a debtors' prison. By the time all his lightning raids are over, the whole has been rifled, and another sort of mind than his, a mind more like Scott's, could assemble it from the fragments. He gives us the God's plenty that we get from Chaucer, Shakespeare, and Scott, but gives us it divided up and scattered over his fiction, sometimes without any special care as to which particular personage a particular instance of it is attached.

Dickens is interested in classifying people by trade, or profession, or gainful or ungainful occupation. One paragraph of *Nicholas Nickleby*, recounting the occasion of the coach's departure for Yorkshire, specifies the executives concerned, and their actions: the coachman and guard (who are 'comparing notes for the last time

[1] R. H. Hutton, *Sir Walter Scott* (1878), pp. 101–2.

before starting, on the subject of the way-bill' and whose heavily clothed bodies make the coach sway to one side when they mount it), the 'porters ... screwing out the last reluctant sixpences', and the 'itinerant newsmen making the last offer of a morning paper'. Here common types are shown in action, that action being characteristic. Occasionally we get pictures the completeness of which is particularly welcome for present-day readers—like those of the occupants of the Fleet Prison. Sam Weller divides them into two types for the benefit of Mr. Pickwick:

There were many classes of people here, from the labouring man in his fustian jacket, to the broken down spendthrift in his shawl dressing-gown, most appropriately out at elbows; but there was the same air about them all—a kind of listless, jail-bird, careless swagger; a vagabondish who's-afraid sort of bearing, which is wholly indescribable in words; but which any man can understand in one moment if he wishes, by just setting foot in the nearest debtor's prison, and looking at the very first group of people he sees there, with the same interest as Mr. Pickwick did.

'It strikes me, Sam,' said Mr. Pickwick, leaning over the iron-rail at the stair-head, 'It strikes me, Sam, that imprisonment for debt is scarcely any punishment at all.'

'Think not, Sir?' inquired Mr. Weller.

'You see how these fellows drink, and smoke, and roar,' replied Mr. Pickwick. 'It's quite impossible that they can mind it much.'

'Ah, that's just the wery thing, Sir,' rejoined Sam, '*they* don't mind it; it's a reg'lar holiday to them—all porter and skettles. It's the t'other vuns as gets done over vith this sort o' thing: them down-hearted fellers as can't svig away at the beer, nor play skettles neither; them as vould pay if they could, and gets low by being boxed up ...'

Here we are nearer to humanity in general than to individuals. Miss Snevellicci, in her naïve attempt to attract Nicholas Nickleby, becomes a type of a larger and more long-lived class:

'I beg your pardon,' said Miss Snevellicci, sidling towards Nicholas, 'but did you ever play at Canterbury?'

'I never did,' replied Nicholas.

'I recollect meeting a gentleman at Canterbury,' said Miss Snevellicci, 'only for a few moments, for I was leaving the company as he joined it, so like you that I felt almost certain it was the same.'

'I see you now for the first time,' rejoined Nicholas with all due gallantry. 'I am sure I never saw you before; I couldn't have forgotten it.'

'Oh, I'm sure—it's very flattering of you to say so,' retorted Miss Snevellicci with a graceful bend. 'Now I look at you again, I see that the gentleman at Canterbury hadn't the same eyes as you—you'll think me very foolish for taking notice of such things, won't you?'

'Not at all,' said Nicholas. 'How can I feel otherwise than flattered by your notice in any way?'

'Oh! you men, you are such vain creatures!' cried Miss Snevellicci. Whereupon she became charmingly confused, and, pulling out her pocket-handkerchief from a faded pink silk reticule with a gilt clasp, called to Miss Ledrook—

'Led, my dear,' said Miss Snevellicci.

'Well, what is the matter?' said Miss Ledrook.

'It's not the same.'

'Not the same what?'

'Canterbury—you know what I mean. Come here, I want to speak to you.'

But Miss Ledrook wouldn't come to Miss Snevellicci, so Miss Snevellicci was obliged to go to Miss Ledrook, which she did in a skipping manner that was quite fascinating, and Miss Ledrook evidently joked Miss Snevellicci about being struck with Nicholas, for, after some playful whispering, Miss Snevellicci hit Miss Ledrook very hard on the backs of her hands, and retired up, in a state of pleasing confusion.

Similarly with Mrs. Kenwigs becoming for the nonce the typical hostess, preparing for her party by getting together all that has to be got together, and getting out of the way all that has to be got out of the way, the party itself being authenticated by such human phrases as

'Everybody having eaten everything . . .' Much of what Dickens shows us in his personages we recognize as existing in our superficially different selves. Scattered actions and remarks spread from an individual so that they illustrate something like a law of human nature. When Mr. Pickwick falls through the ice, Mr. Tupman rushes from the pond crying 'Fire!' This action is fixed on Mr. Tupman, but could well be fixed on others—many people are capable of seeing urgent action as called for (from others), without considering precisely what sort of action.

What may seem remote from ourselves, we recognize as near to other people. Mr. Bung, the beadle in *Sketches by Boz*, contrasts himself with 'one of those fortunate men who, if they were to dive under one side of a barge stark-naked, would come up on the other with a new suit of clothes on, and a ticket for soup in the waist-coat-pocket'; instead he is 'just one of the careless, good-for-nothing, happy fellows, who float, cork-like, on the surface, for the world to play at hockey with'. The fat boy watches other people eating with 'a kind of dark and gloomy joy'. Mr. Wititterly, 'in the ardour of his description, had flourished his right hand to within something less than an inch of Mrs. Nickleby's bonnet, drew it hastily back again, and blew his nose as fiercely as if it had been done by some violent machinery'. Mrs. Squeers 'seizing Mr. Squeers by the throat gave him two loud kisses, one close after the other, like a postman's knock'. Mrs. Gradgrind, on her deathbed, remarks: 'I think there's a pain somewhere in the room . . . but I couldn't positively say that I have got it'. Esther Summerson says, 'falling ill, I seemed to have crossed a dark lake, and to have left all my experiences, mingled together by the great distance, on the healthy shore . . . I had never known before how short life really was, and into how small a space the mind could put it.'

Furthermore Dickens knows how human beings

express themselves. Conspicuous among his speakers are those who use language splendidly and expressively, without having learned how to use it accurately. Some of the recurrent comedy of the novels lies in the grandiose but frustrated attempts of people who have no sure footing along the syntax of the sentences they earnestly propel forward. He sees, as Newman did, that at a crisis 'the whole man moves', even though the whole man, when moving no further than to words, cannot say where his moving has brought him to in a form that would be countenanced by a schoolmaster. An obvious instance is Miss Pross in *A Tale of Two Cities*: 'If it was ever intended that I should go across salt water, do you suppose Providence would have cast my lot in an island?' Miss Pross well knows what she wants her speech to convey—it exists in her heated mind, a blob of insularity. Moreover, what she wants to convey is conveyed effectively. On the other hand, the straight logic behind the speech has become tortured before it reaches that Laocoon group of words. Again, what passes for conversation in Dickens is often little more than an alternation of two or more monologues, exhibiting merely individual cleverness, and people's liking to air their mental possessions. Dickens's personages use language that not only seems right for them, but turns out to be the equivalent of something in ourselves, however wide the apparent difference. Dickens knows that we all use the jargon of a particular set, without remembering how odd it is in itself, and how odd it therefore seems to outsiders. On one occasion Mr. Crummles addresses his troupe as follows: '"Ladies and gentlemen," said Mr. Vincent Crummles, who had been writing on a piece of paper, 'we'll call the Mortal Struggle to-morrow at ten; everybody for the procession. Intrigue and Ways and Means you'll all be up in, so we shall only want one rehearsal ... Everybody at ten, if you please.'" Or there is the disgruntled Mr. Folair: '"Why I *know* of fifteen and sixpence that came to Southampton one night last month to see me dance the Highland Fling, and what's the consequence? I've never been put up in it since—never once—while the 'infant phenomenon' has been grinning through artificial flowers at five people and a baby in the pit, and two boys in the gallery, every night."'

Mrs. Nickleby's mind when expanding itself is not merely at the mercy of the association principle. Her associative links form the one chain of her obsession—her wish to relive her earlier life, 'with your poor dear father', but more affluent and happier.

Mr. Pecksniff soon draws us into deep water. He is supposed to represent pompous egotism, self-right-eousness, and hypocrisy: those failings may be at the centre of him, but a whole geometry is netted like cob-webs elusively architected around them. We are intro-duced to him as he sits with his two daughters over an ample meal (after his undignified entrance in a howling gale), first in his role as 'a moral man'—'his very throat was moral'—and then as a professional architect. Each aspect is then illustrated in conversation, the first scrap leading to a plausible and amazing conclusion:

'Even the worldly goods of which we have just disposed,' said Mr. Pecksniff, glancing round the table when he had finished, 'even cream, sugar, tea, toast, ham,—'

'And eggs,' suggested Charity in a low voice.

'And eggs,' said Mr. Pecksniff, 'even they have their moral. See how they come and go! Every pleasure is transitory. We can't even eat, long. If we indulge in harmless fluids, we get the dropsy; if in exciting liquids, we get drunk. What a soothing reflection is that!'

'Don't say *we* get drunk Pa,' urged the eldest Miss Pecksniff.

'When I say, we, my dear,' returned her father, 'I mean mankind in general; the human race, considered as a body, and not as individuals. There is nothing personal in morality, my love.'

And the second:

'I have again been fortunate in the attainment of my object. A new inmate will very shortly come among us.'

'A youth, papa?' asked Charity.

'Ye-es, a youth,' said Mr. Pecksniff. 'He will avail himself of the eligible opportunity which now offers, for uniting the advantages of the best practical architectural education, with the comforts of a home, and the constant association with some who (however humble their sphere, and limited their capacity) are not unmindful of their moral responsibilities.'

'Oh pa!' cried Mercy, holding up her finger archly. 'See advertisement!'

'Playful—playful warbler,' said Mr. Pecksniff.

To which Dickens adds this comment:

It may be observed in connection with his calling his daughter 'a warbler', that she was not at all vocal, but that Mr. Pecksniff was in the frequent habit of using any word that occurred to him as having a good sound, and rounding a sentence well, without much care for its meaning. And he did this so boldly, and in such an imposing manner, that he would sometimes stagger the wisest people with his eloquence, and make them gasp again.

And then this further comment: 'His enemies asserted, by the way, that a strong trustfulness in sounds and forms, was the master-key to Mr. Pecksniff's character.' On this occasion, Pecksniff acts like an impressionist poet, hesitating over the choice of a pretty word, but one designed to throw mist around the true light of which Mercy has saucily let in a blighting gleam. But though Dickens points out the significance of Pecksniff's verbal tactics, he does not tell us what is even deeper than his choice of sounding words. Deeper than that is his need to be speaking. This need shows itself at its neatest in his use of the sound represented by 'Umph!', which concludes one speech and constitutes the whole of another ('in his most winning tone'). Most of his speechifying, however, takes the form not of impressionistic poetic diction or mellow purrings, but of chains of logical sentences. But his logic is itself impressionistic, as in the speeches about Tom Pinch just before Tom makes his first appearance:

'Ay, ay,' returned her father, raising his hand mildly: 'it is very well to say what can we expect from Mr. Pinch, but Mr. Pinch is a fellow-creature, my dear; Mr. Pinch is an item in the vast total of humanity, my love; and we have a right, it is our duty, to expect in Mr. Pinch some development of those better qualities, the possession of which in our own persons inspires our humble self-respect. No,' continued Mr. Pecksniff. 'No! Heaven forbid that I should say, nothing can be expected from Mr. Pinch; or that I should say, nothing can be expected from any man alive (even the most degraded, which Mr. Pinch is not, no really); but Mr. Pinch has disappointed me: he has hurt me: I think a little the worse of him on this account, but not of human nature. Oh no, no!'

Because many of his persons speak from so rich and strange a nature, they do more than serve the purpose Dickens had, or supposed he had, in mind. His accounts of what he proposed, and what in fact he did, are wildly out. So far as *Martin Chuzzlewit* goes, he set out, as the preface to the first edition tells us, 'with the design of exhibiting, in various aspects, the commonest of all vices'. In the preface to the first Cheap edition this vice is named as selfishness, which is like saying that Cleopatra on the Cydnus shows the use of boats for locomotion. It is often so with his explanations, and the same when he tries to claim his pictures as lifelike in the simplest sense, as he implicitly did with Pecksniff:

I have never touched a character precisely from the life, but some counterpart of that character has incredulously asked me: 'Now really, did I ever really, see one like it?'

All the Pecksniff family upon earth are quite agreed, I believe, that Mr. Pecksniff is an exaggeration, and that no such character ever existed.[1]

Could there be a more glorious instance of the failure of a writer to grasp retrospectively what he had done?

[1] Preface, Charles Dickens edn. (1867).

Most of Dickens's people, like ourselves, do not wish
to undergo any change: and yet critics are rejoiced when
fictional personages are 'convincingly' represented as
undergoing one. Because of his love for the changes that
overtake bad men in fairy-tales Dickens effected quick
changes in some of his own bad men. (Like their fellows
in those tales some of his own are bad for no discoverable
reason.) In the story inserted in *Pickwick Papers* Gabriel
Grub, the wicked sexton, undergoes a horrifying experience with a goblin, and then during a bout of delirium
tremens becomes 'an altered man'. The formula was
reapplied with a difference for the benefit of Scrooge in
the *Christmas Carol*: Grub and Scrooge may only be dismissed as unreal, if we are prepared to dismiss fairy-tales
as unreal. In *Dombey and Son*, however, we have done
with fairy-tale conventions, and are virtually in a novel of
Thackerayan truth. The humanizing of Dombey is
plotted carefully, step by step, almost as it would have
been by Trollope or George Eliot. His change forms the
spine of the novel, and cannot but have existed in
Dickens's mind from the start. In a letter to Forster after
he had written the first number, he outlined his plans, and
we see him thinking in terms of personages complete as
human beings are, and even designing the story to subject
their natures to some sort of change, whether developing
what was latent in them, or vivifying what was
atrophied, or making them throw out new shoots.

From that time, I purpose changing his feeling of indifference
and uneasiness towards his daughter into a positive hatred . . .
So I mean to carry the story on, through all the branches and
off-shoots and meanderings that come up; and through the
decay and downfall of the house, and the bankruptcy of Dombey, and all the rest of it; when his only staff and treasure, and
his unknown Good Genius always, will be this rejected daughter, who will come out better than any son at last, and whose
love for him, when discovered and understood, will be his
bitterest reproach. For the struggle with himself, which goes

on in all such obstinate natures will have ended then; and the sense of his injustice, which you may be sure has never quitted him, will have at last a gentler office than that of only making him more harshly unjust.[1]

Several less important people also undergo the sort of change we have found happening in ourselves—Mrs. Gummidge is one of them, all supine complainings and misery until jerked into effective activity by Em'ly's flight with Steerforth. Changes like this Dickens brings to the pitch of a generalization. In the *Tale of Two Cities* comes the author's comment on Sydney Carton: 'All of us have like wonders hidden in our breasts, only needing circumstances to evoke them'.

Mr. Micawber is a special case. Most people join Chesterton in raising the laugh against Dickens, who makes the emigrant Mr. Micawber end up as mayor of an Australian township. It may be claimed that Dickens had made subtle preparations for the change, but if so, they are too subtle to affect the view of Micawber we have already unshakeably formed. What we have been laughing at cannot be nullified: we insist, even against some evidence to the contrary, that Micawber is as Dickens made him to begin with, and we know that in that capacious and glorious breast all that was hidden was further eloquence in proof of his inefficiency in business matters.

Eccentrics like Micawber are narrative versions of those creations of satiric dramatists like Jonson and Molière, and satiric poets like Pope in his epistles on the characters of men and women. Satirists often see the people they choose to write of as each having a single passion ruling his actions. We honour Dickens, as we honour Pope and Jonson, because they have expressed this view of man so vividly. They are concerned to present human beings 'methodized', stripped of everything

[1] Letter to Forster, 25 July 1846; Forster, VI. ii.

else that exists round about the ruling passion. In creating them, they are critics of human beings rather than recorders. But along with this simplified or clarified psychology goes something that satiric poets have no chance to give us, and which even playwrights cannot give us as abundantly as a novelist can—endlessness of illustration. Dickens multiplies the occasions when the ruling passion is exhibiting itself, and delights us by the infinite variety of its unpredictable antics. How many errors crowd in that account given by the *Saturday Review* of what it considers a fault of Dickens: 'that of exaggerating one particular set of facts, a comic side in a character, or a comic turn of expression, until all reality fades away, and the person who is the centre of the extravagance becomes a mere peg or clothes-horse on which the rags of comedy hang loosely and flutter backwards and forwards'.[1] One error is that the person to whom exaggeration is ascribed never was a 'real' person. Reality is not in question if reality means the faithful record of a complete personage. Another sort of reality, however, does present itself—that achieved by detaching and laying bare what exists somewhere in us all.

No one can miss the human truth in *Dombey and Son*, and that just because it is made more in accordance with plain Thackerayan truth. Even Thackeray, devoted as he was, missed some of the 'nature' in at least the comic parts of the novels:

I think Mr. Dickens has in many things quite a divine genius so to speak, and certain notes in his song are so delightful and admirable, that I should never think of trying to imitate him, only hold my tongue, and admire him. I quarrel with his Art in many respects: [which] I don't think represents Nature duly; for instance Micawber appears to me an exaggeration of a man, as his name is of a name. It is delightful and makes me laugh: but it is no more a real man than my friend Punch is.[2]

Spedding was badly misled by his laughter, thinking

[1] 20 July 1861.   [2] *Letters*, II. 772 (letter of May 1851).

he saw a danger in Dickens's having come into fame as a *comic* writer: '... such a man will always be tempted to study society, with a view to gather suggestions and materials for his creative faculty to work upon, rather than simply to consider and understand it. The author of "Pickwick" will study the present as our historical novelists study the past—to find not what it is, but what he can make of it.'[1] That is brilliantly said, but Lewes in 1837 went deeper: Dickens's 'works', he said, 'are volumes of human nature, that have a deep and subtle philosophy in them, which those who read only to laugh may not discover; but an attentive reading (and we have read some of the numbers three or four times) will convince any one that in nothing he has written has amusement been his only aim'. To which Richard Monckton Milnes, in his memorial address on Thomas Hood in 1854, made an addition:

The gift of humour is, as it were, the balance of all the faculties. It enables a man to see the strong contrasts of life around him; it prevents him being too much devoted to his own knowledge, and too proud of his own imagination ... It is thus that humourists such as Hood has been, and as Dickens is now, are great benefactors of our species, not only on account of the amusement they give us but because they are great moral teachers.

The 'fifty men and women' of a Dickens novel are engaged in an action of shorter or longer length. The shorter length is that of *Oliver Twist, The Old Curiosity Shop, Barnaby Rudge, Hard Times, A Tale of Two Cities,* and *Great Expectations,* and the longer is long indeed, being that of twenty numbers each of thirty-two tall pages of small type. The task of filling these big spaces was formidable. From the evidence of his 'Number plans' we know how carefully Dickens kept in mind both the

[1] *Edinburgh Review* (Jan. 1843).

whole and the temporary unity of the monthly part. In his obituary of Thackeray he spoke with fellow-feeling of the novelist's having to make 'careful preparation for long roads of thought ... for shining goals'. Perhaps he was attempting the impossible if he wished his readers, as they closed one of his books, to feel the aesthetic satisfaction of holding something shapely as the 'vase' to which George Moore compared a novel of Jane Austen. This hope, which some of his fellow novelists might have entertained more reasonably, could scarcely be his. Quite apart from the immensity of twenty parts, readers were slowed down by the Dickensian intensity that burned on almost every page. To read him, experiencing what he was saying as it asked to be experienced, was to be taxed extraordinarily. The serial publication of the novels had a peculiar advantage for him. Even when we have the completed book before us, it is usually in short stints that we still must read him. The impression that we have read a shapely novel can never be predominant. And yet though we are always vividly in possession of a part, and a part only, we always know, and not merely by signs of personage and action, that the part belongs to a particular novel. Like Shakespeare, Dickens provides each fiction with its own 'world' or 'atmosphere' or 'climate' or 'colour'. Freud said that *Hard Times* 'was a cruel book which left him as if he had been rubbed all over by a hard brush', and the aesthetic effect of the longer books is as homogeneous, if much more subtle and complex. Dickens's amalgam of widely separate things has been made harmonious by their having issued from a mind that for each novel limited itself to one inexhaustible range of details—things of one complex colour—differing as different continents differ for a geographer. It is significant that Chesterton called *Bleak House* 'not a string of incidents' but a 'cycle': 'The whole story strays from Bleak House and plunges into the foul fogs of Chancery and the autumn mists of Chesney Wold; but the whole story comes back to Bleak House. There is in it this sense of something pivotal and permanent.' Even if we prefer to think of it as having three centres, those centres are related.[1] We can allow Henry James his image descriptive of novels of Dickens (and Thackeray) when, from his pitch of exquisiteness, he spoke of 'large loose baggy monsters', but only if he concedes that even a monster enjoys a unified being, and that each of Dickens's 'monsters' is quite unlike any other.

If a distant homage is all we can pay to Dickens's immense plots, we can happily disport ourselves for ever among their methods of narration and component details of all sizes. They are so various that one feels he could have written any sort of novel he cared to.

The sort he favoured had this unique charac-teristic—they are as like plays as possible. They represent not life directly, as it were, so much as life mounted on the stage. Dickens may be said to have provided his per-sonages with a 'book of words', and described them acting it, brilliantly got up and lit, the reader having been obliged with a seat in the stalls. Further, the author has himself produced the plays, the text itself carrying minute stage descriptions. To him as to Wilkie Collins, 'the Novel and the Play are twin-sisters in the family of fiction'.[2] Planning *Oliver Twist*, he noted that 'several important scenes lie ahead', 'scenes' having an almost professional sense for him. His personages often strike us as acting a part, and sometimes in scenes more appro-priate to play than novel—Pecksniff overhears Tom Pinch and Mary conversing in the church, and the descriptions of his postures are like stage-directions:

Looking like the small end of a guillotined man, with his chin on a level with the top of the pew, so that he might duck

---

[1] See p. 92.   [2] Dedication of *Basil* (1852).

down immediately in case of either of them turning round, he listened. Listened with such concentrated eagerness, that his very hair and shirt-collar stood bristling up to help him. . . .

Mr. Pecksniff brought up to the top of the pew, by slow degrees, his hair, his forehead, his eyebrow, his eye.

When Smike has attached himself to Nicholas Nickleby, as a squire to his knight, Nicholas answers his 'I only want to be near you' with: '"And you shall," cried Nicholas. "And the world shall deal by you as it does by me, till one or both of us shall quit it for a better. Come."' That is almost at the end of Chapter xiv. Six chapters later another stage effect is allotted to Nicholas. His wicked uncle Ralph, acting on information received from Dotheboys Hall, is accusing Nicholas in his absence, and ends by flinging this rhetorical question at his weeping mother and sister: '"Assault, riot, theft, what do you call these?" "A lie!" cried a furious voice, as the door was dashed open, and Nicholas burst into the centre of the room.' Dickens remembers, no doubt just in time, not to write 'into the centre of the stage'. And indeed the chapters on the Crummleses in this same novel read like a comment, sometimes a satire, on parts of the rest of it, so much in them seeming to be directed to bringing the house down:

'I glanced at the French copy last night,' said Nicholas. 'It looks very good, I think.'

'What do you mean to do for me, old fellow?' asked Mr. Lenville, poking the struggling fire with his walking-stick, and afterwards wiping it on the skirt of his coat. 'Anything in the gruff and grumble way?'

'You turn your wife and child out of doors,' said Nicholas; 'and in a fit of rage and jealousy, stab your eldest son in the library.'

'Do I though!' exclaimed Mr. Lenville. 'That's very good business.'

'After which,' said Nicholas, 'you are troubled with remorse till the last act, and then you make up your mind to destroy yourself. But, just as you are raising the pistol to your head, a clock strikes—ten.'

'I see,' cried Mr. Lenville. 'Very good.'

'You pause,' said Nicholas; 'you recollect to have heard a clock strike ten in your infancy. The pistol falls from your hand—you are overcome—you burst into tears, and become a virtuous and exemplary character for ever afterwards.'

'Capital!' said Mr. Lenville: 'that's a sure card, a sure card. Get the curtain down with a touch of nature like that, and it'll be a triumphant success.'

At the end of a novel, sometimes with brilliant contrivance, the personages accumulate as at the end of a pantomime, till everybody is present. Some, at least, of what has been called exaggeration may be due to the way Dickens has of bringing nature up to the pitch of art—to the peculiar pitch of art that the contemporary stage existed for, the civilization which, whether tawdry or splendid, was glowingly islanded away from the drabness of urban existence.

Some things in the novels that need explaining, either because they are wrong or because they proceed according to obsolete method, are readily ascribable to Dickens's having the mind of a dramatist as well as of a novelist. Some of his places are like places in plays. They do not seem to have environs. Though he tells us that 'popular rumour' asserted this or that about Dotheboys Hall we are not convinced that it had a neighbourhood; it is a stage-set, in which Nicholas Nickleby spent some time. Again, Jingle pops in and out of *Pickwick Papers* as if he had been waiting in the wings for his cue. Such things suffice a playgoer, but leave a novel-reader with the claustrophobic sense that what is shown is all that exists. It may have been this insulation of his places that moved George Eliot to try to provide a full account of 'the medium in which a character moves'; but no medium could be more dense than those of *Bleak House* and *Little Dorrit*.

Larger matters also have their root in the stage and its plays. Contemporary audiences liked a play to provide comic and pathetic scenes. The form was felt to have cheated them if laughs and tears were not elicited. Perhaps they appreciated the therapeutic value of those physical releases, which we acknowledge in the phrases 'a good laugh' and 'a good cry'. Dickens honoured their wishes as often as possible.[1] The laughs Dickens provides are among the great things in literature. His pathos is too much in accord with the practices noticed in *Pickwick Papers* when Sam Weller's mimicry of something 'wery affectin' to one's feelings' is compared to 'the manner of actors when they are in domestic pathetics'. We need a stout historical sense to see them for what they originally were.

It may also have been through plays and their audiences that Dickens was attracted to the Idealist side of the fence.[2] Many personages in Dickens are presented incomplete so as to be more consistently pleasant or unpleasant than human beings can be. Freud in 1882 wrote of his 'mannerisms':

those flawless girls, selfless and good, so good that they are quite colourless; then the fact that all the good people immediately become friends as soon as they meet and work together throughout the whole book; then the sharp distinction between virtue and vice which doesn't exist in life (where should I be, for example?); finally, his easy toleration of feeble-mindedness, represented in almost every novel by one or two blockheads or crazy people, who belong to the side of the 'good ones', and so on. Oh, I had almost forgotten the philanthropist, who has such a frightful lot of money and is available for any noble purpose.[3]

---

[1] 'Humour and pathos' were often specified at this time as among the constituents of a novel: compare George Eliot on 'How I came to write Fiction' and the discussion of her first attempts with Lewes—'There still remained the question whether I could command any pathos' (*Letters*, II. 408).

[2] See p. 161.        [3] Ernest Jones, *Sigmund Freud* (1953), I. 190.

And Gissing had this comment on Sam Weller: 'Sam is the incarnation of common sense and common good-ness, tricked out with all manner of personal and local singularities. In the flesh, we know, he never walked the streets of London ... That we accept Sam Weller is the result of Dickens's power of creative illusion.'[1]

Dickens's stage-mindedness had no ill effect on the way he gripped his personages and the humanity, whole or part, he provided them with. It had, indeed, certain advantages, the main one being that of encouraging him to go on achieving the intensity expected of a dramatist. For some of his readers, probably the vast majority, the theatrical element in the novels carried no disadvantages whatever. Nowadays, when plays are made so differently from what they were a century ago, we recoil from some of it, though we ought not as critics, having responsibly acquired a competent historical sense. Even critics not so schooled will agree that what for them is the most flagrant theatricality—the operatic outbursts of lan-guage—can be true to the psychology of the personages in a way that people of today in the same situation lack the means of to their disadvantages. We are no longer allowed to rant in 'real' life, but there are times when what we have to say would be better for that sort of expression. Dickens gives his operatics mainly to women, as Pope did to his Eloisa, women requiring this sort of linguistic outlet more often and completely than men do. No one is going to say that the operatics of Rosa Dartle are untrue to life, stage or no stage, merely because they do not now happen to be socially possible for us:

'Aye!' cried Rosa, smiting herself passionately on the breast, 'Look at me! Moan, and groan, and look at me! Look here!' striking the scar, 'at your dead child's handiwork!'
... Look at me, marked until I die with his high displeasure; and moan and groan for what you made him!'
'Miss Dartle,' I entreated her. 'For Heaven's sake——'

[1] Introduction to *Pickwick Papers*, Rochester edn. (1899).

'I *will* speak!' she said, turning to me with her lightning eyes. 'Be silent you! Look at me, I say, proud mother of a proud false son! Moan for your nurture of him, moan for your corruption of him, moan for your loss of him, moan for mine!'

'. . . My love would have been devoted—would have trod your paltry whimpering under foot!'

With flashing eyes, she stamped upon the ground as if she actually did it.

As if to show his range Dickens in this same novel gave a completely different style of speech to Miss Mowcher, the dwarf, every one of whose sentences (if that is what they are) is as wholly unpredictable as its implications are subtle: for instance:

'What! My flower!' she pleasantly began, shaking her large head at [Steerforth]. 'You're there, are you! Oh, you naughty boy, fie for shame, what do you do so far away from home? Up to mischief, I'll be bound. Oh, you're a downy fellow, Steerforth, so you are, and I'm another, ain't I? Ha, ha, ha! You'd have betted a hundred pound to five, now, that you wouldn't have seen me here, wouldn't you? Bless you, man alive, I'm everywhere. I'm here, and there, and where not, like the conjurer's half-crown in the lady's hankercher. Talking of hankerchers—*and* talking of ladies—what a comfort you are to your blessed mother, ain't you, my dear boy, over one of my shoulders, and I don't say which!'

Not all Dickens's first readers liked his theatricals. Ruskin regretted his 'circle of stage fire' though he did not see it as impairing Dickens's truthfulness.[1] Lewes contrasted his novels with Thackeray's, in which 'no glare from the footlights is thrown upon exaggerated human nature'.[2] Harriet Martineau deposed in her *Autobiography* that 'few miss as I do the pure plain daylight in the atmosphere of Dickens's scenery'.

---

[1] '*Unto this Last*', i, in the *Cornhill Magazine* (Aug. 1860).
[2] See p. 167.

The most obvious illustrations of stage effects are found in the earlier novels; it goes without saying that Dickens also took advantage of the many effects available only to the novelist, especially as he grew more practised in the form. As a novelist he was free to make observations and deliver occasional authorial harangues. He could interpret as well as report. He could call attention to what a playgoer might miss. For instance, he likes to centre a personage in a physical detail of body or clothing, which thereby acquires moral or psychological status, the recurrent presentation of that detail attaining to a narrative on its own. Mrs. Merdle in *Little Dorrit* has a bosom apparently designed like a jeweller's tray for the display of jewels, and much is heard of that triumphant bosom. Mr. Pancks, in the same novel, is presented by the running image of a tug. Then again he ties together whole scenes by methods not open to dramatists, methods which he passed on to later novelists. For instance, at the end of *A Tale of Two Cities*: 'The same shadows that are falling on the prison, are falling at that same hour of the early afternoon, on the Barrier with the crowd about it, when a coach going out of Paris drives up to be examined.' Towards the close of *Great Expectations* a larger unification is accomplished by the reader who is alive to such things. Pip is waking up on the great day that is to see his convict-benefactor safely escaped out of England:

Wednesday morning was dawning when I looked out of window. The winking lights upon the bridge were already pale, the coming sun was like a marsh of fire on the horizon. The river, still dark and mysterious, was spanned by bridges that were turning coldly grey, with here and there at top a warm touch from the burning in the sky. As I looked along the clustered roofs, with church towers and spires shooting into the unusually clear air, the sun rose up, and a veil seemed to be drawn from the river, and millions of sparkles burst out upon its waters.

That phrase 'a marsh of fire' is so striking that we cannot but link it with the actual marsh with which the story started.

The passage of time is recorded in this way by David Copperfield in the chapter 'Retrospect':

Once again, let me pause upon a memorable period of my life. Let me stand aside, to see the phantoms of those days go by me, accompanying the shadow of myself, in dim procession.

Weeks, months, seasons, pass along. They seem little more than a summer day and a winter evening. Now, the Common where I walk with Dora is all in bloom, a field of bright gold; and now the unseen heather lies in mounds and bunches underneath a covering of snow. In a breath, the river that flows through our Sunday walks is sparkling in the summer sun, is ruffled by the winter wind, or thickened with drifting heaps of ice. Faster than ever river ran towards the sea, it flashes, darkens, and rolls away.

Not a thread changes in the house of the two little bird-like ladies. The clock ticks over the fireplace, the weather-glass hangs in the hall. Neither clock nor weather-glass is ever right; but we believe in both, devoutly.

As a final instance of subtlety of narrative method, consider the way Mr. Tulkinghorn's death is conveyed—in contrast to the telegraphese in which he has hitherto been described:

Rustily dressed, with his spectacles in his hand, and their very case worn threadbare. In manner, close and dry. In voice, husky and low. In face, watchful behind a blind; habitually not uncensorious and contemptuous perhaps . . .

Always at hand. Haunting every place. No relief or security from him for a moment.

For many years, the persistent Roman has been pointing, with no particular meaning, from that ceiling. It is not likely that he has any new meaning in him to-night. Once pointing, always pointing—like any Roman, or even Briton, with a single idea. There he is, no doubt, in his impossible attitude, pointing unavailingly, all night long. Moonlight, darkness, dawn, sunrise, day. There he is still, eagerly pointing, and no one minds him.

But, a little after the coming of the day, come people to clean the rooms. And either the Roman has some new meaning in him, not expressed before, or the foremost of them goes wild; for, looking up at his outstretched hand and looking down at what is below it, that person shrieks and flies. The others, looking in as the first one looked, shriek and fly too, and there is an alarm in the street.

And so on for half the closely printed page, in a calculated delirium of showmanship, running hither and thither with poetic diction and undulant rhythm, with this as the paragraph that brings the chapter to the close:

So, it shall happen surely, through many years to come, that ghostly stories shall be told of the stain upon the floor, so easy to be covered, so hard to be got out; and that the Roman, pointing from the ceiling, shall point, so long as dust and damp and spiders spare him, with far greater significance than he ever had in Mr. Tulkinghorn's time, and with a deadly meaning. For, Mr. Tulkinghorn's time is over for evermore; and the Roman pointed at the murderous hand uplifted against his life, and pointed helplessly at him, from night to morning, lying face downward on the floor, shot through the heart.

Such effects as this are not possible for a dramatist. Nor is the constant centring upon inanimate objects almost independently of the narrative. To some extent, this is a general feature of the nineteenth-century novel, which grew more and more full of objects named and described: furniture, houses, streets, landscape, weather, figure far more prominently and variously than in a novel by Fielding. There was a danger, for writers and readers, of being overwhelmed by what Arnold called 'multitudinousness'; but for Dickens, any page of whose novels contains more things than any other writer's, it was kept in control. The inanimate in his novels is pressed into swelling his general homage to human life. He uses things as an explanation of his people, choosing to create for them an environment that typifies them, and represents their mental being: Mr. Dombey's house is an extended embodiment of him, as Chesney Wold is of Sir Leicester Dedlock and his class. The details of any environment are humanized, animated, as in the garret bedroom at Mrs. Clennam's on Arthur's return after fifteen years' absence:

Meagre and spare, like all the other rooms, it was even uglier and grimmer than the rest, by being the place of banishment for the worn out furniture. Its moveables were ugly old chairs with worn out seats, and ugly old chairs without any seats; a threadbare patternless carpet, a maimed table, a crippled wardrobe, a lean set of fire-irons like the skeleton of a set deceased, a washing stand that looked as if it had stood for ages in a hail of dirty soap-suds, and a bedstead with four bare atomies of posts, each terminating in a spike, as if for the dismal accommodation of lodgers who might prefer to impale themselves.[1]

His undeflectable interest in man explains why there is so much in his description of what Ruskin called the 'pathetic fallacy', relating, for example, the falling of the day to the coming fall of the French aristocracy: 'the carriage slid downhill . . . the red glow departed quickly; the sun and the Marquis going down together'.[2]

The wider context that he preferred for man was that of London; indeed it was Dickens who took up London where Lamb had left it, and eventually helped to create the late nineteenth-century cult of 'London' poetry. The description of the sunrise over the Thames, and such comparisons as 'smoke, which is the ivy of London',[3] or the street-lamps in the Strand which under the

[1] *Little Dorrit*, I. iii.
[2] *Tale of Two Cities*, II. viii; cf. Chs. xvi ('Darkness closed around') and xxiii.
[3] *Bleak House*, Ch. x.

lamplighter's hand 'blurred by the foggy air, burst out one after another, like so many blazing sunflowers',[1] suggest that he saw London sometimes as Ruskin might have done, had Ruskin thought it worth while to open his eyes as widely in urban London as in the Alps.

Critics are right in their insistence that if, in the midst of his fiction, a novelist speaks *in propria persona*, he speaks as author rather than as man. This canon, however, loses some of its force when the author is the immense public figure Dickens was. When, after the death of Jo the crossing-sweeper, the author breaks out with 'Dead, your Majesty. Dead, my lords and gentlemen. Dead, right reverends and wrong reverends of every order. Dead, men and women, born with heavenly compassion in your hearts. And dying thus around us every day',— when the author so breaks out, it must have been taken as a blast from Dickens himself. The might of such an utterance we can estimate by recalling its circumstances. *Bleak House* had now reached its fifteenth number. It was being read by the world at large; everybody had experienced vicariously the horrors of Jo's life. What a moment, then, for an appeal for public action, rolling out like a great speech in a history play of Shakespeare's! Few articles, pamphlets, or books on burning issues could ever hope to attain such force; the nearest equivalent in its time is in the rhetorical addresses in Carlyle's *Past and Present* and *Latter-Day Pamphlets*.

In 1853 the *Westminster* could remark that 'The novelist has a high and holy mission, for his words frequently reach ears which will hear no others.' It was fitting, therefore, for that tireless educator, Charles Knight, to dedicate *The Old Printer and the Modern Press* (1854) 'To Charles Dickens, one of the most earnest labourers in that popular literature which elevates a people.'

[1] *Little Dorrit*, II. ix.

Though Forster held that Dickens's genius led him to comedy, we note nevertheless that even among the earliest and largely comic writings there is evidence that he was drawing on his own painful knowledge of what was far from comic. Those writings show the two sorts of thought he had for down-and-outs, whether they were born so or had come to be so by fault or ill luck. In *Pickwick Papers* he enters into the full wretchedness of the inmates of the Fleet. In *Nicholas Nickleby*, however, he accepts the comforting view that physical want can be lived down. When Nicholas is setting out dejectedly for Dotheboys Hall we read: 'By the time he had found a man to carry his box it was only seven o'clock, so he walked slowly on, a little in advance of the porter, and very probably without half as light a heart in his breast as the man had, although he had no waistcoat to cover it with, and had evidently, from the appearance of his other garments, been spending the night in a stable, and taking his breakfast at a pump.' Dickens does not wince at the relation of Nicholas and the porter; he found a man to carry his box, as he might have found a pack-horse. And the man himself is shown as enviable by one who is downcast at leaving home—*he* is not downcast even though his home is a stable. We are not far from Newman's belief that the poor could be saints, though they were being made to live like animals—or worse, for the contrast was often being drawn between the care employers took of their horses and of their workmen. Dickens's view of the condition of the poor becomes less rosy: the ill-clad, half-starved, cheerful porter becomes the Jo of *Bleak House*. And yet Dickens never ceased to believe that once the minimum bodily comfort is secured, cheerfulness has the power to break in, if the being, now to be counted human, will let it. He was not asking Her Majesty and the Lords and Commons for very much; merely for the equivalent of what horses got in the stable of a kind owner.

Nor did Dickens always need to forgo his comic genius in seriously working for reform. With Bumble, Squeers, even Mrs. Gamp, he contrived to make comedy a spear, transfixing them for all time; so that their images are part of the popular consciousness and of the public conscience which he helped to awaken.

# 4. THACKERAY

THACKERAY HAD enough of the Dickensian power to have parodied Dickens and such a parody would have crowned that brilliant work *Punch's Prize Novelists*, as he wished; but it was vetoed by the publishers, who were also Dickens's. He had enough of the Dickensian power to have done that parody, but rather as a *tour de force*. He admitted, frankly and freely, that his own genius was more humdrum than Dickens's. What amazed him about Dickens was his fountaining fecundity. When in a *Roundabout Paper* he confessed that he would have liked 'to be able to feed a reader so spicily as to have him hungering and thirsting for more at the end of every monthly meal'[1]—that is, the meals provided by the monthly 'numbers'—he was thinking of thriller-writers like Dumas, but also of Dickens's sort of stories, of which part of the thrill is provided by what I have called the colour found in, or added to, men and things. His own sort of novels were much more like those of Trollope, who admired him so much as to call *Esmond* the 'first and finest novel in the English language'.[2] But even if he had had more than a streak of the Dickensian power, he might not have chosen to allow it free vent. It was by choice that he wrote as he did, and his choice was dictated by the philosophy of life he had come to hold. All men, including Dickens, hold some sort of a philosophy of life, but Thackeray had a more conscious grasp of his than most men, including Dickens, have of theirs. A conscious

[1] 'De Finibus'.
[2] 'W. M. Thackeray', *Cornhill Magazine* (Feb. 1864).

grasp of a philosophy of life implies the possession of intellect. Thackeray was given to belittling his own: he disclaimed the possession of any 'head above [his] eyes'.[1] In the very wording of that, however, gleams at least a trace of intellect. Thackeray had more intellect than Dickens had. If readers fail to acknowledge its quality, that may be because they underrate the profundity of statements which being expressed lucidly are received by the mind without effort. Readers are too often more impressed by grandiose obscurity. Thackeray's philosophy of life was a more articulate version of the common reader's. Dickens—to take him for a comparison—loved mankind, and wanted to excite it, with wild laughter or tears or suspense. Reading Dickens, the common reader finds himself greater than he knew, a more glorious specimen of a man. Thackeray also loved mankind, but wanted rather to honour them as they existed during the level intervals between excitements, unaided by stimulus and exaltation. Thackeray draws man as he comes, 'unromantic as Monday morning' (to use Charlotte Brontë's phrase). He praises him as the possessor of a memory stacked with faint pencilled sketches, very few of them coloured. He reminds him how satisfactory are his quietly collected possessions, just as they lie in the mind. The reader returns the love both of Dickens and of Thackeray, the one for bringing out the best, the genius in him, the other for confirming him in the love of his human ordinariness, making him more conscious of the pleasure he gets merely out of spending his life, as he must mainly spend it, among his ordinary fellows.

The big novels of Dickens and Thackeray swarm with people. Every novel of Thackeray's, said one critic, 'brings us into contact with from fifty to a hundred new

[1] *Harper's Magazine* (Jan. 1856).

and perfectly distinct individuals'.[1] Not content with people in the present, he goes back into the past for more, and into other countries. His account of the people of England and America stretches back as far as into the seventeenth century, all his personages being shown at their posts in the social scheme. To each of them he applies his ethical measuring-rod. All novelists must be aware of ethical standards, but Thackeray was particularly aware, and shows it. If we compare him with Dickens, we see Dickens to be even richer in materials for consideration. Dickens would provide psychologists and moralists with endless material, which its discoverer and recorder cannot or does not choose to assess. He leaves the hundreds of discoveries he makes in human nature and in social and national organization as they lie—as the reader does who, along with him, is rushing on to the next vivid moment. Dickens is a sensationalist. For him it is enough to give the reader a wealth of unanalysed sensations. He has a less mixed view of the novel than Thackeray, seeing the action as an endless file of sensational moments stretching ahead, all of which would invite analysis if it were the job of the novelist as he writes, or the reader as he reads, to attend to them. It is enough for Dickens to provide a rich impression for the reader, some part of which may be of interest to the intellect, but only provisionally. Thackeray, on the other hand, takes on the role of thinking about what is present in his imagination. His idea of the novel is less pure than Dickens's, for he sees it as verging on the essay or the sermon.

One item in his completeness was the account he gave of marriage, a topic often neglected by novelists who saw their work as 'romances' and so gave accounts only of courtships. If Thackeray shows little of 'married bliss' he

[1] W. C. Roscoe, *National Review* (1856). This and other reviews cited below are included or quoted in *Thackeray, the Critical Heritage*, ed. G. Tillotson and D. Hawes (1968).

takes in most of what marriage includes otherwise. The young Burne-Jones, reviewing *The Newcomes* in the *Oxford and Cambridge Magazine*, saw its 'central purpose' as 'reaching to the very core of social disease, unhappy wedded life'. The most extensive account of marriage at its most loveless comes in *Barry Lyndon*, where we get this version of 'living happily ever after': Lyndon begins as he means to go on: 'Lady Lyndon was a haughty woman, and I hate pride, and I promise you that ... I overcame this vice in her. On the third day of our journey I had her to light my pipe-match with her own hands, and made her deliver it to me with tears in her eyes.' On which follows this sort of general advice to would-be husbands:

Get a friend, sir, and that friend a woman—a good household drudge, who loves you. *That* is the most precious sort of friendship, for the expense of it is all on the woman's side. The *man* needn't contribute anything. If he's a rogue, she'll vow he's an angel; if he is a brute, she will like him all the better for his ill-treatment of her. They like it, sir, these women. They are born to be our greatest comforts and conveniences; our—our moral bootjacks, as it were.

Husbands more ordinary than Barry Lyndon are represented abundantly and fairly and squarely throughout his writings. They are often appealed to in the passages of commentary:

'I think of a lovely reader laying down the page and looking over at her unconscious husband, asleep, perhaps, after dinner. Yes, madam, a closet he hath; and you, who pry into everything, shall never have the key of it.'[1]

It was during his account of bachelordom, however, that Thackeray was prevented from supplying as much truth as he would have liked to. The preface to *Pendennis* shows him wishing that Mrs. Grundy allowed him more freedom. It also shows him as having gone further than

[1] *The Newcomes*, Ch. xi.

Mrs. Grundy did in fact permit: 'Many ladies have remonstrated and subscribers left me, because, in the course of the story, I described a young man resisting and affected by temptation. My object was to say, that he had the passions to feel, and the manliness and generosity to overcome them.' And so to the crux of the matter:

A little more frankness than is customary has been attempted in this story; with no bad desire on the writer's part, it is hoped, and with no ill consequence to any reader. If truth is not always pleasant; at any rate truth is best, from whatever chair—from those whence graver writers or thinkers argue, as from that at which the story-teller sits as he concludes his labour, and bids his kind reader farewell.

Thackeray, we can but feel, would have liked the freedom allowed to French novelists; but the completeness of his human material still gives him a more European air than English novelists commonly have.

One of the ways Dickens and Thackeray differ as narrators is in the role they assign to people subsidiary to principals. While Thackeray is narrating, as distinct from commenting, he never takes his eyes off his principals, which means that subsidiaries are introduced only when they concern them. Subsidiaries exist in their hundreds, and yet are numbered. What they contribute would be evidence in a court of law. Such a role may be assigned to subsidiaries by Dickens, or it may not—he does not seem to mind. In the passage quoted earlier from *Nicholas Nickleby*[1] the genial nod of a word or two was devoted to anybody who happened to catch his eye while he imagined the likely scene as the coach was preparing to set out. The *likely* scene—Dickens is thinking of *any* such scene. The itinerant newsman had nothing to do with Nicholas; Dickens takes his eyes off Nicholas in order to describe him. The newsman was a wheel revolving in adjacent space, whereas in Thackeray any wheel men-

[1] See p. 127.

tioned, however small, would have cogged in with whatever other wheels were turning. Take as a fair sample of
Thackeray's method a comparable passage from Chapter
vii of *Vanity Fair*, where the orphan Becky Sharp is taking
up her post as governess in the household of Sir Pitt
Crawley:  ·

John, the groom, who had driven the carriage alone, did not
care to descend to ring the bell; and so prayed a passing
milk-boy to perform that office for him. When the bell was
rung, a head appeared between the interstices of the dining-
room shutters, and the door was opened by a man in drab
breeches and gaiters, with a dirty old coat, a foul old neck-
cloth lashed round his bristly neck, a shining bald head, a
leering red face, a pair of twinkling grey eyes, and a mouth
perpetually on the grin.
    'This Sir Pitt Crawley's?' says John, from the box.
    'Ees,' says the man at the door with a nod.
    'Hand down these 'ere trunks then,' said John.
    'Hand 'n down yourself,' said the porter.
    'Don't you see I can't leave my hosses? Come, bear a hand,
my fine feller, and Miss will give you some beer,' said John,
with a horse-laugh, for he was no longer respectful to Miss
Sharp, as her connexion with the family was broken off, and as
she had given nothing to the servants on coming away.

The principals here are Becky and Sir Pitt (whom she
quite understandably mistakes for the porter), and the
other people get a look in because they are vitally connected with the principals. John is necessary to Becky
because she and her baggage could not have arrived on
the scene without his agency, and his enlisting the
services of the milk-boy is necessary because Becky
does not rate a carriage fully manned and John is in sole
charge of it.
    Throughout the narrative part of his fiction Thackeray
exercises economy. While narrating he is saying that
the people whose story he has chosen to tell are all in
all to him till that story is told, whatever their general

importance or non-importance. His exclusive concentration on them is the return he makes to them for
their being so kind as to have provided him with a story.
Intervening between stretches of narrative are the
stretches of commentary. They have themselves received
much comment from critics: at this point I note only their
function as a relaxation. They accord with the narrator's
right to relax his strenuous concentration on the story, a
right no sensitive reader will dispute. The relaxation,
however, as far as people go, is of the busman's holiday
sort. The economy exercised in the narrative is itself
carried over into the commentary, since no one of the
many personages introduced into it lacks the credentials
of those who figure in the narrative proper. There is no
credit for Thackeray in this, economy being inevitable
when the only reason for bringing people into the commentary at all is as illustration. Credit is conspicuously
due, however (and was especially in the nineteenth century), when economy is exercised in the narration. To
provide it was to be brought into collision with that
widely applied contemporary principle making for multitudinousness. In the eighteenth century there had been
much interest in 'plenitude', the divine principle by
which the world was furnished with a complete range of
things, but things in the nineteenth century seemed
denser still, the scientists now bringing so many more of
them into significance. Moreover, people in the
nineteenth century—those at least in the upper of the
'Two Nations'—had many more things in their personal
possession. Their lives were crowded with bric-à-brac
and larger furniture as never before. Dickens and Browning, to name the two chief rejoicers in this density, honour as much of it in their writings as they can. Some other
writers, Thackeray and Emily Brontë being the most
noteworthy, prefer to exercise the right to select strictly.
The extraordinary thing is that, exercising this right,
Thackeray represents multitudinousness so adequately,

simply by dint of writing so much. And yet things are introduced only as they serve the vital purposes of narrative or commentary. Keeping his eye steadily on people meant that things are mentioned only as people intimately attach themselves to them. He never relaxed hold of his principle by taking time off to paint a scene for its own sake, which meant forgoing the exercise of a power much indulged at the time, and which he himself possessed in abundance—as we know from the descriptions supplied in his travel books. Thackeray's novels are like the fir trees on the hillside, vital with trunks, stems, and needles before they receive all the glittering additions Dickens liked to hang on them, out of pure perpetual Christmas spirit. Dickens will describe anything that happens to belong to a scene, Thackeray only what intimately concerns the people in it.

Economy over wide stretches—practicable only for a writer of strong intellect, which it is not customary to claim for Thackeray—is evinced over the whole of his writings. If he selects economically it is according to a principle. He is a conscious critic at the same time as a rapt creator, the critic in him directing the creation, giving it, as it were, a spine. Whatever else he is doing, he is making a point, sometimes a point in favour of a reform. The title-pages of the novels announce a theme, or at least an intellectual interest: *Vanity Fair. A Novel Without a Hero*; *The History of Pendennis. His Fortunes and Misfortunes, His Friends and His Greatest Enemy*, that greatest enemy being himself; that of *Philip* is related to the parable of the Good Samaritan—*The Adventures of Philip, on his way through the world, shewing who robbed him, who helped him, and who passed him by. The Book of Snobs* is built on a single idea. When a description is called for in the novels it is called for because the account of one or more human beings will not be complete without it: the description itself, however, has its theme: here is the Newcomes' family home at Clapham:

It was a serious paradise. As you entered at the gate, gravity fell on you; and decorum wrapped you in a garment of starch. The butcher-boy who galloped his horse and cart madly about the adjoining lanes and common, whistled wild melodies (caught up in abominable play-house galleries), and joked with a hundred cookmaids, on passing that lodge fell into an under-taker's pace, and delivered his joints and sweetbreads silently at the servant's entrance. The rooks in the elms cawed sermons at morning and evening; the peacocks walked demurely on the terraces; the guineafowls looked more quaker-like than those savoury birds usually do. The lodge-keeper was serious, and a clerk at a neighbouring chapel. The pastors who entered at that gate, and greeted his comely wife and children, fed the little lambkins with tracts. The head-gardener was a Scotch Cal-vinist, after the strictest order, only occupying himself with the melons and pines provisionally, and until the end of the world, which event he could prove by infallible calculations, was to come off in two or three years at farthest.[1]

Thackeray's intellect made him a fighter. The first half of the huge amount of his writings was a battlefield with occasional lulls in the fighting. If, in his later work, which includes all the novels after *Vanity Fair*, he was less com-bative, that was not only because combativeness cannot readily make the organizing principle of the long novel, but because his campaign had been a success. Partly, or largely, because of him, other great novelists—Trollope, Mrs. Gaskell, the Brontës, George Eliot, Reade, Meredith—wrote with due regard for what he called 'truth'. Indeed, it was the promoting of this principle that made him the prime reformer of mid-century fiction. Where it had erred and strayed, he conspicuously helped to bring it back on to the right path. He belonged to the same school as Marryat, Harriet Martineau, and Surtees. They all wrote, as Jane Austen and Maria Edgeworth had, about what they could vouch for, as it were in a court of law. This is how, they say, we have noticed ordinary

---

[1] Ch. ii. 'Serious' was a recognized term in the Evangelical vocabulary.

men and women behaving, and what by observation we
have adduced as to their moral character, moral character
being the prime interest of a novelist. They achieved
what they called 'truth' by the use of their eyes and any
other of the senses—including their common sense!—
that were called for.

In adopting this principle they were opposing the
'idealism' popular at the time. The most that could be
allowed idealism by a novelist was allowed by George
Eliot: 'Art', she said in a letter, 'must be either real and
concrete, or ideal and eclectic. Both are good and true in
their way, but my stories are of the former kind.'[1] We all
practise a certain amount of idealism as we exist from day
to day. At certain times we see things flatteringly—after a
good meal, for instance, or when we are in love. The
idealists, of whom Bulwer Lytton was the chief, were for
writing as if they were always slightly intoxicated or head
over heels in love. People when actually in those states
may sometimes write, but they seldom read, and accordingly readers expect the sobriety they almost always get
from writers who are great. Thackeray, more wholly
than Dickens, wanted to see and write as if sober. He
believed with Horace that 'fictions meant to please
should be as like actuality as possible';[2] he believed that
novelists should take to heart what Carlyle had said in
praise of Burns, that 'he does not write from hearsay, but
from sight and experience';[3] that, as Ruskin said, 'the
greatest thing a human soul ever does in this world is to
*see* something and to tell what it *saw* in a plain way';[4] that
the writer should take 'human faces', again to quote
Ruskin, 'as God made them'; should work as Balzac did,
and ignore Joubert's remark that 'Fiction has no business
to exist unless it is more beautiful than reality'.[5] He

---

[1] *George Eliot Letters*, II. 362 (12 June 1857).
[2] *Ars Poetica*, 338.    [3] *Edinburgh Review* (Dec. 1828).
[4] *Modern Painters*, vol. III, Ch. xvi.
[5] Quoted in Matthew Arnold's 'Joubert', *Essays in Criticism* (1865).

believed that novelists, or anybody else for that matter, should ignore German philosophers, who, like Kant, were for finding an ideal world under or within the actual world; should dissociate themselves from what Ruskin called 'Purist Idealism', which 'results from unwillingness of pure and tender minds to contemplate evil', and of which his illustration was Fra Angelico;[1] and that instead they should proceed as the painters Thackeray himself commended, who 'do not generally attempt what is called the highest species of art, and content themselves with depicting nature as they find her, and trusting to the poetry and charms of the scenes which they copy, rather than to their own powers of invention, and [of] representing ideal beauty'.[2] Many powerful statements were made on this burning question, one of the most remarkable being this comment on George Sand's 'transcendentalism':

a term which we take to mean the science of proving that everything is something else, rejecting Bishop Butler's contrary axiom that 'everything is the thing it is, and not another thing'. Persons who profess an especial enlightenment come naturally to assimilate whatever they admire to something in themselves; the object contemplated is not so much on its own account as for advancing a cause; it is not studied for its simple merits, but as proving some point peculiar to the observer. By some magic process of transformation it loses its identity, and only subscribes to his fancies and ideas. ... And yet all the while there need not have been any real proper appreciation at all, for the mind has been too full of itself for the humble learner's part.[3]

Florence Nightingale herself could not forgo a hit at the idealists in her *Notes on Nursing* (1859):

---

[1] *Modern Painters*, vol. III, Ch. vi.
[2] *Morning Chronicle* (29 Apr. 1844; *Contributions to the Morning Chronicle*, ed. G. N. Ray, 1955, p. 27).
[3] Anne Mozley, in *Bentley's Quarterly Review* (1860).

In writings of fiction, whether novels or biographies, these death-beds are generally depicted as almost seraphic in lucidity of intelligence. Sadly large has been my experience in death-beds, and I can only say that I have seldom or never seen such. Indifference, excepting with regard to bodily suffering, or to some duty the dying man desired to perform, is the far more usual state.

Thackeray was prominently on the side of such realists, believing that a novelist writes, as a scientist does, about what he has found for himself, his imagination existing to create a world as nearly indistinguishable from the actual one as possible. In his preface to *Pendennis* he made his prime principle clear: 'this person writing strives to tell the truth. If there is not that, there is nothing.' The compliment Thackeray must have prized most comes quietly in a review of *Vanity Fair* by Forster: the person-ages of the novel 'are drawn from actual life, not from books and fancy'. It was the compliment paid to the great scientists, who, like Thackeray, ignored books and fancy except as things to confirm, modify, or contradict from their own experience of men and things.

One of Thackeray's most entertaining pieces of journal-ism is his account of a provincial performance of *The Warlock of the Glen*,[1] in which his main purpose was to ridicule the action of the play, to rule it out from serious

---

[1] 'A Brighton Night Entertainment', *Punch* (18 Oct. 1845). The play is by C. E. Walker, and dates from 1820. Thackeray's description begins: 'In a paste-board cottage, on the banks of the Atlantic Ocean'; the climax he reports as follows: 'Haste we to the Castle of Glencairn. What ceremony is about to take place? What has assembled these two noblemen, and those three ladies in calico trains? A marriage! But what a union! The Lady Adela is dragged to the chapel door by the truculent Clanronald. "Lady," he says, "you are mine. Resistance is unavailing. Submit with good grace. Hence-forth, what power on earth can separate you from me?"
"MINE CAN", cries the Warlock of the Glen, rushing in.'
For the Warlock is the long-lost husband of Adela.

consideration as a truthful story. His second purpose, however, was to show how the meagre audience, including himself, enjoyed it. Preposterously unlike the lot of most human beings, its action could not but give rise to human feeling, and so provide the actors with interesting things to do with faces, voices, and indeed bodies complete. If few countesses experience a 'Warlock' dénouement, yet on more ordinary occasions many women do explode with this particular woman's 'scream of joy'. That was truthful enough, whatever gave rise to it. Thackeray enjoyed attending the theatre, when contemporary plays were on the boards, because, like other ordinary human beings, he could put up with silliness for the sake of the fierce or tender human truth tangled up in it. In introducing his account, he says:

I have always had a taste for the second-rate in life. Second-rate poetry, for instance, is an uncommon deal pleasanter to my fancy than your great thundering first-rate epic poems. Your Miltons and Dantes are magnificent,—but a bore: whereas an ode of Horace, or a song of Tommy Moore, is always fresh, sparkling, and welcome. . . . I like second-rate theatrical entertainments—a good little company in a provincial town, acting good old stupid stock comedies and farces; where nobody comes to the theatre, and you may lie at ease in the pit, and get a sort of intimacy with each actor and actress, and know every bar of the music that the three or four fiddlers of the little orchestra play throughout the season.

When Thackeray introduced a play into the action of one of his novels he found a specimen which, though higher in the literary scale than *The Warlock*, still lacked greatness. It was in an adaptation of Kotzebue's *Stranger* that Pen confronted the Fotheringay. The apostle of truth, however, pauses to give it its due:

The Stranger's talk is sham, like the book he reads, and the hair he wears, and the bank he sits on, and the diamond ring he makes play with—but, in the midst of the balderdash, there runs that reality of love, children, and forgiveness of wrong, which will be listened to wherever it is preached, and sets all the world sympathising.[1]

Thackeray's indulgence towards the theatre was that of the many who did not want it changed. In an essay, 'English History and Character on the French Stage',[2] he noted that the Revolution had had small effect inside the theatre: 'those who are at all acquainted with the stage know well how sedulously it obeys its routine habits and traditions. The stage but little adapts itself to sudden changes in society'. Social changes had also happened in England, if not so violently, and with as little effect as far as the stage was concerned. When, however, the theatre did change, with Robertson, it was in the direction of Thackerayan truth. Thackeray's stand for truth in prose fiction may have helped the English stage towards realism.

Thackeray's criticism of contemporary drama was crowned by his treatment of the Fotheringay in *Pendennis*. When on the stage she stood, walked, and spoke as no woman off it would, and yet through all the art, her flesh and blood remained uneclipsed:

She was of the tallest of women, and at her then age of six-and-twenty—for six-and-twenty she was, though she vows she was only nineteen—in the prime and fulness of her beauty. Her forehead was vast, and her black hair waved over it with a natural ripple ... She never laughed, (indeed her teeth were not good), but a smile of endless tenderness and sweetness played round her beautiful lips, and in the dimples of her cheeks and her lovely chin. ... But it was her hand and arm that this magnificent creature most excelled in, and somehow you could never see her but through them. They surrounded her. When she folded them over her bosom in resignation; when she dropped them in mute agony, or raised them in superb

---

[1] *Pendennis*, Ch. iv.
[2] *Foreign Quarterly Review* (Apr. 1843).

command; when in sportive gaiety her hands fluttered and waved before her ...[1]

Her acting might be a perversion, but perversion designed to enhance the truth of the human body.

This human body carried the Fotheringay off the stage into her father's lodgings, where Pen meets her, and finds her altogether human. What truth she exhibited on the stage was now partly cancelled and partly expanded into completeness. Even in his description of her stage presence Thackeray had admitted defects. For Pen she was 'complete and beautiful' despite her poor teeth and rather big feet. Off the stage she is completer still, the daughter of a 'shabby-looking', Irish 'buck', choleric and besotted.

She cannot justly be called a romantic person: nor were her literary acquirements great: she never opened a Shakespeare from the day she left the stage, nor, indeed, understood it during all the time she adorned the boards: but about a pudding, a piece of needle-work, or her own domestic affairs, she was as good a judge as could be found; and not being misled by a strong imagination or a passionate temper, was better enabled to keep her judgement cool.[2]

Whatever truth was discoverable in acted plays, novels, when truthful, represented people in their homes, where a Fotheringay was plain Milly Costigan. The stage was one thing and ordinary life another. This meant that Thackeray had no use for the theatre mouthings that often intruded into 'untruthful' mid-century novels. So much of this theatre elocution existed that when Whitwell Elwin reviewed *The Newcomes* in 1855 he found Thackeray's truth 'surprising'. One item in the surprise is that 'Men, women, and children talk ... in his pages exactly as they are talking ... at every hour of every day'. That word 'exactly' is probably nearer the truth for Thackeray than for any one else, even for Trollope, whose characters usually speak with a little more of

---

[1] *Pendennis*, Ch. iv.    [2] Ibid., Ch. xii.

Trollope's own grace than they could command if left to themselves. An explicit rejection of the high-flown is made in Thackeray's long story *The Ravenswing* (1843) when Morgiana, the singer, receives a proposal from her ridiculous music master, and meets it with 'Don't be a fool, Baroski!'; whereupon Thackeray points out that schooled in the fiction of the time, the reader might have expected her to 'rise with cold dignity, exclaiming "Unhand me, Sir!"' Something further is added: 'It is not my fault that my heroine's sensibilities were not more keen, that she had not the least occasion for sal-volatile or symptom of a fainting fit'. More truth is provided when Morgiana and her mother decide not to tell her father: 'So when he came home not a word was said; and only that his wife met him with more warmth than usual, you could not have guessed that anything extraordinary had occurred'. Characteristically, this further truthful development affects the plot; not having been alerted, Mr. Walker takes no precaution against Baroski's having him arrested for debt—for the cost of the music lessons.[1]

Thackeray's usual method of criticizing dramatics is less explicit. Contemporary readers must have been aware of all the occasions in his stories and novels for the theatre rhetoric that he avoided. In Chapter xlix of *Vanity Fair*, for instance, Lord Steyne treats his ladies to a 'vigorous elocution', but there is no theatre in it, any more than in the women's high-and-mighty replies. Thackeray's avoidance of theatrical falsity was appreciated at least by one lover of the stage, G. H. Lewes, who pointedly commended him: 'No glare from the footlights is thrown upon exaggerated distortions of human nature.'[2]

Other falsities he also enjoyed attacking: for example, the theory and practice of the travel books now becoming numerous. In pleading for truth he had the companionship of his friend Kinglake, whose *Eothen* was published in 1844, and who wrote in his preface:

[1] *Miscellanies*, IV (1857), Ch. iv.    [2] *Morning Chronicle* (6 Mar. 1848).

My excuse for this book is its truth ... My narrative is not merely righteously exact in matters of fact ... but ... conveys—not those impressions which *might have been* produced upon any 'well-constituted mind', but those which were really, and truly received at the time of his rambles, by a headstrong, and not very amiable traveller, whose prejudices in favour of other people's notions, were exceedingly slight.

Thackeray himself produced three truthful travel books, out of Irish journeys, visits to France, and his trip 'from Cornhill to Cairo'. In *The Irish Sketch Book* comes this typical whiff of realism, in a visit to a ruined abbey: 'But depend on it, for show-places and the due enjoyment of scenery, that distance of cold chickens and champagne is the most pleasing perspective one can have.'

Then there were the book illustrations, a topic of more importance now that the illustration of novels and even poems was much in demand. Thackeray himself had some gifts as a draughtsman, and had even had training when he was hesitating about the profession he should take up. The importance of his gift for the literary student is that, in the event, he did drawings for several of his works, so providing them with double expression. Like Edward Lear's, his illustrations make a contribution to the text not merely aesthetic but intellectual. Reading *Vanity Fair* as illustrated with the author's plates and interspersed woodcuts, we find the verbal meaning supplemented, as when we read Lear's 'Nonsense' books. *Vanity Fair*, therefore, and the rest of the works Thackeray both wrote and illustrated, achieved what might be called 'composite form', a form that he seems to have inaugurated, and which enriches the literature of the mid-century, several of the great writers of the time being also gifted draughtsmen. Thackeray's own drawings are often comical, and so when they exaggerate do so frankly. But whatever their degree of truth, it is plain that it is truth that is being honoured. Not so in the *Annuals*, which distorted the human body more drastically than the actors, and which he reviewed in *The Times* in 1838: 'Their beauties nowadays are not women at all. They have not bodies and limbs like women, their eyes are too large, their waists are far too small, the beauty of the annuals is the modern English *improvement* upon a woman. Nature does not know how to make them, that is clear.' Or there is this outburst in another review:

Oh, Medora, Zuleika, Juana, Juanina, Juanetta, and Company!—oh ye of the taper fingers and six-inch eyes! shut those great fringes of eyelashes, close those silly coral slits of mouths. Avaunt, ye spider-waisted monsters! who have flesh, but no bones, silly bodies, but no souls. And ye, O young artists! who were made for better things than to paint such senseless gimcracks, and make fribble furniture for tawdry drawing-room tables, look at Nature and blush![1]

Some of Thackeray's own drawings, and many of Cruikshank's and Doyle's, point a distinction applicable also to fiction. An artist might freely choose for some purpose or other *not* to provide truth, this reversal being acceptable so long as the intention was made clear. An obvious instance is that 'composite' work, his *Rose and the Ring*, which is offered for what it is—a fairy-tale for children illustrated by Thackeray's pictures of the man-based monsters who figure in the tale—and another his 'Sultan Stork', a story in the manner of *The Arabian Nights*. In both these stories there was no question of truth direct and unmanipulated. But though not representing the sort of truth Thackeray put into his novels, they imply it. Many of Cruikshank's drawings were offered as fantastic—he helped to show the way for Lear and Lewis Carroll. What offended Thackeray in some of the wall pictures and the book illustrations of the day was what offended him in many fashionable novels—their taking the false, the fantastic, and offering it as truth. And like the mid-century dramatists, the painters and

[1] *Fraser's* (Jan. 1839).

draughtsmen came to apply the Thackerayan principle to themselves. The Pre-Raphaelites owed something to the art of the Middle Ages, but also something to contemporary scientists, and to Thackeray.


It was in the *Morning Chronicle*, as a reviewer of novels, that Thackeray held forth most plainly, vigorously, and extensively about what he saw to be the novelist's *modus operandi*. He had the wit to see as ridiculous what many novel-readers were still taking seriously. Even Dickens and George Eliot did not see the falsity of Bulwer Lytton as clearly as Thackeray did—their respectfulness may, however, be partly due to non-literary considerations.

Thackeray backed up his adverse criticism with fiction of his own. Late in the day—for by 1847 his own *Vanity Fair* was making grape-shot unnecessary—he produced his *Punch's Prize Novelists*, ridiculing the chief offenders in turn in the most brilliant series of parodies before Max Beerbohm's *Christmas Garland*. As early, however, as 1839–40 he was contributing to *Fraser's* a short novel, *Catherine*, intended as a counterblast to the 'Newgate' fiction of the time, to which, in its way, *Oliver Twist* contributed. His experience over *Catherine* may have contributed to his own education in the sense of reminding him that when his immediate literary purpose was achieved there awaited him another less temporary purpose—that of showing truth in its completeness. He took for his subject an eighteenth-century murderess in order to demonstrate what a brute she was, and in the passages discussing his doctrine spoke as if he had succeeded. It was one thing, however, to ridicule the falsity being offered by the offending novelists, and another to claim, as he did, that the truth consisted wholly of the evil and sordid. Where Bulwer Lytton and Dickens went wrong was not in showing their rogues as not wholly vicious, brutal, and sordid, but in not fusing the mixture. What

was wrong with Bulwer Lytton's Eugene Aram was not
that he possessed intellect and learning, but that he
possessed them apart from his crime and unaffected by it.
What was wrong with Dickens's Nancy was not her
access of belated good-heartedness, but her acquiring
refinement along with it. Thackeray did not truly point
out where the offence lay. Bulwer Lytton and Dickens
had failed to make their personages the literary equivalent
of human beings. His Catherine was human, but only
because she had more to her than her criminality. While
telling her story he came to see that truth cannot consist
wholly of the bad. He admitted privately to having 'a
sneaking kindness' towards her. Rogues, in practice and
on long acquaintance, were found not wholly bad, and
Thackeray as theorist should have said so, insisting only
that their goodness and badness and the relationship between them should all be seen for what they were. By the
time he wrote *Barry Lyndon* four years later he had ample
materials for a true judgement. When that novel, which
purports to be the autobiography of a villain, reappeared
in the *Miscellanies* of 1856, Fitzjames Stephen reviewed
it perceptively, pointing to Barry's courage: 'Mr.
Thackeray seems to us to have shown his unusual acute-
ness in exposing the fallacy of the common notion that a
bully and a braggart is generally a coward', and to his
affection for his son: 'There is something not only
touching, but deeply true, in such a representation. It
recognises the fact that a strong, unbridled character, full
of fierce appetites and ungoverned passions, is not utterly
devilish . . .'[1]

If his theory in some of its applications did not go
deep enough, it nevertheless achieved, along with his
own practice as a writer of fiction, the reform he advocated, to which Theodore Martin paid him tribute in an
anonymous review in the *Westminster*:

---

[1] *Saturday Review* (27 Dec. 1856).

sham sentiment, sham morality, sham heroism, were everywhere rampant; and romance-writers every day wandering
farther and farther from nature and truth. . . . In criticism and in
parody, Mr. Thackeray did his utmost to demolish this vicious
state of things. The main object of his *Luck of Barry Lyndon*,
and his *Catherine Hayes*, was to show in their true colours the
class of rogues, ruffians, and demireps, towards whom the
sympathies of the public had been directed by Bulwer,
Ainsworth, and Dickens.[1]

In his obituary of Thackeray in the *Reader*, David Masson
summed up his achievement as a public benefactor: 'the
apostle and representative of Realism ... a tendency to
keep close to nature and fact, and to bring into fiction a
surcharge of actual matter of observation, which has
certainly been one of the intellectual phenomena of our
time'.

   Thackeray had every right to expect that what he called
truth would interest readers, including reviewers.
Among his readers were some of the choicest. Clough
kept pace with his publications; Mrs. Carlyle preferred
him to Dickens; Charlotte Brontë admired him beyond
all other novelists; Ruskin read him gratefully; on the sole
basis of his writings, Newman felt a 'piercing sorrow' at
his premature death in 1863; George Eliot (writing in
1857, when the Brontë sisters were dead) supposed that
'the majority of people with any intellect [think him] on
the whole the most powerful of living novelists';[2] Carlyle
quoted a letter of John Sterling's: 'I got hold of the two
first numbers of the *Hoggarty Diamond*; and read them
with extreme delight. What is there better in Fielding or
Goldsmith? The man is a true genius ... There is more
truth and nature in one of these papers than in all ——'s
Novels together.'[3]

---

[1] April 1853.                                    [2] *George Eliot*, II. 349.
[3] *Life of John Sterling* (1851), III. iii. The name suppressed by Carlyle is
probably Bulwer, but possibly Dickens.

When Ruskin read *The Newcomes* he found in it 'some pieces of wonderful power', to which he added, 'and, I fear, wonderful truth'.[1] His double response was according to the pattern of Newman's youthful response to Voltaire: 'How dreadful, but how plausible!'[2] At bottom his response was that of all readers. All of us mix realism and idealism in our private philosophies, and most of us attend to the realism in the mixture as little as possible. Newman attended to it as much as possible, making Sunday cover the whole week. His view of life was as realistic as possible, if we are to take as final such statements as this from one of his Dublin sermons: 'Generation passes after generation, and there is on the one side the same doleful, dreary wandering, the same feverish unrest, the same fleeting enjoyments, the same abiding and hopeless misery; and on the other, the same anxiously beating heart of impotent affection.' Later, at the close of the *Apologia*, his tune was the same: 'I look out of myself into the world of men, and there I see a sight which fills me with unspeakable distress'. Most of those who would subscribe to this view would do so only at times and seasons. Thackeray aimed at keeping men mindful of what they mainly like to forget. As a thinker he is in the company of Newman and Swift. What was found most offensive, therefore, was the thinking expected of a satirist or priest operating not only in a novel, but in the whole of one. Whereas a satirist and priest are paid, as it were, to be 'truthful' and 'realistic', a novelist is paid to be entertaining, entertainment ensuring a forgetting of the truth about hell or molecules. Readers of poems or novels are self-convicted idealists in that by the act of reading they are not, or not usually, attending to the 'duty that lies nearest', let alone the many duties lying further afield. That was why Newman in one of his Anglican sermons, 'The Danger of Accomplishments', preached against reading. *Vanity Fair* broke

[1] Not traced.          [2] *Apologia*, Ch. i.

the compact between novelists and their readers. Thackeray had attracted them into a pew when they expected a chair by the fireside. They felt tricked. A *Spectator* reviewer of *The Paris Sketch Book in* 1840 described its 'vein of humour' as 'too severe and biting to be pleasant', and, when it came to *Vanity Fair*, the complaint was repeated more widely and weightily. 'The life that is here painted is not that of high comedy, but of satiric farce; and it is the business of the artist to shew you all its deformities, its cringing affectations, its paltry pride, its despicable finery, its lying, treachery, and penury of soul in the broadest light.'[1]

The rest of the reviewers, both of *Vanity Fair* and the later work, concerned themselves with the philosophy in them. That philosophy softened a little as time went on, mainly because Thackeray's *literary* aim was fulfilled—he had cleared the air of sickly odours, and novelists were now free to be truthful.

Among the many nineteenth-century accounts of his philosophy one of the most generally interesting is that of W. S. Lilly, who lectured on him in 1895 to the Royal Institution, his lecture becoming part of his *Four English Humourists of the Nineteenth Century*. It deals with topics that recur from the first reviews onwards, and which accordingly testify to the interest the novels have always had for such readers as like to ponder the upshot even of a novel. 'Thackeray's philosophy of life I find underlain by three great philosophical principles which most probably he could not have formulated, and which are distinctly Kantian. The first is the cardinal truth of human personality ...' He then quotes at length the passage on 'isolation' which concludes Chapter xvi of *Pendennis*. 'Next, I find Thackeray holding fast to the great verity that life is a state of moral probation. Kant's doctrine—it is the very kernel of his ethical philosophy—is that knowledge is not man's highest attribute; that the will is higher

[1] Robert Bell, reviewing *Vanity Fair* in *Fraser's* (1848).

than the understanding; that practice is higher than theory.' This he illustrates from the passage on the effects of scepticism in *Pendennis*, Chapter lxi:

Again, Thackeray felt in his inmost soul that human life is inadequate to satisfy human aspirations; that the bottom of everything, in the phenomenal order, is that 'inexorable ennui' of which Bossuet speaks. . . . Kant judged that the realization of the highest good which the ethical faculty prescribes, implies an order above nature. There *must* be, he argues, a life beyond the phenomenal where the triumph of the moral law will be assured, where its rewards and penalties shall be adequately realized; there *must* be a Supreme Moral Governor who will bring about that triumph. It appears to me that some such conviction as this was to Thackeray an anchor of the soul—sure and steadfast. It breathes throughout his writings. I find it most shortly and simply stated in one of his letters. 'I don't know about the unseen world. The use of this world is the right thing, I am sure . . . waiting for the completion of my senses and the fulfilment of His intention towards me, after-wards, when this scene closes over me.'

At one point Lilly exaggerates. Kant's idea of the isolation of the individual often appears in nineteenth-century literature, but only as a passing thought, as a nod in the direction of that reach of realism we acknowledge but usually forget. This further reach Thackeray's novels usually ignore. For him, as for most people, appearance is much more important in that daily life of which novels are made than such an item of reality as our isolatedness. If the reality is isolation, the appearance is connection—the wounded traveller did not feel isolated from the Good Samaritan, who bound up his wounds, pouring in oil and wine, nor vice versa. Even the priest and Levite were connected with the man they passed by since he continued to exist for them in their conscience. For Thackeray the very realism itself came to include pleasant as well as unpleasant things. Lilly overlooked the plain fact that Thackeray, realist or part-realist as he may be, does not leave us to the worst of it, after *Vanity Fair* at least, without recommending a more valiant course than that of forgetting it as much as possible. He recommends—and his recommendation surprises us only if we have not been attending closely, even in *Vanity Fair*—that we cherish the Carlylean 'nobility' that exists in bits and scraps in ourselves and our neighbours, never existing amply enough to earn its possessor the name of hero, but just amply enough to serve the particular purpose. His final view of man, which is at least implicit in the most 'unpleasant' of his works, but explicit in the later, and especially in the *Roundabout Papers*, is that for all man's sins of omission and commission he has good somewhere in him, feeble, but just sufficing to make him at least a passable member of his society. Thackeray would not have agreed that life was as dark as Newman made out, mainly because 'affection' was *not* 'impotent' (it is impossible, on the evidence, to believe that Newman finally thought this). Like Browning, he would have seen in human love something to experience and remember and allow a place for in the general summing up, even a prominent place. He closed his *Book of Snobs* in February 1847—that is, just after *Vanity Fair* had begun its long monthly course—with what he called a 'concluding benedictory paragraph': 'To laugh at [snobs] is *Mr. Punch's* business. May he laugh honestly, hit no foul blow, and tell the truth when at his very broadest grin—never forgetting that if Fun is good, Truth is still better, and Love best of all.' Love was the best thing men could attain to. For the rest, it was seemliest if they acknowledged their shortcomings. His great and final hope was that his novels would help people to see themselves more accurately. Sinful they could not but be, being human, but what saddened him most was not men's many sins, but their not taking them into account in their self-estimates. If they hoped for forgiveness by grace of what he calls the 'Divine Tenderness', they might practise some of it themselves. He was sorry there was so little regard for the parable of the Good Samaritan, and such sayings of Jesus as that about not casting a stone unless you yourself were faultless, and about attending to the beam in your own eye before attending to the mote in your neighbour's. What he liked best in Christianity was the human goodness of Jesus, and those things he had said that accorded with the Golden Rule of the ancients, which commanded men and women to do as they would be done by. Ignoring, as beyond his interests and powers, the German idealism that had saved Carlyle from suicide, he saw another, very different idealism that he could not ignore—looking into themselves and their deeds, people saw a picture rosier than the facts warranted. He disliked the shams and humbug that Carlyle disliked, but for him they existed more painfully in private than in public life. In this he more resembled Dr. Johnson than Carlyle—Dr. Johnson, who had noted the superior usefulness of the moral of the *Rape of the Lock* over that of Boileau's *Le Lutrin*, because men and women suffer more from discord in the home than from the quarrels of ecclesiastics. The worst of sins was for Thackeray that of hypocrisy with its attendant pride, self-satisfaction, and unkindness. He could never have been a parson because he had no interest in dogma, but it is easily possible to imagine him assuming the human, more pastoral, duties of the office. There was, however, another deterrent from his becoming an actual parson. He could never have raised his voice from an actual raised-up pulpit. In *Vanity Fair* he pictures himself as a clown on a barrel. When the Reverend Charles Honeyman preaches a sermon to a congregation including members of the Newcome family, he takes occasion to allude to the impending departure of the Colonel, who is accordingly discomforted at hearing his merits alluded to 'in that sacred place'. To have been in a pulpit would have been to have had merit accorded to him—so Thackeray would have thought. The less said about merit the better, while any demerits existed. Thackeray felt too much the need to be preached to rather than to preach. Whatever he charges against his fellows he acknowledges as simultaneously existing in himself. The preacher and the satirist speak at people, but Thackeray remains one of themselves, and even when denouncing them never fails to include himself in the denunciation, having a hundred ways of attaching to his diatribes the airy phrase that includes himself among the offenders. On one occasion he says 'I do not scourge sinners! I am true to my party'. To say things like that and to say them that way, makes him not only a great moralist but a unique one. Despite the low claims he made for himself, he was a 'serious' novelist in that he wanted his novels to be a tribute to life, even if it were no more high-flying than the tribute that would readily be paid by the ordinary man. Even if we pitch our demand low, life (he saw) gives us plenty to be thankful for. Charlotte Brontë rejected the comparison between him and Fielding, thinking him—as, all told, we should hesitate to do—Fielding's superior. Many links, however, did exist between the two, the strongest being that each of them wrote as a man rather than merely as an entertainer. He was the last to underrate the genial merits of the entertainer, and he wished his own books had been more fully entertaining than they were. But what he said about *Esmond* must also be brought into the picture: 'Here is the *very* best I can do . . . I stand by this book, and am willing to leave it, when I go, as my card'—that is, as his visiting-card with his name on it. If he had not lived to write *Esmond*, however, he could have said the same about any books of his in that they all expressed the best self he had in him. On this score he differed from Sterne, with whom many, since Bagehot, have happily compared him, especially as to manner. It was noted by Harold Williams, however, in his *Two Centuries of the English Novel*, that though the death of Le Fevre in

*Tristram Shandy* 'has much in common with the call home of Colonel Newcome', there is an important difference—'we cannot escape the consciousness that Sterne is writing for the sake of the scene'. Thackeray found fault with Byron who 'got up rapture' for his public, and with Bulwer Lytton and even Dickens. He was not a Miss Braddon, who cheerfully manufactured what her easy-going public wanted, though he would have admired her cheerfulness and honesty in saying so, and the skill with which she turned out her tawdry thrillers. If he speaks of the novelist as a humorist, a clown, a showman, he also honours him with the name of the historian. It was not only in recognition of eighteenth-century practice that he called two of his novels *The History of Pendennis* and *The History of Henry Esmond*, and he represents *The Newcomes* as *Memoirs*.

Having a philosophy consciously held meant that Thackeray was never inside the narrative. This apartness affected the account he gave of his personages. For him Carlyle's behest to see for yourself had peculiar cogency. He liked to restrict his material to what the eye can see, and what the mind can infer from the sight without losing hold of it. Aristotle had noted the evidence of character afforded by the body, and Bacon had particularly noted that 'a number of subtle persons, whose eyes do dwell upon the faces and functions of men, well know the advantage' of observing those 'lineaments of the body [that] disclose the disposition and inclination of the mind'. If human beings, then novelists. Thackeray, writing his novels, was looking not at human beings but at their counterparts in his imagination. Yet more than most novelists he restricted himself to the role of the 'subtle persons' remarked by Bacon. His eyes were supplemented by his ears. Introducing *The Virginians* he remarks: 'I have drawn the figures as I fancied they were;

set down conversations as I think I might have heard them.' This testimony assumes that the novelist's eyes and ears are those of Everyman—which brings us back to the problem about what we see and what a genius makes of what he sees. Whatever the participation of Thackeray's genius in the record of what he sees and hears, the result as it strikes the reader resembles what he himself experiences. What he sees and hears is all weighed.

Reviewers were divided as to whether or not his method led to representing people completely. Writing in 1848, when *Vanity Fair* was before him, Abraham Hayward in the *Edinburgh* declared: 'He can skim the surface, and he can penetrate to the core'. It is noticeable, however, that those who think his province to be mainly 'surface' are the idealists. The eloquent W. C. Roscoe can speak for them:

Man is his study; but man the social animal, man considered with reference to the experiences, the aims, the affections, that find their field in his intercourse with his fellow-man: never man the individual soul. He never penetrates into the interior, secret, *real* life that every man leads in isolation from his fellows, that chamber of being open only upwards to heaven and downwards to hell. He is wise to abstain; he does well to hold the ground where his pre-eminence is unapproached,—to be true to his own genius. But this genius is of a lower order than the other.[1]

Such criticism is obtuse, being true only if we cannot read, as Hayward could, the signs that imply the core, without describing it. It is true that the core is usually that of ordinary people, whom Thackeray deliberately preferred to write of, and who would not themselves lay claim to the possession of much core. And it is also true, even of these ordinary people, that Thackeray deliberately refrains from prying into the most private secrets—again in accordance with his philosophy, which demanded of him reverence towards the naked human

[1] *National Review* (1856).

heart. When we have allowed for these two things we may well have as much implied as even the greatest analysts provide. If he deprecated a describing of those dark places, this did not mean that he did not know what they contained. Thackeray represents mankind profoundly, I find a Shakespearian depth in his simplicities. When Becky concludes, after making her monetary calculations, that if Rawdon should be killed at Waterloo she can 'look her [widow's] weeds steadily in the face', when a 'sexual jealousy' is discovered in the mother as her son meditates marriage, when Laura Bell, during Pen's neglect of her or worse, practises the piano for long spells—those things and a thousand more tally with our own reading of life. The famous instance, however, is provided by *Esmond*, of which George Eliot reported in a letter to a friend: '"Esmond" is the most uncomfortable book you can imagine. You remember, Cara, how you disliked [George Sand's] "François le Champi". Well, the story of Esmond is just the same. The hero is in love with the daughter all through the book, and marries the mother at the end.'[1] Forster thought the marriage 'incredible'.[2] Mrs. Oliphant called it 'monstrous': 'our most sacred sentiments are outraged, and our best prejudices shocked by the leading feature of this tale'.[3] Nevertheless, George Brimley, in his review in the *Spectator*, felt himself equal to demonstrating its psychological truth, as 'a complex feeling, in which filial affection and an unconscious passion are curiously blended,' and shows how Thackeray turns the difficulty into triumph, with 'beauties which a safer ambition would not have dared to attempt'.[4] And the last words are Saintsbury's: 'there is ... nothing for it but to confess that it is very shocking—and excessively human'.[5]

The personages he imagines are mainly ordinary.

[1] *George Eliot Letters*, II. 67.    [2] *Examiner* (6 Nov. 1852).
[3] *Blackwood's* (Jan. 1855).    [4] *Essays*, ed. W. G. Clark (1860), p. 258.
[5] Introduction in the Oxford Thackeray (1908), xiv, pp. xii–xiii.

When he goes back in time, and brings in the great people whom his more ordinary people come up against, he reduces their greatness. He might have acknowledged that the idea of the heroic was proving useful for Carlyle in his campaign to bring out the best in ordinary people, but he found no use in it himself. The idea smacked too much of idealism. As Trollope said of him: 'The heroic ... appeared contemptible to him, as being untrue'.[1] In his *Second Funeral of Napoleon* Thackeray had given a brilliant account of the ceremonies in Paris, which *The Times* objected to as irreverent, and to which Thackeray replied: 'O, you thundering old *Times*! Napoleon's funeral was a humbug, and your constant reader said so. The people engaged in it were humbugs, and this your Michael Angelo hinted at. There may be irreverence in this, and the process of humbug-hunting may end rather awkwardly for some people.'[2] It is significant that the sub-title of *Vanity Fair* is 'A Novel without a Hero' and when he himself writes a historical novel in *Esmond* he produced what Trollope hailed as 'the first truthful historical novel'. After *Esmond* came *The Virginians* as sequel, with, finally, a dip into French history in *Denis Duval*. Nor does any of it degrade the term 'historical', Thackeray being as close a student of the past as Carlyle. The only serious criticism brought up against its factual truthfulness pertains to his picture of the Old Pretender, which is held to malign an upright and honourable man. Thackeray's truthfulness may here have been the victim of political and religious prejudice. Usually, however, he had no difficulty in giving an authentic humanity to his historical personages.[3]

Action as well as personages is kept at a distance. We are made aware of it as lying outside the narrator, sometimes no farther than at the tip of his pen, but sometimes

---

[1] *Thackeray* (1879), p. 91.

[2] 'On Men and Pictures', *Fraser's* (July 1841).

[3] See Appendix, and Preface, p. viii.

as far away as the sun and moon. Thackeray saw the world represented in his novels as spectacle rather than as an arena in which the author and his personages interlock. He felt that Charlotte Brontë was too much embroiled in the moments as they came. He himself is not embroiled. He judges, if that is not too harsh a term, thinks about, comments on the moments, even when they are of the exciting kind. He is sometimes so detached that he notices the motion of the heavens above the card-tables. He is so much aware of what lies around the action that he can describe himself as a showman working his puppets. He shows us himself keeping pace with the implications of what is taking place in his imagination.

His distance from the narrative is furthest when narrative gives place to commentary, extended sometimes to the length of a long paragraph. It has been this extended commentary that has led critics to allege breaks in the continuity. To think so, however, is to have failed to respond duly to the nature of Thackeray's particular kind of narrative. That kind is never pure, or rather it is more impure than narrative need be. Attended to closely, pure narrative does not exist, simply because whatever is written has a writer whose existence is noticed in the very choice of the words, the style being the man. Thackeray's narrative, however, while having this authorial existence inevitably noticeable in it, has also a more tangible sign of it. To existence is joined participation. I have said that he keeps the narrative at a distance, and the most continuous means of his doing so lies in the constant bestowing of epithets denoting comment, appraisal, sometimes judgement. A favourite epithet is 'little', which evinces his function as showman of puppets. Because of the constant comment, appraisal, judgement, conveyed in epithets of this sort, the narrative already includes criticism before narrative gives place to comment at paragraph length.

The very prose of his novels witnesses to his

philosophy in being the prose we should all write if we could—unassuming, easy, comfortable, elegant, making the fewest demands on the reader, as limpid when its sense is profound as when not. One of his reviewers noted that he makes his personages speak as ordinary people speak every hour of their lives, and for his own prose he takes theirs, and gives it a supple continuity. The result has always been admired; his prose is the most distinguished in the whole range of our fiction. Its distinction, however, is in making us receive its art as completely natural. It has many marks of the colloquial. Thackeray likes to end a sentence with 'though' or 'very likely', and write such a one as 'And a very good thing too', or 'And so they went on in *Arcadia* itself, *really*', or '... as far away as Clive's almost'. It is a style without fuss. Its deadly remarks are said quietly. The almost unnoticeable way in which he makes tremendous statements reminds one of Dryden's praise for the kind of satirist who cuts off a man's head and leaves the body standing in its place.

His philosophy also led him to reject the well-made plot. The kind he preferred were those that dispensed with what he called 'tricks of art', and so he helped to revolutionize the concept of the novel form. We give him full credit for this only when we see how strong was the contemporary addiction to the plot so elaborately contrived as to collide sometimes or often with the improbable. We get an idea of this addiction when we discover that the publisher's reader complained of deficiency of plot in Trollope's *Barchester Towers*, and that Clough, praising *The Newcomes*, admits that 'there is certainly no story nor very much anything' in it.[1] Clough's remark is particularly illuminating—he must

[1] Letter of 3 Mar. 1854 (*Correspondence of Clough*, ii. 478). Writing from Cambridge, Mass., Clough could hardly have read further than Ch. xvi.

have felt that *The Newcomes* was so lifelike as to be vaguely confusing and intangible to a novel-reader. Thackeray subscribed to Hazlitt's desideratum that the story-teller should 'invent according to nature', and would have applauded Zola's remark that a well-made plot is the sort of work expected of 'women and children'. It was not a 'man's job'. He would also have applauded Trollope's view that plot was 'the most insignificant part of a tale'[1] because, as Reade put it, 'in my experience a complete plot rarely exists except in a drama or story'. Life itself having no plots, novels should not. In the obituary published in *Fraser's*, Thackeray is represented as himself laughing at the way he ended *Philip*: the old coach is made to upset and the lost will to come to light among the debris, which 'discovery' sends 'the necessary fortune ... in the right direction'. He rejected the ingenious plot from conviction. It was not an instance of sour grapes. Structural ingenuity exists brilliantly in the ten tales that make up *Punch's Prize Novelists*, and one of the best critics of the shapely *Barry Lyndon* is Fitzjames Stephen, who remarks that 'the story is as natural and easy as if it were true'. Thackeray's kind of plots prompted Roscoe to invent a phrase that was later modified into the technical term, a 'slice of life'—he says that Thackeray 'cuts a square out of life, just as much as he wants, and sends it to [his publishers] Bradbury and Evans'.

Thackeray, then, writes for people in their maturity, fulfilling Ruskin's wish that novels should deal with adult subjects rather than 'the narrow aims, vain distresses or passing joys of youth'.[2] One young reviewer objected to my saying this in my book on Thackeray, not realizing that the conditions for entry into that particular dispute ruled him out. He claimed that youth could fully

---

[1] *Autobiography*, Ch. vii.
[2] Letter to *Daily Telegraph* (15 Jan. 1888; *Works*, XXIV. 615).

appreciate, shall we say, the melodies of Mozart's slow movements. Youth, however, cannot yet know how it will appreciate these same melodies as it grows older. It does not see that by then it will have acquired a different and a finer mental instrument for them to be played on. Thackeray's sadness is the sort that men feel worth attending to for all its painfulness. It is the sadness that supervenes on the experience of youth. Often, he takes up the Horatian theme of time and its changes, softening it with the grey and silver of his moonlight and candlelight. James Hannay wrote of how 'inside his fine sagacious common-sense understanding' there was 'a pool of poetry', like 'the *impluvium* in the hall of a Roman house'.[1] Hannay's instances were from such verse as the 'Ballad of Bouillabaisse' and the lines on Charles Buller; but Thackeray, like Newman, provides even more of these poetic moments in his prose, as in the close of 'De Finibus' in the *Roundabout Papers*:

Another Finis written; another milestone on this journey from birth to the next world ... Oh, the sad old pages, the dull old pages; oh, the cares, the *ennui*, the squabbles, the repetitions, the old conversations over and over again! But now and again a kind thought is recalled, and now and again a dear memory. Yet a few chapters more, and then the last; after which, behold Finis itself comes to an end, and the Infinite begins.[2]

[1] *A Brief Memoir* (1864), first published as an obituary notice in the *Edinburgh Evening Courant* (5 Jan. 1864).

[2] The first sketch of the passage in manuscript has 'Another Finis, another slice of life which *Tempus edax* has devoured! And I may have to write the word once or twice more, perhaps, and then an end of Ends. Oh the troubles, the cares, the *ennui*, the disputes, the repetitions, the old conversations over and over again, and here and there oh the delightful passages, the dear, the brief, the ever remembered!' (Quoted in full by Dr. John Brown in 'The Death of Thackeray', first published in *North British Review*, Feb. 1864; see also *John Leech and other Papers*, pp. 193–4).

# 5. CHARLOTTE AND EMILY BRONTË

*Charlotte Brontë*

JANE EYRE, as the new novel of an unknown author, was
sent by its publisher to Thackeray, who at once 'lost (or
won if you like) a whole day in reading it at the busiest
period, with the printers waiting for copy [of the next
number of *Vanity Fair*]'. He was 'exceedingly moved and
pleased', to the point of crying over 'some of the love-
passages, to the astonishment of John who came in with
the coals'.[1] His high opinion increased his sense of the
'enormous compliment', a few months later, of the dedication of the second edition and the fervent preface liken-
ing him to the prophet Micaiah before the kings of Israel
and Judah;[2] 'he speaks truth as deep ... with a mien as
dauntless and as daring'. Such a public tribute from the
mysterious 'Currer Bell' produced some embarrassment,[3] but this is unimportant beside the instinctive
and immediate response of each author to the other's
truth.

To Charlotte Brontë the good word of Thackeray
was 'worth pages of praise from ordinary judges'.[4]
She admired not only what she saw as his fearless

---

[1] *Letters*, II. 318–19.

[2] I Kings 22: 7–27.

[3] Though offered from a 'total stranger', the dedication gave colour to the
absurd rumour that the author was a former governess in Thackeray's
family; see *The Brontës, their Lives, Friendships, and Correspondence*, ed. J.
Symington and T. J. Wise (1932), II. 183–4 (hereafter *Brontë Letters*), and
Elizabeth Rigby's review of the two novels in the *Quarterly* (Dec. 1848).

[4] *Brontë Letters*, II. 150.

denunciation of the falsehood and follies of the world, but his firm control of his power, the 'charm of majesty and repose in his greatest efforts; *he* borrows nothing from fever'; at its most forcible and exciting, his narrative was still 'as quiet as reflection, as quiet as memory'.[1] Her discernment may have been sharpened by her own experience, in life and art, that such control was not easily attained. Her own writing owes something to 'fever' both in emotion and experience. But Thackeray was not far out when he said (in the letter already quoted) that 'she knows her language better than most ladies do or has had a "classical" education'.

Louis Moore in *Shirley*, wandering about Fieldhead, comes upon an open desk that bears the marks of Shirley's recent presence, and sees therein: 'a pretty seal, a silver pen, a crimson berry or two of ripe fruit on a green leaf, a small, clean, delicate glove—these trifles at once decorate and disarrange the stand they strew. Order forbids details in a picture: she puts them tidily away; but details give charm.'[2] The distinction indicates two principles of description, both characteristic of Charlotte Brontë's writing: accumulation of detail, the 'multitudinousness' that Arnold deplored in Browning; and the ordered, sparse, and selective.

In her preface to *The Professor*[3] she had deprecated her former taste for 'ornamented and redundant composition', the staple of the romances about the imaginary country of Angria which she had continued to write until a few years before she began that novel. Such 'ornament' is, however, often extended into the novels and is sometimes 'redundant': as in 'what dark-tinged draught might she now be offering? What Genii-elixir or Magi-

---

[1] Ibid., II. 201 (29 Mar. 1848).
[2] Ch. xxix.
[3] Written when it was again submitted for publication in 1851; after its rejection, she used some of its material in *Villette*.

distillation?'[1] or when Lucy Snowe contrasts Dr. John with Paul Emanuel, 'as the fruit of the Hesperides might be unlike the sloe in the wild thicket; as the high-couraged but tractable Arabian is unlike the rude and stubborn "sheltie"',[2] or dwells on the 'solid joy' of his longed-for letter;

not a dream, not an image of the brain, not one of those shadowy chances imagination pictures, and on which humanity starves but cannot live; not a mess of . . . manna . . . neither sweet hail, nor small coriander-seed—neither slight wafer nor luscious honey, [but] the wild savoury mess of the hunter, nourishing and salubrious meat, forest-fed or desert-reared, fresh, healthful, and life-sustaining.[3]

Contrast the neat shapeliness of the summary that concludes the same chapter: 'Really that little man was dreadful: a mere sprite of caprice and ubiquity: one never knew either his whim or his whereabout.' Or the many places where an equal richness of fancy is pared down to its essentials—'the dubious cloud-tracery of hope',[4] the 'proper happiness for early morning—serene, incomplete, but progressive',[5] Mme Beck coming in 'like a living catherine wheel of compliments, delight, and affability'.[6] When, as often, phrases from the poetry and drama that she read are merged into her prose, they seem at home there; one paragraph in *Villette* closes with 'scalded my cheek with tears as hot as molten metal';[7] and Shirley looks out at the stormy forest in the moonlight 'touched, if not rapt—wakened, if not inspired',[8] a line (not in quotation marks) from Pope's *Eloisa to Abelard*. Passing references—to an 'inky mass of shrubbery', 'sun-bright nasturtiums', the curtain that 'shrivelled up to the ceiling'[9]—are often more telling than her rhetorical set

---

[1] *Villette*, Ch. xvii.
[2] Ibid., Ch. xx.
[3] Ibid., Ch. xxii.
[4] Ibid., Ch. viii.
[5] *Shirley*, Ch. xxxvi.
[6] *Villette*, Ch. xix.
[7] Ibid., Ch. xv.
[8] *Shirley*, Ch. xxxi.
[9] *Villette*, Chs. iv, xii, xiv.

pieces. And her dialogue is almost invariably economical and forceful, engaging us (especially in *Shirley*) in the conflict of ideas and attitudes as well as personalities.

Charlotte Brontë stands with such writers as Browning, George Eliot, and Meredith, as one of the pioneers in the expression of matter discovered, or newly enhanced, in the nineteenth century. They all explored the 'dark passages' Keats had spoken of, doing exploits of Drakean proportions and hazard rather than joining the many who were paddling round the Isle of Dogs.[1] They wrested their materials out of chaos—the multitudinousness of the psyche and of the intellect fully aware of 'this nineteenth century', of the 'condition of England', of changing morality. If they did not strive hard enough for lucidity, some blame must be set down to the *Zeitgeist*, and some, more precisely, to Carlyle. The defect of his greatness was to encourage writers to eager piling up and excess, rather than to restriction. Writers had too much encouragement to embrace multitudinousness without discriminating what they could master of it.

Charlotte could not have accepted Arnold's counsel to learn 'clearness of arrangement, rigour of development, simplicity of style', nor Thackeray's dictum (evoked by a reading of *Villette*) that 'novelists should not be in a passion with their characters, but should regard them, good or bad, with a like calm'.[2] Her feelings ran high, and she endowed her creatures with them—particularly the two women, Jane Eyre and Lucy Snowe, whose experiences were most like her own. She was gifted to read her own feelings as few can—perhaps, indeed, no other writer has read them so closely. And she could represent the feelings of personages quite outside herself—of a Ginevra Fanshawe or Mme Beck, of a Paul Emanuel or even a Rochester. Her authority is evinced by the firmness of the line she draws between what she grasps and what she does not try to grasp. The *Tablet* reviewer

[1] See p. 86.         [2] *Letters*, III. 67.

of *Jane Eyre* exaggerated, but pardonably, in alleging that 'the story invites the reader into the recesses of the human heart, and by its force detains him there until he has unravelled all the mysteries of that miraculous organ'; Charlotte knew enough not to claim so much, for she knew that some mysteries remain 'ravelled'—she did not claim to explain all that she presented.

Feelings constitute the inner strength of the novels, and are the main source of that 'almost preternatural power' that George Eliot responded to in *Villette*.[1] But it so happened that she was writing at a time when for a writer with feelings to spare there was a temptation other than those noted by Arnold and Thackeray: a time when there were inducements (financial and other) not only to multiply feelings in novels but to give them a merely fashionable expression. There was the feeling accompanying physical suspense, ranging from horror at ghosts and marvels to the 'sentimental admiration' analysed by Ruskin: 'the kind of feeling which most travellers experience on first entering a cathedral by torchlight, and hearing a chant from concealed choristers; or in visiting a ruined abbey by moonlight, or any building with which interesting associations are connected, at any time when they can hardly see it'. He noted that 'it was apt to rest in theatrical effect', and 'was wholly unable to distinguish truth from affectation'.[2]

Such feelings were fashionable throughout the mid-century; and along with them went what survives all (or most) fashions and was honoured by the name of 'romance'. In Mrs. Radcliffe's novels, still popular when Charlotte wrote, courtship is treated as a long drawn-out occasion for a masquerade of superfine politeness and delicacy and, in its expression, an occasion for the

[1] *George Eliot Letters*, II. 87.
[2] Preface to 2nd edn. of *Seven Lamps of Architecture* (1855).

practice, as on a spinet, of the language of conduct manuals. (People have every right to conform to contemporary fashions in expression, but fashions vary in their worth for posterity.) Mrs. Radcliffe's personages court each other in questions such as 'Is it possible I can be less than sincere?' or 'Can you then wish, lovely Adeline, to fly from him who adores you?' It is to this kind of thing that Thackeray opposed Morgiana's 'Don't be a fool' to her kneeling suitor in *The Ravenswing*[1], and for which Charlotte more subtly substitutes the exchange between Mr. Rochester and Jane Eyre: '"You examine me, Miss Eyre; do you think me handsome?" ... "No, sir".'

Along with the 'Gothick novels' and their leisure for superfine sentiments there were also, for Charlotte, the early novels of George Sand, in which feelings, if superfine, are part of a larger humanity than Mrs. Radcliffe's. Charlotte deeply respected her 'grasp of mind', even if she appeared to 'couple strange extravagance with wondrous excellence'.[2] Some of the 'grasp of mind' was shown in her knowledge of music and the arts, for instance, which may have encouraged Charlotte to take the important step of introducing such pleasures seriously into English fiction. George Sand's novels were altogether more intelligent than Mrs. Radcliffe's (and *Consuelo*, which Charlotte thought 'the best', is a recognizable influence in *The Professor*); but 'extravagance' is evident in their elaborate plots, showing love in conflict with law and prejudice through complications of 'blood', involving at least two generations, and with the usual French load of sexual complications. Too many skeletons from aristocratic cupboards walk about dressed up as people, only showing themselves as skeletons when other people have fallen hopelessly in love with them.

In effect it was Mrs. Radcliffe's novels and George Sand's as well as her own Angrian stories that Charlotte was ridiculing when, in all her own novels, she halted

[1] See p. 167.　　　　　[2] *Brontë Letters*, II. 180.

momentarily to contrast them with those she called 'romantic': as when Lucy Snowe, like William Crimsworth, first sees 'the wide difference that lies between the novelist's and the poet's ideal "jeune fille", and the said "jeune fille" as she really is'.[1] (Later she provides a further observation: 'Many of these girls ... were not pure-minded at all' adding the Carlylean 'very much otherwise'.) As for Mrs. Radcliffe's ghosts, they are slain for ever by her comment on the 'vague tale' of the nun once buried alive, and supposed to be seen in a certain part of the school garden: 'The ghost must have been built out some ages ago, for there were houses all round now'.[2] And in Chapter xxiii of *Shirley* her rejection of Mrs. Radcliffe is explicit, though tender: Rose Yorke, a child of 12, is absorbedly reading *The Italian*; Caroline kneels beside her and reads too, 'making no remark'.

'Do you like it?' inquired Rose, ere long.

'Long since, when I read it as a child, I was wonderfully taken with it.'

'Why?'

'It seemed to open with such promise,—such foreboding of a most strange tale to be unfolded.'

Where Caroline stands is defined in her dialogue a little later with Rose's mother, who accuses her of 'romantic ideas' and a 'habitually lackadaisical expression, better suited to a novel-heroine than to a woman who is to make her way in the real world'; bidden to look in the glass and compare her face with 'that of any early-rising, hardworking milkmaid', she retorts:

'My face is a pale one, but it is *not* sentimental, and most milkmaids, however red and robust they may be, are more stupid and less practically fitted to make their way in the world than I am. I think more and more correctly than milkmaids in general do; consequently, where they would often, for want of reflection, act weakly, I, by dint of reflection, should act judiciously.'

[1] Ch. viii.          [2] Ch. xii.

'Oh, no; you would be influenced by your feelings; you would be guided by impulse.'

'Of course, I should often be influenced by my feelings; they were given me to that end.'

So with Louis Moore, alone in the stormy moonlit night writing his heart-searching memories of Shirley: '"I know this is the talk of a dreamer—of a rapt, romantic lunatic: I *do* dream: I *will* dream now and then; and if she has inspired romance into my prosaic composition, how can I help it?"'

Charlotte recognized the truth of some of the Radcliffean matter and made her own discriminating selection from it—like the 'ghost' in *Villette*, with its eventual rational explanation. Even in the opening of *Shirley*, promising (or threatening) 'something unromantic as Monday morning, when all who have work wake with the consciousness that they must arise and betake themselves thereto', she adds the hint of 'a taste of the exciting, perhaps towards the middle and close of the meal'—fulfilled in the account of the riots in the second volume, but arising from the problems of 'work'. The 'romance' of the undivulged blood-relationship, which opens the third volume (possibly an afterthought), is alone touched with what to us seem the unrealities of the theatrical. It was the sheer amount of the romantic and strange that made the romantic novels seem 'untrue', and its remoteness from the work of Monday morning; horrors await Mrs. Radcliffe's young people in the castles and wastes of foreign countries, but it is the unvisited upper floor of a country-house in the north of England that harbours the madwoman in *Jane Eyre*. More often, 'strangeness' comes from the inner life: Lucy says she 'seemed to hold two lives', one nourished with 'the strange necromantic joys of fancy' and the other with 'daily bread, hourly work, and a roof of shelter'.[1] Hers is the strangeness of dreams, nightmares, 'sleeping fan-

[1] Ch. viii.

tasies', of the night-wandering under the influence of the drug that 'instead of stupor' brings 'excitement'. It is at night that strange experiences come, or are sought—like Lucy's visit to the confessional, and her swoon on the steps of the Béguinage.

*Jane Eyre* was commended by one reviewer because the author wisely avoided 'any startling expedients or blue fire colouring, so prominent in modern literature'.[1] In that novel, however, she touched the edge of the supernatural, and went further into true mystery than could be imagined by a 'blue fire' novelist: Mr. Rochester's cry is heard, and answered, by Jane, in a distant county, when she is almost yielding, from a sense of duty, to St. John Rivers's proposal; when she learns that he did call her name and heard her reply, she does not disclose her own experience; 'the coincidence struck me as too awful and inexplicable to be communicated'. At the time, she had rejected 'superstition', and called it 'the work of nature' who 'was roused and did—no miracle— but her best'.[2] The reader (who, as often, is invoked) may be left in doubt, perhaps believing no more than that the desperation of intense love may bring identical experience to those far separated; the 'electric chord of sympathy' imagined by Lucy Snowe as 'sustaining union through a separation of a hundred leagues'.[3] Each had entreated Heaven, Jane to be shown the right path, and Rochester in 'remorse and repentance' for forgiveness. Meanwhile we do not forget that we are still within the novel, that Charlotte has provided fiction with one of its supreme climaxes—supreme, because whether supernatural or not, the 'visitation', the 'unspeakable strangeness', falls upon a world that we have come to inhabit.

Usually what we are given is truth as Thackeray approved it, and the crucial specimen is Mr. Rochester:

[1] *Weekly Chronicle* (23 Oct. 1847).
[2] *Jane Eyre*, Chs. xxxv and xxxvii.
[3] Ch. xvi.

crucial, as nearest to Angrian heroes like Lord Ebrington in 'The Foundling', who 'though scarcely a man, is not yet altogether a monster'. But Rochester's humanity is secured partly by what is imputed by Jane's lively treatment of him; you cannot, for instance, joke with a monster. '"Am I hideous, Jane?"' he inquires with an anxiety attested by the added vocative, to be met with, '"Very, sir,"', and the teasing and good-humoured conversational addition '"You always were, you know".' A possible departure from truth is in the last pages of the novel, summarizing the 'perfect concord' of their ten years' marriage. But this is an ending like a 'coda' in music, an appended idyll suggested by what has gone before yet distinct from it. And it has one individualizing touch: 'We talk, I believe, all day long; to talk to each other is but a more animated and an audible thinking.'

Marriage marks the end of her novels; only in *The Professor* does she devote as much as a whole chapter to it. But this does not make her vulnerable to Thackeray's criticism of the conventional novelist who 'drops the curtain' when the 'matrimonial barrier is past . . . as if the drama of life were over then'.[1] Her heroines (and heroes too) constantly discuss and reflect upon what they expect or hope from marriage. It is notably unconventional for the essentials of marriage to be fully discussed by Shirley, who explains in some detail to her uncle and guardian why his candidate as suitor falls short of her requirements, describing, he tells her, 'with far too much freedom for your years and sex, the sort of individual you would prefer as a husband';[2] and in the penultimate chapter Louis Moore records her long dialogue with him on the same topic—to be continued, we assume, after this marriage. For marriage is seen, in part, as a continuing, unending conversation. It supervenes on friendship, 'the minds' and affections' assimilation';[3] when Lucy is

---

[1] *Vanity Fair*, Ch. xxvi; cf. *Rebecca and Rowena*, Ch. i.
[2] Ch. xxxi.                        [3] *Villette*, Ch. xli.

assured that Paul Emanuel is her friend, that is the crucial step into happiness: 'I envied no girl her lover, no bride her bridegroom, no wife her husband; I was content with this, my voluntary, self-offering friend.'[1]

If marriage is the further extension of a growing friendship, it is so for people who have never denied that the body exists with all its rights, rights not of its own but of the whole person. Charlotte's account of the feelings of her lovers could hardly be further intensified. Of course there are aspects of love that she could not, even if she had wished to, have given a full account of; but we do not miss them. An exchange of glances is a momentous event; the unobserved scrutiny of a face a strange delight: 'I looked, and had an acute pleasure in looking—a precious yet poignant pleasure; pure gold, with a steely point of agony.'[2]

While [Dr. John] sat in the sunshine ... I was observing the colouring of his hair, whiskers, and complexion—the whole being of such a tone as a strong light brings out with somewhat perilous force (indeed I recollect I was driven to compare his beamy head in my thoughts to that of the 'golden image' which Nebuchadnezzar, the king, had set up).[3]

To his kindly letters (which seemed then a 'divine vintage' though in later retrospect 'a beverage of milder quality') feeling bids her reply with the full expression of her 'attachment', 'a passion of solicitude'; Reason forbids. But Reason is powerless in the seven long blank weeks when no letters come: the post hour is her 'hour of torment ... the rack of expectation and the sick collapse of disappointment which daily preceded and followed that well-recognised ring', and as the days pass and the nerves are 'almost gnawed through with the unremitting tooth of a fixed idea', 'I muffled my head in my apron and stopped my ears in terror of the torturing clang'.[4] The

[1] Ch. xxxv.　　　　　　　　　　[2] *Jane Eyre*, Ch. xvii.
[3] *Villette*, Ch. x.　　　　　　　　[4] Chs. xxiv–v.

joys and agonies of her first, one-sided attachment, born of loneliness, are remembered later and contrasted with 'a Love that laughs at Passion, his fast frenzies and his hot and hurried extinction'. But this second and less 'romantic' love does not lack its 'frenzies'; when it seems that Paul Emanuel has gone without a farewell, 'What wonder that the second evening found me ... untamed, tortured, again pacing a solitary room in an unalterable passion of silent desolation?'; and when she witnesses unseen what she supposes a love scene, 'something tore me so cruelly under my shawl, something so dug into my side, a vulture so strong in beak and talon'. She has now far more to lose—a love 'venturing diffidently into life after long acquaintance, furnace-tried by pain, stamped by constancy, consolidated by affection's pure and durable alloy, submitted by intellect to intellect's own tests'.[1]

The moment of revelation for Lucy is the disclosure, next day, of the house he has taken for her and his presentation of copies of a prospectus for the school she is to establish: 'It was the assurance of his sleepless interest which broke on me like a light from heaven; it was his (I will dare to say it) his fond, tender look, which now shook me indescribably. In the midst of all, I forced myself to look at the practical.'[2] This is no anti-climax; economic independence is as important to Lucy as affection.

The insistence that women as well as men need fulfilment in work is one of the new elements of reality in Charlotte Brontë's novels, and must have found an echo in many hearts. In *The Professor* even marriage does not rule it out; Frances Henri in her quiet way makes claims that would be startling in the 1840s. After consenting to pass her life with William, it is she who first breaks the silence of 'stirless ... happiness': 'I wished merely to say, that I should like, of course, to retain my employment of teaching'.[3] She supports this with feeling as well

[1] Chs. xl–xli.  [2] Ch. xli.  [3] Ch. xxiii.

as reason: unemployed, she would be 'depressed and sullen'; and those who work together like and esteem each other better. As for single women, their need for worth-while occupation is one of the leading themes of *Shirley*, breaking the surface at an interesting point in the second long exchange of thoughts between Caroline and Shirley.[1] It follows Caroline's muted confession of her sense of dependence on Robert, who, she knows, seldom thinks of her when he is away: '"Women have so few things to think about, men so many ... however my thoughts might adhere to him, his were effectively sundered from me"'.

'Caroline,' demanded Miss Keeldar abruptly, 'don't you wish you had a profession—a trade?'
'I wish it fifty times a day.'

Thereafter the subject recurs in almost every chapter, most markedly in Caroline's long soliloquy, culminating in Carlylean apostrophes to 'Men of England' and 'Fathers'.[2] Shirley, with the firm basis of an independent fortune, masculine, as she says, in name and position, is more explicit in her defiance of conventional views about women; condemnation of the 'marriage market' makes her uncle think her unfit to associate with his daughters, and her assertion of freedom to choose a husband for herself he attributes to a mind 'poisoned with French novels'.[3] But it was her own experience and observation rather than the novels of George Sand that made Charlotte almost an avowed feminist—a generation before the word appeared in English. It is her chief contribution to the public thought of her time, and is part of the 'grasp of mind' that she missed (though mistakenly) in the novels of Jane Austen.

In reaction against both her own Angrian stories and the still popular fashionable novels of the time, Charlotte determined in her first novel, *The Professor*, that her hero

[1] Ch. xi.     [2] Ch. xxii.     [3] Ch. xxxi.

should 'work his way through life as I had seen real living
men work theirs—that he should never get a shilling he
had not earned—that no sudden turns should lift him to
sudden wealth or high station'.[1] To this she adheres also
in *Jane Eyre* and *Villette*, equally concerned with the
struggle for existence by impoverished members of the
middle class (Jane's inheritance comes too late, and she
renounces most of it). Crimsworth 'must travel in search
of money'; 'My business is to earn a living where I can
find it', is Lucy's justification for her journey to Labas-
secour. Their struggles are hard, but zestful; they see
earning a living partly as an athlete sees a gymnasium,
and both in *The Professor* and *Villette* the teachers' first
experience of taking a class of girls is a crucial challenge of
their capacity and courage. They do not envy the more
fortunate; 'Miss Ingram was a mark beneath jealousy; she
was too inferior to excite the feeling'.[2] 'Still, Miss Fanshawe, hapless as I am, according to your own showing,
six pence I would not give to purchase you, body and
soul'.[3] Most of the settings, and the point of view, are
confined within the range of the middle class, prosperous
or struggling; but the servants are kept in view, and
presented as individuals. Bessie in *Jane Eyre* is a substantial and reassuring figure at Gateshead Hall, and John
and Mary at Ferndean contribute to the sublimity of the
climax; Rosine at Mme Beck's plays a conspicuous and
vivacious part. In *Shirley* the turbulent industrial matter
further stretches the social range; Joe Scott argues with
Shirley and Caroline on equal terms, and William Farren
is Caroline's chosen companion in convalescence. Mrs.
Pryor, who 'felt as if a great gulf lay between her caste and
his' warns Caroline that 'he may presume', and 'smiled
sceptically at the naive notion' of his having 'fine feelings'. With none of the radical views of Mrs. Gaskell,
Charlotte has something of her respect, sympathy, and

[1] Preface.                          [2] *Jane Eyre*, Ch. xviii.
[3] *Villette*, Ch. xiv.

interest in the workers. But she was well aware of the novelty of such an attitude in the eyes of genteel southern readers, whom she ironically warned about 'low persons being here introduced' in the title of Chapter xviii.

Lucy Snowe chose to read few books, 'preferring always those on whose style or sentiment the writer's individual nature was plainly stamped' to those that were 'characterless, however meritorious'.[1] Charlotte Brontë's individual nature is stamped upon all her novels, and most plainly upon *Villette*, where her earnestness, her emotional intensity, and perceptions are concentrated on a single and unusual point of view. Some readers were repelled; Arnold saw 'nothing but hunger, rebellion, and rage',[2] Harriet Martineau was struck by the unwholesome influences of seclusion, a mind preying upon itself—both, perhaps, blurring the distinction which the author always maintained between herself and her creature. What puts Lucy among the most fully realized persons in fiction (until we come to Miriam in Dorothy Richardson's *Pilgrimage*, on which *Villette* is one of the few discernible influences) is partly the successive sharply defined particulars of her response to her total experience: particulars vivid and multitudinous but directed and controlled by psychological truth. Swinburne hardly exaggerated when he saw in her creator:

the highest and rarest quality ... a power to make us feel in every nerve, in every step forward which our imagination is compelled to take under the guidance of another's, that thus and not otherwise, but in all things altogether even as we are told and shown, it was and it must have been with the human figures set before us in their action and their suffering; that thus and not otherwise they absolutely must and would have felt and thought and spoken under the proposed conditions.[3]

[1] Ch. xxi.
[2] *Letters of Matthew Arnold 1848–1888*, ed. G. W. Russell (1895), I. 29.
[3] *A Note on Charlotte Brontë* (1877), pp. 12–14.

## Emily Brontë: Wuthering Heights

In the 'Editor's Preface' supplied by Charlotte for the second edition of *Wuthering Heights* and *Agnes Grey*, Emily is shown as a recluse, and the psychological, moral, and intellectual character we deduce for ourselves from her writings, including her most famous poem, is one of self-sufficiency. From other sources we also know how business-like she was in the fulfilling of household tasks—like the other women novelists of the time she had all her wits about her. The one novel she completed concerned personages wilder than those of Richardson's *Pamela* or of *Jane Eyre*, not to mention the pallid palpitating creatures of Mrs. Radcliffe; *Wuthering Heights* is the one English novel that stands within hailing distance of *King Lear* and *Macbeth*. But whatever wildness flamed up in her mind, it coexisted with the mighty wits she had about her. Accordingly, *Wuthering Heights* respected the reader's everyday interests as much as it excited him with strangeness. Emily saw that her particular farmhouse, its inmates and their predecessors, were not to be thrown in the reader's face. She took pains to propitiate him, even though the means she favoured might seem cumbersome and creaking. If she insisted on the farouche, she did not omit an admixture of the familiar.

She may be assumed to have learned from the authors of *Robinson Crusoe*, *Gulliver's Travels*, and *The Ancient Mariner* that when the matter of a story is strange, the reader needs to be introduced to it by way of the familiar. And yet her problem was not quite that of Defoe and the rest, whose matter was strange for all possible readers. Emily's was strange only for southerners. Carlyle had seen England as divided into two nations according to wealth. It was divided, however, as widely between North and South—a division that Mrs. Gaskell endorsed in the title of one of her novels. W. C. Roscoe, himself a Lancashire man, recorded with amusement the remark of the 'timid lady who, after a perusal of some of the Brontë novels, declared she would rather visit the Red Indians than trust herself in Leeds society'.[1] West Riding people needed no introduction to Wuthering Heights and its inmates. Their like were known already, or known about. In the 'Editor's Preface' accompanying her 'Biographical Notice' Charlotte described the setting of Emily's story as 'the outlying hills and hamlets of the West Riding of Yorkshire', and the actors its local 'inhabitants', ranging from gentry to hinds, complete with their 'customs'. All these things were familiar to northerners, but strange to southerners, whose introduction had therefore to be as gentle as possible.

It had to be all the more gingerly because Emily would not tamper with the northernness itself. There was no question of conciliating the southerners in that respect; indeed she let them know in her very title what she had waiting for them. Never before had a word of English dialect figured with that prominence; and in the text itself came the dialect speech of Joseph and Zillah, accurate in diction and in phonetic spelling. Not only that, there was the earthiness abundant in rustic speech. The remarks of most of Emily's personages are littered with references to all those 'rats and mice and such small deer' that town people have no experience of. On a single page come an 'eft' and a 'cockatrice',[2] it being an easy transition from actual brutes to those legendary ones familiar to people whose book education came mainly, if not wholly, from the Bible. And Mrs. Dean's account of Heathcliff's moral character—'Rough as a saw-edge, and hard as whinstone'—is followed by her description of one of his victims, Hareton, as 'cast out like an unfledged dunnock!'[3] Whinstone was the stone used for bruising gorse to soften

[1] *National Review* (July 1857); *Poems and Essays* (1860), II. 314.
[2] Ch. xxvii.     [3] Ch. iv.

it to a condition suitable for cattle fodder, and Catherine herself hits on the same comparison when trying to convince the infatuated and babyish Isabella Linton of Heathcliff's true nature: 'an unreclaimed creature, without refinement, without cultivation: an arid wilderness of furze and whinstone. I'd as soon put that little canary into the park on a winter's day, as recommend you to bestow your heart on him!'[1] Charlotte, acting as editor in 1850, felt it prudent, in Emily's interests, to soften the edges of at least the dialect by removing what was most outlandish in it. As Emily made her novel, and as it was first published, the north remained inviolate in it, and southerners approached it having been warned.

Emily, however, was also willing to take them by the hand. The part of the framework that readers encountered first was 'southern' and familiar. Lockwood, the new tenant of Thrushcross Grange, pays a social call on his landlord, and so stumbles on the whole household of Wuthering Heights. (The adjective being unfamiliar to him, he notes its meaning.) He is in happy mood, greeting the region he has chosen as his temporary retreat from the 'stir of society' with 'This is certainly a beautiful country'. Heathcliff he finds 'a dark-skinned gypsy in aspect', but 'in dress and manners a gentleman; that is, as much a gentleman as many a country squire'. He even speaks of a 'sympathetic chord' as being resonant between them. What the reader is launched into is the witnessing of Lockwood, an idling southerner, being drawn almost casually into a fascination. Lured by natural curiosity to make inquiries, he—and the reader with him—comes on the story bit by bit. Moreover, there is a second screen between the reader and the story, for most of Lockwood's narration is an account of what Nelly Dean told him. He receives the story by way of his housekeeper, an altogether civilized body, who has lived on the edge of the Heathcliff–Linton whirlpool. Let me

[1] Ch. x.

hear how it came to pass' is how he words his curiosity when almost the last stage of the story is pending.[1] He (and the reader) is agog to hear the story of the last three generations who have inhabited the stately, ancient, but fallen farmhouse. Nelly's 'screen', it is true, often resembles the fence North Americans allude to in hard weather ('There's a fence between us and the North pole, and it's down'). Nevertheless, her screen has some tempering effect on the narration. If it often falls down, she keeps on propping it up.

We can see the screens neatly in place towards the close of the story, when they receive an addition from Joseph—Heathcliff's 'heart' may well be what Joseph calls it, an 'earthly hell', but what we are *shown* is Heathcliff's words, Nelly's thoughts and words, and Joseph's guess:

He [Heathcliff] began to pace the room, muttering terrible things to himself, till I was inclined to believe, as he said Joseph did, that conscience had turned his heart to an earthly hell. I wondered greatly how it would end. Though he seldom before had revealed this state of mind, even by looks, it was his habitual mood, I had no doubt: he asserted it himself; but not a soul, from his general bearing, would have conjectured the fact. You did not, when you saw him, Mr. Lockwood: and at the period of which I speak, he was just the same as then, only fonder of continued solitude, and perhaps still more laconic in company.

With Lockwood and Nelly interposing, Emily maintained her own reserve as narrator. Third-person narrative, in those days, demanded authorial commentary, or at least comments, and Emily may have thought it wise to spare the reader hers. (Poems were a different matter—in them she could say offensive things like 'Vain are the thousand creeds', but not in a novel.) The donning of her double mask may have also seemed advisable for the sort of reasons that prompted Swift to write as few

[1] Ch. xxxii.

things as possible *in propria persona*. Emily, whose imagination Charlotte in her preface described as 'sombre' and 'powerful' (epithets that fit Swift), is bottled up in *Wuthering Heights* behind glass doubly thick. It was according to her genius to impose control on her sombreness and power. Charlotte did not feel the same degree of need to control what called for it in herself—her own particular genius, though as powerful as Emily's, was hotter and more claustrophobic, and she could not resist showing herself 'in a passion' with her characters.[1] Emily, who needed no advice from outside, needed no screens herself as far as Heathcliff went. She could stand up to him as Catherine herself could. Indeed, as we shall see, there was a part of him and his cruelty that unduly fascinated her. Even so, she was a more wholly objective creator than Charlotte. Most of what there is in *Wuthering Heights* of Emily, the individual genius, was made to exist as far outside the Haworth parsonage as possible. Like all writers, she put her whole genius into her book, but, more than Charlotte, did so for the most part without seeming to. She was a recluse from choice, being self-sufficient. Accordingly, she did not need to make use of her fiction to unload much turmoil of private personality. It was her intellect rather than her feelings that found Lockwood and Nelly useful as a screen.

Furthermore, Emily, in parts of her novel, provided narration of a sort that Thackeray felt the novel had now outgrown, something, however, that novel-readers were still finding comfortable. Nelly's narration, by the new standard of Thackerayan truth, is quite impossible. How *could* she have spoken for so long at a time, and so coherently, and indeed so beautifully, in English as distinguished as anything in nineteenth-century literature? In other words, the narrative method is as primitive on this score as that of *The Ancient Mariner*. Moreover, into the midst of her story protrudes a further glaring impos-

[1] See p. 190.

sibility—the narrative elaboration in the long letter written by Isabella, which describes her reception at Wuthering Heights after her marriage to Heathcliff—a letter necessary both for Nelly and the story. A letter might well be as informative and as long as Isabella's—the age in which long letters were the norm had not yet passed—but the extension into it of the narrative method we have already been asked to accept as Nelly's, allowing of the reproduction of dialogue verbatim, throws fiction back to its Richardsonian stage, when every personage figured as an autobiographical novelist. It may be urged that these were established eighteenth-century conventions, appropriate in a novel of eighteenth-century life; but they were falling out of use by the 1840s, and some reviewers found Emily's novel unskilfully constructed. Nevertheless, that Emily's methods of narration were not felt by Charlotte to be so old-fashioned as to need excuse is attested by her making no reference to them in her partly defensive preface.

Narrative method apart, however, Emily stands with Thackeray, Trollope, Mrs. Gaskell, and the rest of the great novelists in providing 'Thackerayan truth'. To make that statement throws on its maker the onus of proof, particularly as it applies to personages. It will be conceded at once that most of them—Linton and his sister, Nelly Dean, Hindley, and even both Catherines —are plainly in the same truthful class as personages in Thackeray, Trollope, or George Eliot. Hareton and Joseph also, though southerners would not find it so easy to see this—southerners, who (to use Charlotte's words again): 'will hardly know what to make of the rough, strong utterance, the harshly manifested passions, the unbridled aversions, and headlong partialities of unlettered moorland hinds and rugged moorland squires, who have grown up untaught and unchecked, except by mentors as harsh as themselves'.[1]

It is Heathcliff alone who might be thought to defy the Thackerayan standard. He combines the fiercest hate and the fiercest love. The hate is so fierce that Isabella reaches the point of withdrawing her prior assumption that he is a human being at all:

'I can recollect yet how I loved him; and can dimly imagine that I could still be loving him, if—no, no! Even if he had doted on me, the devilish nature would have revealed its existence somehow. Catherine had an awfully perverted taste to esteem him so dearly, knowing him so well. Monster! would that he could be blotted out of creation, and out of my memory!'

'Hush, hush! He's a human being,' I said. 'Be more charitable: there are worse men than he is yet!'

'He's not a human being,' she retorted; 'and he has no claim on my charity. I gave him my heart, and he took and pinched it to death; and flung it back to me. People feel with their hearts, Ellen: and since he has destroyed mine, I have not power to feel for him: and I would not, though he groaned from this to his dying day, and wept tears of blood for Catherine! No, indeed, indeed, I wouldn't!'[2]

Isabella almost loses her own humanity in dwelling on his lack of it. It needs a Nelly Dean to keep the standard firm: 'Hush, hush! He's a human being'. But her remark comes from her heart rather than her head—she is willing to thrust aside categories in the desperate hope of keeping somebody, anybody, from going mad. The 'man' they are dealing with is completely represented by Nelly's account of his treatment of Isabella and the purpose behind it: '"Whatever he may pretend," [says Isabella to Nelly] "he wishes to provoke Edgar to desperation: he says he has married me on purpose to obtain power over him; and he shan't obtain it—I'll die first!"' Her threats play into Heathcliff's hands:

[1] Editor's Preface (1850).
[2] Ch. xvii.

'No; you're not fit to be your own guardian, Isabella, now; and I, being your legal protector, must retain you in my custody, however distasteful the obligation may be. Go up stairs; I have something to say to Ellen Dean in private. That's not the way: upstairs, I tell you! Why, this is the road up-stairs, child!'

He seized, and thrust her from the room; and returned muttering—

'I have no pity! I have no pity! The more the worms writhe, the more I yearn to crush out their entrails! It is a moral teething; and I grind with greater energy, in proportion to the increase of pain.'

'Do you understand what the word pity means?' I said, hastening to resume my bonnet. 'Did you ever feel a touch of it in your life?'[1]

The ferocity of his hate, however, is made 'truthful' by being accounted for. Emily had some of Galton's special intelligence. She saw that people are largely explained by heredity and training. Heathcliff's parents were unknown, but thought (from his appearance) to have been gipsies—or he might be 'a little Lascar, or an American or Spanish castaway'. When Nelly is trying to bring the best out of the child, she suggests: 'You're fit for a prince in disguise. Who knows but your father was Emperor of China, and your mother an Indian queen, and you were kidnapped by wicked sailors and brought to England?'[2] But usually his origins are assumed to be the basest: 'But where did he come from, the little dark thing ...?'

If his parentage remains obscure, there is no doubt of the part played by nurture in completing his character and personality. Picked up and brought home by old Mr. Earnshaw, doing what Nelly Dean calls a 'good deed', the treatment he received from the son and heir, Hindley, was a 'plague' and a 'persecution', so malicious that at one point it is called 'vivisection'.[3] Heathcliff had 'bred bad

[1] Ch. xiv.    [2] Ch. vi; Ch. vii.
[3] See Chs. iv and vi.

feeling in the house' and when he becomes master, as a result of chance, contrivance, and the weakness that time reveals in his oppressor, he retaliates. What had been done to him he does to others, and he does it the more thoroughly because of his inborn powers of intellect and his good fortune in living on to continue his revenge on Hindley's son, Hareton. After Hindley's funeral, Heathcliff 'lifted the unfortunate child on the table and muttered, with peculiar gusto, "Now, my bonny lad, you are *mine*! And we'll see if one tree won't grow as crooked as another, with the same wind to twist it!"'[1] We are told how he treats the animals he subdues—Linton winces to recall how hard he laid it on to dogs and horses—and people with money and rank are for him simply stubborn wild animals, against whom he has equipped himself for the business of taming them into giving him satisfaction.

Heathcliff is an indication of what happens when hate is pursued single-mindedly, as Swift's Yahoos are of what would happen if men reverted to the brute. Only if revenge is inhuman does Heathcliff lack 'truth'.

The good in him is accounted for by its being the same power meeting its match in Catherine.[2] She calls out in him feelings strong as hate but now reversed in as extreme a love. The coin has two sides, but is made of the same metal; without Catherine that second side might never have been known to exist. Through this revelation we come upon love in all its fire, purity, and lack of the self-seeking—like the love of Eloisa for Abelard, a thing of the spirit even more than of spirit and flesh combined. On that level the two cannot be united: this is ruled out first by the accident of Heathcliff's overhearing only part of Catherine's confidential outburst ('He had listened till he heard Catherine say it would degrade her to marry

[1] Ch. xvii.

[2] Catherine Earnshaw (later Linton) will be referred to here as 'Catherine' (though to Heathcliff she is always 'Cathy'), and her daughter Catherine as 'Cathy'.

him, and then he staid to hear no further')[1] and his consequent flight and long absence, during which she marries Edgar Linton. At their last meeting (with Nelly as witness)—in Swinburne's words 'the last fierce rapturous passage of raging love and mad recrimination'—Catherine is already dying and about to bear Edgar's child. 'An instant they held asunder, and then how they met I hardly saw, but Catherine made a spring, and he caught her, and they were locked in an embrace from which I thought my mistress would never be released alive; in fact, to my eyes, she seemed directly insensible.'[2] Physical consummation is neither here nor there when love is at the pitch of theirs. When they talk about what they are thinking of constantly, they say things like 'If all else perished, and he remained, I should still continue to be; and if all else remained, and he were annihilated, the universe would turn to a mighty stranger', and 'he's in my soul', and he 'is more myself than I am' and 'Whatever our souls are made of, his and mine are the same'. Those are words of Catherine's,[3] but Heathcliff speaks the same dialect. This is the moment when he hears from Nelly how she died:

'And—did she ever mention me?' he asked, hesitating, as if he dreaded the answer to his question would introduce details that he could not bear to hear.

'Her senses never returned: she recognised nobody from the time you left her,' I said. 'She lies with a sweet smile on her face; and her latest ideas wandered back to pleasant early days. Her life closed in a gentle dream—may she wake as kindly in the other world!'

'May she wake in torment!' he cried, with frightful vehemence, stamping his foot, and groaning in a sudden paroxysm of ungovernable passion. 'Why, she's a liar to the end! Where is she? Not *there*—not in heaven—not

---

[1] Ch. ix.
[2] Ch. xv.
[3] In Chs. ix and xv.

perished—where? Oh! you said you cared nothing for my sufferings! And I pray one prayer—I repeat it till my tongue stiffens—Catherine Earnshaw, may you not rest as long as I am living! You said I killed you—haunt me, then! The murdered *do* haunt their murderers. I believe—I know that ghosts *have* wandered on earth. Be with me always—take any form—drive me mad! only *do* not leave me in this abyss, where I cannot find you! Oh, God! it is unutterable! I *cannot* live without my life! I *cannot* live without my soul!'

He dashed his head against the knotted trunk; and, lifting up his eyes, howled, not like a man, but like a savage beast getting goaded to death with knives and spears.[1]

He cannot live, he says, without his soul. There is no mention of any body, or even of earth: he is a disembodied thing in an abyss. When he is on the point of dying—or rather melting into his image of Catherine —he thinks of the body, but then it is with 'my soul's bliss kills my body'. Catherine and Heathcliff—or this half of him—do not think on the same plane as most of us. Their sort of love impresses us as no other sort does. We honour it as we honour the self-sacrifice of heroes; it is humanity at its most exalted. The rest of us, if we ever reach this pitch, reach it only rarely. Heathcliff and Catherine live in its fierce light without a break, without guessing that there is any alternative. What we see by an occasional flash of lightning, they gaze at as a settled light—though after her marriage Catherine at least has to pretend that she wholly inhabits the 'light of common day'. Arnold said:

> So, in its lovely moonlight, lives the soul . . .
> We visit it by moments, ah! too rare.

But how inconvenient to visit it often! We retire into our ordinariness. At the close of her epistle to Abelard Eloisa imagines two lovers gazing at their tomb and exclaiming:

> Oh may we never love as these have lov'd!

[1] Ch. xvi.

We say the same thing at the close of the first half of *Wuthering Heights*, when Catherine is dead, and Heathcliff is vowing his revenge on the innocent family into which he has married. We see the blessed comfortableness of being ordinary. Nevertheless, most of us recognize the 'truthfulness' of the love between Catherine and Heathcliff, having felt some of it ourselves.

'Thackerayan truth', finally, is a term literally appropriate for Heathcliff—he exists in essence in Thackeray's *Barry Lyndon*. The Brontë sisters do not refer to that particular novel of Thackeray's, but we can be sure they had read it, since they took in *Fraser's* in which it appeared, and since Charlotte spoke of Thackeray as she did in dedicating the second edition of *Jane Eyre* to him. What Fitzjames Stephen says of Barry Lyndon[1] applies to Heathcliff in kind and almost in degree. In the natures of both hate and love coexist, both in extremes, Barry's only love being for his son. If further demonstration is called for, no reader can feel Heathcliff to belong to the literary class to which, say, Dickens's Quilp belongs, Dickens here being out to make a monster, not a man at all.

It is also in accord with 'truth' that Heathcliff's evil is finally overcome: the normal life of two of its victims is assured, even before his death. The goodness of the grandfather—as might be expected on the Galtonian view—reasserts itself also in Hareton: 'Earnshaw was not to be civilised with a wish; and my young lady was no philosopher, and no paragon of patience; but both their minds tending to the same point—one loving and desiring esteem, and the other loving and desiring to be esteemed—they contrived in the end to reach it.'[2] And with this effect: '"It is a poor conclusion, is it not?" he observed, having brooded a while on the scene he had just witnessed [the happiness of Hareton and Cathy] "An absurd conclusion to my violent exertions! ... I don't care for striking: I can't take the trouble to raise my

[1] See p. 171.          [2] Ch. xxxii.

hand!"'[1] Like Macbeth, he goes to pieces towards the end; being like him obsessed with his one idea, Macbeth's idea being that he is unkillable, and Heathcliff's that he must merge himself into the dead Catherine. Even earlier, under his threats, Cathy Linton can confound him with her claim to immunity:

'Linton is all I have to love in the world, and, though you have done what you could to make him hateful to me, and me to him, you *cannot* make us hate each other! and I defy you to hurt him when I am by, and I defy you to frighten me.' ...

'I know he has a bad nature ... he's your son. But I'm glad I've a better, to forgive it; and I know he loves me, and for that reason I love him. Mr. Heathcliff, *you* have *nobody* to love you; and however miserable you make us, we shall still have the revenge of thinking that your cruelty arises from your greater misery! ...'

There is a further range of truth, quite apart from Heathcliff, to which the novel contributes as it were by accident. By virtue of 'seeing' with eye and mind a writer, like anyone else, sets up a standard. He discovers what constitutes a man, and so what falls short of it. Truth abhors the 'poseur'. His mere existence gives him right of entry into a truthful novel, but, having got in, he has to be truthfully shown for what he is—a whole man pretending to be only part of a man. In the thirties and forties there was still need to expose Byronism as a sham, as a pose of the idle well-to-do that could not stand the light of perennial seriousness and earnestness for which Carlyle had given people a new sense. Lockwood announces himself as a misanthrope. Misanthropy had drawn him to the great northern 'desolation' which, by being 'completely removed from the stir of society', makes a 'perfect misanthropist's heaven'. His misanthropy is a pose, and his experience within the novel cures him of it. When towards the end he again uses the word, it does not occur to him to connect it with

[1] Ch. xxxiii.

himself; he applies it to the inmates of Wuthering Heights—'clowns and misanthropists'.[1] In Heathcliff he has seen something worthy of a terrible name he had lightly applied to himself. Moreover, he had found that misanthropy, even when at the Heathcliff pitch, is not the whole man, Heathcliff's love of Catherine being anything but that. Lockwood is educated by Heathcliff to discard the false, and become more wholly true, even as the superior of the two nations had been educated by Carlyle, or as the readers of Disraeli's high-society novels and Bulwer Lytton's pretentious ones had been educated by Thackeray. And within the story proper another education proceeds from the same quarter. Isabella Linton's infatuation for Heathcliff drove her to abandon all the 'elegancies, and comforts, and friends' of Thrushcross Grange, 'under a delusion' which, as Heathcliff contemptuously observes, led to her 'picturing in me a hero of romance, and expecting unlimited indulgences from my chivalrous devotion'. He adds, 'I can hardly regard her in the light of a rational creature, so obstinately has she persisted in forming a fabulous notion of my character, and acting on the false impressions she cherishes.'[2] Isabella's delusion, like Lockwood's misanthropy, was in itself 'true' enough: it existed as a fact. Like a pose, then, it is legitimate material for a truthful novel, but in order to show that the novel is fully truthful, it must be shown to be only a 'piece of a man'. The truth about Isabella that was missing during her infatuation comes to light in her married suffering and repentance. If truth in 'real' life is the result of seeing, and seeing steadily and whole, Isabella achieved it too late for her general happiness. She was merely cured of her misjudgement of Heathcliff, who pointedly sums it up with 'It was a marvellous effort of perspicacity [for her] to discover that I did not love her.'

Towards the end of the novel Lockwood sees how

[1] Ch. xxxii.   [2] Ch. xiv.

very far is the sort of life being led at Wuthering Heights from the sort of dream that is common elsewhere: '"How dreary life gets over in that house!" I reflected, while riding down the road. "What a realization of something more romantic than a fairy tale it would have been for Mrs. Linton Heathcliff, had she and I struck up an attachment ... and migrated together into the stirring atmosphere of the town!"'[1] Even now he is not fully educated. A Cathy Lockwood could not, any more than could her mother, have left those 'solitudes', where 'In winter nothing is more dreary, in summer nothing more divine, than those glens shut in by hills, and those bluff, bold swells of heath.'[2]

In *Wuthering Heights*, then, there is the truth that takes in what exists, and the truth that comes of criticizing some of it by reference to truth as a whole.

There was another ground on which truth was vindicated—that of the scientific legitimacy of its sensation. Instead of ghosts we get the nightmares we all know to be facts. The novice Lockwood, putting up in Wuthering Heights in a snowstorm, reads before dropping asleep part of Catherine Earnshaw's diary, and as a result passes 'a terrible night'—but he also ascribes it to 'bad tea and bad temper'. The sensations Emily provides are unsurpassed in power, but they are all due to nature. They are created by Heathcliff and other natural causes, not imposed by super-nature.

Eighteen years after, Heathcliff recalls, as if it had just happened, the day of Catherine's burial:

In the evening I went to the churchyard. It blew bleak as winter—all round was solitary: ... Being alone, and conscious two yards of loose earth was the sole barrier between us, I said to myself—'I'll have her in my arms again! If she be cold, I'll think it is this north wind that chills *me*; and if she be motionless, it is sleep.' I got a spade from the toolhouse, and began to delve with all my might—it scraped the coffin; I fell to work

[1] End of Ch. xxxi.    [2] Ch. xxxii.

with my hands; ... when it seemed that I heard a sigh from some one above, close at the edge of the grave, and bending down. 'If I can only get this off,' I muttered, 'I wish they may shovel in the earth over us both!' and I wrenched more desperately still. There was another sigh, close at my ear. I appeared to feel the warm breath of it displacing the sleet-laden wind. I knew no living thing in flesh and blood was by; but as certainly as you perceive the approach to some substantial body in the dark, though it cannot be discerned, so certainly I felt that Cathy was there: not under me, but on the earth. A sudden sense of relief flowed, from my heart, through every limb. I relinquished my labour of agony, and turned consoled at once: unspeakably consoled. Her presence was with me: it remained while I re-filled the grave, and led me home. You may laugh, if you will; but I was sure I should see her there. I was sure she was with me, and I could not help talking to her.

Returning to Wuthering Heights—

'I looked round impatiently—I felt her by me—I could *almost* see her, and yet I *could not*! I ought to have sweat blood then, from the anguish of my yearning—from the fervour of my supplications to have but one glimpse! I had not one. She showed herself, as she often was in life, a devil to me! And, since then, sometimes more and sometimes less, I've been the sport of that intolerable torture! ... When I sat in the house with Hareton, it seemed that on going out, I should meet her; when I walked on the moors I should meet her coming in. When I went from home, I hastened to return: she *must* be somewhere at the Heights, I was certain!

The roots of this lie in natural human experience.

What has been said and implied about Emily's achievement contradicts certain things said by Charlotte. When in 1847 *Wuthering Heights* was first published, along with *Agnes Grey*, it was imperfectly understood,[1]

---

[1] [The first edition, though much less widely reviewed than *Jane Eyre* (partly owing to the parsimony of Newby, the publisher), still attracted a fair amount of notice, being reviewed, sometimes with extensive quotation, in at

and after her sisters' ensuing deaths, Charlotte saw the chance offered by the fame she had herself won with *Jane Eyre* to recommend and defend their work. Her recommendation took the solid form of a 'Biographical Notice of Ellis and Acton Bell' and an 'Editor's Preface' to *Wuthering Heights* (and *Agnes Grey*) in a new edition three years after the first. The former of these is as precious to the biographer of either sister as the latter is to the critic of Emily. The critic, however, will misread the preface unless he allows full weight to Charlotte's purpose in writing it—that of winning from a hitherto unresponsive or baffled public the due response to genius at a high pitch. What she says of *Wuthering Heights* and its author puts them in the light that would most commend them to the readers, mainly southerners, of 1850.

Evidently the screens placed within the novel between Heathcliff and the reader had failed of their purpose, and Charlotte's two pieces are held up as further screens. Charlotte, therefore, presents the novel as the best that could have been expected in extraordinary circumstances, as a precious thing despite repulsive defects. Her difficult position is plain from the twistings and turnings of her defensive argument. The only point at which she can speak freely is when she recommends Emily's account of place. Counting on the contemporary worship of scenery, she can emphasize Emily's picture of the Haworth moors, one item in the general 'rusticity', the novel being admittedly 'rustic all through':

---

least fifteen periodicals, English and American. It was seen as 'strangely original' in its setting and characters (the epithets 'strange' and 'wild' recur in several reviews, and are not inept) and 'powerful' ('we are spell-bound, we cannot choose but read'), but painful, coarse, and even 'disagreeable': the characters were 'savage' and 'degraded', and the author's purpose obscure. Most reviewers were impressed by the settings, and two were reminded of Salvator Rosa; but 'provincialisms' and oaths were occasionally objected to. The early reception of the novel is well summarized in John Hewish, *Emily Brontë* (1969), pp. 160–4, with a list of reviews and earlier comments on them on p. 188. *Ed.*]

It is moorish, and wild, and knotty as the root of heath. Nor was it natural that it should be otherwise; the author being herself a native and nursling of the moors ... Ellis Bell did not describe as one whose eye and taste alone found pleasure in the prospect; her native hills were far more to her than a spectacle; they were what she lived in, and by, as much as the wild birds, their tenants, or as the heather, their produce. Her descriptions, then, of natural scenery, are what they should be, and all they should be.

Otherwise she vacillated between her two minds. She thought *Wuthering Heights* an inspired work; its attribution to her she regarded as an honour. Yet she seems at one point to suggest that a Lockwood, say, would have written a better novel than was possible for the underprivileged Emily:

Had Ellis Bell been a lady or a gentleman accustomed to what is called 'the world,' her view of a remote and unreclaimed region, as well as of the dwellers therein, would have differed greatly from that actually taken by the homebred country girl. Doubtless it would have been wider—more comprehensive: whether it would have been more original or more truthful is not so certain.[1]

Emily's 'practical knowledge' of the people of the locality, Charlotte explains, was slight:

Though her feeling for the people round was benevolent, intercourse with them she never sought; nor, with very few exceptions, ever experienced. And yet she knew them: knew their ways, their language, their family histories; she could hear of them with interest, and talk of them with detail, minute, graphic, and accurate; but *with* them she rarely exchanged a word. Hence it ensued that what her mind had gathered of the real concerning them, was too exclusively confined to those tragic and terrible traits of which, in listening to the secret annals of every rude vicinage, the memory is sometimes compelled to receive the impress.

[1] [But this may be her characteristic, rather heavy irony, directed at Emily's more 'worldly' reviewers. *Ed.*]

Charlotte then proceeds to yield up Heathcliff to those critics who saw him as a 'strange' unnatural being, a 'deformed monster', or 'an incarnation of evil': 'Heathcliff, indeed, stands unredeemed; never once swerving in his arrow-straight course to perdition'. Except for 'solitary traits' of human feeling 'we should say he was child neither of Lascar nor gipsy, but a man's shape animated by demon life—a Ghoul—an Afreet'. Contradictions abound. At one turn Emily is learned, at another ignorant. All that Charlotte really meant was that Emily's human learning came from observation and report rather than from bodily participation, but that it was, Emily being Emily, none the worse for that.

Charlotte does not allow enough weight to Emily's rejection of the experience that could have been hers. Allowing that Emily might have had more if she had wanted it, she did not allow (or pretended not to) that she knew what she was doing, knew that her genius happened to be of the hoarding and treasuring sort, that she gained enough knowledge of human beings to see what all the gossip she drank in—full-flavoured and strong as all country gossip then was, and still is—implied as to the persons concerned, to see what sort of people could have done what she heard reported of them. Charlotte had forgotten (or pretended to have) what Lockwood learned, that the mind will find what it needs in little or in much. When Nelly Dean wants to telescope certain stretches of her narrative Lockwood interposes:

'No, no, I'll allow nothing of the sort! Are you acquainted with the mood of mind in which, if you were seated alone, and the cat licking its kitten on the rug before you, you would watch the operation so intently that puss's neglect of one ear would put you seriously out of temper?'

'A terribly lazy mood, I should say.'

'On the contrary, a tiresomely active one. It is mine, at present: and, therefore, continue minutely. I perceive that people in these regions acquire over people in towns the value that a spider in a dungeon does over a spider in a cottage, to their various occupants; and yet the deepened attraction is not entirely owing to the situation of the looker-on. They *do* live more in earnest, more in themselves, and less in surface change, and frivolous external things.'[1]

Emily saw to it that, denied the cottage, she found ample compensation in the spider. She contributed to that nineteenth-century rediscovery or reassertion that there is no dearth of quantity of matter when there exists the power to make a full use of the eyes. 'Take what God has given,' Ruskin was saying, 'and really look at that'. Keble was assuring people that

> The trivial round, the common task
> Would furnish all we ought to ask.

Emily attains to quantity of matter by way of intensity. Denied some of the kind of first-hand experience that Charlotte sought out, or choosing to deny it for herself, she used what she had as a basis for imagining the rest, and was greatly helped, we must suppose, by the vivid minds of the Haworth natives.

Charlotte said splendid things of Emily and her novel; but not all that she could have said to later, unscared readers.

It goes without saying, the style being the man himself, that no writing can be 'seraphically free / From taint of personality', and even the 'screens' were all made by Emily. Otherwise, she is among the writers least involved, apart from the involved imagination, in her people and their doings. In parts of her novel, however, there are signs of a person who likes to take the horrid and linger over it, like the witches of *Macbeth* when they detail the ingredients of their cauldron. At points in the action Emily comes near to invoking the imps of comedy—we

[1] Ch. vii.

even occasionally recall the brilliant fun of *Cold Comfort Farm*. When Nelly Dean has stung Heathcliff to the quick by referring to the lately dead Catherine as one who would never have put up with his ill-treatment as a wife, he attacks her;

he snatched a dinner knife from the table and flung it at my head. It struck beneath my ear, and stopped the sentence I was uttering; but, pulling it out, I sprang to the door and delivered another which I hope went a little deeper than his missile. The last glimpse I caught of him was a furious rush on his part, checked by the embrace of his host; and both fell locked together on the hearth. In my flight through the kitchen I bid Joseph speed to his master; I knocked over Hareton, who was hanging a litter of puppies from a chair-back in the doorway; and, blest as a soul escaped from purgatory, I bounded, leaped, and flew down the steep road ...[1]

We do not need those hanged puppies. Emily sometimes recalls her own Isabella, according to Heathcliff's reading of her: 'I suppose she has an innate admiration of [brutality], if only her precious person were secure from injury'. That physical security is enjoyed by any novelist. Some of the detail of pain and horror is Pre-Raphaelite in its cool clarity. Heathcliff's account of the escapade at the Lintons' from which he has to flee, leaving Catherine behind, contains this description of the bulldog which has been released to foil his escape:

'I got a stone and thrust it between his jaws, and tried with all my might to cram it down his throat. A beast of a servant came up with a lantern, at last, shouting—"Keep fast, Skulker, keep fast!" He changed his note, however, when he saw Skulker's game. The dog was throttled off; his huge, purple tongue hanging half a foot out of his mouth, and his pendant lips streaming with bloody slaver ...'[2]

Emily had made the most of her confined education. Haworth had taught her language, as Prospero taught it

[1] Ch. xvii.                    [2] Ch. vi.

to Caliban, and her profit on't was that she knew how to curse. She had enough knowledge for her purposes, which included this dwelling on horror. Again, there is this incident shared between Catherine, Heathcliff, and Isabella; Catherine is speaking:

'Isabella swears that the love Edgar has for me is nothing to that she entertains for you. I'm sure she made some speech of the kind; did she not, Ellen? And she has fasted ever since the day before yesterday's walk, from sorrow and rage that I despatched her out of your society under the idea of its being unacceptable.'

'I think you belie her,' said Heathcliff, twisting his chair to face them. 'She wishes to be out of my society now, at any rate!'

And he stared hard at the object of discourse, as one might do at a strange repulsive animal: a centipede from the Indies, for instance, which curiosity leads one to examine in spite of the aversion it raises. The poor thing couldn't bear that: she grew white and red in rapid succession, and, while tears beaded her lashes, bent the strength of her small fingers to loosen the firm clutch of Catherine; and perceiving that as fast as she raised one finger off her arm another closed down, and she could not remove the whole together, she began to make use of her nails; and their sharpness presently ornamented the detainer's with crescents of red.[1]

It is possible that even here the personal involvement may be less than we first think. Emily may, like Thackeray, have planned those passages as criticism of the sham and rose-water of contemporary novelists.

Lockwood, at one point, handsomely declares that he could not improve on the English of Nelly Dean's narrative—though he believed (quite unnecessarily on the evidence) that he might condense it a little. That the prose is Emily's own, we have some of the great lines in the

[1] Ch. x.

poems as a reminder. One of its principles is economy. She selects single-mindedly: this is how Nelly acts when she is brought the news of the birth of Hindley's son, 'the last of the ancient Earnshaw stock', and the dangerous state of the mother: '"But is she very ill?" I asked, flinging down my rake and tying my bonnet.'[1] She is neat and concise: 'while I ironed, or pursued other stationary employments'. To be economical among pots and pans may seem easy, but Emily, without gainsaying her principles, can also master complexities of behaviour by what is apparently mere observation:

Catherine frowned, and retreated to the window-seat, chewing her lip, and endeavouring, by humming an eccentric tune, to conceal a growing tendency to sob.

If he [Heathcliff] stirred to touch anything in compliance with my entreaties, if he stretched his hand out to get a piece of bread, his fingers clenched before they reached it, and remained on the table, forgetful of their aim.

Or, with the observer brought into the picture, though unregarded; Lockwood, unseen, watches Cathy standing behind Hareton:

her light shining ringlets blending, at intervals, with his brown locks, as she bent to superintend his studies; and her face—it was lucky he could not see her face, or he would never have been so steady—I could, and I bit my lip, in spite, at having thrown away the chance I might have had, of doing something besides staring at its smiting beauty.

Still unseen, and (unusually) 'feeling very mean and malignant', he 'skulked round' to the kitchen and Nelly Dean.

All these passages come from the closing chapters,[2] when the views and voices of the narrators and those of the author more clearly converge. The scene between the young lovers is also the reader's preparation for the

---

[1] Ch. viii.          [2] Chs. xxxii and xxxiv.

happy ending: when Lockwood sees them again, that same evening, he has heard Nelly's account of Heathcliff's last days and death, and knows of their coming marriage:

the garden gate swung to; the ramblers were returning.

'*They* are afraid of nothing,' I grumbled, watching their approach through the window. 'Together they would brave satan and all his legions.'[1]

Emily Brontë does much with simple means. '*They* are afraid of nothing'; Lockwood, like the reader, is still afraid. Until he stands beside 'the three headstones on the slope next the moor' and brings the novel to its memorable quiet close.

---

[1] Ch. xxvii. Quotations and chapter-references are from the World's Classics edition, the best modern text until the appearance of the novel in the Clarendon Brontë, too late in 1976 to be used here.

# 6.  MRS.  GASKELL

W HEN  G EORGE  E LIOT  read Mrs. Gaskell's *Life of Charlotte Brontë* she found it as 'poetic as one of her own novels'.[1] Those novels provide a special aesthetic experience. Charlotte Brontë said of 'The Moorland Cottage', that it opened like a morning daisy, and in his review of *Wives and Daughters* Henry James was reminded of 'the divine blue of the summer sky'.[2] Those happy images honour subtle Gaskellian things—the naturalness of her writings, or their freedom from any effect of art and artifice, their water-colour airiness, their blitheness and, as it were, 'bonniness', and the gentle progressiveness of the action, whenever Mrs. Gaskell is free to take her own time.

Mrs. Gaskell's fiction is poetical in the gentlest, most loving, particularizing sense, which might be called the 'feminine', a sense suggested by a contrast drawn by Newman in his early essay 'Poetry with Reference to Aristotle's Poetics', in which he equates what is 'especially poetical' with the 'virtues peculiarly Christian'—'meekness, gentleness, compassion, contentment, modesty, not to mention the devotional virtues'—contrasting them with what issues in rhetoric rather than poetry ('anger, indignation, emulation, martial spirit, and love of independence'). Amiability and sweetness flourished in her mind, and the quality George Eliot described as 'charming' is unmatched at the time. As the editor of the *Cornhill* put it in his postscript to the last instalment of *Wives and Daughters* Mrs. Gaskell lived to write: 'few minds showed less of base earth' than hers.

[1] *George Eliot Letters*, II. 319.
[2] *Nation* (1 Mar. 1866); *Notes and Reviews* (1921), p. 154.

After a holiday from Manchester in 1857, she sums up her likings in mock defiance: 'I like a smelling and singing world. Yes I do. I can't help it. I like Kings and Queens, and nightingales and mignonettes and roses. There!'[1]—a list which Ruskin could have subscribed to. And her motto exists in Ruth's words when she goes out nursing the typhus patients: 'Any fastidiousness I shall have to get rid of, and I shall be better without; but any true refinement I am sure I shall find of use . . .'[2] There is much 'true refinement' in Mrs. Gaskell's free and easy genius.

One way in which she differed from Ruskin lay in the strength of her preference for finding beauty in nooks and crannies rather than in Alps and piled clouds. She speaks for herself when, in her introduction to the English edition of *Mabel Vaughan* (1857) she remarks that novels 'unconsciously reveal all the little household secrets; we see the meals that are put on the table, we learn the dresses which those who sat down in them wear . . .' (It is like her humility to preface that remark with 'Of course novels are not one of the highest forms of literature'.) *Mabel Vaughan* was the work of Maria Susanna Cummins, a New Englander, and Mrs. Gaskell always responded warmly to her many American admirers, noting in this very introduction the 'pleasant intercourse that we English are having with our American relations, in the interchange of novels, which seems to be going on pretty constantly between the two countries'. Plainly New England readers would take Mrs. Gaskell to their bosoms—that flourishing country had long since achieved the good sense to cherish the niceties of domestic well-being. It is a love that women are born to or aspire to, and, as the many men know who have a touch of the feminine in them, the happiness the exercise of this gift brings is unending.

[1] *Letters*, ed. J. A. V. Chapple and A. Pollard (1966), p. 492 (letter to Charles Eliot Norton, 7 Dec. 1857, describing her autumn visit to Oxford).
[2] *Ruth*, Ch. xxix.

Not surprisingly, Mrs. Gaskell from early days had loved and imitated the poems of Crabbe, many of which tell homely country stories, and she began her own writing by imitating them in verse and prose. But the quality of her poeticalness rather resembles that of Goldsmith or of a twentieth-century writer, the author of *Lark Rise to Candleford*. Flora Thompson's life, in comparison with Mrs. Gaskell's, was hard, being that of the very poor and the very rural. Mrs. Gaskell's was mainly that of the comfortable Cranfordian and then, after her marriage to William Gaskell, a Unitarian minister in Manchester, that of the comfortably urban. In *Mary Barton* she was to show herself more conscious of the horrors of Manchester than of its comforts, but those comforts formed the ground from which the horrors were seen—it is to a middle-class audience that that timely book was expressly offered. Outside *Mary Barton* and *North and South* Mrs. Gaskell found much of her subject-matter in something near the Flora Thompson milieu, to which the title of that juvenile poem—'Sketches among the Poor'—pointed the way. When she proposed to follow Crabbe, she added that she would do so 'in a more seeing-beauty spirit'.[1] As far as opportunities could be come by in her stories, she saw and sketched beauty. She saw and sketched as much of it as possible even in the Manchester of *Mary Barton*, though it was the point of that novel to show the mill-workers existing day and night in filth—filth that she particularizes without blinking: 'As they passed, women from their doors tossed household slops of *every* description into the gutter'; in the Davenports' cellar-dwelling 'the smell was so foetid as almost to knock the two men down'.[2] Nevertheless, it is a prime article in her reading of man that he prefers to make the most of what is clean and healthful in his hard-won civilization. And so the first chapter of *Mary Barton* is not about the infamous civil-

[1] *Letters*, p. 33.
[2] Ch. vi.

ization of the meanest streets but about the wholesome civilization of trim fields:

There are some fields near Manchester, well known to the inhabitants as 'Green Heys Fields,' through which runs a public footpath to a little village about two miles distant. In spite of these fields being flat, and low, nay, in spite of the want of wood (the great and usual recommendation of level tracks of land), there is a charm about them which strikes even the inhabitant of a mountainous district, who sees and feels the effect of contrast in these common-place but thoroughly rural fields, with the busy, bustling manufacturing town he left but half an hour ago. Here and there an old black and white farm-house, with its rambling outbuildings, speaks of other times and other occupations than those which now absorb the population of the neighbourhood. Here in their seasons may be seen the country business of haymaking, ploughing, &c., which are such pleasant mysteries for townspeople to watch; and here the artisan, deafened with noise of tongues and engines, may come to listen awhile to the delicious sounds of rural life: the lowing of cattle, the milkmaid's call, the clatter and cackle of poultry in the old farm-yards.

Even Manchester had its pastoralities, as Birmingham people for Newman had their souls. Her writings are accordingly the climax of the homely-aesthetic as well as being, like George Eliot's, climaxes of the homely-moral. Mrs. Gaskell would have had something amiable to say about a chimney-sweep or a dunghill. The milking of a cow is made as pleasant a chore as picking flowers, given the senses of a Mrs. Gaskell, who can light on clauses like 'a capricious cow ... letting her fragrant burden flow' (with its rekindling of the almost obsolete 'poetic diction'), and 'the milky down-pour came musical and even from the stall next to Black Nell'. Those descriptions, predecessors of Hardy's in *Tess*, come from *Sylvia's Lovers*, which in its quiet parts is the masterpiece in the pastoral line—many rungs further down the social ladder than *Cranford*. With unimportant exceptions everybody in *Sylvia's Lovers* speaks dialect, and Sylvia has the honour of being the first dialect-speaking heroine in English, as distinct from Scots: nor does she aspire to leave her class, as Hetty Sorrel did. In dialect speech, as Burns, Scott, and Barnes knew, there is more poetry than in town speech, the speakers of it being free to be as creative, up to the limit of their powers, as Shakespeare. One of the inducements to write *Sylvia's Lovers* must have been its opportunities of this sort, and it now seems a pity that fifteen years earlier she evidently felt that she could not give dialect speech to Mary Barton, though she gave a mild version of it—milder than that in *Sylvia's Lovers*—to all her associates. As we have seen, two years after *Mary Barton* Charlotte Brontë thought it advisable to tone down the dialect when republishing *Wuthering Heights*, in the hope of winning more readers.

As well as the beauty of rural speech there is in all the novels, as far as may be, the beauty of scene. The Monkshaven of *Sylvia's Lovers* is Whitby, and about it are cliffs and sea, and 'Haysterbank Gulley opening down its green entrance among the warm brown bases of the cliffs'. And there is the beauty of common things in farmhouse and shop, things ranging from Victoria and Albert exhibits to the homeliest pots and pans:

At the Corneys', the united efforts of some former generations of the family had produced patchwork curtains and coverlet; and patchwork was patchwork in those days, before the early Yates and Peels[1] had found out the secret of printing and parsley-leaf. Scraps of costly Indian chintzes and palempours were intermixed with commoner black and red calico in minute hexagons; and the variety of patterns served for the usual purpose of promoting conversation as well as the more obvious one of displaying the work-woman's taste. Sylvia, for instance, began at once to her old friend, Molly Brunton, who had accompanied her into this chamber to take off her hat and

[1] Robert Peel of Accrington invented printing on calico in the mid-eighteenth century, and his first pattern was a 'parsley sprig'. William Yates was an eminent follower of his.

cloak, with a remark on one of the chintzes. Stooping over the counterpane ... she said to Molly,

'Dear! I never seed this one afore—this—for all the world like the eyes in a peacock's tail.'[1]

Indeed in that phrase 'seeing-beauty spirit' there was a touch of defiance, of showing the worth of what was usually ignored. Mr. Benson in *Ruth* takes a conscious pleasure of an aesthetic sort when reduced to shrunken finances:

The little re-arrangements of the household expenditure had not touched him as they had done the women. He was aware that meat-dinners were not now every-day occurrences; but he preferred puddings and vegetables, and was glad of the exchange. He observed, too, that they all sat together in the kitchen in the evenings; but the kitchen, with the well-scoured dresser, the shining saucepans, the well-blacked grate, and whitened hearth, and the warmth which seemed to rise up from the very flags, and ruddily cheer the most distant corners, appeared a very cozy and charming sitting-room.[2]

And this is what awaited a Dissenting congregation as well as a sermon in their little meeting-house: 'The walls were white-washed, and were recipients of the shadows of the beauty without; on their "white plains" the tracery of the ivy might be seen, now still, now stirred by the sudden flight of some little bird.'[3] What becomes of the Puritan provision against the beautiful when a Mrs. Gaskell can find it, as Vermeer and Utrillo could, on the whitewashed walls of a conventicle? It is because of Mrs. Gaskell's habitual cherishing of whatever offered that she can make do with less literary grandeur than Dickens or Charlotte Brontë. Occasionally she feels that the narration demands a set piece of description—of Monkshaven, for instance—and then we get something which for her is conscientious and plodding. When free to sketch, however, as for most of the time she is, we get the

[1] Ch. xii.    [2] Ch. xxix.
[3] Ch. xiv.

best from her, and the soul of a sketch is economy. By instinct she prefers economy to clutter.

This economy of hers, unlike that of, say, Landor, carries with it no scent of art. It is plain that art must be much used by any writer, but either Mrs. Gaskell used as little as possible or devoted a great deal of it to making her writings seem not only artless but careless. Her grammar is sometimes that of hasty speech; and she will sometimes interpose a remark like 'as I may have said before', just as if she was talking to us as she swayed about dreamily in a rocking-chair. 'I told the story [*Mary Barton*] according to a fancy of my own; to really SEE the scenes I tried to describe . . . and thus to tell them as nearly as I could, as if I were speaking to a friend over the fire on a winter's night.'[1] The reader is more alert than she—he *knows* she is repeating herself. The title she gave to one strung-together collection of stories, *Round the Sofa*, witnesses to what Newman would call her 'undress' manner. Whether artful or not, this manner coexists with her sweetness and elegance, and contributes to her feminine charm, on which float the habitually precise and concise phrases of description. Her economy is as plainly applied to people as to things: 'It was the longest sentence he [Sylvia's father] said that day'.[2] The point about economy is that it suggests the whole from which the representative has been selected.

This power is most congenially employed in her nouvelles. Along with Thackeray she is the true inventor of this important form, the form which asks no more persons or events than a short story but records them at something like the pace of a novelist. The finest is 'Cousin Phillis', which is a story of hopes raised and then left to wither. The most ambitious is 'Lois the Witch', which treats a New England theme of great power—we

1 *Letters*, p. 82.                    2 Ch. xii.

are made eye-witnesses of the hundred steps by which an innocent girl comes to be hounded as a witch. The psychology of mob persecution is laid bare. We recognize hideous superstition as understandable, seeing how a community can share a single, partly sexual character and be dominated by a 'fixed idea' (Mrs. Gaskell borrows Carlyle's term) and how communal imagination can supply itself with evidence for its mistaken purposes. Another of the nouvelles, 'The Crooked Branch', which may be said to retell Wordsworth's 'Michael' with additions, does something rare in its time. In the course of the last tragic pages it quietly indicates an event beyond the ending, suggesting that after the scene at the trial and Mrs. Huntroyd's paralysis and death, and perhaps not until after the death of old Mr. Huntroyd, his niece Bessy, who is now nearing 30, and was to have married the prodigal son, will marry John Kirkby, the 'hard featured, short-spoken' bachelor neighbour in his forties. The very last words of the story descend like a benediction, as do the last words of 'Michael': 'But the broken-hearted go Home, to be comforted of God.'

Among other things these nouvelles make us accept nobility as possible for a human being, a feat which a Scott could achieve, but not so many of the novelists of the 'noble school of fiction'. Calamity has sovereign power only over externals for the saints Mrs. Gaskell places in her stories. Shattered and tortured, even killed, they may be, but they endure with the inner resources of martyrs. Lois, Ellinor in 'A Dark Night's Work', Maggie—and also the invalid Mrs. Buxton—in 'The Moorland Cottage' retain something like peace. For the entering into that sort of matter Mrs. Gaskell has no rival.

In these nouvelles, more consistently than in some of the novels, we experience that felicity of novel-readers—the sense that even amid the 'sensational' we are witnessing the probable. When the Mortons of Morton Hall are brought low, and one of the survivors dies of proud starvation in a tumble-down cottage, the narrator (a former tenant gifted with Mrs. Gaskell's power of sad weighty detail) comments: 'We should not have dared to think that such a thing was within the chances of life'. But Mrs. Gaskell does not herself believe in more chances than she needs to. The poverty of the Mortons is due to the extravagance of the heir. For Mrs. Gaskell, as for 'truthful' novelists, many chances are ascribable to human agency. When they are not, when chance strikes from the skies, it can still satisfy the reader as probable, provided it does not happen too often, or too plainly help the story out of a fix. Stories, it is plain, are all the better for getting themselves into a fix, and sound sense lay behind the mid-nineteenth-century insistence on elaboration of plot. The provisos, however, were equally to be insisted on—that the elaboration should not be excessive, and that it should proceed in accordance with what in *The City of Dreadful Night* Thomson called 'life's laws'. The provisos against excess and improbability were much flouted in that age, especially by the 'Sensation Novelists', who put the sensational first. In these very nouvelles comes an instance of such a preference. The climax of 'The Moorland Cottage' is both thrilling and probable—Maggie is being asked to renounce her engagement with Frank because Frank is being urged by his father to marry 'well', such a renunciation carrying with it the hushing-up of the crime of Maggie's brother Edward, who has cheated Frank's father by a forgery. On this something equally powerful and inevitable follows—that when Maggie, who refuses to renounce the engagement, offers to accompany Edward on his connived flight to America, her lover joins the boat incognito so as to look after her. How smoothly Mrs. Gaskell, using her wits, could have reached the end she has in view—the reconciliation of Maggie, Frank, and his father. Instead she invokes sensation—as if we had not had enough of it already! She has the boat catch fire and drowns the brother. That supererogatory horror spoils what would otherwise have been a superb nouvelle.

What then of the novels? We do not understand Mrs. Gaskell unless we see her drawn to the sensational as by a fascination. She had all the virtues as a writer that Newman held to be both 'peculiarly Christian' and 'especially poetical', and in addition all those other characteristics he contrasted with them,[1] though these were perhaps acquisitions rather than gifts at birth. To her love of the exquisite she added a love of devilry. Wordsworth, some of whose choicest gifts she shared, had consciously avoided going outside the field in which he was sure he had authority—'The moving accident is not my trade; / To freeze the blood I have no ready arts'. Mrs. Gaskell also lacked some of those arts, but was not so content with the deprivation. She darkly enjoyed making a grab at them, a splendid daring that cost her more than one masterpiece. She wanted to do more than interest and move her reader, however closely, however profoundly. She wanted to thrill him as—for example—Dickens had done in *Oliver Twist*, Thackeray in *Barry Lyndon*, and Trollope in *The Macdermots of Ballycloran*. The idea that the novel was a complication of the comic was giving way to the idea that it was a complication of the thrilling. How well Mrs. Gaskell grasped what was expected of a novelist is attested by the letter she sent in 1859 to Herbert Grey:

You say you do not call The Three paths a novel; but the work is in the form which always assumes that name, nor do I think it is one to be quarrelled with. I suppose you mean that you used the narrative form merely to introduce certain opinions and thoughts. If so you had better have condensed them into the shape of an Essay.

[1] See p. 226.

But if he does wish to 'narrate', then:

I think you must observe what is *out* of you, instead of examining what is *in* you ... we ought not to be too cognizant of our mental proceedings, only taking note of the results ... Just read a few pages of De Foe &c and you will see the healthy way in which he sets *objects* not *feelings* before you. ... every day your life brings you into contact with live men & women,—of whom yr reader knows nothing ... Think if you cannot imagine a complication of events in their life which would form a good plot. Your plot in The Three paths is very poor; you have not thought enough about it,—simply used it as a medium. The plot must grow, and culminate in a crisis; not a character must be introduced who does not conduce to this growth & progress of events. The plot is like the anatomical drawing of an artist; he must have an idea of his skeleton, before he can clothe it with muscle & flesh, much more before he can drape it. Study hard at your plot. I have been told that those early Italian Tales from which Shakespeare took so many of his stories are models of plots,—a regular storehouse. See how they—how the great tragedies of all time,—how the grandest narrations of all languages are worked together,— and really make this sketch of your story a subject of labour and thought. Then set to and imagine yourself a spectator & auditor of every scene & event! Work hard at this till it become a reality to you,—a thing you have to recollect & describe & report fully & accurately as it struck you, in order that your reader may have it equally before him. Don't intrude yourself into your description. If you but think eagerly of your story till *you see it in action*, words, good simple strong words, will come,—just as if you saw an accident in the street that impressed you strongly you would describe it forcibly.[1]

Her idea of the novel, we note, has its place for the sensational—she speaks of Cinthio's Italian tales, and the 'great tragedies of all times' and an 'accident in the street'. That place, however, is wholly legitimate because she sees the need to make the novel grow into shape in

---

[1] *Letters*, pp. 541–2; the text is a draft, here slightly emended. Grey's novel was published in 1859.

accordance with 'life's laws'. Unfortunately she did not always heed her own advice. Even in a nouvelle she exceeded the allowable amount of 'sensation', and in constructing *Sylvia's Lovers* as she did spoilt a masterpiece on the big scale. She spoilt it with her eyes open—she always had her wits about her even when fatally driven on the rocks.

The construction of some of her novels is wholly right: even that of *Cranford*. The history of the making of that work resembled, in essentials, the history of *Pickwick Papers* by beginning as detached sketches and achieving as it proceeded a plot (or what would now be called such), Dickens having asked for more of it than had appeared in *Household Words*. Like *Pickwick*, it started and continued unambitiously as to structural complications. To its great advantage, *Cranford* does find room for the 'sensational', in the episode of Peter's flight and return. Then there is her last, almost completed novel, *Wives and Daughters*, about which Gerard Manley Hopkins exclaimed 'if that is not a good book I do not know what a good book is'.[1] It is a long leisurely novel, its scale admitting the ample exercise of a personage, (Cynthia Kirkpatrick), whose character is as complex as anybody's in our literature—Mrs. Gaskell excels in the creation of complex characters—and has everything that is good except depth and moral integrity.

Nor is there anything to complain about in *Mary Barton*, which Mrs. Gaskell described as meeting her 'idea of a tragic poem'[2]—words that suggest moods of hers when the novel form did not seem necessarily inferior to the highest. More than in *Cranford* and even *Wives and Daughters*, she was now up against the demands of a complicated plot. Its complexities, however, are contrived in a way the reader freely grants to be likely, achieving a cat's-cradle climax that painfully relates the heroine to all three important male personages. Young

[1] *Letters to Robert Bridges*, p. 251.  [2] *Letters*, pp. 68, 70.

Henry Carson, the mill-owner's son, has been dazzling
Mary with his attentions, but is murdered by her father,
John Barton, who has been conscripted to the deed by his
desperate fellow trade-unionists. The man accused of the
murder, however, is Jem Wilson, her honourable lover,
whom she was coming to favour. To have engineered
that fix for Mary by firm steps was to be a successful if
eager maker of plots. Nor is *Ruth* far from being wholly
satisfactory. Its only structural defect is the five years' gap
which Mrs. Gaskell could have filled so beautifully with
the *process* of Ruth's education The ending is soundly
conceived. Ruth dies. She has not succumbed to the fever
infection while she spent the weeks of nursing in the
hospital, but she has been exhausted by the experience,
physically and mentally. This Mrs. Gaskell thoroughly
shows—the household at Mr. Benson's are intent on
nursing her, making her rest and be quiet. It is then that
she hears of the illness of Mr. Bellingham (now Mr.
Donne), her seducer. In spite of all warning she goes to
nurse him and catches the fever from him and dies. All
this is made to seem inevitable. It is in character because
the unselfish Ruth is still in love with Bellingham. After
the terrific interview on the sands when she refuses to
marry him, and rushes away up the cliff-side to safety,
she cannot resist the impulse to look out over the sands to
see the retreating figure, in vain: and her look is a look of
love. The plot then garners in the subsidiary advantages
of Ruth's death. That death throws a clear light on Bellingham's character. Mr. Benson takes him upstairs to see
the body—Bellingham thinks he is going up into the
drawing-room, which he expects to be more comfortable
than the study. The experience essentially means nothing
to him and he chatters away about finding provision for
the boy. This Mr. Benson rejects with the quiet scorn of
the good man; there are some insults that the best men
cannot brook.

And what is all to the good is that the links in the chain

of events sometimes look frail as cobweb: when the attractive Bellingham takes Ruth to the inn just before the fatal step, she would have escaped him, but she had no money on her to pay her part of the bill for tea, and the landlord was standing in the doorway—'all dilemmas appeared of equal magnitude to her'.

Nor is there anything questionably false in the course of *North and South*, which achieves the bringing-together of the southerner Margaret Hale and John Thornton, the stubborn northern mill-master much in need of humanizing. At one late point Margaret looks back on a year of her life:

'. . . But I am very miserable! Oh, how unhappy this last year has been! I have passed out of childhood into old age. I have had no youth—no womanhood; the hopes of womanhood have closed for me—for I shall never marry; and I anticipate cares and sorrows just as if I were an old woman, and with the same fearful spirit. I am weary of this continual call upon me for strength. I could bear up for papa; because that is a natural, pious duty. And I think I could bear up against—at any rate, I could have the energy to resent, Mrs. Thornton's unjust, impertinent suspicions. But it is hard to feel how completely he must misunderstand me. What has happened to make me so morbid to-day? I do not know. I only know I cannot help it. I must give way sometimes. No, I will not, though,' said she, springing to her feet. 'I will not—I *will* not think of myself and my own position. I won't examine into my own feelings. It would be of no use now. Some time, if I live to be an old woman, I may sit over the fire, and, looking into the embers, see the life that might have been.'

That year had been sensational enough—worst of all, she had had her brother, whom she was shielding from justice, mistaken for a lover by the man she loves. Yet the sensations had been found plausible by the reader.

It is in *Sylvia's Lovers* that there is elaboration for the sake of piling on the sensational illegitimately. We are presented with two coincidences, one crucial. The first we grant without strain: Philip Hepburn, the good, steady, undervalued suitor, happens to be the only person to see his rival Kinraid carried off on the sea-shore by the ambushed press-gang, and therefore is free to concur in the universal assumption that he has been drowned, and so reap the advantage of marrying Sylvia. The second we cannot grant, nor is it vital to the story. After years have passed, Philip and Kinraid are brought together on the battlefield, when Philip saves Kinraid's life, with resulting complications. Would it not have been simpler to have let Kinraid return by more probable means? All that the saving of his life contributes to character is that to Philip's already sufficient virtues it adds that of heroism. The effect it produces could have been produced by other means, the sort which Mrs. Gaskell uses so beautifully. By other means she could have enabled Philip to win back the respect and love of his wife, and made her ashamed of the curse which, when Kinraid turned up alive, she laid on him, especially as she is now disillusioned over Kinraid's lack of heroic passion for her— he marries an heiress too soon after his discovery that Sylvia is bound to Philip. If Mrs. Gaskell had desperately wanted to endow Philip with physical heroism, she could have waited for the act by which he meets his death—the rescue of his little daughter from the rising tide.

As with all great writers, however, their deficiencies are knitted in with their greatness, which may even be enhanced by means of them. However much we deplore some of Mrs. Gaskell's contrivances, it does make a difference when she is found not only providing them for the sake of excitement but in order to face up to their effects on the characters; it further increases the difference when the coincidences and revelations are not engineered at the expense of their consistency. In the sensation novels of Wilkie Collins, let alone those of the multitude of his inferiors, the novelist is satisfied by providing excitement; Mrs. Gaskell, on the other hand, almost seems to favour contrivances because she can rise to face what follows from them, and to face it with a queenly power.

Whatever may sometimes go wrong in her handling of action, nothing goes wrong in her handling of people. Each person she has to dwell on is, to quote *Sylvia's Lovers*, a 'living, breathing, warm human creature', and each person who makes only a momentary appearance is nicely hit off as Dickens himself would have done it. All the persons she dwells on she finds complex as an opal, so that we scarcely can determine the predominant colour. Mary Barton is summarized as 'the same sweet, faulty, impulsive, lovable creature she [Margaret] had known in the former Mary Barton, but with more of dignity, self-reliance, and purpose'; and Cynthia Kirkpatrick has everything good about her except her shallowness and her lack of integrity and power to love. One of Mrs. Gaskell's favourite epithets is 'deep', and because of its context in her sentences the word loses the tinniness familiar in such cant phrases as 'deeply religious'. She can tell us much about the depths of personality and character in spite of her belief that 'we ought not to be too cognizant of our mental proceedings'. She does speak in *Mary Barton* of analysis: at first, Mary's grief after she has rejected Jem 'was too sudden for her to analyse'; presently, 'it was as if two people were arguing the matter'.[1] But she seems to achieve her own knowledge rather by the means of intuition. As an instance of her hold on psychology, take the account of the party on Old Year's Night at the Corneys'.[2] She shows here as elsewhere that the feelings of the common herd are as opalescent, fine, and changing as those of the high-born heroines of George Sand. Sylvia is in love with the brilliant Kinraid—who is 'not unaccustomed', we learn later, 'to women'—but is deeply loved by the staid Philip. Her

[1] Ch. xi.  [2] *Sylvia's Lovers*, Ch. xii.

own feelings are complex, but not for a moment obscure, whether Mrs. Gaskell describes them by a deft series of touches or whether they shine behind her acts. A climax comes when a 'forfeit'—plainly of sexual significance—is claimed of Sylvia who has had the ribbon Philip gave her snatched from her. The forfeit is to 'kiss the candle-stick'—that is, the man who has been the first to grab a candle and hold it as its candlestick. Sylvia cannot face the kiss, and is disgraced. At this 'Philip's spirits rose'. He did not see that her inability to give Kinraid a light kiss is just because of her love for him. In the equally weighty chapter that follows, 'Perplexities', Philip is eager to take courage from seeing Kinraid merry with the Corney girls, assuming from this that he does not love Sylvia. He makes the error of judging Kinraid by himself. Kinraid's merriment, had he known it, is because of 'a secret triumph in his heart', a triumph that he had felt at the party—he is secure of Sylvia's love. Another instance: a girl notices that the inconvenience of rain is spoken of in reference to others not to her, and so feels a 'cold shadow pass[ing] over her heart', knowing that the speaker loves another.[1] These evince the sort of depth Mrs. Gaskell searches out. Most events in the novels are 'small events', as she puts it, but not to those they concern. She makes discoveries in human nature, or, if that is too much to credit anybody with, is the first writer to put them into literature. A girl like Esther, who has become a prostitute, cannot accept the helping hand offered by Jem Wilson, Mary Barton's lover: '"If you will know all," said she, as he still seemed inclined to urge her, "I must have drink"'.[2] Or we learn that 'a mother only gives up her son's heart inch by inch to his wife, and then she gives it up with a grudge',[3] or that a manly fellow like Jem Wilson is only manly on balance:

[1] Ibid., Ch. xxv.
[2] *Mary Barton,* Ch. xiv.
[3] Ibid., Ch. xxxiii.

Mrs. Gaskell 243

He had been absent and abstracted all day long with the thought of the coming event of the evening. He almost smiled at himself for his care in washing and dressing in preparation for his visit to Mary; as if one waistcoat or another could decide his fate in so passionately a momentous thing. He believed he only delayed before his little looking-glass for cowardice, for absolute fear of a girl. He would try not to think so much about the affair, and he thought the more.[1]

Or, to descend to those minutiae we all welcome because they exist in ourselves unnoticed: 'Jem was pondering Mary's conduct; but the pause made him aware he ought to utter some civil listening noise; so he said, "Very true"':[2] or, again: 'Mrs. Kirkpatrick was rather weary of girls as a class'.[3] (That remark implies the whole of Mrs. Kirkpatrick as a person.) Mrs. Gaskell sees it as a primary human error that we assume others to be like ourselves, and judge things by the same scales on which we judge ourselves. She sees how precarious is our boasted 'niceness'. It may not have needed the Manchester of the Hungry Forties to show her this, but it helped to make the knowledge strike deep. She shows how being 'out of work', with all that that meant, transforms, while it lasts, John Barton:

Then came a long period of bodily privation; of daily hunger after food; and though he tried to persuade himself he could bear want himself with stoical indifference, and did care about it as little as most men, yet the body took its revenge for its uneasy feelings. The mind became soured and morose, and lost much of its equipoise. It was no longer elastic, as in the days of youth, or in times of comparative happiness; it ceased to hope. And it is hard to live on when one can no longer hope.

The same state of feeling which John Barton entertained, if belonging to one who had had leisure to think of such things, and physicians to give names to them, would have been called monomania; so haunting, so incessant, were the thoughts that pressed upon him.[4]

[1] Ch. xi.　　　　　　　　　　[2] Ch. viii.
[3] *Wives and Daughters*, Ch. xi.　　[4] *Mary Barton*, Ch. xv.

In his new state he seems two fathers to Mary: when her sweetheart Jem is wondering whether or not he should inform him of Mary's illness,

> It was true that he was Mary's father, and as such had every right to be told of all concerning her; but supposing he were, and that he followed the impulse so natural to a father, and wished to go to her, what might be the consequences? Among the mingled feelings she had revealed in her delirium, ay, mingled even with the most tender expressions of love for her father, was a sort of horror of him; a dread of him as a blood-shedder, which seemed to separate him into two persons,—one, the father who had dandled her on his knee, and loved her all her life long; the other, the assassin, the cause of all her trouble and woe.
>
> If he presented himself before her while this idea of his character was uppermost, who might tell the consequence?[1]

Mrs. Gaskell sees the part played by mere physique in the assertion of personal superiority, in this instance between the brother and sister, Thurstan and Faith Benson; Faith has suggested that it would be better if Ruth were to die in her confinement:

> 'Faith!'
> That one word put them right. It was spoken in the tone which had authority over her; it was so full of grieved surprise and mournful upbraiding. She was accustomed to exercise a sway over him, owing to her greater decision of character; and, probably, if everything were traced to its cause, to her superior vigour of constitution; but at times she was humbled before his pure, child-like nature, and felt where she was inferior. She was too good and true to conceal this feeling, or to resent its being forced upon her. After a time she said,—
> 'Thurstan, dear, let us go to her.'
> She helped him with tender care, and gave him her arm up the long and tedious hill; but when they approached the village, without speaking a word on the subject, they changed their position, and she leant (apparently) on him.[2]

[1] Ch. xxxiii.
[2] *Ruth*, Ch. xi.

To which I add a later exchange between the two: Miss Benson says:

'You look tired and weary dear. You should blame your body rather than your conscience at these times.'
'A very dangerous doctrine.'[1]

Dangerous, yes; but impelling belief. Mrs. Gaskell, more than most of us, sees, as a practical thing, that circumstances alter cases, and from some things she lets drop, one might conclude *all* cases. In *Sylvia's Lovers* she can see just why Quakers countenance smugglers in Monkshaven, and 'drinking was hardly a sin against morals, in those days, and in that place'.[2]

She seems to feel with great sadness that if only we could each live in solitude all might be well, our happiness depending too much on others for it to be safe. A loving nature meets with deception or rebuff, and sometimes wastes painful years before it can find its mate. The 'tears of things' are everywhere. What are we to think when we come upon the conclusion of this piece of commonplace dialogue between Sylvia and Philip about their child, whose birth has brought her the first happiness since her marriage:

'Philip,' said Sylvia, one night, as he sate as still as a mouse in her room, imagining her to be asleep. He was by her bed-side in a moment.

'I've been thinking what she's to be called. Isabella, after mother; and what were yo'r mother's name?'

'Margaret,' said he.

'Margaret Isabella; Isabella Margaret. Mother's called Bell. She might be called Bella.'

'I could ha' wished her to be called after thee.'

She made a little impatient movement.

'Nay; Sylvia's not a lucky name. Best be called after thy mother and mine. And I want for to ask Hester to be god-mother.'

[1] Ch. xviii.
[2] Ch. xi.

'Anything thou likes, sweetheart. Shall we call her Rose, after Hester Rose?'

'No, no!' said Sylvia, 'she must be called after my mother or thine, or both. I should like her to be called Bella, after mother, because she's so fond of baby.'

'Anything to please thee, darling.'

'Don't say that as if it didn't signify; there's a deal in having a pretty name,' said Sylvia, a little annoyed. 'I ha' allays hated being called Sylvia. It were after father's mother, Sylvia Steele.'

'I niver thought any name in a' the world so sweet and pretty as Sylvia,' said Philip, fondly; but she was too much absorbed in her own thoughts to notice either his manner or his words.

'There, you'll not mind if it is Bella, because you' see my mother is alive to be pleased by its being named after her, and Hester may be godmother, and I'll ha' t' dove-coloured silk as yo' gave me afore we were married made up into a cloak for it to go to church in.'

'I got it for thee,' said Philip, a little disappointed. 'It will be too good for the baby.'

'Eh! but I'm so careless, I should be spilling something on it! But if thou got it for me I cannot find i' my heart for t'wear it on baby, and I'll have it made into a christening-gown for mysel'. But I'll niver feel at my ease in it, for fear o' spoiling it.'

'Well! an' if thou does spoil it, love, I'll get thee another. I make account of riches only for thee; that I may be able to get thee whativer thou's a fancy for, for either thysel', or thy mother.'

She lifted her pale face from her pillow, and put up her lips to kiss him for these words.

Perhaps on that day Philip reached the zenith of his life's happiness.[1]

Is not such a power the one thing needful for a great teller of stories?

A further distinction of hers is that, like Emily and Charlotte Brontë, she can show us what human love is when at what most of us honour as its best, however unattainable inferior human beings find it—the love that

[1] End of Ch. xxx, 'Happy Days'.

has no obvious sex in it, and the sexual love that has no lust in it. Mrs. Gaskell has much of the 'heavenly' in her. She is so good herself that we feel she underrates the bad in others. She is always ready to seize on the good, however small the quantity, being a sort of God out to seek for and value all the good discoverable. She invokes God, her simple version of Him, often. Mr. Benson in *Ruth* is a Christian she admires:

In the Bensons' house there was the same unconsciousness of individual merit, the same absence of introspection and analysis of motive, as there had been in her mother; but it seemed that their lives were pure and good, not merely from a lovely and beautiful nature, but from some law, the obedience to which was, of itself, harmonious peace, and which governed them almost implicitly, and with as little questioning on their part, as the glorious stars which haste not, rest not, in their eternal obedience. This household had many failings: they were but human, and, with all their loving desire to bring their lives into harmony with the will of God, they often erred and fell short; but, somehow, the very errors and faults of one individual served to call out higher excellencies in another, and so they re-acted upon each other, and the result of short discords was exceeding harmony and peace. But they had themselves no idea of the real state of things; they did not trouble themselves with marking their progress by self-examination; if Mr. Benson did sometimes, in hours of sick incapacity for exertion, turn inwards, it was to cry aloud with almost morbid despair, 'God be merciful to me a sinner!' But he strove to leave his life in the hands of God, and to forget himself.[1]

More characteristic of the common people is Job Legh in *Mary Barton* who finds God a friend, but only a friend in need: '"Well, Mary! I'll give you my prayers," said Job. "It's not often I pray regular, though I often speak a word to God, when I'm either very happy, or very sorry; I've catched myself thanking him at odd hours when I've found a rare insect, or had a fine day for an out; but I

[1] Ch. xiii.

cannot help it, no more than I can talking to a friend."[1] God is an 'abyss of mercies', as for Sir Thomas Browne, the Deity of the superstitious common people. It was this indispensable but only occasional relation that people like Newman were damaging with their talk about dogma. George Eliot said her own books scourged her. The scourge is heavier still in Mrs. Gaskell's. Her stories shame us.


Mrs. Gaskell exploited her femininity, for which we are grateful. But she felt that her novels had to enter the man's world, not only as it is a violent world, but as it is a business world and a world facing unusually acute political problems, and where because of the 'laicism' and 'liberalism' deplored by Newman there was need of sage counsel, counsel to help people deal with 'conduct' which Matthew Arnold was to rank as three-fourths of life.

She faced this man's world with her first novel, the novel which partly because of this achievement made her promptly famous. Her entry into that world would have been more emphatic if her publishers had allowed her to retain the title she first favoured—*John Barton*. For Mary, who has all Mrs. Gaskell's 'charm' and goodness, rather suffers than helps to bring about the climax of the story. Its being a man's world is attested by the male controversies it started. It makes a plea for the sort of Carlylean knowledge that comes in at the eyes—knowledge of how the life visibly being endured in Manchester felt to those enduring it, and so for sympathy. And her plea seemed beside the point to those whose eyes conned books of political economy and who talked the new language of those books, and put their faith in *laissez-faire*. Mrs. Gaskell took her readers out of the textbooks into life. She had felt the effects of *laissez-faire* with all a

[1] Ch. xxiii.

woman's feelings, as had Carlyle,[1] who therefore saw the importance of *Mary Barton* as furthering the work he held so dear. Of much later testimony to the same effect I single out that of F. D. Maurice in his lecture of 1865:

There are some admirable writers, female writers especially, who have supplied our best antidote to such morbid excitements ['Sensation Novels']. They have lifted the veil which conceals from us the struggles and sufferings of those whom we are meeting every day; they have shown us something of the hearts of those whom we only knew by their want of the good things upon which we pride ourselves. There is nothing sensational in such revelations; but they may be more terrific, and more cheering, than all fantastic enormities ever were. One such writer has just gone from us, and will be long remembered by those who know that her Mary Bartons and her Libbie Marshes describe what she knew, and express inward, not fictitious, sympathies. I am sure she rejoiced once, and must still rejoice, that she made a few persons understand better the condition of a great English town—forgive the offences and sins, and honour the manliness and womanliness, of those who toil and groan in it; and that she was never tempted to seek a temporary and mischievous reputation by catering to the appetites of any of her sex or ours who prefer sentiment to humanity, falsehood to truth.[2]

This meant that in *Mary Barton* Mrs. Gaskell had achieved a true purpose novel. Of the many such novels during this period few are so splendidly a novel as well. Mrs. Gaskell was so constituted that she could not possibly forget that the only vital 'purpose' for a novelist is that of showing the interest of a chain of human events. The events of *Mary Barton*, like the human arguments of Carlyle's *Past and Present*, appealed to the reader as a

[1] Letter of 8 Nov. 1848 (quoted by A. B. Hopkins, *Elizabeth Gaskell*, 1952, and elsewhere). He called the novel, whose feminine authorship he at once recognized, 'a real contribution (about the first real one) toward developing a huge subject, which has lain dumb too long'. When harassed by the controversies about it, she said, 'Mr Carlyle's letter remains my real true gain' (*Letters*, p. 68).

[2] *The Friendship of Books, and other lectures*, ed. T. Hughes (1874), p. 90.

human being. What had been the preserve of the political economist was peopled as Carlyle had peopled it—she refers to him more than once in the novel—with 'living, breathing, warm human creatures'. She is herself surprised at her temerity, and when her story erupts into authorial discussion admits that she cannot use the right 'technical terms'. Her passages of argument are what anyone would expect who has read up to the point at which they break out. She pleads on behalf of the workers for the reason that would have been Swift's, and which had been Carlyle's—that they are inevitably reverting to animalism, which cannot be right in England in the nineteenth century. She admits that the 'condition-of-England question', the terrible contrasts between wealth and poverty, is now 'the mysterious problem of life', but it is not too mysterious to become so much less of a problem if food can be guaranteed to the workers. Like Carlyle she sees the power-looms as the gifts of God, but like him again sees also that life is another of His gifts, and that it is being denied the workers. Astonishingly, some of these workers are, or were, learned men:

In the neighbourhood of Oldham there are weavers, common handloom weavers, who throw the shuttle with unceasing sound, though Newton's 'Principia' lies open on the loom, to be snatched at in work hours, but revelled over in meal times, or at night. Mathematical problems are received with interest, and studied with absorbing attention by many a broad-spoken, common-looking factory-hand. It is perhaps less astonishing that the more popularly interesting branches of natural history have their warm and devoted followers among this class. There are botanists among them, equally familiar with either the Linnaean or the Natural system, who know the name and habitat of every plant within a day's walk from their dwellings; who steal the holiday of a day or two when any particular plant should be in flower, and tying up their simple food in their pocket handkerchiefs, set off with single purpose to fetch home the humble-looking weed. There are entomologists, who may be seen with a rude-looking net, ready to catch any winged insect, or a kind of dredge, with which they rake the green and slimy pools; practical, shrewd, hard-working men who pore over every new specimen with real scientific delight.[1]

Intellect, however, is neither here nor there since the mindless also suffer hunger. The two nations must be one at heart simply because they are one at belly. *Mary Barton* therefore is more than a novel, as *Gulliver's Travels* is more than an account of adventures. And yet, just as Disraeli discovered politics to be excellent material for part of a novel otherwise containing much falsity—a discovery that led Trollope and Meredith to build masterpieces out of it—so Mrs. Gaskell discovered in the condition-of-England question the material for great fiction. No wonder her book started controversies—the masters were attacked as it were bodily by a woman who would so much have preferred to nurse her kindliness in Cranford.

Another of her thoughtful novels is *Ruth*. It could not strike its first readers as timely in the way *Mary Barton* had done, because its theme is the timeless one of the girl who is seduced by circumstances rather than by choice. Again Mrs. Gaskell makes a plea for knowledge, confident, as so many were in her time, that knowledge is power to put right—or in this instance, power not to misjudge. But that it had some special relevance to its time is again attested by the controversy it aroused. Mrs. Gaskell aimed her novel not into the heart of industry but into the heart of church and chapel. It fell into what was at that time a numerous class, the class of the 'religious' novel. The *Athenæum* reviewer pointed out the appropriateness of the seventeenth-century verses on the title-page, which ended with

> Nor let His eye
> See Sin, but through my tears.

[1] Ch. v.

There was nothing to start controversy in Ruth's repentance. What was offensive was Mrs. Gaskell's making a
minister of religion act a lie. Mr. Benson, a Dissenting
minister (of a sect that is left unspecified), takes the preg-
nant Ruth into the home he shares with his sister, and
passes her off as a widow. The *Athenæum* reviewer liked
the vagueness of Mr. Benson's religion, and liked the
absence from the novel of the polemical, 'not tempt[ing]
into controversy by dogmas put forth as infallible truth'.
Mrs. Gaskell had made the poor folk of the place think
that 'the faith which made [Mr. Benson] what he was
could not be far wrong'—which had been Pope's
philosophy a hundred years before: 'he can't be wrong
whose life is in the right'. Mr. Benson is a splendid man of
the quiet kindly sort, and even the prim Miss Benson, his
sister, reaches the point of saying that 'our telling a lie has
been the saving of her. There is no fear of her going
wrong now.' The Bensons' servant Sally had been
brought up Church of England, her father being a parish
clerk; though she cannot but think the ways of Dissenters
odd, this does not prevent her worshipping in her master's chapel. One wonders what Clough meant when he
found it at first 'rather cowardly—and "pokey" in its
views I think', a judgement tempered when he had
finished it: 'it is really very good—but it *is* a little too
timid, I think'.[1] Evidently he would have preferred a
more defiant attitude to the judgement of the world; but
Mrs. Gaskell went further than most of her public would
take. There was Mrs. Pearson to reckon with:

'Oh ma'am! she cannot be the young person I mean... holding
the position she does in your establishment. I should hardly
say I knew her myself; for I only saw her two or three times at
my sister's house; but she was so remarked for her beauty, that
I remember her face quite well—the more so, on account of her
vicious conduct afterwards.'[2]

[1] *Correspondence of Clough*, pp. 417–18.
[2] Ch. xxv.

Mrs. Pearson had recognized Ruth as the girl once apprenticed to her sister, and cunningly lets out the knowledge to the daughter of the house where Ruth is employed as a governess. This undoes the rescue that the Bensons had secured, and the third of the three-volume novel that has still to run is taken up by showing Ruth's further and more painful course of expiation.

In general Mrs. Gaskell's philosophy is that nothing whatever should be allowed to prevent people being kind to one another. The vicar of Monkshaven in *Sylvia's Lovers* is a better man than his beliefs about Church and State suggest:

... a kindly, peaceable old man, hating strife and troubled waters above everything. He was a vehement Tory in theory, as became his cloth in those days. He had two bugbears to fear—the French and the Dissenters. It was difficult to say of which he had the worst opinion and the most intense dread. Perhaps he hated the Dissenters most, because they came nearer in contact with him than the French; besides the French had the excuse of being Papists, while the Dissenters might have belonged to the Church of England if they had not been utterly depraved. Yet in practice Dr. Wilson did not object to dine with Mr. Fishburn, who was a personal friend and follower of Wesley's; but then, as the doctor would say, 'Wesley was an Oxford man, and that makes him a gentleman; and he was an ordained minister of the Church of England, so that grace can never depart from him.' But I do not know what excuse he would have alleged for sending broth and vegetables to old Ralph Thompson, a rabid Independent, who had been given to abusing the church and the vicar, from a Dissenting pulpit, as long as ever he could mount the stairs.[1]

But the matter is not simple, and the gently humorous tone is partly misleading. The vicar has to preach at the funeral of the returning sailor who was killed resisting the press-gang; his sympathies as a man are 'all on the bereaved father's side', but are overcome by his

[1] Ch. vi.

conviction of his duty to support 'due subordination and loyalty'. He preaches a conventional, perfunctory sermon—though at one moment, catching the 'up-turned, straining gaze of the father . . . seeking with all his soul to find a grain of holy comfort in the chaff of words, his conscience smote him'.

But again the discord between the laws of man and the laws of Christ stood before him; and he gave up the attempt to do more than he was doing, as beyond his power.

His simple hearers do not blame him for their 'dull feeling of disappointment'; his goodness and kindness 'made him beloved by all'. But that is not enough.

In these few paragraphs, concerned with a character on whom the narrator's light falls only this once, Mrs. Gaskell touches one of the underlying themes of her novels: the discord between 'the laws of man and the laws of Christ'. As Job Legh says of John Barton, ' "You see he were sadly put about to make great riches and great poverty square with Christ's gospel" '. To resolve the discord might be beyond human power, but Mrs. Gaskell did not give up the endeavour: and she knew that kindness, the prime essential, must be fortified by fearlessness of offending authority and common opinion.[1] Much has always been made of the charm of her character and her writing; not enough of her independence, her courage, and what Carlyle at the outset of her career called her 'veracity and devout earnestness of mind'.

[1] How firmly entrenched this was is evident from the outcry against Ruskin's *'Unto this Last'*.

# 7. TROLLOPE

IN HIS *Autobiography* Trollope records that in 1858, when he was in his forty-fourth year, he was commissioned by the General Post Office to visit the West Indies. During his absence from home he produced not only official reports but a travel book, *The West Indies and the Spanish Main*, published in 1859 'by Anthony Trollope, author of "Barchester Towers," "Doctor Thorne," "The Bertrams" etc.' Looking back, he deemed it 'on the whole... the best book that has come from my pen', adding by way of explanation 'it is short [i.e. by the standard set by most of his novels], and, I think I may venture to say, amusing, useful, and true'.[1] Egregious misjudgement!—as if Dickens had awarded the palm to *Pictures from Italy* or *American Notes*. And yet the seemingly slighted novels are not so different as might be thought from the travel book. To mark the overlapping at its most obvious: when their action leaves England for foreign parts it is into foreign parts that Trollope himself has visited. *The Bertrams*, published in the same year, is the prime example, partly based on his own experiences in the Holy Land. Much in its first volume is the fictional counterpart of a travel book he did not write, and it would have been still more like Thackeray's *From Cornhill to Cairo* if he had felt that what he calls the 'light pages' of a novel was the place for discussing religious faith, as Thackeray had done—all that Trollope permits himself is a sigh, in the manner of Matthew Arnold, over its decay in the nineteenth century. In the *Autobiography* he recounts that he began writing *The Bertrams* in Egypt, the day after he finished writing *Doctor Thorne*, and that

[1] *Autobiography*, Ch. vii.

from there he went to the Holy Land, the new novel accordingly being written 'under very vagrant circumstances,—at Alexandria, Malta, Gibraltar, Glasgow, then at sea, and at last finished in Jamaica'. Now that we know of his sojourn in the East, we see why some of the action of *The Bertrams* takes place in Jerusalem. His personages share their maker's experience as a tourist—indeed one of its chapters describes at length a dance of dervishes, which is as much a piece of reporting as the description of the sugar plantation in the *West Indies*. Trollope's fiction—though at one point he refers to his writing as pulling out 'long reels of gossamer literature'[1]—is sometimes scarcely distinguishable from his travel books.[2] It is pinned down in fact as firmly as possible. What is fiction in the novel is fact outside it, and vice versa.

That nineteenth-century doctrine of 'seeing' found no more unflagging disciple than Trollope. In his account of novel-writing in the *Autobiography* nothing is said about invention—that faculty of the literary mind that Dryden and Johnson placed highest, and which the novelist needs even more than the epic poet. Trollope speaks only of the novelist's need for 'observation'. In the nineteenth century writers often insisted on the need for that —Wordsworth had placed it first in a list of what went to make poetry, and Henry James counselled the novelist to 'Try to be one of the people on whom nothing is lost'. None, however, went so far as Trollope did, ascribing to observation the whole of his power—his power to invent, to think, to write. The creative process, as he experienced it himself, seemed to him the result of holding up the mirror to as much of the world of men and things as had come his way.

[1] *The West Indies*, Ch. vii.

[2] As he admitted, many of the stories in *Tales of all Countries* (1861, 1863) are founded on his travel experiences. The tragic event on which one, 'Returning Home', was based had occurred just before he reached San José (*The West Indies*, Ch. xx).

The 'facts' of Trollope's novels, then, were for the most part contemporary facts. He did write one historical novel, *La Vendée*, an early work, but regarded it as 'certainly inferior to those which had gone before;—chiefly because I knew accurately the life of the people in Ireland, and knew, in truth, nothing of life in the La Vendée country, and also because the facts of the present time come more within the limits of my powers of story-telling than those of past years'.[1] And the contemporary facts he noticed were those he noticed in his maturity. His younger days, it would seem, were devoted rather to quiet preparing to see and understand what he was to put into his novels. He differed, therefore, from the many among his fellow novelists who preferred to write of what they had seen as children, Thackeray often going still further back into the memories of his seniors. Trollope hardly started to notice England till the railway had come and changed it. His genius was as much that of the leader writer as of the novelist. He could not but withdraw to his desk for the writing of his stories, but he knew that his place was among his fellow countrymen as they dealt with each day as it came up. As a novelist he is 'a man speaking to men' in a plainer sense than is true of Wordsworth's poet. He speaks as men do in the street or market-place, in the saddle, on the doorstep or at the tea-table, and about what concerns them as they muse or speak. His fiction qualifies better than does Pope's poetry for Crabbe's description of it: 'Actuality of narration ... nudity of description ... without an atmosphere', and that because those are the characteristics of ordinary conversation. Trollope approves normal conversation as being 'reticent and dry'.[2] It was for the sake of reticence and dryness that Mrs. Trevelyan, when Lady Milborough came to remonstrate with her about the proposed marital separation, declined to have her child with her: '"It would be stagey," she had said, "and

[1] *Autobiography*, Ch. v.     [2] See p. 271.

clap-trap. There is nothing I hate so much as that."'[1]
Trollope's own conversation with the reader is often
'dry' compared, for example, with Thackeray's, which
he himself thought had 'a certain affected familiarity' and
'absence of . . . dignity'.[2] The following from *The Three
Clerks* is a typical piece, typical because of the interest of
what has been observed and the reticence of what is said
to have been felt; Norman is meeting his sister-in-law,
who had rejected him for Alaric, now ending a term of
imprisonment for fraud:

I should exaggerate the fact were I to say that he would not
have known her; but had he met her elsewhere, met her where
he did not expect to meet her, he would have looked at her
more than once before he felt assured that he was looking at
Gertrude Woodward. It was not that she had grown pale, or
worn, or haggard; though, indeed, her face had on it that
weighty look of endurance which care will always give; it was
not that she had lost her beauty, and become unattractive in his
eyes; but that the whole nature of her mien and form, the very
trick of her gait was changed. Her eye was as bright as ever, but
it was steady, composed, and resolved; her lips were set and
compressed, and there was no playfulness round her mouth.
Her hair was still smooth and bright, but it was more brushed
off her temples than it had been of yore, and was partly
covered by a bit of black lace, which we presume we must call
a cap; here and there, too, through it, Norman's quick eye
detected a few grey hairs. She was stouter too than she had
been, or else she seemed to be so, from the changes in her dress.
Her step fell heavier on the floor than it used to do, and
her voice was quicker and more decisive in its tones. When
she spoke to her mother, she did so as one sister might do
to another; and, indeed, Mrs. Woodward seemed to exercise
over her very little of the authority of a parent. The truth
was that Gertrude had altogether ceased to be a girl, had
altogether become a woman. Linda, with whom Norman
at once compared her, though but one year younger,

[1] *He Knew He was Right*, Ch. xi.
[2] *Thackeray*, Ch. ix, p. 201.

was still a child in comparison with her elder sister. Happy, happy, Linda![1]

If Trollope's own commentary calls on the reader at all, it is for the sort of corroboration we solicit when checking our watches.

Like Dr. Johnson, he trusts the 'common reader', blissfully ignorant of the 'refinements of subtilty and the dogmatism of learning'. He thinks better of the novel kind because novels have pleased many and pleased often. What all men do is rightly done. Louis Trevelyan 'knew he was right', but his dogmatic certainty was fatal because his rightness was not that of ordinary folk. Trollope stands with Frank Greystock—that far from wholly admirable 30-year-old in *The Eustace Diamonds*—who had the sense to see that 'It doesn't do to be wiser than other men'. Trollope puts his faith in what in *Phineas Finn* he calls the 'ordinary honest man of the world'. He does not mind having ordinary people occupying prominent places in his stories. Indeed he prefers that it should be so, simply because ordinary people occupy prominent places in life. He allows that very occasionally ordinary people speak poetry—that is, speak exaltedly and with imagery. In their sore trials characters will use biblical phrases, as Mr. Crawley does, and more unexpectedly, Dr. Thorne, Lady Mason in *Orley Farm*, and Mr. Peacocke in *Dr. Wortle's School*. But the obviously 'poetical' is slightly suspect: Luke Rowan's rhapsodies over the sunset when he is beginning to court Rachel Ray are not unconnected with 'that Byronic weakness which was ... prevalent among young men', and Lizzie Eustace's reading of Shelley is an item in her untrustworthiness. Otherwise his personages speak Trollopean prose, being commonplace. For him their very ordinariness is precious. He suffers his intellectual inferiors gladly: he treats the humble Mrs. Brattle in the

[1] Ch. xliii.

*Vicar of Bullhampton*, as Beatrice Curtis Brown has
pointed out, beautifully, 'accord[ing] her inarticulate distress an understanding which few novelists accord to
characters they do not consider their intellectual equals'.[1]
More than once a character is enlightened by the truer
instincts of an intellectual inferior: Mrs. Grimes in 'The
Spotted Dog'[2] overrides the editor's doubts about her
lending the marital bedroom to Julia Mackenzie to write
in:

'Mr. Grimes will be sure to dislike it.'
    'What,—John! Not he. I know what you're a-thinking of
Mr. ——. But we're different in our ways than what you are.
Things to us are only just what they are. We haven't time, nor
yet money, nor perhaps edication, for seemings and thinkings
as you have. If you was travelling out amongst the wild
Injeans, you'd ask any one to have a bit in your bed-room as
soon as look at 'em, if you'd got a bit for 'em to eat. We're
travelling among wild Injeans all our lives, and a bed-room
ain't no more to us than any other room . . .'

Trollope knows that the warm, vague, seldom sharp
minds of ordinary folk contain everything that more
brilliant or learned people have the power of making clear
to themselves. Ordinary folk have no power to analyse
states of mind. Sir Peregrine Orme could not analyse
either his own or his daughter's, but 'he felt that her
woman's ideas of honour and honesty were in some way
different from his ideas as a man',[3] and the feeling was
enough. It is for *our* sake that Trollope analyses tirelessly,
whatever the person whose mind is before him at the
moment.
    In *The Macdermots of Ballycloran* he says of Thady Mac-
dermot, who though innocent is fated to die by hanging,
that 'He knew little of the Grecian's doctrine of necessity;
but he had it in his heart that night'.[4] In *Ayala's Angel*

---

[1] *Anthony Trollope* (1950), pp. 28–9.
[2] *An Editor's Tales* (1870).
[3] *Orley Farm*, Ch. xvi.                    [4] Ch. xxix.

comes this characteristically profound moment—Ayala has the idea that only a veritable angel of a man is a fit mate for her, and Captain Stubbs does not come up to that pitch:

She would fain have told him, had she known how to do so, that her heart was very gentle towards him, was very kind, gentle and kind as a sister's;—but that she could not love him, so as to become his wife. 'You are not he,—not he, not that Angel of Light, which must come to me, radiant with poetry, beautiful to the eye, full of all excellences of art, lifted above the earth by the qualities of his mind,—such a one as must come to me if it be that I am ever to confess that I love. You are not he, and I cannot love you. But you shall be the next to him in my estimation, and you are already so dear to me that I would be tender to you, would be gentle,—if only I knew how.' It was all there, clear enough in her mind, but she had not the words. 'I don't know what it is that I ought to say,' she exclaimed through her sobs.[1]

It is almost as if Trollope were grateful to the unlearned Ayala for proving over again that literature is about life.

When ordinary people do read books they often try to escape from their ordinariness, preferring to read of heroes rather than men. Why do not ordinary folk love their ordinariness? he asks, and in Chapter xxxv of the *Eustace Diamonds* devotes a couple of unusually brilliant pages of energetic argument with them, of which the following is a sample:

It is very easy to depict a hero,—a man absolutely stainless, perfect as an Arthur,—a man honest in all his dealings, equal to all trials, true in all his speech, indifferent to his own prosperity, struggling for the general good, and, above all, faithful in love. At any rate, it is as easy to do that as to tell of the man who is one hour good and the next bad, who aspires greatly, but fails in practice, who sees the higher, but too often follows the lower course. There arose at one time a school of art, which delighted to paint the human face as perfect in beauty; and

[1] Ch. xxv.

from that time to this we are discontented unless every woman is drawn for us as a Venus, or, at least, a Madonna. I do not know that we have gained much by this untrue portraiture, either in beauty or in art. There may be made for us a pretty thing to look at, no doubt;—but we know that that pretty thing is not really visaged as the mistress whom we serve, and whose lineaments we desire to perpetuate on the canvas.

His readers' wish 'that a hero should be heroic' is the only fault he can find with them. On every other topic they agree.

At a time when the choosing of poets or 'literary' people for heroes and heroines was beginning Trollope sticks to the old eighteenth-century idea, that a novel is about a Tom Jones or a Vicar of Wakefield. He could not have created a convincing poet, as Tennyson did for *Maud*. His own aesthetic sense is that of ordinary people. There are few occasions in his novels when he exclaims on the superlative beauty of the scene. In *Orley Farm* comes this: 'I do not know anything more pleasant to the eye than a pretty country church, decorated for Christmas-day'.[1] Chapter xvii of *Can You Forgive Her?* opens:

Of all sights in the world there is, I think, none more beautiful than that of a pack of fox-hounds seated, on a winter morning, round the huntsman, if the place of meeting has been chosen with anything of artistic skill. It should be in a grassy field, and the field should be small. It should not be absolutely away from all buildings, and the hedgerows should not have been clipped and pared, and made straight with reference to modern agricultural economy. There should be trees near, and the ground should be a little uneven, so as to mark some certain small space as the exact spot where the dogs and servants of the hunt should congregate.

This in the century of Ruskin! But the common folk would have plumped for Trollope.

[1] Ch. xxii.

At the centre of the novels, and radiating out to their distant circumference, is this normality of their author, looking outward, and if inward, only for confirmation of what he had found outside.

Looking outward, he was most aware of human nature. He took in what he saw, and gave it a fair hearing. He did not impose his own nature on it, as Dickens or Meredith may be said to do. In Chapter xii of the *Autobiography* he lays down the law for the benefit of the neophyte novelist:

In all this human nature must be the novel-writer's guide. ... But in following human nature he must remember that he does so with a pen in his hand, and that the reader who will appreciate human nature will also demand artistic ability and literary aptitude.

The young novelist will probably ask, or more probably bethink himself how he is to acquire that knowledge of human nature which will tell him with accuracy what men and women would say in this or that position. He must acquire it as the compositor, who is to print his words, has learned the art of distributing his type—by constant and intelligent practice. Unless it be given to him to listen and to observe,—so to carry away, as it were, the manners of people in his memory, as to be able to say to himself with assurance that these words might have been said in a given position, and that those other words could not have been said,—I do not think that in these days he can succeed as a novelist.

The study of human nature may lead to modifications of accepted views. For instance, in *Mr. Scarborough's Family* comes this:

A lover who is anxious to prevail with a lady should always hold up his head. Where is the writer of novels, or of human nature, who does not know as much as that? And yet the man who is in love, truly in love, never does hold up his head very high. It is the man who is not in love who does so. Nevertheless it does sometimes happen that the true lover obtains his reward. In this case it was not observed to be so.

But now Mr. Anderson was sure of his fate, so that there was no encouragement to him to make any attempt at holding up his head. 'I have come once more to see you,' he said.[1]

A wish to give a true account of human nature, then, is behind his novels, and he is as much interested in people's practical affairs, down to the last entry in the laundry-book, if that is called for. When he showed his satisfaction with what he thought his 'best book', it was not merely with a travel book but with a travel book as he himself had made it. Trollope's travel books are so much more than pictorial, than sketches of places and people. They come as near to the great newspapers as possible, newspapers that report, and comment, as weightily as possible, on what they report. They see everything, and comment on everything—the social organization, the economic, the political, the legal. As a tourist, he got the hang of the place. And not being able to write travel books about the England that endlessly fascinated him, and which for all its faults and failings he admired so deeply, he wrote novels that should be the convenient and much-read evidence that he had got the hang of it, as he had of the West Indies, and as he had of human nature. Money—whether in shillings (the coin he refers to most often) or in the unprecedented piles of international financiers, professions, primogeniture, entails, the grow-ing importance of America, principles of the political parties that shaded into each other, the 'reforms' achieved, painfully and even cursedly—to quote one of his old Tories:

All interference with prerogative has been bad. The Reform bill was very bad. Encroachment on the estates of the bishops was bad. Emancipation of Roman Catholics was the worst of all. Abolition of corn-laws, church-rates, and oaths and tests were all bad. The meddling with the Universities has been grievous. The treatment of the Irish Church has been Satanic.

[1] Ch. lxiv.

The overhauling of schools is most injurious to English education. Education bills and Irish land bills were all bad. Every
step taken has been bad.[1]

—all such things, including more premature reforms
such as decimal coinage, are prominent in his pages as the
physical and moral presence of his hundred memorable
characters. Trollope was a Walter Bagehot among the
mid-century novelists, or a Defoe, but a Defoe who
brought all his knowledge into his fiction.

The experience of men and women that came Trollope's way and to which, as a novelist, he looked for
guidance, was mainly that of men and women of the
middle and upper classes, which was also the experience
of the bulk of his readers. Mid-century literature was
about the middle class, with top and bottom thrown in
where called for. Trollope's experience was mainly that
of the upper middle class, and he was as much a figure on
the hunting-field as in his room in the Post Office. He had
had enough experience of the aristocracy to write authen-
tically of them, and to startle the readers of 'silver-fork'
novels, as Thackeray had done with his Sir Pitt Crawley.
'Very eccentric, and very cross' proved to be the true
report of the Marquis in *The Bertrams* whom the Wil-
kinsons felt they had enough claim on to visit with a
request! Adolphus Crosbie, too, finds a March wind
blowing when asking Lady Alexandrina's hand of her
father, Lord de Courcy:

'I believe you have not any fortune, have you? She's got none;
of course you know that?'
   'I have a few thousand pounds, and I believe she has as
much.'
   'About as much as will buy bread to keep the two of you
from starving. It's nothing to me. You can marry her if you
like; only, look here, I'll have no nonsense. I've had an old
woman in with me this morning,—one of those that are here in

---

[1] *The Eustace Diamonds*, Ch. iv.

the house,—telling me some story about some other girl that you have made a fool of. It's nothing to me how much of that sort of thing you may have done, so that you do none of it here. But,—if you play any prank of that kind with me, you'll find that you've made a mistake.'

Crosbie hardly made any answer to this, but got himself out of the room as quickly as he could.

'You'd better talk to Gazebee about the trifle of money you've got,' said the earl. Then he dismissed the subject from his mind, and no doubt imagined that he had fully done his duty by his daughter.[1]

It is a moment of high comedy, in which moral mode Trollope excels, for Crosbie, who has meanly jilted Lily Dale, has been trapped by his own worship of rank into a marriage that only too truly promises discomfort.

For Trollope the upper classes are beautiful examples of Arnold's 'barbarians'. In a way all Trollope's personages are that, because of his ignoring of the schooled intellect. All his plots are to do with morals, and the powers, often splendid, of his personages are wholly concerned with what remains the same for learned and unlearned, clever or humdrum. He is not concerned with how the possession of intellect or a book-stocked mind affects the way everyday problems are tackled. If a young man is said to be brilliant as Harry Clavering is, Trollope gives no direct evidence of it, any more than Thackeray would. Harry is a double first, and Fellow of his College, but only as another personage may have red hair. His intellect hardly participates in the action. When his father, the Rev. Henry Clavering, rector, airs the suggestion that for profession Harry should go into the ministry, Harry declines to do so because of distaste—he also mentions that though he has no 'doubts' he would probably have them if he thought about them. His father himself is a nice specimen of the ecclesiastical barbarian.

Whenever Trollope brings in members of the 'other

[1] *The Small House at Allington*, Ch. xxiv.

nation', as he does now and again, they are hit off to the life, complete with dialect. Except in the Irish novels, they are seldom distressed, unless by their own fault. Trollope's comfortable lower classes are represented by the bedesmen of Hiram's Hospital in *The Warden*, or by the rustics of *John Caldigate*, who are indistinguishable from common folk in Shakespeare, George Eliot, or Thomas Hardy. Trollope takes a line about them which is that taken in the sixties by Balliol College, when they chose as Latin inscription for their new dining-hall the smug words of the Psalmist: 'I have been young, and am now old: and yet never saw I the righteous forsaken, nor his seed begging their bread.' In *The Three Clerks* Trollope interposed this comment:

There was something noble in this courage, in this lack of prudence. It may be a question whether men, in marrying, do not become too prudent. A single man may risk anything, says the world; but a man with a wife should be sure of his means. Why so? A man and a woman are but two units. A man and a woman with ten children are but twelve units. It is sad to see a man starving—sad to see a woman starving—very sad to see children starving. But how often does it come to pass that the man who will work is seen begging his bread? we may almost say never—unless, indeed, he be a clergyman. Let the idle man be sure of his wife's bread before he marries her; but the working man, one would say, may generally trust to God's goodness without fear.[1]

The condition of the poorest was a little better in the second half of the century, but Trollope and Balliol were deceiving themselves.

In the huge class falling between the aristocrats and the peasantry there is social turmoil. When Mr. Saul, the curate, wishes to marry Fanny Clavering there are two objections, over and above his physical unattractiveness—his indigence (his curacy brings him in £80 a year) and his not being the right social grade:

[1] Ch. xxxi.

Mr. Saul was a gentleman; but that was all that could be said of him. There is a class of country clergymen in England, of whom Mr. Clavering was one, and his son-in-law, Mr. Fielding, another, which is so closely allied to the squirearchy as to possess a double identity. Such clergymen are not only clergymen, but they are country gentlemen also. Mr. Clavering regarded clergymen of his class—of the country-gentlemen class—as being quite distinct from all others,—and as being, I may say, very much higher than all others, without reference to any money question. When meeting his brother rectors and vicars, he had quite a different tone in addressing them,—as they might belong to his class, or to another. There was no offence in this. The clerical country gentlemen understood it all as though there were some secret sign or shibboleth between them; but the outsiders had no complaint to make of arrogance, and did not feel themselves aggrieved. They hardly knew that there was an inner clerical familiarity to which they were not admitted. But now that there was a young curate from the outer circle demanding Mr. Clavering's daughter in marriage, and that without a shilling in his pocket, Mr. Clavering felt that the eyes of the offender must be opened. The nuisance to him was very great, but this opening of Mr. Saul's eyes was a duty from which he could not shrink.[1]

What was proving most troublesome, however, was the status of those who had recently risen into the upper middle class by wealth, coming from trade or from success in a profession other than those recognized as gentlemanly. The Burtons in *The Claverings* are engineers. Trollope admires them—Theodore Burton, as a man, is a hero after his own heart (go-ahead, sensible, effective, hard-working, standing no nonsense), but the social gap between Harry Clavering and him is unhappily wide. Harry's 'soft manners' attract Mrs. Burton, Theodore's wife, as a pleasant thing in a proposed brother-in-law. Much is made (even to the point of a chapter-heading) of Theodore's irritating way of dusting his shoes with his pocket handkerchief. Nevertheless,

[1] *The Claverings*, Ch. xxxiii.

Trollope leaves us in no doubt as to his superiority over young Clavering in point of moral character.

Trollope saw that, in addition to giving the general picture of Barsetshire, and much of the rest of England, his novels could be practically 'useful' in the way his *West Indies* had proved to be, and especially to the much-exercised middle class. He would have agreed with Arnold that conduct is three-fourths of life, and his utility was aimed largely at recommending what he called 'purity of manners'. The manners he recommended were a purification of those of the middle and upper classes, or where purity had been attained already, a picture of it. A better word than 'picture', however, would be 'moving picture' because Trollope's medium is narrative; and also because he sees life as a struggle, as Carlyle or Browning did. Even bidding farewell to his characters in the hard-won happy ending of *Dr. Wortle's School* he 'cannot pretend that the reader shall know . . . [their] future fate and fortunes . . . They must be left still struggling. But then is not such always in truth the case, even when the happy marriage has been celebrated?' It is a painful yet bracing and enlivening struggle, that of attaining to or preserving what is seen as the right thing. There is an unusually vehement passage in *Orley Farm*: he begins by giving a letter from Mrs. Furnival to her lawyer husband, a sadly complaining letter referring to less prosperous, but happier, days, when they lived in humbler quarters in the street, where, as it happens, Trollope himself was born:

'I wonder whether you ever think of the old days when we used to be so happy in Keppel Street?' Ah me, how often in after life, in those successful days when the battle has been fought and won, when all seems outwardly to go well,—how often is this reference made to the happy days in Keppel Street! It is not the prize that can make us happy: it is not even the winning of the prize, though for the short half-hour of triumph that is pleasant enough. The struggle, the long hot hour of the honest fight, the grinding work—when the teeth are set, and the skin moist with sweat and rough with dust, when all is doubtful and sometimes desperate, when a man must trust to his own manhood knowing that those around him trust it not at all,—that is the happy time of life. There is no human bliss equal to twelve hours of work with only six hours in which to do it. And when the expected pay for that work is worse than doubtful, the inner satisfaction is so much the greater. Oh, those happy days in Keppel Street, or it may be over in dirty lodgings in the Borough, or somewhere near the Marylebone workhouse;—anywhere for a moderate weekly stipend. Those were to us, and now are to others, and always will be to many, the happy days of life.[1]

What his heroes are trying to achieve is the status of being a 'gentleman'. Trollope decides that the definition of the old term in its changing connotations is impossible. When Mrs. Callander assures John Caldigate with: 'Of course we all know that you are a gentleman', he replies: 'I am much obliged to you; but I do not know any word that requires a definition so much as that'.[2] The missing definition Trollope provided in his novels as a whole. Its content had a solid moral core. The gentleman is a man of honour. His word must be his bond. That being so, there are few gentlemen about. In *The Eustace Diamonds* we read:

When Lord Fawn gave a sudden jump and stalked away towards the house on that Sunday morning before breakfast, Lucy Morris was a very unhappy girl. She had a second time accused Lord Fawn of speaking an untruth. She did not quite understand the usages of the world in the matter; but she did know that the one offence which a gentleman is supposed never to commit is that of speaking an untruth. The offence may be one committed oftener than any other by gentlemen,—as also by all other people; but nevertheless, it is regarded by the usages of society as being the one thing which a gentleman never does.[3]

[1] Ch. xlix.                          [2] Ch. vii.
[3] Ch. xxix.

But there is an aesthetic content to the term that is almost as important as the moral, and more easily seized on. It is well discussed at the point in *Rachel Ray* where Mr. Prong is introduced:

He was a devout, good man; not self-indulgent; perhaps not more self-ambitious than it becomes a man to be; sincere, hard-working, sufficiently intelligent, true in most things to the instincts of his calling,—but deficient in one vital qualification for a clergyman of the Church of England; he was not a gentleman. I do not mean to say that he was a thief or a liar; nor do I mean hereby to complain that he picked his teeth with his teeth with his fork and misplaced his 'h's'. I am by no means prepared to define what I do mean,—thinking, however, that most men and most women will understand me. Nor do I speak of this deficiency in his clerical aptitudes as being injurious to him simply,—or even chiefly,—among folk who are themselves gentle; but that his efficiency for clerical purposes was marred altogether, among high and low, by his misfortune in this respect. It is not the owner of a good coat that sees and admires its beauty. It is not even they who have good coats themselves who recognize the article on the back of another. They who have not good coats themselves have the keenest eyes for the coats of their better-clad neighbours. As it is with coats, so it is with that which we call gentility. It is caught at a word, it is seen at a glance, it is appreciated unconsciously at a touch by those who have none of it themselves. It is the greatest of all aids to the doctor, the lawyer, the member of Parliament,—though in that position a man may perhaps prosper without it,—and to the statesman; but to the clergyman it is a vital necessity. Now Mr. Prong was not a gentleman.

Bidding adieu to Mrs. Prime, 'his favourite sheep', he pressed her hand, 'and invoked a blessing on her head in a warm whisper. But such signs among such people do not bear the meaning which they have in the outer world. These people are demonstrative and unctuous,—whereas the outer world is reticent and dry.'[1] In *The Prime Minister*

[1] Ch. vi.

Trollope ascribes much to tradition, and his sympathy with it is attested by the exquisiteness of his imagery; when Mr. Wharton is examining his feelings about Lopez as a suitor to his daughter:

But then was he sure that he was right? He of course had his own way of looking at life, but was it reasonable that he should force his girl to look at things with his eyes? The man was distasteful to him as being unlike his idea of an English gentleman, and as being without those far-reaching fibres and roots by which he thought that the solidity and stability of a human tree should be assured. But the world was changing around him every day.[1]

The discussion is carried on in *Phineas Redux*, the topic having shifted to 'manliness'. Newman thought manliness to consist in self-control. Trollope asks for more than that:

A composure of the eye, which has been studied, a reticence as to the little things of life, a certain slowness of speech unless the occasion call for passion, an indifference to small surroundings, these,—joined, of course, with personal bravery,—are supposed to constitute manliness. That personal bravery is required in the composition of manliness must be conceded, though, of all the ingredients needed, it is the lowest in value. But the first requirement of all must be described by a negative. Manliness is not compatible with affectation. ... A man cannot become faithful to his friends, unsuspicious before the world, gentle with women, loving with children, considerate to his inferiors, kindly with servants, tender-hearted with all,—and at the same time be frank, of open speech, with springing, eager energies,—simply because he desires it. These things, which are the attributes of manliness, must come of training on a nature not ignoble.[2]

'Purity of manners' was most conspicuous on the girl's side. She has to fall in love once and once only, but, until she has got her cue, without showing that she has done so. The young man may have to be forgiven a certain

[1] Ch. ix.                    [2] Ch. lxviii.

amount of sexual experiment, of one degree or another, but once he has fixed on his choice it has to be final, and, from that point onwards, he should face any obstacles, in the main financial, that are likely to be placed in his way. The reasons why finance must be above board, and why it achieves something like parity with affection, are of a Trollopean obviousness—marriage meant children, and, as one of his heroines puts it, no mother wants to be running an 'impoverished nursery'.

It has been already stated that Nora Rowley was not quite so well disposed as perhaps she ought to have been, to fall in love with the Honourable Charles Glascock, there having come upon her the habit of comparing him with another gentleman whenever this duty of falling in love with Mr. Glascock was exacted from her. That other gentleman was one with whom she knew that it was quite out of the question that she should fall in love, because he had not a shilling in the world; and the other gentleman was equally aware that it was not open to him to fall in love with Nora Rowley—for the same reason. In regard to such matters Nora Rowley had been properly brought up, having been made to understand by the best and most cautious of mothers, that in the matter of falling in love it was absolutely necessary that bread and cheese should be considered. 'Romance is a very pretty thing,' Lady Rowley had been wont to say to her daughters, 'and I don't think life would be worth having without a little of it. I should be very sorry to think that either of my girls would marry a man only because he had money. But you can't even be romantic without something to eat and drink.'[1]

As we have seen, the novelist of Barsetshire recognized that aristocratic and middle-class manners were changing in his time. With the change he kept pace, almost completely—he does not quite keep up with the fastest-paced of the women, as Reade does—and part of the interest of the great series of political novels, which with several novels interspersed occupied him from the early sixties until 1880, lies in the new manners, mainly metropolitan, and the contrast they afford to the 'purity' of the older

[1] *He Knew he was Right*, Ch. iv.

Barsetshire manners. In *The Duke's Children* it becomes
clear that a girl has to fight her own battles—Lady Mabel
Grex is speaking of Silverbridge to Frank Tregear:

'. . . when I taxed him with his falsehood,—for he has been
false,—he answered me with those very words! "I have
changed my mind." He could not lie. To speak the truth was a
necessity to him, even at the expense of his gallantry, almost of
his humanity.'
    'Has he been false to you, Mabel?'
    'Of course he has but there is nothing to quarrel about, if
you mean that. People do not quarrel now about such things.
A girl has to fight her own battle with her own pluck and her
own wits'.[1]

The degree of change is indicated by *The Way We Live
Now* (1875); for if Carlyle tells us most about the England
of the first half of the mid-century, Trollope, with
Meredith and Reade, tells us most about the England of
the second. This late novel is so much in the thick of new
things that it cannot but lack the fullness of calm and
control that is the glory of the Barsetshire series. Its very
title shows that Trollope was growing with the times. In
*Phineas Finn* he speaks with awe of the 'majestic growth
of the English people'. Yes, as a spectacle it was majestic,
even what he had seen of it since he began writing in the
forties. But it had its sadnesses too—so much that he had
most sympathy with seemed to be being superseded. The
'purity of manners' was in the dark melting-pot. The
most striking personage in that novel is Melmotte, the
Great Financier. (Dickens had already done something on
the same lines with Mr. Merdle in *Little Dorrit*.) In English metropolitan life, the life that was in the news, big
money was now openly supreme. The words 'finance'
and 'financier' had only recently become commonly used
in the modern sense: at one point the shallow Georgiana
Longstaffe, telling her mother that she has become

[1] Ch. lxxvii.

engaged to Brehgert the Jew, writes ingratiatingly: 'He is a very wealthy man, and his business is about banking and what he calls finance. I understand they are among the most leading people in the City.' Melmotte himself towers above Brehgert, and, having sprung from the shadiest antecedents and not being above the forging of documents, comes to be called 'The Merchant Prince', and is accorded supreme social distinction. He even entertains the Emperor of China at a dinner so grand that members of the English royal family are present. He successfully stands for Parliament as Conservative candidate for Westminster, and tells a crowd of electors, who are mainly mechanics, that it is the 'proudest boast of his life to be an Englishman and a Londoner'—he hails from Eastern Europe. His spectacular end is suicide. While he lasts, however, Trollope does him well. He is a jovial brute, and has no regrets. There is a sort of Trollopean manliness about his love for dishonesty on the biggest scale. As the Secretary of State for the Home Department puts it to the Chancellor of the Exchequer, 'he has been about the grandest rogue we've seen yet'. In this finance-ridden world Roger Carbury, the head of the Carbury family, is contrasted with the Brehgerts and Melmottes, a sort of *ultimus Romanorum*, intent on keeping together the estate despite all money difficulties, holding it in trust for those who come after him, even though he has himself no prospect of marrying—since his cousin Hetta, as it turns out, rejects him. The complications for poor Roger have their wheels within wheels: the next heir is the dissipated Sir Felix Carbury, a baronet, but Roger thinks ill of his title as well as his character:

He thought that a gentleman, born and bred, acknowledged as such without doubt, could not be made more than a gentleman by all the titles which the Queen could give. With these old-fashioned notions Roger hated the title which had fallen upon a branch of his family. He certainly would not leave his property to support the title which Sir Felix unfortunately possessed.

But Sir Felix was the natural heir, and this man felt himself constrained, almost as by some divine law, to see that his land went by natural descent. Though he was in no degree fettered as to its disposition, he did not presume himself to have more than a life interest in the estate. It was his duty to see that it went from Carbury to Carbury as long as there was a Carbury to hold it, and especially his duty to see that it should go from his hands, at his death, unimpaired in extent or value. There was no reason why he should himself die for the next twenty or thirty years,—but were he to die Sir Felix would undoubtedly dissipate the acres and then there would be an end of Carbury. But in such case he, Roger Carbury, would at any rate have done his duty. He knew that no human arrangements can be fixed, let the care in making them be ever so great. To his thinking it would be better that the estate should be dissipated by a Carbury than held together by a stranger. He would stick to the old name while there was one to bear it, and to the old family while a member of it was left. So thinking, he had already made his will, leaving the entire property to the man whom of all others he most despised, should he himself die without child.[1]

The Barsetshire traditions are not forgotten in the new hubbub, though more temptations are now put in the way of their continued peaceful existence. Keeping up to date, Trollope had to write of a metropolitan world as violent as the Irish world he put into his first novels, a world so largely unlike that of Barsetshire. As a novelist, he is in two minds about what he sees. The new world has its own sublimity for him, simply because it taxed all those powers he had so happily employed in the wild West Indies. But if happiness of the best and most lasting sort is the end and aim most people set before themselves, the achieving of it had had so much better a chance in the Barsetshire of the earlier novels. Fortunately, even in the milieu of Melmotte, moral character does persist, and with all the old quiet ferocity he had admired in his Barset heroines. It persists in Melmotte's daughter, Marie.

[1] Ch. xiv.

Over all Trollope's stories extends the moral Johnson elaborated in *Rasselas*. We are wisest when we do not hanker after leaving our birthplace and rank in society. It happens to some that they do leave it, but not after hankering. Friends and lovers should come 'naturally', that is, from among those round and about us in our native haunts. As a young man John Caldigate had led a wild life in New South Wales, and his 'natural' life in his father's 'moderate house called Folkings, in the parish of Utterden, about ten miles from Cambridge', was thereby interrupted. Without that interruption none of his sensational troubles would have come upon him. At one point John has to stand such sneering as that of his stern Aunt Polly:

'... You have inveigled your cousin's affections and now you say that you can do nothing for her. This comes from the sort of society you have kept out at Botany Bay! I suppose a man's word there is worth nothing, and that the women are of such a kind they don't mind it. It is not the way with gentlemen here in England; let me tell you that!'[1]

Things are best left as they are when they are comfortable for most of those concerned. Indeed that word 'comfortable' must be Trollope's favourite. When one or more of those concerned—or when one or more of those *not* concerned—are for stirring them up, let them think twice, since they often see themselves as persons of goodwill. Comfort was scattered to the winds when well-meaning John Bold felt moved to point out that, owing to an increase in the value of land, the wording of the bequest under which the warden and bedesmen of Hiram's Hospital were paid no longer represented the benefactor's intentions, the warden accordingly being now in receipt of disproportionate emoluments. When Mr. Harding was brought to see Bold's point all his comfort fled. Nor did Bold, as it turned out, benefit the

[1] Ch. xvi.

bedesmen. If things are quiet and comfortable, may it not
be better, even in the nineteenth century, to leave them
so? Trollope knew as well as anybody that change must
come. A noisier, faster life had already overtaken London. One half of him responded as Macaulay, Kingsley,
and Charles Reade did, feeling braced and alive, but,
more than they, he loved what was being lost. His deepest sympathies lay with Mrs. Ray and Rachel in their
disagreement with Dorothea Prime, Mrs. Ray's married
daughter:

'. . . If you had really wanted advice, mamma, I would sooner
have heard that you had gone to Mr. Prong.'

'But I didn't go to Mr. Prong, my dear, and I don't mean.
Mr. Prong is all very well, I dare say, but I've known Mr.
Comfort for nearly thirty years, and I don't like sudden
changes.' Then Mrs. Ray stirred her tea with rather a quick
motion of her hand. Rachel said not a word, but her mother's
sharp speech and spirited manner was very pleasant to her. She
was quite contented now that Mr. Comfort should be
regarded as the family counsellor. She remembered how well
she had loved Mr. Comfort always, and thought of days when
Patty Comfort had been very good-natured to her as a child.

'Oh, very well,' said Mrs. Prime. 'Of course, mamma, you
must judge for yourself.'

'Yes, my dear, I must; or rather, as I didn't wish to trust my
own judgment, I went to Mr. Comfort for advice. He says that
he sees no harm in Rachel going to this party.'

'Party! What party?' almost screamed Mrs. Prime. Mrs. Ray
had forgotten that nothing had as yet been said to Dorothea
about the invitation.

'Mrs. Tappitt is going to give a party at the brewery,' said
Rachel, in her very softest voice, 'and she has asked me.'

'And you are going? You mean to let her go?' Mrs. Prime
had asked two questions, and she received two answers. 'Yes,'
said Rachel; 'I suppose I shall go, as mamma says so.' 'Mr.
Comfort says there is no harm in it,' said Mrs. Ray; 'and Mrs.
Butler Cornbury is to come from the parsonage to take her
up.'[1]

[1] Ch. v.

He did not see much likelihood that the Ten Commandments would be widely broken in Baslehurst or in
Barsetshire, and many of their number not at all. The
temptations such people needed to pray against were
rather, to quote *John Caldigate*, 'evil thoughts, hardness of
heart, suspicions, unforgiveness, hatred'. In other later
novels the decalogue was still wholly relevant. In *Phineas
Redux* there is a murder, as in *The Way We Live Now* there
is a suicide. These were sensations forced on him, as it
were. He preferred them to be of the homely sort—a
sensation like that when Miss Todd discussed a certain
matter with Mr. O'Callaghan, the curate at Littlebath:

'I fear you do not approve of cards?' said Miss Todd.
   'Approve! Oh no, how can I approve of them, Miss Todd?'
   'Well, I do with all my heart. What are old women like us to
do? We haven't eyes to read at night, even if we had minds fit
for it. We can't always be saying our prayers. We have nothing
to talk about except scandal. It's better than drinking; and we
should come to that if we hadn't cards.'
   'Oh, Miss Todd!'
   'You see you have your excitement in preaching, Mr.
O'Callaghan. These card-tables are our pulpits; we have got
none other. We haven't children, and we haven't husbands.
That is, the most of us. And we should be in a lunatic asylum in
six weeks if you took away our cards. Now, will you tell me,
Mr. O'Callaghan, what would you expect Miss Ruff to do if
you persuaded her to give up whist?'
   'She has the poor with her always, Miss Todd.'
   'Yes, she has; the woman that goes about with a clean apron
and four borrowed children; and the dumb man with a bit of
chalk and no legs, and the very red nose. She has these, to be
sure, and a lot more. But suppose she looks after them all the
day, she can't be looking after them all the night too. The mind
must be unbent sometimes, Mr. O'Callaghan.'[1]

In theory a novel for Trollope was what it was for
Henry James. He admitted that he lacked the power to

[1] *The Bertrams*, Ch. xxii.

construct elaborate plots—the word 'plot' in the mid-century implied elaboration, mysteries, secrets. He thought his deficiency no fatal disadvantage. He was not averse, however, any more than James was, to 'sensations'. Indeed he advised the novelist to provide as many as possible, with the crucial proviso that the account of the actors' minds kept pace with them. For the true business of the novelist was not the elucidation of mysteries so much as of character. However furnished, the form of a novel should be one thing—though it 'may have many parts' including 'subsidiary plots', they should all 'elucidate the main story', which 'should be all one'. Henry James did not ask for more or for other things.

Among the fifty or so of Trollope's novels some few have all the virtues he aspired towards. *Rachel Ray* was one of them: in George Eliot's happy phrase, 'as natty and complete as a nut on its stem'. In criticizing the work of an author, however, who proliferates novels, many of them of mammoth size, it seems pedantic to apply the Jamesian standard Trollope himself subscribed to. Who cares if among the thousands of chapters some few drag? The worst morass of sluggishness comes in *Orley Farm*, the all but motionless action of Chapters xxi–iv representing what happened in four different places during the Christmas season—and Trollope did not even have the excuse of seasonable part-publication, for this sixth of twenty monthly parts appeared in August. In *John Caldigate* the whole Bolton strand of the story is tedious, especially towards the end of the novel; so also in *Can You Forgive Her?* the Widow-Greenow–Cheesacre strand, as farcical as much in the novels of Anthony's mother, Frances. Swinburne spoke of the 'slovenly superfluity of underplot which is the damning fault' of Caroline drama, and the phrase fits some of Trollope's novels. Not all his 'subsidiary plots' meet his own requirement that they should 'all tend to the elucidation of the main story'.[1]

---

[1] *Autobiography*, Ch. xii.

Sometimes, too, a big scene is skimped, and there results a lack of proportion: after his wife's discovery of Mrs. Houghton's compromising letter to Lord George in *Is He Popenjoy?* her forgiveness should have come more slowly than it does, and only during the course of the long colloquy that we are denied. Many mid-century novels are of mammoth size merely because they consist of an alternation of two or more shorter ones. In several of Trollope's the various strands have very little to connect them. No doubt they can be justified, as it were mechanically—they do actually touch at various points.[1] But by his own standards for unity they fail. When, however, he does unify multitudinousness, it is sometimes at the expense of verisimilitude. In *The Way We Live Now* it is merely for the ready convenience of the author that when Ruby Ruggles, in flight from a steady lover she does not want (John Crumb) in hopes of securing one she does want (Sir Felix Carbury), takes refuge in the house of her aunt, it should turn out that that aunt is landlady to Mrs. Hurtle, who is in love with Paul Montague, who is in love with Hetta Carbury, who is Felix's sister; or that when John Crumb is walking the streets of London by night he should come across the very man, Sir Felix, whom he wants to knock out, and come on him at a moment when he most invites a knock-out blow—Sir Felix is in altercation with a girl whose scream advertises her as Ruby. This sort of plot-luck, if one can coin a word, puts the reader of a big novel of Trollope into a difficulty—he wants to discount the defects because of their minimal proportion to the whole at the same time as he wishes that a designer usually so scrupulous in verisimilitude should have devised the offending events more happily. Then again, Trollope can annoy by

[1] [Newman, a devoted reader of Trollope, saw another reason 'why skilful novelists like Trollope have underplots. Such a contrivance obliges events to go slowly—also it gives opportunity for variety and repose' (letter of 10 Jan. 1874; ed. C. S. Dessain, *Letters*, xxviii, 1975, p. 8). *Ed.*]

repetitions and recapitulations, perhaps justified when publication, as it often was for him, was by instalment, but which needed to be reduced before the novel was presented complete. Sometimes it seems that they exist because they were necessary for him physically, so to speak, as a means of getting squarely placed towards the tackling of what lay immediately ahead of him as he seated himself at his desk. He had no time to fuss over a novel once it was published.[1] By then he was too busy over his next.

Two of the novels are in part misconceived. Both *Orley Farm* and *He Knew He Was Right* get bogged down in painfulness. Arnold, when he withdrew *Empedocles on Etna*, was right, in principle at least: he said that readers miss the indispensable poetical 'enjoyment' when the story offered is one 'in which the suffering finds no vent in action; in which a continuous mental distress is prolonged, unrelieved by incident, hope or resistance; in which there is everything to be endured, nothing to be done'. Arnold states his case in extreme terms, but by and large it applies to both these novels. In *Orley Farm* Lady Mason's guilt is shown weighing on her heart immovably and for a long time; and in *He Knew He Was Right* we live through two years while Louis Trevelyan nurses his belief that an 'inexorable Fate' has 'utterly destroyed his happiness without any fault of his own'.

It is best, however, when the novelist is a Trollope, to leave a listing of defects, for fear they should loom too large in the general estimate. When the less well-made novels are part of a series—a series Trollope invites us to keep unbroken by making some of his personages, after the fashion of Balzac and Thackeray, crop up in later

---

[1] There is little evidence of revision in later editions: a polemical chapter dropped from *The Three Clerks*, and some reduction and rewriting in *The Macdermots of Ballycloran*, are the main instances. Neither was published in parts.

novels—defects count far less because of our sense of 'God's plenty'. We turn away from most of the novels singly and all of them together with the glowing satisfaction that we have been watching a world steadily revolving. The unity he sought settled over his work, good or less than good, as it settles over the vast series of Bach's cantatas.

What Trollope excels in is narration. He can make an action scud, as if before a stiff breeze. In *He Knew He Was Right* he speaks of his 'somewhat uneven story'. He likes the progress to be on an even keel, and as brisk as possible, and there are few of his stories that do not give us spells of this scudding progress, sometimes for long stretches at a time. It is matched by certain things in music—the finale of Brahms's trio in C major, for instance, where the piano part evenly scampers forward bearing without noticing it the weight of the urgent strings. An instance of this power comes in Chapter x of *The Three Clerks,* and is almost detachable as a supreme short story. Mr. Fidus Neverbend, the stolid and starchy senior civil servant, is to write a memorandum in collaboration with Alaric Tudor, his brilliant junior, on the state of the mine named Wheal Mary Jane. Alaric falls into a trap (set by shady financial interests), and drinks too much; he is therefore late for the descent of the mine, much to the satisfaction of the jealous Neverbend, who, however, is chagrined to see, as the bucket he is standing in descends the shaft, the arrival of Alaric. In the grim depths of the mine Neverbend's nerve gives out at the point when further descent is by ladder. It is accordingly the nimbler and more intrepid Alaric who gets the information necessary for the memorandum. Neverbend signs it without criticizing its contents (which are in the interests of the financiers who have compromised Alaric) in return for Alaric's suppression of what would compromise Neverbend's dignity. Trollope ties up every end: the action concerns a number of people, including the servants at the inn, and every move they make has its adequate psychological reasons.

Another of Trollope's virtues is his power to concentrate an issue into a great scene, and to do so frequently. Such a scene is that in *Framley Parsonage* where Lady Lufton and Fanny Robarts discuss Fanny's sister-in-law Lucy, who is in love with Lord Lufton, Lady Lufton's son. Fanny keeps her head and has a firm lawyer-like grip on all the fine points, nothing being scamped, every point being made in order, clearly, distinctly, beautifully.[1] Or that scene in which Mrs. Grantly lords it over Mrs. Proudie because her daughter is to marry a Viscount whereas Mrs. Proudie's is to marry only a Mr. Tickler. Or, again, the great scene in *The Last Chronicle* where Mr. Crawley suppresses Mrs. Proudie; or that in *Can You Forgive Her?* where Burgo Fitzgerald tries to persuade Lady Glencora at the ball to an adulterous elopement.

Particularly interesting are the scenes where rights are in dispute, rights that are assumed rather than claimed. In Chapter xxvi of *Doctor Thorne* Lady Arabella, eldest daughter of Lord de Courcy, visits the doctor to try to impose stricter terms on their two families so as to prevent Frank Gresham's courtship with Mary, the doctor's ward. And in *He Knew He Was Right* it is assumed that Nora's aunt, because she is keeping her niece, can control her correspondence, but the right is disputed.

If good plays were scarce in the mid-century the lack was amply supplied by the novelists, and conspicuously by Trollope. In his *Autobiography* Trollope himself singled out one of these scenes, and, un-self-assertive as he was, was not afraid to place it in the best of company. The whole context is interesting as an uncharacteristic instance of authorial pride. At the present day, he says (writing in 1876), there is supposed to be a marked division between 'realistic' novelists such as himself

[1] Ch. xli.

and 'sensational' novelists such as Wilkie Collins, and between their readers. But this is a mistake, arising from

the inability of the imperfect artist to be both realistic and sensational. A good novel should be both, and both in the highest degree ... Let those readers who believe that they do not like sensational scenes in novels think of some of those passages from our great novelists which have charmed them most:—of Rebecca in the castle with Ivanhoe; of Burley in the cave with Morton; of the mad lady tearing the veil of the expectant bride, in *Jane Eyre*; of Lady Castlewood as, in her indignation, she explains to the Duke of Hamilton Henry Esmond's right to be present at the marriage of his Grace with Beatrix;—may I add, of Lady Mason, as she makes her confession at the feet of Sir Peregrine Orme?

He goes on to distinguish between the mere accumulation of horrors and the sufferings of 'men and women with whom we can sympathise', claiming that

he who can deal adequately with tragic elements is a greater artist and reaches a higher aim than the writer whose efforts never carry him above the mild walks of everyday life ... Truth let there be,—truth of description, truth of character, human truth as to men and women. If there be such truth, I do not know that a novel can be too sensational.

This is the highest claim that Trollope makes for his own work, and it is surely justified.

# 8.  TENNYSON

No contemporary pair have ever proffered credentials more diverse than Browning and Tennyson. Whereas the author of *Men and Women* and *The Ring and the Book* presents us with a vast rambling Gothic building, strong as a fortress, if it were not for its looped and windowed raggedness, Tennyson presents us rather with a saloon of water-colours leading on to further saloons. He becomes great by accumulation of exquisite things of many different sizes, some of which form sequences impressive in their totality. Reading his *Poems, chiefly Lyrical* (1830), published when he was not quite 21, we greet a writer obviously endowed with the characteristic gifts of a poet—the capacity to feel, to lead a sensuous existence, to think about common things, to put together words as pictorial as possible in felicitous metre. To that first volume he added much, for he lived long. It was said of him that he never fulfilled his early promise. He had no need to, his promise being already achievement. All that was necessary for him was to go on making additions. Even in that youthful volume came things perfectly Tennysonian; in 'Mariana', in the 'Ode to Memory':

> . . .   the brook that loves
> To purl o'er matted cress and ribbéd sand,
> Or dimple in the dark of rushy coves,
> Drawing into his narrow earthen urn,
>     In every elbow and turn,
> The filtered tribute of the rough woodland.

and

A spirit haunts the year's last hours
Dwelling amid these yellowing bowers:
    To himself he talks;
For at eventide, listening earnestly,
At his work you may hear him sob and sigh
    In the walks;
    Earthward he boweth the heavy stalks
Of the mouldering flowers:
    Heavily hangs the broad sunflower
      Over its grave i' the earth so chilly;
    Heavily hangs the hollyhock,
      Heavily hangs the tiger-lily.

Tennyson was taken notice of from the first; this volume was reviewed at length in the *Westminster* and *Blackwood's*, and Leigh Hunt wrote in the *Tatler* that the author could 'take his stand at once among the first poets of the day'[1]. Some of this notice took the form of attacks on what seemed affectation and eccentricity—notably (on his second volume, in 1833) from the powerful *Quarterly*. Nevertheless, delighted readers slowly multiplied until by the 1860s it seemed as if the whole nation was reading him. He wrote for the few and the many, often by means of the same poem; he had the common touch, as well as a sense for what was delicate and rare.

This very popularity was turned against him: in his own words 'Then they cried at the turn of the tide, / You're no poet—why, you're popular!' Those who came to 'doubt' him—Hopkins uses the word in 1864[2]—did so mainly on intellectual grounds: representative of many, before and since, is the minor poet John Payne, who in his *Autobiography* avowed that Tennyson 'owed his popularity mainly to the way in which he pandered to the weaknesses of the intellectually lower classes and to his

[1] Feb. 1831.
[2] 'Do you know a horrible thing has happened to me. I have begun to *doubt* Tennyson' (*Further Letters of Gerard Manley Hopkins*, ed. C. C. Abbott, 1938, p. 68).

cunning fashion of adorning and idealizing the grossest gospel of disguised materialism and crass optimism'[1]. Tennyson was vulnerable because he chose to offer thinking on the problems of the time (as many poets do not), both in his own person and through fictitious personages; and his choice is an index of his sensitiveness to the claims of the Carlylean era. And some of his thinking, as on matters being urgently raised by the scientist, far from echoing the thought of the intellectually lower classes, won and can still win the admiration of the higher.[2]

But on some other topics his thinking has suffered the fate of all who express views—the topics being so complex, and so much at the mercy of times and seasons. For example, it may be counted against him that on the topic of war he wrote some loudly patriotic songs, such as 'English Warsong' and 'National song', which appeared in *Poems, chiefly Lyrical*. They have flashes of splendour:

> On the ridge of the hill his banners rise;
> They stream like fire in the skies;
> Hold up the Lion of England on high
> Till it dazzle and blind his eyes.

These songs, however, are boyish efforts, and were not reprinted. Even so, loudly patriotic songs will have their uses so long as patriotism survives, and accordingly it is satisfactory when they are written by a poet.

More damaging, because affecting a major poem, is the criticism of the thinking about war and peace offered by the hero of *Maud*, which appeared early in the Crimean War. Yet much of it is of excellent quality as well as dramatically valid. Objections concentrate upon and isolate the conclusion of the poem; but the theme is present from the beginning. It enters as early as the sixth verse,

[1] *The Autobiography of John Payne (1842–1916)*, ed. Thomas Wright (1926), p. 13.
[2] See pp. 311–13.

which (along with the fourth section) sees nature at strife:

For nature is one with rapine, a harm no preacher can heal,
The mayfly is torn by the swallow, the sparrow spear'd by the
    shrike,
And the whole little wood where I sit is a world of plunder and
    prey . . .

In the same way 'Mammonist' society is always at war: 'lust of gain in the spirit of Cain'—'Is it peace or war? Civil war . . . / The viler, as underhand, and not openly bearing the sword'. The martial song that he hears Maud singing (I. v) shames him into wishing his own life were less 'languid' and 'base'; then, in contrast, the anti-war preaching of the electioneering cotton-spinner:

> This huckster put down war! Can he tell
> Whether war be a cause or a consequence?
> Put down the passions that make earth Hell!
> . . . Down too, down at your own fireside,
> With the evil tongue and the evil ear,
> For each is at war with mankind.

and the longing to hear Maud's song again—'The chivalrous battle-song / That she warbled alone in her joy'. The duel in which he kills his rival represents 'the Christless code / That must have life for a blow', contrasted, after his flight, with the killing of the soldier in battle:

> Friend, to be struck by the public foe,
> Then to strike him and lay him low,
> That were a public merit, far,
> Whatever the Quaker holds, from sin;
> But the red life split for a private blow—
> I swear to you, lawful and lawless war
> Are scarcely even akin.

In the final section 'lawful war' brings 'a hope for the world'—though this may be 'but a dream'

> yet it lighten'd my despair
> When I thought that a war would arise in defence of the
>       right,
> That an iron tyranny now should bend or cease,
> The glory of manhood stand on his ancient height,
> Nor Britain's one sole God be the millionaire.

All this is convincing in the context not only of
the poem, but of the contemporary situation—the opening months of a war which still looked like a 'cause';
Tennyson, who is not wholly invisible behind the screen
of his drama, expresses the view that many were taking.
But it is not the view expressed through 'The Passing
of Arthur', nor in the late 'Epilogue' to 'The Charge of
the Heavy Brigade at Balaclava':

> And who loves War for War's own sake
> Is fool, or crazed, or worse ...

nor, forty years earlier, in the vision of the future in
'Locksley Hall' where the speaker sees beyond 'the
nations' airy navies grappling in the central blue' to a time
when 'the war-drum throbb'd no longer, and the battle-
flags were furl'd / In the Parliament of man, the Fed-
eration of the world'. This 'vision' of Tennyson's was the
result of thinking, and must have given 'the intellectually
lower classes' in 1842 reason for gaping at new ideas. The
same could be said of his thinking on woman's education
and his concluding hope for the future in *The Princess*:

> The woman's cause is man's; they rise or sink
> Together, dwarf'd or godlike, bond or free.

The Prince's whole speech, also written in the 1840s,
needs no defence as forward-looking thinking about
marriage and the social role of woman; it is not narrowed
by the time like the conclusion of *Maud*, but leaves room
for much that has happened.

The scene near the end of 'The Two Voices' has often
been attacked by later critics: the resolution of the

speaker's conflict comes with the Sabbath morn, the sweet church bells, and the sight of a man walking to church with his wife and child:

> With measur'd footfall firm and mild,
> And now and then he gravely smiled.
>
> The prudent partner of his blood
> Lean'd on him, faithful, gentle, good,
> Wearing the rose of womanhood.
>
> And in their double love secure,
> The little maiden walk'd demure,
> Pacing with downward eyelids pure.

—and the heavenly toned voice of hidden hope, which leads him (not to church) but 'forth into the fields' to rejoice in the spring. These stanzas are preceded by 400 lines of thinking as solid as exists in English verse. At bottom that thinking concerns the worth of life. It asks 'Were it not better not to be?' Emerging from his long black tunnel of thinking, it is not surprising that when the 'I' comes on the Sabbath sight it is as if on the opening of the gates of paradise. In its place, therefore, his sight of the family of three going to church is a psychological event, though it also contributes to the argument, showing him that life is worth living, at least for some people, and so perhaps for him. In its context the ending of the poem is right. Even out of it, there is nothing wrong with the subject itself. Even atheists must approve a family knitted together, though by means they cannot approve. What offends us is the family's smugness. And yet Tennyson's contemporaries found no smugness in their visible piety. Hopkins, praising the poem as it deserves, as 'a philosophical poem written with the greatest flow, lucidity and point', and 'bright with imagery,'[1] made no exception of its ending. Whatever is to be charged against

---

[1] *Correspondence with R. W. Dixon*, p. 62.

the picture is rather to be charged against the mid-century.

Allowance must always be made for an author's place in time. Some authors are ahead of their time, but for the rest, no less dear to literature, allowances are necessary. Tennyson was sometimes ahead of his age, often abreast of what was most advanced in it, but not so in a passage like this. Surely, however, he cannot be blamed for taking over what we can call the furniture of his time, any more than Chaucer for the conventions of Courtly Love, or some writers of mid-twentieth-century poems and novels for the use of 'four-letter words'. Every age is crowded with approved furniture that writers bring into their work as a matter of course. Having acquired new, a later age by that token cannot complain of furniture now obsolete. It sufficed in its day. It gave the same pleasure as the spick-and-span novelties are giving today. Tennyson has borne much misplaced criticism on this score. The expression on the faces of his church-going family is that of hundreds of contemporary pictures. That such pictures were painted, and that such ways of behaving existed, argue that they were admired. They were admired because fashionable, and the looks that offend us may as often have been assumed without design, automatically as fashions usually are adopted, as with it. Dickens's novels have many similar instances of admirable people wearing looks that we ourselves avoid: what we should now call smugness should be seen as an item of historical furniture.

Unfairly, again, the last line of 'Enoch Arden' has been much ridiculed or grieved over. Harold Nicolson called it 'fatal', though he admired the rest, which seemed to him 'well-constructed' and 'moving'. The ending of the poem tells of the death of Enoch, who had returned to his home town after being presumed lost at sea, and who, on finding his 'widow' married to his rival, had remained incognito until his death:

> So past the strong heroic soul away.
> And when they buried him, the little port
> Had seldom seen a costlier funeral.

Tennyson's own defence was 'The costly funeral is all that poor Annie could do for him after he was gone. This is entirely introduced for her sake, and, in my opinion, quite necessary to the perfection of the Poem and the simplicity of the narrative.' The costliness of that funeral is a detail of social history. The fashion for display in the funerals of a hundred years ago was seized on by Tennyson, as it would have been by the little seaport, as a means, luckily to hand, of honouring the heroic in Enoch.

A knowledge of the times will also help to reinstate 'The May Queen' in favour. The mid-twentieth century dislikes the putting of death-beds into poems or novels, unless it can dilate, as mid-nineteenth-century writers did not, upon their physical horrors. Again this is fashion, and nothing else. Making allowance for it, we are freed to see the poem more for what it is—three lyrical monologues by a young girl, 'little Alice', first in health, than at an early and late stage of a very common fatal disease. Tennyson thoroughly understands Alice. She begins as 'wild and wayward', self-centred and enjoying her power over the opposite sex. The first line of the poem shows her as imperious:

You must wake and call me early, call me early, call me early
> mother dear.

When the disease has come on her, its good effect on her character is shown by the new version of that first line, which introduces the second stage of the poem:

If you're waking call me early, call me early, mother dear.

Alice speaks at length, and that also is fitting—the landlady, who is the recipient of Enoch Arden's dying confession, responds with 'voluble' sympathy, words sometimes being all the help that can be given to a death-bed, or the only possible occupation of the dying. It is even possible that Alice's Tennysonian touches are in character: in health she describes herself as running past her slighted lover 'like a flash of light', and she also speaks lines like:

And the wild marshmarigold shines like fire in swamps and
     hollows grey.

When the disease is on her there is more of this, and indeed, as Walter de la Mare for one noticed, some stanzas that are Tennyson supreme:

All in the wild March-morning I heard the angels call;
It was when the moon was setting, and the dark was over
     all;
The trees began to whisper, and the wind began to roll,
And in the wild March-morning I heard them call my
     soul . . .

O look! the sun begins to rise, the heavens are in a glow;
He shines upon a hundred fields, and all of them I know.
And there I move no longer now, and there his light may
     shine—
Wild flowers in the valley for other hands than mine.

True, we should have to think of Alice as gifted with unusual expressiveness to allow that these Tennysonian things are 'authentic'. Such things, however, have not so much literal authenticity as accordance with literary convention: a poet or novelist writing of a second person usually endows him with something of his own literary powers, as Dickens does in *Bleak House* when he allots part of the narration to Esther Summerson. We accept this as a matter of course, as we accept metrical speech in a poem. 'The May Queen' is a good poem, some of its goodness being accessible only to the reader who can transport himself back to Tennyson's times.

The detractors who assailed Tennyson, particularly

from the sixties onwards, had one ground that cannot be wholly removed. He is not always successful with his human beings. In 'The Dream of Fair Women' the dreamer meets Cleopatra:

> A queen, with swarthy cheeks and bold black eyes,
>   Brow-bound with burning gold.

> She, flashing forth a haughty smile, began:
>   'I govern'd men by change, and so I sway'd
> All moods. 'Tis long since I have seen a man.
>   Once, like the moon, I made

> 'The ever-shifting currents of the blood
>   According to my humour ebb and flow.
> I have no men to govern in this wood;
>   That makes my only woe.

Tennyson's account, though it improves later, is so far at least an insult to Shakespeare s 'serpent of old Nile'. More important is the unsatisfactoriness of Arthur in the *Idylls of the King*. The defect may be put down to irreconcilable aims, the writing being partly in the manner of the epic, and partly in that of the novel. Goldwin Smith found the *Idylls* 'impregnated with the spirit, not of the age of chivalry, but the age of Goethe': in which actions are referred to the moral character and psyche of the actors.[1] This course Tennyson might well have been equal to; there is 'Enoch Arden' to support the possibility. To have handled the matter of Arthur, Guinevere, and Lancelot, however, as a novelist, would have detracted from something else that Tennyson had at heart, the creation of a kingly figure completely noble. As epigraph for his poem Tennyson chose the exalted words of Joseph of Exeter: 'Flos Regum Arthurus'. Perhaps in justice his poem should be placed among the poems of patriotism, and its central defect of characterization explained on that score. A version of pure epic written with all Tennyson's

[1] In his review of Thackeray's *Virginians*, *Edinburgh Review* (Oct. 1859).

splendour and grandeur might have carried his ideal king. To depart from epic, however, into novel was to mistake. Epic meant speechifying: but not in the mode of Arthur's long speech of accusation to Guinevere. It did not occur to Tennyson's exalted Arthur that he may have asked too much of his queen as of his knights. His bitterness should have been at least partly levelled against his own over-weening expectations. The *Idylls of the King* tells of a romantic enterprise, romantic in the sense of forlorn; in a novel Arthur would have seen this, and behaved differently. He would have belonged more fully to the post-Goethean world. The characterization of Guinevere and Lancelot is much better done, because epic nobility is not there so much at stake.

Against these partial failures in characterization may be opposed the many shorter poems in which the grip on character, especially as it stands for its portrait to be painted, is strong. Instances are numerous, for Tennyson was prolific of what in the nineteenth century came finally to be called the dramatic monologue. There are the many people re-created out of classical poetry—Ulysses, Oenone, Tithonus, Demeter—and the many created out of what he found round about him, the northern farmer, the elderly spinster, the grandmother, the old woman lamenting the death of her son by hanging. Such things we commend because they show a grip on simple character, and also because of the Chaucerian distance separating one from the other: on the one hand, Tithonus, beloved of the Dawn that had conferred on him immortality but not eternal youth:

> Alas! for this gray shadow, once a man—
> So glorious in his beauty and thy choice,
> Who madest him thy chosen, that he seem'd
> To his great heart none other than a God!
> I ask'd thee, 'Give me immortality.'
> Then didst thou grant mine asking with a smile,
> Like wealthy men who care not how they give.

But thy strong Hours indignant work'd their wills,
And beat me down and marr'd and wasted me,
And tho' they could not end me, left me maim'd
To dwell in presence of immortal youth,
Immortal age beside immortal youth,
And all I was, in ashes.

And on the other hand, the 'new style' northern farmer:

Doesn't thou 'ear my 'orse's legs, as they canters awaäy?
Proputty, proputty, proputty—that's what I 'ears 'em saäy.
Proputty, proputty, proputty—Sam, thou's an ass for thy
paäins:
Theer's more sense i' one o' 'is legs nor in all thy braäins.

Woa—theer's a craw to pluck wi' tha, Sam: yon's parson's
'ouse—
Dosn't thou knaw that a man mun be eäther a man or a
mouse?
Time to think on it then; for thou'll be twenty to weeäk.
Proputty, proputty—woä then woä—let ma 'ear mysen
speäk.

Me an' thy muther, Sammy, 'as bean a-talkin' o' thee;
Thou's beän talkin' to muther, an' she beän a tellin' it me.
Thou'll not marry for munny—thou's sweet upo' parson's
lass—
Noä—thou'll marry for luvv—an' we boäth on us thinks
tha an ass.

Such human simplicities—or rather comparative simplicities—Tennyson can do well.

It was to Tennyson's credit that he was wholly and
frankly up to date in the furniture of those of his poems,
the great majority, in which he spoke on contemporary
matters. Writing them as he did, he related them to the
controversy between the idealists and the realists. This
controversy had arisen because of the uneasiness felt in

some quarters now that the old idea of decorum had been abandoned, and a poem of any literary kind whatever was free to draw its words from as much of the dictionary as it liked. Some writers saw the new freedom as a threat to the honour of poetry. The importance of what was felt to be at stake is attested by the spread of the controversy to take in novels and blank-verse plays. The idealists, principal among whom was Bulwer (novelist, dramatist, poet), were for limiting the scope of literature to things dignified and beautiful in man and the external world, including the objects man had made by recombining parts of it. Thackeray's stand for 'truth' was made in the interests of the sum of things, and his turning up the seamy side was his response to idealist provocation. To a writer of novels 'truth' or realism mainly meant a clearer look at men's motives and morals.

The conflict between idealism and realism posed a sharper problem for poets than for novelists, and was at its sharpest where diction was concerned. We can best understand it by looking back over the history of English poetry, especially during its latter centuries. Pope had used diction according to the rules imposed by the 'kinds', which over and above words common to writing in whatever kinds allowed the use of the whole dictionary for satire, essay, and epistle, but not for epic, pastoral, and related kinds, which limited themselves to words judged to be dignified and beautiful. During the latter half of the eighteenth century certain poets turned away from Pope, or at least from his *Pastorals*, *Homer*, satires, essays, and epistles, and by the beginning of the new century had achieved a new concept of poetry requiring it to limit its subject-matter as much as possible to the dignified and beautiful, and so to use only words appropriate to that end. They accepted the principle by which their epic and pastoral predecessors had used only words of dignity and beauty, but now had another idea as to which words qualified to be so described: they now spoke of the 'sea' rather than of the 'liquid plain' (though Tennyson spoke of 'placid ocean-plains') but it was still about dignified and beautiful things like the sea that they preferred to speak, and to speak in words aesthetically appropriate. Keats preferred 'poesy' to 'poetry' for use in verse, and his preference typified the poet's new limitation of topic and expression. The idealists of the mid-century preferred to compose 'poesy' rather than poetry, and this preference led the young Arnold in 1849, while allowing that the 'age and all one's surroundings' was, as he put it in Carlylese, 'not unprofound, not ungrand, not unmoving', to lament that it was 'deeply *unpoetical*'. The idealists had accordingly to find their poesy elsewhere. In other words, poets could not be expected to cope with railways and the other 'deeply unpoetical' novelties that were helping to make the nineteenth century the *saeculum mirabile*. Ruskin had declared in *Modern Painters*, III, that 'energetic admiration may be excited in certain minds by a display of fireworks, or a street of handsome shops; but the feeling is not poetical, because the grounds of it are false, and therefore ignoble'. He proceeded in explanation: 'There is in reality nothing to deserve admiration either in the firing of packets of gunpowder or in the display of the stocks of warehouses. But admiration excited by the budding of a flower is a poetical feeling, because it is impossible that this manifestation of spiritual power and vital beauty can ever be enough admired.' This is not an instance of Ruskin being successfully persuasive; to refer a display of fireworks to packets of gunpowder is like referring one of Turner's pictures to tubes of paint. But his remarks accord well with the theory of the idealists. The very words 'railway', 'train', 'junction', and so on were impossible in poesy, nor could poets resort to periphrasis, which had now become available only for comic or satiric purposes.

The problem of a poet's topic and diction had been well aired during the long controversy of whether or not Pope

was a poet, and was continued over the group of verse
dramatists who in the forties called themselves the
'Syncretics'. It could not be expected that a topic so wide
and subtle would be analysed to the bottom, but a notable
·paper on it was contributed to the *Westminster* of 1842 by
Lewes, in which he reviewed the printed text of two
recent tragedies, *Nina Sforza* by R. Zouch Troughton
and *The Patrician's Daughter* by John Westland Marston.
This latter boasted a prologue by Dickens by way of
manifesto:

> Awake the Present! Shall no scene display
> The tragic passions of the passing day?

Lewes noted that blank verse was not a suitable medium
for M.P.s in 1841, even if it might be allowed to seem so
for remoter legislators. His alternative, however, was
more encouraging for novelists than for poets: 'there is
stuff of tragedy in the age of civilisation—but the
tragedy, in its treatment, must be different from that of
one placed in a distant era. Instead of being poetical, it
must be prose.' The old sort of tragedy was no longer
fully possible. The nineteenth century preferred 'hard-
luck' stories, and if a poet wished to write one, he could
do so without embarrassment by retelling or inventing a
story of long ago, a 'Sohrab and Rustum' or an item in an
*Idylls of the King*. To specify the tragic, however, was to
limit the discussion, which when unlimited concerned
the admission of modern things into any poem other than
a comic one. Lewes asked what a poet would do with a
man called Wiggins. He forgot that such a name had not
embarrassed earlier poets. Waller had started a poem of
compliment with 'Ingenious Higgons ...', and Wordsworth another with 'Spade! with which Wilkinson hath
till'd his Lands'—it may still be well to add that, the poem
being by Wordsworth, the poetry only suffers for those
who still need poetry to be poesy. They had been unem-
barrassed because poesy with its restrictions was as yet

unknown. They were free to put life before a particular
view of art, as Johnson had advocated when he deplored
those epitaphs that did not embody the name of the
lamented, and so insulted his memory by suggesting that
the tribute was 'stock'. An idealist poet would have had
to risk insult, and hedge, as Arnold did in calling Clough
'Thyrsis', and as Swinburne did when he named the
subject only in the title. In 'real life' we accept Wiggins
without noticing what we are accepting, though we may
grant that it makes a difference if Wiggins is the name
selected by a poet, or even a novelist, for a fictitious
personage. The choice of it would argue some particular
literary purpose such as Masefield had in the early 1900s.

Various mid-nineteenth-century poets solved the
problem variously. Browning took it by the horns,
having no use for poesy. He rejoiced in trailing his coat
before the idealists, insisting that poets were as free as
prose-writers to talk of Hobbs, Nobbs, Stokes, and
Nokes as any man might. He even outstripped Dickens
by giving one of his Englishmen the impossible name of
Gigadibs. Clough saw that poetry unrestricted as to
words could still please its readers merely by being in
metres more or less elaborate, and through a gay alertness
of mind and trenchancy of word. Arnold often chose to
write of ancient matters, but for contemporary ones
usually preferred 'free verse' as being nearer to conversation and so further from poesy.

Tennyson struck his readers as having solved the problem with an easy felicity. The dignity and beauty of his
poetry was never in question, even when its topic, before
he came to treat it, would have struck the idealists as
incorrigibly unpoetical. Arthur Hallam, like anybody
else, was unpoetical outside *In Memoriam*, but became
poetical inside it, even without the help of Corydon
or Thyrsis, when frankly invoked as 'my lost Arthur'.
(Not that Tennyson could have proceeded as frankly if
Hallam's name had been Jabez Wiggins; but he would

have got over the difficulty without recourse to poesy.)
That excellent critic George Brimley,[1] in a passing comment on 'The Brook, an Idyl', remarked its 'handling of
modern names, things, habits, boldly and as a matter of
course, yet so simply and gracefully as to avoid the
slightest jar of vulgarity or laughableness'. Here is the
opening of the poem:

> Here, by this brook, we parted; I to the East
> And he for Italy—too late—too late:
> One whom the strong sons of the world despise;
> For lucky rhymes to him were scrip and share,
> And mellow metres more than cent for cent ...

And Ruskin's fears about 'fireworks' in poetry had
already been dispelled by the Prologue to *The Princess*,
where the garden fête is described:

> a fire-balloon
> Rose gem-like up before the dusky groves
> And dropt a fairy parachute and past:
> And there thro' twenty posts of telegraph
> They flash'd a saucy message to and fro
> Between the mimic stations; so that sport
> Went hand in hand with Science; otherwhere
> Pure sport: a herd of boys with clamour bowl'd
> And stump'd the wicket; babies roll'd about
> Like tumbled fruit in grass ...

In such things modernity glows with the poetry seen in it
by a poet, others having to wait until shown it. Even that
everyday diminutive 'babies', which would have been
proscribed by the idealists as too unpoetical for poesy, did
not trouble Tennyson, whose simile bestows on them the
sort of poetical richness we associate with the canvases of
Renoir.

Whenever nineteenth-century things are brought into
Tennyson's poems they deserve such praise as Brimley

---

[1] *Fraser's* (1855), p. 264.

gave to the 'idylls of the hearth' or such as *Fraser's* in 1872
gave to poems on another sort of modern theme:

There is a curious repugnance in these new poets to deal with
the tangible facts of modern life. With few exceptions their
figures, their ideas, their expression, belong to regions remote
from us in time and thought. They are Greek, or Italian, or
French, occasionally old English or Scotch; only the England
in which we now live is a sort of forbidden ground. And here
Mr. Tennyson's superiority comes out with unquestionable
force. He has a power of laying hold on the living sympathies
of his fellow-men from which those who set themselves to
write only for the elect body or church who share with them a
peculiar incommunicable gift of artistic insight have deliberately cut themselves off. ... [*In the* Charge of the Light
Brigade] the poet spoke with the voice of the nation and ... has
fixed the memory of that ride in the hearts of this generation of
Englishmen.

The same idealist-realist shadow fell over the matter of
science, if a poet wished to write of it in verse now so far
removed from the couplets and Miltonic blank verse
favoured for the topic in the eighteenth century. Here
again Tennyson triumphed. His introduction of it into
his dignified and beautiful poetry never offended with the
smell of technicalities. The close of Section 10 of *In
Memoriam*, for instance, reads:

> O to us,
> The fools of habit, sweeter seems
>
> To rest beneath the clover sod,
>   That takes the sunshine and the rains,
>   Or where the kneeling hamlet drains
> The chalice of the grapes of God;
>
> Than if with thee the roaring wells
>   Should gulf him fathom-deep in brine;
>   And hands so often clasp'd in mine,
> Should toss with tangle and with shells.

'Tangle' is Tennyson's version of the name 'oar-weed' (a sort of seaweed), which botanists know as *laminaria digitata*. His name for it is not only pleasant, but integrates the thing into the very grief of the poem: he cannot bear the thought that seaweed might clasp with its fingers (*digitata*) the hands so often clasped in his. Newman, who said that 'Poetry . . . is always the antagonist of science',[1] and Arnold, who found the age 'deeply unpoetical', did not see that the mind was widening its operations to take in large and small items of the physical world hitherto ignored, that fact was being met, as it always must be, with feeling.

One of the firmest indications of Tennyson's greatness is the evidence in his poems of the strength of his relation to external nature. Not even Ruskin or Hopkins is greater in this kind. His relation to it varies. Faithful to the values of the common man, he prizes his link with it as it lies subdued in the vicinity of village or mansion. In reading *Maud* we gather bit by bit the complete layout of the countryside, sloping down to the sea—the moor, the Hall above the meadow and the wood, and the village below; and in the opening of 'Enoch Arden' the topography of the seaport is presented all at once, complete except for one detail added later—'leafy lanes behind the down' where stands 'a lonely Hall' with its 'portal-warding lion-whelp, / And peacock-yewtree'. In describing the scene Tennyson has hit on the method much employed nowadays by the film:

> Long lines of cliff breaking have left a chasm;
> And in the chasm are foam and yellow sands;
> Beyond, red roofs about a narrow wharf
> In cluster; then a moulder'd church; and higher
> A long street climbs to one tall-tower'd mill;

[1] *Historical Sketches*, III. 386 (written in 1858).

And high in heaven behind it a gray down
With Danish barrows; and a hazelwood,
By autumn nutters haunted, flourishes
Green in a cuplike hollow of the down.

It is unnecessary to illustrate his many felicitous accounts of hundreds of places, some of them named with their map-names. Eighteenth- and nineteenth-century poetry was leading the way for novelists, who were now giving a full account of where their fictional events were supposed to take place. Tennyson was both their supreme guide and standard. His description of gardens is worth dwelling on. He could be claimed as a great poet merely on the evidence of his many pictures of them, just as Monet could be as a great painter merely on the evidence of his many paintings of the pool of water-lilies. James Joyce's joking reference to 'Lawn Tennyson' implies gardens of a high civilization that are worth the name, complete with the happiness found in cultivated flowers. The garden in *Maud* is perhaps what a reader remembers most vividly. The one preferred by the narrator of 'The Gardener's Daughter; or, the Pictures' is not sealed off, as Maud's is, from its surrounding pastures:

Not wholly in the busy world, nor quite
Beyond it, blooms the garden that I love.
News from the humming city comes to it
In sound of funeral or of marriage bells,
And, sitting muffled in dark leaves, you hear
The windy clanging of the minster clock;
Although between it and the garden lies
A league of grass, wash'd by a slow broad stream,
That, stirr'd with languid pulses of the oar,
Waves all its lazy lilies, and creeps on,
Barge-laden, to three arches of a bridge
Crown'd with the minster-towers.

'Lawn Tennyson' may be allowed to epitomize Tennyson's many accounts of nature civilized, but not

those equally numerous accounts of nature at its wildest
and largest: one or two instances will suffice to recall the
rest:

> in my own dark garden ground,
> Listening now to the tide in its broad-flung ship-wrecking
>     roar,
> Now to the scream of a madden'd beach dragg'd down by the
>     wave,
> Walk'd in a wintry wind by a ghastly glimmer, and found
> The shining daffodil dead, and Orion low in his grave.

The word-painting Tennyson did was almost wholly
the sort that might have been done 'with the eye on the
object', as Wordsworth counselled. What happened
when his eye had not seen the object he wanted to
describe for the sake of a particular poem has been well
put by Harold Nicolson:

*The Voyage of Maeldune*, which takes him necessarily very far
from Lincolnshire, Cornwall, or even Cauteretz, does not
tempt him to wander from the safe ground of his own experience. The trees met with on that romantic Odyssey are
confined to the poplar, the cypress and the pine; the fauna does
not extend beyond the lark, the cock, the bull and the dog; the
flowers are not more exotic than the clematis, convolvulus,
passion-flower, lily, poppy, tulip, gorse and rose.

In other words, Tennyson does his best in a dilemma,
having to choose between the new scientific principle and
the needs of a topic he was intent on writing on, and
which he could only hope to supply by means of the
imagination prompted by books—and perhaps by paintings.[1] His great feat when he chose to rely on books was
the description of Enoch's island, which travellers
applauded for its accuracy.

---

[1] In 'The Palace of Art', 72–84, he may be recalling successively Samuel
Palmer's *Cornfield by Moonlight*, Constable's *Salisbury Cathedral from the
Meadows*, and Crome's *Slate Quarries*; see Alethea Hayter, *Opium and the
Romantic Imagination* (1968), p. 92.

The delights of describing with eye on object resulted in passages that achieved little more poetry than comes of accuracy and its neat expression, as in the minor term in this description of Katie Willows's hair in 'The Brook':

> her hair
> In gloss and hue the chestnut, when the shell
> Divides threefold to show the fruit within.

Such things were received as delightful novelties: in Cranford Mrs. Gaskell shows Mr. Holbrook marvelling that ash buds, now that a reading of 'The Gardener's Daughter' had opened his eyes, are indeed superlatively black. Tennyson, less pedagogically than Ruskin, gave his readers eyes for the appearance of the face of nature in all its grandeur and beauty. We can call these descriptions by the name that was now coming to be given to them—'word-painting', of which at the time there were so many that Hopkins exclaimed 'Word painting is, in the verbal arts, the great success of our day'.[1]

Sometimes those descriptions are pictures held, as it were, at arm's length. Often, however, Tennyson represents the poet, or the person he is writing of, as concerned with the external world much more intimately. There was nothing novel about that—indeed Ruskin found enough of it in literature to warrant his creation of a literary category, that of the 'pathetic fallacy'—the fallacy being that by which men ascribe their own feelings to natural things that happen to be round about them. The most striking instance in Tennyson is the opening of *Maud* where the almost morbidly sensitive hero floods the landscape with his own haunted memory of his father's financial disaster and violent death:

I hate the dreadful hollow behind the little wood,
Its lips in the field above are dabbled with blood-red heath,
The red-ribb'd ledges drip with a silent horror of blood ...

[1] *Letters to Bridges*, p. 267.

And out he walk'd when the wind like a broken worldling
   wail'd,
And the flying gold of the ruin'd woodlands drove thro' the
   air.

The hero of *Maud* almost makes a way of life of this
attracting of the external world to himself—in 'Go not,
happy day', and in such lines as: 'The silent sapphire-
spangled marriage-ring of the land', 'The planet of Love
... beginning to faint in the light that she loves / On a bed
of daffodil sky'.

   Another sort of triumph is evident when Tennyson
renders the impact of external nature on his senses by
means for which word-painting is inept. Section 95 of *In
Memoriam* is an account of a family party on the lawn 'by
night' in genial summer weather, after which the poet
lingers on, rereading letters of his dead friend and
experiencing a sense of his friend's presence. Then the
external world around him, which had been described at
the outset, comes again on his senses, night now giving
way to dawn:

> Till now the doubtful dusk reveal'd
>    The knolls once more where, couch'd at ease,
>    The white kine glimmer'd, and the trees
> Laid their dark arms about the field:
>
> And suck'd from out the distant gloom
>    A breeze began to tremble o'er
>    The large leaves of the sycamore,
> And fluctuate all the still perfume,
>
> And gathering freshlier overhead,
>    Rock'd the full-foliaged elms, and swung
>    The heavy-folded rose, and flung
> The lilies to and fro, and said
>
> 'The dawn, the dawn,' and died away;
>    And East and West, without a breath,
>    Mixt their dim lights, like life and death,
> To broaden into boundless day.

Among other things, that passage illustrates what almost amounts to a law—that the poet who, like Pope or Tennyson, lives with words as with the air he breathes, finds those he needs for his meaning to be just those he needs for his music, finding in this instance that the common English word for daybreak is a scrap of music that a stirring of the air might be appropriately imagined as saying. (In the same way in *Maud* the name of the heroine was chosen, we must suppose, quite independently of its lucky usefulness for reproducing the cry of rooks:

> Birds in the high Hall-garden
>  When twilight was falling,
> Maud, Maud, Maud, Maud,
>  They were crying and calling.)

Like many poets before him, but with superior materials to hand, Tennyson occasionally enjoyed sporting with nature in the elegant manner of Ovid's *Metamorphoses* rivalled by Pope in his 'Fable of Dryope':

> ... the creeping rind invades
> My closing lips, and hides my head in shades ...
> And all the nymph was lost within the tree.

Early instances are 'The Dying Swan', 'Amphion', and 'The Sleeping Beauty'. These fantasies are outdone by 'The Voyage of Maeldune', which recounts the experience of sailors who visit in turn an island of silence, of shouting, of flowers, and so on. The description, which manipulates for 'magic' purposes materials Tennyson had gathered with eye on object, is accomplished with a godlike ease—Tennyson was 'born', as we say, to write this poem; and his version of the natural world is more ravishing—brilliant, vivid, and thrilling—than any other poet's:

> And we came to the Isle of Flowers: their breath met us
>  out on the seas,

For the Spring and the middle Summer sat each on the lap
  of the breeze;
And the red passion-flower to the cliffs, and the dark blue
  clematis, clung,
And starr'd with a myriad blossom the long convolvulus
  hung;
And the topmost spire of the mountain was lilies in lieu of
  snow,
And the lilies like glaciers winded down, running out
  below.
Thro' the fire of the tulip and poppy, the blaze of gorse,
  and the blush
Of millions of roses that sprang without leaf or a thorn
  from the bush;
And the whole isle-side flashing down from the peak
  without ever a tree
Swept like a torrent of gems from the sky to the blue of
  the sea.

Tennyson also excelled as a describer of external nature
as it was becoming known about by the great scientists,
who unlike painters and most poets are not content with
the appearance of things. Much had been done of this
kind in the eighteenth century—by Pope, for example,
and Thomson; and Shelley had daringly made scientific
fact the matter for lyrics. It was Tennyson, however,
whose mind and imagination were most tightly gripped
by the deeply exploring scientists, especially Lyell and the
astronomers. Even in *Poems of Two Brothers* he showed an
interest in books of science, the annotations naming
works like Sir William Jones's *Eastern Plants* and 'Baker
on animalculæ'. By 1842 the evidence was mounting
impressively, witness in particular 'The Two Voices'. In
*The Princess*, *In Memoriam*, and in many later poems
everything is admitted that bore on what Huxley called
the question of questions for the nineteenth century—
man's place in nature. Man encloses 'the ape and the
tiger', he walks on a planet that had been cast off by the
sun as a drop of water might be by a waterfall, a planet

that may be destined to lose its human beings by the freezing-up or explosion of the sun—'sun-flame or sun-less frost'—that sun itself being a mere drop in what Carlyle phrased as the 'sea of stars', and which Tennyson worded in passages such as this in the Epilogue to 'The Charge of the Heavy Brigade':

> The fires that arch this dusky dot—
>     Yon myriad-worlded way—
> The vast sun-clusters' gather'd blaze,
>     World-isles in lonely skies,
> Whole heavens within themselves ...

Contemporary scientists were grateful to Tennyson as the 'poet of science', as a poet worthy of the grandeur of science in the nineteenth century. The startling prophecy made in the famous preface to the *Lyrical Ballads* had come true earlier than even Wordsworth expected—that as science comes home to men's business and bosoms poets 'will be at [the scientists'] side', expressing man's new interest. Oliver Lodge acted as spokesman for his fellow scientists when he wrote of Tennyson: 'It is generally admitted ... that whenever reference is made to facts of nature in the poems or the fringe of Science touched on,—as it so often is,—the reference is satisfying and the touch precise.' As a scientist he was also impressed by the poet's 'clear comprehension of the fundamental aspects' of the controversial questions discussed in his time.[1] But Tennyson is more than 'satisfying' and 'precise'.

[He] put into his poems all the new things that men had just learned to see and to make, and his greatness as a poet is that he put in with them his grasp of their distance, their age, their size (immense or infinitesimal), their appearance, their sudden power to stretch the mind, their meaning for mankind. The geologists had taught Tennyson that where London stands had once stood sea. Tennyson responded to that fact as a scientist, and also as a poet:

[1] Hallam Tennyson, *Tennyson and his Friends* (1911), p. 281.

> There where the long street roars, hath been
> The stillness of the central sea.

He states a fact so as to start a sublime emotion. In the minds of scientists and ordinary men scientific facts prompt an emotion which may be sublime but which they can express, if by words at all, only by words that are inadequate.[1] ... Tennyson always brings age and immensity within our human reach. The highest pitch to which human words have climbed seems to me ... Tennyson's translation of a scrap of the *Iliad*:

> As when in heaven the stars about the moon
> Look beautiful, when all the winds are laid,
> And every height comes out, and jutting peak
> And valley, and the immeasurable heavens
> Break open to their highest. ...

Homer could not get so high because he had not read the books Tennyson had read, because his eye had not haunted, as Tennyson's had the telescope. Science helped Tennyson to be a greater poet.[2]

It is never true that 'brooding over scientific opinion ... often extinguishes the central flame in Tennyson.'[3]

Tennyson's thought about the way expanding scientific truth was now coming home to men's business and bosoms, as distinct from delighting their newly awakened eyes, was embraced by some for the comforts it gave them as men by the time that Tennyson had reached the conclusions of his arguments, while others found that they did not themselves need that final leap into Optimism—found that 'science' (not necessarily in

---

[1] In his *Malay Archipelago* (1869), II. 223, Alfred Russel Wallace, confronted with a new range of glorious things, wishes there were a poet at hand to record their glory.

[2] [G. Tillotson, *Criticism and the Nineteenth Century* (1951), pp. 224, 226–7; from 'English Poetry in the Nineteenth Century', Inaugural lecture, 1945, where the theme is more fully developed. The most thorough recent treatment is in M. Millhauser, 'Fire and Ice, the Influence of Science on Tennyson's Poetry', Tennyson Society, 1971. *Ed.*]

[3] W. B. Yeats, 'The Symbolism of Poetry' (1900), collected in *Essays* (1924), p. 200.

the professional sense) furnished them with a philosophy satisfactorily complete. Henry Sidgwick, the Cambridge philosopher, was one of the latter. In a letter to Tennyson's son in 1895 he wrote that his own generation in the 1860s 'absorbed in struggling for freedom of thought in the trammels of a historical religion', took 'a more sceptical and less Christian view' than that of *In Memoriam*; but with the passing years its influence had increased.[1] Some years later A. E. Housman rejected Tennyson's conclusion with characteristically scornful imagery: 'He described the argument of *In Memoriam* as being that "things must come right in the end, because it would be so very unpleasant if they did not", adding that, "if God had answered Tennyson out of the whirlwind as he answered Job, he would have said, 'Who is this that darkeneth counsel by words without knowledge?'"[2] His comment, while it overlooked the amount of Tennyson's knowledge that overlapped with Huxley's, was fair towards Tennyson in so far as he claimed as knowledge, as Newman did, what fulfilled the desires of his heart. Huxley paid Tennyson a rare compliment when he 'spoke strongly of the insight into scientific method shown in ... "In Memoriam"'. There came a point, however, where Tennyson, unlike Huxley, threw over 'scientific method', and felt impelled to proceed by Newman's means. For Newman angels, miracles, the supernatural are 'fact': for Tennyson things we know as facts on earth survive elsewhere. Tennyson cannot rest content with thinking beyond a certain point. Thereafter he leaps ahead with hope, or trust. There would be nothing wrong with that were it not that Tennyson sometimes speaks as if the new step had been taken by thinking. What he hopes for he claims as fact. In *In Memoriam* after the long discussion by the mind about man and the æon-old universe, he does frankly admit that

[1] *Tennyson, a Memoir* (1897), I. 301.
[2] Recalled by R. W. Chambers (*Man's Unconquerable Mind*, 1939, p. 371).

the way to avoid materialist conclusions is by allowing
feeling to be supreme:

> If e'er when faith had fall'n asleep,
>   I heard a voice 'believe no more'
>   And heard an ever-breaking shore
> That tumbled in the Godless deep;
>
> A warmth within the breast would melt
>   The freezing reason's colder part,
>   And like a man in wrath the heart
> Stood up and answer'd 'I have felt.'
>
> No, like a child in doubt and fear:
>   But that blind clamour made me wise;
>   Then was I as a child that cries,
> But, crying, knows his father near.

We know how profound Tennyson's feelings were. Even
as expressed in the poems they are often nearer being
suicidal than those of any other great poet. And they had
been stirred to their dark depths by the early death of
Hallam. Tennyson could go on, he testified later, only if
he suspended the pursuit of scientific method and assured
himself of the immortality of the soul. All other Christian
dogmas he questioned, but not that. He assured himself
of its truth—*In Memoriam* gives us some inkling of the
torments prior to that assurance—by claiming it as truth
and fact, as the earth itself was truth and fact, but on the
sole evidence of his own passionate need and hope.
Newman believed because he loved, and held, as Tennyson did, that external truth is discoverable by the heart.
On other occasions, however, Tennyson speaks with
the confidence that thought alone could have given
him. Two poems end by proclaiming immortality as
a fact: 'Parnassus', which admits but defies two new
and 'terrible' Muses, Astronomy and Geology; and
the 'Epilogue' to 'The Charge of the Heavy Brigade at
Balaclava':

> ... Let it live then—ay, till when?
>   Earth passes, all is lost
> In what they prophesy, our wise men,
>   Sun-flame or sunless frost,
> And deed and song alike are swept
>   Away, and all in vain
> As far as man can see, except
>   The man himself remain;
> And tho', in this lean age forlorn,
>   Too many a voice may cry
> That man can have no after-morn,
>   Not yet of these am I.
> The man remains, and whatsoe'er
>   He wrought of good or brave
> Will mould him thro' the cycle-year
>   That dawns behind the grave.

Here we pass from the supposition 'except / The man . . . remain' to the statement that man does remain.

Tennyson thinks profoundly about man, who always comes off well in his general statements. The part of 'Tithonus' already quoted[1] contains the line:

> Man comes and tills the field and lies beneath.

We see at once why Tennyson admired Gray, whose 'divine truisms'—such as 'The paths of glory lead but to the grave'—he said 'make me weep'. The power to bring tears by mere statements is one of the certain marks of a poet. Tennyson speaks of man as often as Pope had done, but, like Gray, sees him as a more intimate part of the earth and its seasons than did Pope:

> Old Yew, which graspest at the stones
>   That name the under-lying dead,
>   Thy fibres net the dreamless head,
> Thy roots are wrapt about the bones.

[1] See p. 296.

> The seasons bring the flower again,
>     And bring the firstling to the flock;
>     And in the dusk of thee, the clock
> Beats out the little lives of men.
>
> O not for thee the glow, the bloom,
>     Who changest not in any gale,
>     Nor branding summer suns avail
> To touch thy thousand years of gloom:
>
> And gazing on thee, sullen tree,
>     Sick for thy stubborn hardihood,
>     I seem to fail from out my blood
> And grow incorporate into thee.

Here there is both Man and the individual man writing. Tennyson writing about himself is as good as Tennyson writing about Man. *In Memoriam* is one of the great confessional poems, a kind of poem Tennyson began to write early, as we have seen, in 'Supposed Confessions of a Second-rate Sensitive Mind' and which produced 'The Two Voices'.

Tennyson's 'common touch' can be seen in his remark that 'he would rather have written Gray's 'Elegy' than the whole of Wordsworth',[1] and in the comments recorded by Palgrave on the manuscript of the *Golden Treasury* (1861): 'he would not hear of the book unless it had . . . Gray's Elegy' and 'he would unfeignedly prefer it to all his own poetry'.[2] One of the reasons for excluding Wordsworth was that Gray knew a surer way, or happened on it, for reaching the heart of the people, for achieving a poem that won Johnson to praise it as he praised no other poem. We know that some of Wordsworth's *Lyrical Ballads* were printed as broadsides, and it would be impossible to imagine a great poem more likely to win the commonest reader than 'The Reverie of Poor Susan'; and

---

[1] Reported by A. H. Clough; *Letters to Allingham*, p. 144.
[2] B.M. Add. MS. 42126, folio 98, 224.

yet Wordsworth's simplicities are rather for the sophis-
ticated reader. Gray may have owed his unlettered public
to his not having written down to it, to his having written
up to the Milton standard, but on a solemn matter of
inescapable interest, and combining warmth and splendour with a golden felicity. Perhaps the unlettered like to
stretch up towards the Miltonic, when they are assured of
their interest in what is being sung—on a principle similar
to that which leads countries emerging from barbarism
to insist that if they are to read English books they should
be Shakespeare's. One contemporary critic of the early
Tennyson charged him with 'out-babying Wordsworth
and out-glittering Keats'.[1] (The charge of infantilism
referred, no doubt, to pieces like 'O Darling Room' and
'The Skipping Rope', which Tennyson later dropped.)
There was more hope in Gray's way. There was much of
Gray in *In Memoriam* and in the non–medieval narratives,
of which 'Enoch Arden' became the most famous. For
Gray, as for Wordsworth, the annals of the poor were
short and simple. Gray may have known, as Wordsworth
and Tennyson did, that the interspaces between the
events recorded on the flyleaf of the family Bible were as
crowded as those of Queen Victoria.

When we study Tennyson's art we are studying one of
the subtlest things in our literature. If his matter is not
uniformly great, his music is. He said that he knew the
quantity of every English word except that of 'scissors',
and where others might disagree with him he let them
know where he stood—a note in the Eversley edition
reads: 'Knowledge, shone, knoll—let him who reads me
always read the vowels in these words long'. His remark
about 'quantity' is best understood as showing that for
him words had sonoral lightness, heaviness, 'colour',
mellifluousness, sharpness, and so on, and that a 'mot'

[1] Bulwer Lytton, *The New Timon* (1846).

was 'juste' not merely because it would have best sufficed the expression of his meaning in prose-writing—it had to suffice also his sense of sound.

The music of some of his lines is perhaps too obviously triumphant:

> The moan of doves in immemorial elms,
> The murmur of innumerable bees.

> The long day wanes, the slow moon climbs, the deep
> Moans round with many voices ...

> the spring, that down,
> From underneath a plume of lady-fern,
> Sang, and the sand danced at the bottom of it.

We are left marvelling at such verbal feats, but marvelling partly at cleverness. These effects, however, are but the posters outside the penetralia and all their mysteries. Some of his devices are built on Gray's. Like Gray, he sometimes lets alliteration show and sometimes as deliberately avoids it. Beside such a phrase as Gray's 'drowsy tinklings' we have Tennyson's 'crimson petal'. Then look at the unbelievable lightness of 'letting' in the following lines from one of his earliest poems:

> Where Claribel low-lieth
> The breezes pause and die,
> Letting the rose-leaves fall;

And the contrasted heaviness of the words in the two lines that follow:

> But the solemn oak-tree sigheth,
> Thick-leaved, ambrosial.

Dorothy Sayers remarked a similar subtlety in the lines describing the dandified priest in *Maud*:

> The snowy-banded, dilettante,
> Delicate-handed priest intone ...

where the ending of 'dilettante' followed by the 'd' that begins the next line supplies the rhyme (as near as matters) with 'banded' and 'handed'. (In speaking the lines the tip of the tongue performs a tattoo on the front part of the roof of the mouth.) On every page there are dozens of such delicacies of sound. His most sustained feat as a user of words is in *In Memoriam* which confines them almost entirely to one or two syllables, the dozen or so exceptions coming therefore with extraordinary salience. In the *Idylls*, as Coventry Patmore noted, the diction is mainly Saxon, and some of his revisions are made in the interests of making it more archaic with words like 'costrel' and 'manchet'. Into the *Idylls* there is also a calculated intrusion of speech at its most 'common': 'Ugh!' appears more than once, and speech like 'You should have seen him blush'—'calculated' because too much of it would have detracted from the flowing dignity.

He is the supreme metrist in English, because though Milton and Gray, Coleridge and T. S. Eliot, are as infallible, they do not operate over so wide a range. Every line of the stanza from 'A Spirit haunts the year's last hours'[1] shows his early mastery, as well as his adventurousness. (This adventurousness, not always sure-footed in that first volume, giving a line like 'And a dark cloud with rich moonlight', led the aged Coleridge to exclaim hastily that Tennyson did not understand metre.) He can supply traditional metres with controlled subtlety of rhythm, and create metres strikingly beautiful. The octosyllabic line in the 'Ballad of Oriana' (also of 1830) has such delicate variations as 'At midnight the cock was crowing' and 'While blissful tears blinded my sight'—irregularities which had decisive force for Rossetti. To show his inventiveness, we need go no further than *Maud*, which would be a *tour de force* if it were not all as easily accomplished as a tree accomplishes leaves. It includes something like a dozen distinct metrical shapes. Some are slender, some

[1] *Poems, chiefly Lyrical*; see p. 287 above.

portly, some buoyant, some explosive. They are treated so flexibly that they sometimes seem to change during their brief existence. Some are free verse. 'Come into the garden, Maud' is planned to imitate the rhythm of a polka. When we have mastered the sense of what they are carrying, all of them read themselves, slippery with perfection.

In the creation of metre he was again indebted to Gray, who had invented metres in which what in other poets would be random irregularities were part of the fixed pattern. In the stanza used for 'The Daisy', a sizeable poem, the bold metrical irregularities recur at appointed intervals. The first two lines of each four-line stanza are as regular as either half of the *In Memoriam* stanza:

> What slender campanile grew
> By bays, the peacock's neck in hue,

but see what follows:

> Where, here and there, on sandy beaches
> A milky-bell'd amaryllis blew,

the third line having a syllable added at the end and the fourth and last, which rimes with lines one and two, a syllable added in the third foot. In his contribution to *Tennyson and his Friends* Alfred Lyall noted that the ripple in the last line was not only accentual (strong-weak-weak)—the only consideration that is vital for English metre—but also often quantitative (long-short-short). We may note something else—that these ripples often coincide with words derived from classical sources, 'Mónaco', '-bell'd amar[yllis]', 'citadel', 'Boboli's', 'avenues', 'Maxume', '[met]ropolis', and so on. That is, they are not only metrical events, but draw attention to words prominent in the Italian theme. In the similar stanza used for 'To the Rev. F. D. Maurice' the last line has its one trisyllabic foot regularly placed first in the fourth line. One need not labour the point: Tennyson was the author of that little group of poems he called 'Experiments', two of which were poems that experimented in metre, and the first of which was 'Boädicea', which Swinburne thought 'the highest if not the sweetest of all the notes he ever struck':

> While I roved about the forest, long and bitterly
>     meditating,
> There I heard them in the darkness, at the mystical
>     ceremony,
> Loosely robed in flying raiment, sang the terrible
>     prophetesses,
> 'Fear not, isle of blowing woodland, isle of silvery
>     parapets!
> Tho' the Roman eagle shadow thee, tho' the gathering
>     enemy narrow thee,
> Thou shalt wax and he shall dwindle, thou shalt be the
>     mighty one yet!
> Thine the liberty, thine the glory, thine the deeds to be
>     celebrated,
> Thine the myriad-rolling ocean, light and shadow
>     illimitable,
> Thine the lands of lasting summer, many-blossoming
>     Paradises,
> Thine the North and thine the South and thine the
>     battle-thunder of God.'

Surely this poem is one of the most wonderful metrical achievements in the English language. As a metrist, Tennyson was as adventurous as Browning, but unlike him had mastered his metres down to the last syllable of their application. Browning's 'Women and Roses' introduces regular irregularities of the kind Tennyson used in 'The Daisy', but they pass unnoticed except by the specialist, whereas Tennyson's are beautifully obvious. When Tennyson is denied his place among the greatest English poets it is by people whose ear for music is irredeemably portion of their 'muddy vesture of decay'. Just as our great pianists vie in their attempts to play

Mozart's concertos and sonatas, so should our actors and reciters vie in reading worthily the thousand pages of Tennyson.

Altogether his expression prompted Patmore, reviewing *Maud* in the *Edinburgh*, to write of 'Tennyson's most fastidious taste in the melody of language, seeking purity of tone, sometimes even at the expense of strength on the one hand, and sweetness on the other, and scarcely ever resting until it has arrived at the reduction of our rough and consonantal English to the bell-like clearness of the Italian.' This point about his Italianization of English was repeated (as if for the first time) by Oliver Elton and Dr. Leavis. Its truth is plain up to a point: but the staple of the *Idylls* is Saxon, and our Saxon words are scarcely musical as Italian words are. Moreover, Tennyson's interest in onomatopoeia (in all its bold and subtle forms) makes for clangour and harshness as often as mellifluousness. Perhaps Latin should be invoked rather than Italian. Classical scholars have noted how readily Tennyson's English goes into Latin, but that is a comment on his use of the language as it consists of concrete diction and syntax. The praise accorded to his expression by the *Eclectic Review* in its review of *In Memoriam* is just: 'As regards words merely, Tennyson is undeniably one of the greatest of *expressers*. His is the master's facility. His are the "aptest words to things". In expert "fitting" of the one to the other, his present practice far exceeds even his original gift.'

Poetic technique includes more than expression in words and metre. It includes the art of setting out the matter. Tennyson never attempts a single vast fully integrated structure like that which made Goethe exclaim of *Paradise Lost*, 'How greatly it is all planned'. The *Idylls of the King* comes nearest to earning this high commendation, but though the separate stories of which it is made are provided with interconnections of many kinds—the career of King Arthur and his court, ideas, people, the course of the seasons—the diversity of it all is as much in evidence as the unity. The unity of *Maud* is on a small scale—Tennyson called it his 'little' *Hamlet*. That of *In Memoriam* is the linear, undulant unit of an argument with circlings, pausings, antiphonal returns. No Miltonic planning for matter worthy of Milton was achieved by Tennyson. Perhaps it was avoided as not suitable in the chaotic nineteenth century. Certainly the reader, to put it negatively, finds no *longueurs* in his poems. They progress at what the reader feels to be the right pace. We cannot accept Lascelles Abercrombie's summary that Tennyson had 'no structural imagination'.

It was an oddity of more recent criticism when T. S. Eliot asserted that Tennyson could not tell a story. His ability that way surely is noticeably good. What he cannot do as well as Browning, say, is the psychologizing of a story, making the personages complex in a way that shows the reader deep things in his own psyche. In a self-analytical poem like *In Memoriam* we feel repeatedly that we are seeing new things in ourselves, but not so often in 'Enoch Arden' or the *Idylls of the King*. We recall Browning's comment on how he himself would have treated the ending of Enoch,[1] and his objections to 'Pelleas and Ettarre'.[2] Tennyson can tell us what would have been presented to our eyes, having a great liking for the picture the thing composes itself into, and making us like it with him, but not much about what our brain can infer from the sight. Nevertheless, the narration of the *Idylls* and of 'Enoch Arden' is sufficient answer to Eliot. 'Enoch Arden' is not a novel in verse, of which there were many in Tennyson's day, since it gives us a blank-verse line where a novel gives us a page; it is, however, a novel boiled down. George Eliot could have made a novel by

[1] See *Robert Browning and Julia Wedgwood: Letters*, ed. Richard Curle (1937), pp. 75–7; Annie remains in ignorance, and Enoch is buried as an unknown pauper.
[2] See pp. 339–40.

filling in Tennyson's sketch, Tennyson having made the bones suggest the whole body. He did this by concentrating on what furthers the steady course of the story, by limiting what he says to the weightiest specification, by calling on a word to convey more than 'it would outside its new context. Some moments warrant treatment more expansive—as when, for instance, Annie fails to catch a sight of Enoch's last wave of the hand as his ship passes his home:

> She when the day, that Enoch mention'd, came,
> Borrow'd a glass, but all in vain: perhaps
> She could not fix the glass to suit her eye;
> Perhaps her eye was dim, hand tremulous;
> She saw him not: and while he stood on deck
> Waving, the moment and the vessel past.

Annie's failure here furthers the story because it is one of the links in the heavy chain of their misfortunes, all the worse because in proposing the spy-glass, Enoch had tried to cheer her up:

> At length she spoke 'O Enoch, you are wise;
> And yet for all your wisdom well know I
> That I shall look upon your face no more.'

> 'Well then,' said Enoch, 'I shall look on yours,
> Annie, the ship I sail in passes here
> (He named the day) get you a seaman's glass
> Spy out my face, and laugh at all your fears.

Again, we do not live through the stages by which the little shop fails—the shop which Enoch, before embarking, had provided for Annie in the front room of their cottage. Its failure is explained by her incapacity for business, which is briefly analysed rather than shown in action, and is clinched by the word 'solitary', placed in the account of the visit paid to Annie by her second husband-to-be:

'Surely' said Philip 'I may see her now,
May be some little comfort;' therefore went,
Past thro' the solitary room in front ...

Enoch's voyage across the world is suggested in a dozen lines:

... prosperously sail'd
The ship 'Good Fortune,' though at setting forth
The Biscay, roughly ridging eastward, shook
And almost overwhelm'd her, yet unvext
She slipt across the summer of the world,
Then after a long tumble about the Cape
And frequent interchange of foul and fair,
She passing through the summer world again,
The breath of heaven came continually
And sent her sweetly by the golden isles,
Till silent in her oriental haven.

'Enoch Arden' is a narrative of Chaucerian shapeliness. Swinburne said that Morris's Muse (in the *Earthly Paradise*) 'drags her robes as she walks; I really think a Muse (when she is neither resting nor flying) ought to tighten her girdle, tuck up her skirts, and step out. It is better than Tennyson's short-winded and artificial concision—but there is such a thing as swift and spontaneous style. Top's is spontaneous and slow ...'[1] One could scarcely call Tennyson's narrative pace swift, but he does 'step out' and not shuffle.

A remarkable, perhaps unique, power of his, a power of a structural sort, is that by which he can keep the top spinning—achieve a long, spreading, developing sentence, covering many stanzas without pausing for breath. Several sections of *In Memoriam* consist of one of these sentences, and one of the longest-drawn, most mounting, triumphantly closes the poem. The same inexhaustibleness along with speed marks the ecstatic 'Go not, happy day ...'

His structural power is at its subtlest in the lyrics, and

[1] *The Swinburne Letters*, II. 68 (letter of 10 Dec. 1869).

in the sections, lyric-short, of *In Memoriam*. Take the greatest of all the lyrics, one of the songs included in the fifth edition of *The Princess*:

> Now sleeps the crimson petal, now the white;
> Nor waves the cypress in the palace walk;
> Nor winks the gold fin in the porphyry font:
> The fire-fly wakens: waken thou with me.
>
> Now droops the milkwhite peacock like a ghost,
> And like a ghost she glimmers on to me.
>
> Now lies the Earth all Danaë to the stars,
> And all thy heart lies open unto me.
>
> Now slides the silent meteor on, and leaves
> A shining furrow, as thy thoughts in me.
>
> Now folds the lily all her sweetness up,
> And slips into the bosom of the lake:
> So fold thyself, my dearest, thou, and slip
> Into my bosom and be lost in me.

Sensuousness, colour, loveliness, sweetness, all these existing along with delicacy to the point of precision—surely, in comparison, other poets seem to have fists without fingers. But my present point is structure. Let the reader note that though there is no rhyme there is instead a bell-like repetition of 'me' at the end of five of the twelve lines, a musical effect binding the whole together. Let him also count up the variety of quality in the half-dozen links between the lover and the things around him.

Take another short lyric, 'In the Valley of Cauteretz', in which Tennyson recalls Arthur Hallam:

> All along the valley, stream that flashest white,
> Deepening thy voice with the deepening of the night,
> All along the valley, where thy waters flow,
> I walk'd with one I loved two and thirty years ago.

All along the valley while I walk'd to-day,
The two and thirty years were a mist that rolls away;
For all along the valley, down thy rocky bed
Thy living voice to me was as the voice of the dead,
And all along the valley, by rock and cave and tree,
The voice of the dead was a living voice to me.

The structure of this needs no demonstration. The melli-fluous phrase 'all along the valley' has an appropriate mooning softness, almost somnolent, as the poet's feet plod onward, his mind remembering and achieving a new experience, expressed with the ironic neatness of logic.

To Tennyson most of all poets we can apply FitzGerald's often-quoted words on Mozart: 'people cannot believe that he is *powerful* because he is so beautiful'.

# 9. BROWNING

IT IS difficult for us in the twentieth century, who are lulled by long familiarity with the effect of Browning on most later English poetry, to credit him with the full brilliance of his novelty. After he had found the principle that governed his mature practice, finding it by writing 'Italy'—the poem later called 'My Last Duchess'—for publication in the third number of *Bells and Pomegranates* (November 1842) and following it up, three years later, with 'Home Thoughts from Abroad', 'The Tomb at St. Praxed's Church', and the twin poems later called 'Meeting at Night' and 'Parting at Morning', he was incapable of putting pen to paper without creating a poem markedly different not only from other people's poems but from his own. This principle, especially as it applied to form, impressed G. K. Chesterton, but he did not see it as novel in its time. It took hold of English poetry, and has not yet relaxed its grip. If any poet or novelist deserved comparison with Lyell and Darwin it was Browning. Even Carlyle's influence spent its force sooner than Browning's has. More thoroughly even than Tennyson, he destroyed what remained of the allegiance, strong in the eighteenth century, to the 'kinds'—to pastoral, satire, elegy, and so on—and showed poets that because matter was inevitably new, as it always had been at least when good poets were treating it, it had a right to a new form. It was partly on that principle that some critics objected to Arnold's mourning his friend Clough—a conspicuously 'new' man—in the traditional form of the elegy complete with swains and reeds, Corydon, Plato, and Proserpine. We cannot imagine

Browning writing so of a dead friend. Rather he wrote a *La Saisiaz*.[1] Clearing poetry of the kinds, he also demonstrated that matter for the new poetry could be picked up anywhere, and that the whole of it, modern and ancient together, was suitable for expression in verse. This was also being demonstrated by Tennyson but more defiantly by Browning, for instead of making what Arnold saw as the 'unpoetical' present take its place in poetry that remained as patently beautiful as Keats's, he accommodated it in a new sort of poetry, whose poeticalness might escape those readers of Keats and Tennyson who were too exclusive and inflexible.

On one occasion he named Keats as the important nineteenth-century poet, crediting him with discovering the precious murex that was to become all the rage:

> Hobbs hints blue,—straight he turtle eats:
> Nobbs prints blue,—claret crowns his cup:
> Nokes outdares Stokes in azure feats,—
> Both gorge. Who fished the murex up?
> What porridge had John Keats?

The continued fertility of Keats was undeniable. By Hobbs, Nobbs, Nokes, and Stokes Browning no doubt denoted the Spasmodics, but greater poets than they were benefiting from the 'azure'. Tennyson incurred a debt to Keats on several counts, however distinct was the scientific flavour of his descriptions from the Shakespearian flavour of Keats's; Rossetti, also, for his medievalism and, later, for the coloured luxuries of his *House of Life*. By 1853—two years before Browning's 'Popularity', which includes the stanza just quoted—Arnold had published 'The Scholar Gipsy', and was later to publish 'Thyrsis', poems in which he provided what in *On the Study of Celtic Literature* he was to call 'natural magic', a thing he associated, as far at least as the nineteenth century went, with Keats, if not with him only. All these

[1] See pp. 356–7.

declare debts to Keats, and it may have been Browning's poem that prompted Saintsbury to the epigram: 'Keats begat Tennyson, and Tennyson begat all the rest'. If so, it made Browning pay heavily for his generosity, and did him, not to mention Wordsworth, a grave injustice. In nineteenth-century poetry the parallel stream of Wordsworth flowed quite as powerfully as that of Keats, and persisted longer, and the powerful Browning stream longer than either.

Browning did not often refer to Wordsworth; but what he took in from him he took in from the circumambient air—by the thirties and forties no writer could escape Wordsworth.[1] One of the accidental links between the two was a liking for the interestingness of things, irrespective of their aesthetic status. When in 'The Female Vagrant' Wordsworth describes nocturnal thieves, he speaks of their hanging on tiptoe as they lift the latch, and of their 'gloomy lantern' and 'dim blue match'. When Browning describes a nocturnal incident in 'Meeting at Night', he also records the 'blue spurt of a lighted match'. What other two poets of their time, who were not writing satires, would stoop so low into the up-to-date 'unpoetical'? To both of them fact, and things as they come, were sacred, their value for the aesthetic sense taking second place to their value for the intelligence. They enlarged their aesthetic sense indeed by taking advantage, as not all poets had dared to, of the law Aristotle had noted, and which Browning's Fra Lippo Lippi has made memorable:

> ... we're made so that we love
> First when we see them painted, things we have passed
> Perhaps a hundred times nor cared to see ...
> ... Art was given for that ...

[1] What he stood for was passing even into the novel, sometimes with his name attached—he was constantly being invoked in title-page and chapter-heading epigraphs. And also into prose of thinking—the title-pages of all five volumes of Ruskin's *Modern Painters* were weighted with a paragraph-long quotation from *The Excursion*.

Wordsworth could not live up to his discovery completely—in 'The Blind Highland Boy', he first set the boy afloat in a 'Household Tub', but was prevailed upon by the reviewers to think again, whereupon he substituted on Coleridge's suggestion a 'Turtle-shell'. Browning was always wholly unrepentant. He saw that poems could be poetical as Brueghel's pictures were, that the oddity of things and their grotesqueness were a delight to men, that when placed in verse a change comes over them, which in the hands of the incompetent is bathos, but not in the hands of a Browning. There is no bathos in him, whatever he lugs into the lines.

Another accidental link with Wordsworth is plain. The *Poems* of 1807 included a group called 'Moods of My Own Mind', and one of its constituents, 'Gipsies', showed him engaged characteristically:

Yet are they here?—the same unbroken knot
Of human Beings, in the self-same spot!
   Men, Women, Children, yea the frame
   Of the whole Spectacle the same!
Only their fire seems bolder, yielding light:
Now deep and red, the colouring of night;
   That on their Gipsy-faces falls,
   Their bed of straw and blanket-walls.
—Twelve hours, twelve bounteous hours, are gone while I
Have been a Traveller under open sky,
   Much witnessing of change and chear,
   Yet as I left I find them here!

   . . . . . .
   Behold the mighty Moon! this way
   She looks as if at them—but they
Regard not her:—oh better wrong and strife,
Better vain deeds or evil than such life!
   The silent Heavens have goings on;
   The stars have tasks—but these have none.

Here Wordsworth records what struck him on a certain actual or imagined occasion, and, being Wordsworth, invokes the universe to support his conclusions—as it happens invoking a principle favoured by Browning, the preference of any activity to sloth. In writing such casual things his practice overlapped with what was to be Browning's. This was most noticeable in poems where Browning's thinking had most bearing on his own times. Such poems as *Christmas Eve and Easter Day*, *La Saisiaz*, and *Parleyings with Certain People of Importance in their Day* are constructed on the lines of 'Gipsies' and the more extended 'Resolution and Independence'—in other words, they represent the poet as thinking while experiencing. Wordsworth, though he has many poems in which he is participating much less than in these, is scarcely ever absent from them entirely. In this Browning differs from him. Whereas Wordsworth often represents himself as thinking about what has come his way, the thinking in Browning's poems is usually entrusted to the people he has put into them, and whom he credits with experience of their own. Wordsworth is royal in his world, Browning more democratic. He would not be found using the phrase 'my own mind' in a poem, let alone in a title. Rather, it is the word 'dramatic' that figures in his collective titles.

The choice of Keats as fisher-up of the murex amounted to a comment on Browning's early passion for Shelley. In that same *Men and Women* in which 'Popularity' appeared Shelley was not forgotten, but was mentioned only as a 'personality':

> Ah, did you once see Shelley plain,
>   And did he stop and speak to you?
> And did you speak to him again?

There had been an allusion to him earlier than this, but not by the plain name that Browning gave him in those striking lines of 'Memorabilia'. In the youthful *Pauline* he had been called magnificently but unexplainingly 'Suntreader'. A passion for Shelley, or for a similar poet, is often a biological necessity for certain adolescents. What the boy Browning saw plain in the poetry was not so much the 'Ode to the West Wind', in which by a great effort Shelley had subdued his weaknesses, as things like 'Alastor', where those weaknesses were indulged. Even in *Pauline* an occasional sharpness of descriptive phrase suggested his later defection, and he soon outgrew his infatuation, though never wholly his Shelleyan verbosity.

There had been much energetic fumbling before Browning achieved at the age of 33 his strikingly original masterpieces. *Pauline*, for all its 'spasms', was a remarkable poem with striking phrases, and the *Paracelsus* of 1835 and the *Sordello* of 1840 are rewarding if we have the patience or sympathy to look among the leaves for the occasional berry. Of the total of eight *Bells and Pomegranates*, the yellow-wrappered series that ran from 1841, when he was 29, to 1846, the six that consist of plays are of mainly minor account—Browning, like so many aspirants, lacked a number of the many gifts that make a great writer of poetic drama. All these impressive writings showed how long he could remain fumbling, and what energy he could put into it. To that generalization *Pippa Passes* is partly an exception. It had appeared as the first of the series, and had had this to commend it, that it adopted the novel procedure of making Pippa, the young silk-weaver on a day's holiday, intervene unwittingly in the lives of the several groups of people who happened to hear her songs. The matter accordingly was provided with a form such as it took a Browning to invent. The matter, however, lets down the brilliance of the form by not being dramatic enough—what it exhibits is animated toys that Browning is playing with rather than human beings so real as to have demanded his help to express themselves. It was the two later *Bells and*

*Pomegranates*—*Dramatic Lyrics* and *Dramatic Romances and Lyrics*—in which by some miracle fumbling had been replaced by its opposite. By and large the poems in these two booklets achieved the classical. They were not so recognized by Arnold—if they came his way—yet 'My Last Duchess' and 'The Tomb at St. Praxed's Church' qualify, *mutatis mutandis*, for the compliment he was to pay to Greek plays, whose alleged effect on the audience he described in the preface to the *Poems* of 1853:

... then came the Poet, embodying outlines, developing situations, not a word wasted, not a sentiment capriciously thrown in: stroke upon stroke, the drama proceeded: the light deepened upon the group: more and more it revealed itself to the rivetted gaze of the spectators: until at last, when the final words were spoken, it stood before him in broad sunlight, a model of immortal beauty.

The plain difference is one of scale; that difference, however, matters less than it might because of the intensity of Browning's human matter. 'Immortal beauty' is not too strong praise for their effect, if it is not too strong for that of a Greek play. From first to last Browning is too often, it may be admitted, 'capricious'—that vice was a *bête noire* for Arnold as also for Newman. But here and elsewhere, Arnold ought to have admitted in return that, with complex matter to deal with, Browning displayed in these poems the opposite virtue of control.

For the production of elegant poems he got little encouragement from his age. The best help—of the kind that the author of the classical 'Pied Piper of Hamelin', which also appeared in *Bells and Pomegranates*, might have been expected to welcome—was offered by the comic poets. It was by contract, as it were, that Praed, Hood, and Barham had written scrupulously—a ragged and clumsy comic poet is rejected at sight as incompetent. Browning, with little to encourage him, wrote 'My Last Duchess'. He might so easily have remained the sort of poet inaugurated by *Pauline*. The Spasmodics did. Accordingly, we must honour whatever it was—a something within him moral and intellectual rather than, first of all, aesthetic—which enabled him to become a great poet, even if he was always liable to lapse into carelessness—frisky, restless, hasty— and so to lack the uniformity of greatness that was Milton's, Pope's, or Tennyson's. All Browning's poems, however, have so many scraps and bones of greatness to them that enough of quantity is added to turn the scale. His good poetry attained the requisite massiveness. Hopkins, who, like so many, learned from him, and who, like everybody else, saw his defects, spoke of the 'great body of genius' presented in *The Ring and the Book*. And his image may be expanded—the great body is indubitably alive if not entirely presentable. In places it is better when seen not too closely. To Dr. Leavis Browning was not a great body of genius but a 'great lump' in the midst of nineteenth-century poetry, but the image can only be accepted if the same term is applied to a mountain, which no climber would allow.

I have called Browning democratic in his love for people. He is among those great poets whose imaginations seek the company of their fellows by the hundred, concerning themselves, to quote *Paracelsus*, with 'the everlasting concourse of mankind'. Landor compared him to Chaucer. Browning struck a balance between the claims of man and nature, not as Wordsworth did, but in the way of many of the greatest novelists. He acknowledged the existence of rocks and stones and trees as intimately part of the common man's experience. Indeed, in his earlier work he often allowed them more than their due importance. This was why Arnold in the late forties saw him (along with Keats) as 'prevailed over by the world's multitudinousness'; and there was one moment in *The Ring and the Book* when he was quite prevailed over—the moment when he spoke of a peacock's egg (III. 63–5). Arnold, however, might have allowed that, if Browning was overwhelmed, it was in that part of the world's multitudinousness which, except for the satirists, poets had badly neglected. It is beautiful things in that multitudinousness that poets usually select. In an essay that was to become famous Bagehot marked Browning off from Tennyson (and Wordsworth) according to the aesthetic criterion of his preference for the grotesque. His poems accordingly righted a balance, the balance that Keats, Tennyson, Arnold, and Swinburne upset, by demonstrating that external nature included many things that interest rather than enchant the eye. While his poems include as many natural things as theirs, they are brilliantly odd things, or brilliantly odd aspects of such things as are usually claimed as wholly beautiful. Some of the quotations I shall make for other purposes illustrate his grip on this brilliance and oddity. Here are examples from his later work: from 'James Lee's Wife':

The swallow has set her six young on the rail,
    And looks sea-ward:
The water's in stripes like a snake, olive pale
    To the leeward,—
On the weather-side, black, spotted white with the wind:
    'Good fortune departs, and disaster's behind,'—
Hark, the wind with its wants and its infinite wail!

from 'Caliban upon Setebos':

Yon otter, sleek-wet, black, lithe as a leech;
Yon auk, one fire-eye in a ball of foam,
That floats and feeds; a certain badger brown
He hath watched hunt with that slant white-wedge eye,
By moonlight;

from the 'Parleying' with 'Gerard de Lairesse':

... morning's laugh sets all the crags alight
Above the baffled tempest: tree and tree

Stir themselves from the stupor of the night,
And every strangled branch resumes its right
To breathe, shakes loose dark's clinging dregs, waves free
Its dripping glory. Prone the runnels plunge,
While earth, distent with moisture like a sponge,
Smokes up, and leaves each plant its gem to see,
Each grass-blade's glory-glitter;

from 'Bernard de Mandeville':

> Let the oak increase
> His corrugated strength on strength, the palm
> Lift joint by joint her fan-fruit, ball and balm,—
> Let the coiled serpent bask in bloated peace,—
> The eagle, like some skyey derelict,
> Drift in the blue, suspended, glorying ...

Unlike his fellow poets in what he chooses, he is unlike
them again in often choosing to speak of the thousands of
things that man has made for himself out of the natural
materials local to his hand. His poems, like a salesman's
catalogue, are crammed with them. In this he resembles
the novelists—only among them is there a comparable
abundance of interesting household and urban artefacts.
When he is playing the descriptive poet, it is not often, as
with the poets, for the sake of describing them, but
because the people he is writing about can only be understood if what they are living alongside is participating in
their lives. It was according to this literary necessity that
in *The Ring and the Book* we are told just where the poet
came upon the book in question:

'Mongst odds and ends of ravage, picture-frames
White through the worn gilt, mirror-sconces chipped,
Bronze angel-heads once knobs attached to chests,
(Handled when ancient dames chose forth brocade)
Modern chalk-drawings, studies from the nude,
Samples of stone, jet, breccia, porphyry
Polished and rough, sundry amazing busts
In baked earth, (broken, Providence be praised!)

A wreck of tapestry, proudly-purposed web
When reds and blues were indeed red and blue,
Now offered as a mat to save bare feet
(Since carpets constitute a cruel cost)
Treading the chill scagliola bedward:

That list, compiled with Dickensian particularity, is
intimately part of a poem on the large scale, because
intimately part of the poet's experience on that 'memorable day'. He looked into the book in which he found his
story because he was in the habit of looking into everything that came his way. Browning's frequent use of a
person other than himself, as in the dramatic monologues, excludes irrelevant description because the person is plausibly a person. In some of Tennyson's poems
of the same kind, the person is implausible, being, as it
were, partly a sight-seeing person, and therefore not so
typical a human being as are Browning's, who attend
only to such things as pertain to their urgent business.
Tennyson's Œnone, for all her grief, has time to paint
pictures of where her grief began. She is partly a sight-
seeing person, whereas Browning's 'Childe Roland',
who has his eyes everywhere, is looking for something.
In 'James Lee's Wife' the much intertwisting of life and
things is according to the sort of life represented—that of
a plausible woman, who, in the absence of her husband,
has no one to talk to, and occupies herself with what her
eye falls on as she stands at the window, by the fireside, in
the doorway, walks along the beach, and so on. This is
the opening of the section of the poem sub-titled 'Among
the Rocks':

> Oh, good gigantic smile o' the brown old earth,
>     This autumn morning! How he sets his bones
> To bask i' the sun, and thrusts out knees and feet
> For the ripple to run over in its mirth;
>     Listening the while, where on the heap of stones
> The white breast of the sea-lark twitters sweet.

> That is the doctrine, simple, ancient, true;
>> Such is life's trial, as old earth smiles and knows.
> If you loved only what were worth your love,
> Love were clear gain, and wholly well for you:

Things participate not only in her feelings, but in her thinking. We note further that the landscape itself is interesting—brilliantly so—rather than beautiful, as another autumn landscape was to Keats, but not for the humane and urban Donne, who found it coloured 'like an oft-dryed garment'. In this poem of Browning's place is described as it is in *Maud*, the poem of Tennyson's that Browning most admired, the two poets writing for once almost to the same principle. Usually Browning reversed the proportions allotted by Tennyson to human and external nature, reversed them so plainly that he was once unfairly charged with having no great love for rocks and stones and trees. Denying the charge, he added, too quickly to please some of his fellow poets, 'But I love men and women better'.[1] He brought out this preference pointedly when, in a letter to Isa Blagden, he contrasted the way Tennyson dealt with the catastrophe in 'Pelleas and Ettarre' and the way he himself would have done.

Pelleas has witnessed the treachery of Gawain and Ettarre, and left them asleep with the 'naked sword athwart their naked throats':

> And forth he past, and mounting on his horse
> Stared at her towers that, larger than themselves
> In their own darkness, throng'd into the moon.
> Then crush'd the saddle with his thighs, and clench'd
> His hands, and madden'd with himself and moan'd:
>> 'Would they have risen against me in their blood
> At the last day? I might have answer'd them
> Even before high God. O towers so strong,
> Huge, solid, would that even while I gaze
> The crack of earthquake shivering to your base
> Split you, and Hell burst up your harlot roofs

[1] W. H. Griffin and H. C. Minchin, *Life of Robert Browning* (1910), p. 39.

Bellowing, and charr'd you thro' and thro' within,
Black as the harlot's heart—hollow as a skull!
Let the fierce east scream thro' your eyelet-holes,
And whirl the dust of harlots round and round
In dung and nettles!

Browning drew the inevitable contrast:

We look at the object of art in poetry so differently! Here is an Idyll about a knight being untrue to his friend and yielding to the temptation of that friend's mistress after having engaged to assist him in his suit. I should judge the conflict in the knight's soul the proper subject to describe: Tennyson thinks he should describe the castle, and the effect of the moon on its towers, and anything *but* the soul.[1]

It is a hasty comment, suggesting a confusion between Pelleas and Gawain. In Gawain's 'soul' there is no room for 'conflict'; and there is more than description of moonlight in the passage. But it is true that if Browning had written the story, there would have been more thinking. At first sight, therefore, it is a surprise to find in 'Memorabilia' that what the 'I' of the poem opposes to the memorability of 'Shelley plain' is that of a 'moulted feather, an eagle-feather', as if the 'I' were a naturalist—until we see that the real subject of the poem is the quirks of human memory. Who would believe that a man's memory, with all that could have loomed large in it, should have given such prominence to a discarded feather! Many writers, since Browning's day, have chimed in with their own instances of this incalculable behaviour of the memory. Many novelists have. And it is with novelists that Browning belongs, even more than with poets. The book in which 'Memorabilia' appeared had for title *Men and Women*. Usually, as usually in Dickens, things perform a function as part of the richly social lives of his personages. That is why there are so few beautiful things in Browning's poetry after 1842—there

[1] *Letters of Robert Browning*, ed. T. L. Hood (1933), p. 134.

had been much description of beautiful things in the earlier work. They are absent for the same reason as they are usually absent from our human lives. Like Dickens, he sees that men and women live among things that match people in mainly being not beautiful but grotesque or odd. When we get what comparatively speaking is a set-piece of description, its presence is often according to a stricter principle than the old one that poetry has always liked descriptions. There is often a firm psychological permission and intellectual justification for it.

Browning's love of things leads him to discover imagery that works as well as sits and smiles. Much of the meaning of 'The Bishop Orders his Tomb at St. Praxed's Church' exists in the images describing the 'lump, ah God, of *lapis lazuli*' hidden away by the bishop against its decorating his tomb:

> Big as a Jew's head cut off at the nape,
> Blue as a vein o'er the Madonna's breast

—the first image is that of a persecuting Christian, and the second shows him not only thinking of the Madonna, but thinking of her as if she were his mistress. The power to speak so powerfully flashes out in the account of how the door opened to the deceiving knock of Guido:

> Wide as a heart, opened the door at once.

For Browning, as for Dickens, people meant first of all individuals. Some of them were more typical than others—that is, they belonged to types that were more plentifully stocked with human beings. To see how similar is Browning's interest to Dickens's, we might compare the lines from 'How it strikes a Contemporary':

> I only knew one poet in my life:
> And this, or something like it, was his way . . .
> He stood and watched the cobbler at his trade,

> The man who slices lemons into drink,
> The coffee-roaster's brazier, and the boys
> That volunteer to help him turn its winch ...
> He took such cognizance of men and things,
> If any beat a horse, you felt he saw;
> If any cursed a woman he took note;
> Yet stared at nobody,—you stared at him,
> And found, less to your pleasure than surprise,
> He seemed to know them and expect as much.

—we might compare those lines with 'how it strikes' Dickens when Nicholas Nickleby's coach is preparing to start for Yorkshire, with the news-vendor offering the travellers their last chance of the morning paper, and the coachman and attendant comparing notes for the last time on the subject of the way-bill.[1] Both writers hit off human types by showing them performing a typical action. The matter Browning excelled in using was the matter he discovered in others by an effort of what might be called the intellectual imagination. In the preface he wrote for a volume of fabricated letters of Shelley, he distinguished (not without dust and heat) poets objective and poets subjective—say, those taking to the dramatic form and the lyric respectively. He was more of the former kind than of the latter, more other-regarding than self-regarding. It was in accord with a sound instinct that he came to look outward as often as possible: he ran the risk of being cloudy—sometimes perhaps fatally—when being least like a novelist.

People, usually people one at a time, who are made so as to seem actual to the reader, but who are shown more briefly and solitarily than in a novel or play—these are among Browning's best creations. Even the more straightforward of them have distinctiveness—by straightforward I mean traditionally of the stock of any poet. Take 'The Flower's Name', the first of the two 'Garden Fancies' (first published in 1844). The synopsis

[1] See pp. 126–7.

of its matter given by Mrs. Orr[1] is as follows: 'A lover's reminiscence of a garden in which he and his lady-love have walked together, and of a flower which she has consecrated by her touch and voice: its dreamy Spanish name, which she has breathed upon it, becoming part of the charm.' At the bottom of this poem, then, is that stock figure, the lover doing homage to his lady in a garden. This is the first stanza:

> Here's the garden she walked across,
>     Arm in my arm, such a short while since:
> Hark, now I push its wicket, the moss
>     Hinders the hinges and makes them wince!
> She must have reached this shrub ere she turned,
>     As back with that murmur the wicket swung;
> For she laid the poor snail, my chance foot spurned,
>     To feed and forget it the leaves among.

The garden is anybody's, and the woman any woman. Even poems that are little more than jingles are about people: the claret-flask cooling in the pond in 'Nationality in Drinks':

> Our laughing little flask, compell'd
>     Thro' depth to depth more bleak and shady;
> As when, both arms beside her held,
>     Feet straightened out, some gay French lady
> Is caught up from life's light and motion,
> And dropped into death's silent ocean!

'Sibrandus Schnafnaburgensis' is the second of the 'Garden Fancies'. The incident related in it takes place mainly in a garden. But the garden is not there for its beauty, but because the process of rapid decay described could happen only there—the book read 'under the

---

[1] In 1855 she published her *Handbook to Browning's Works*, which Browning had seen and consented to; she added to it and revised it at least up to the sixth edition of 1891. Its main usefulness lies in the lucid prose summaries she provides for the poems.

arbute and laurustine' is deliberately dropped down a crevice in the trunk of a plum-tree and 'fished' up again a month later:

> So, I took pity, for learning's sake,
>   And, *de profundis, accentibus laetis,*
> *Cantate!* quoth I, as I got a rake,—
>   And up I fished his delectable treatise.
>
> Here you have it, dry in the sun,
>   With all the binding all of a blister,
> And great blue spots where the ink has run,
>   And reddish streaks that wink and glister
> O'er the page so beautifully yellow:
>   Oh, well have the droppings played their tricks!
> Did he guess how toadstools grow, this fellow?
>   Here's one stuck in his chapter six!

The big shock, however, is not that this is what can happen in that lovesome thing, a garden, but that the import of the laboratory process is criticism of an ancient pedant.

Then, again, the plain course for one writing on drinks would be to write as if autobiographically, recalling occasions when various drinks had meant something worth recalling. This course, or something like it, Browning did follow in the claret poem quoted above—'My heart sank with our claret-flask'. In the next, however, his attention shifted from himself to picturing the swashbuckling Hungarian for whom, he assumes, Tokay was invented. The third recounts the historical incident when beer was drunk to Nelson's health off Cape Trafalgar. Even in the jingles there is solid humanity, and sometimes much of it, and little of Browning. The same is true of a much greater poem, the 'Soliloquy of the Spanish Cloister', greater because, among other things, it finds room for more humanity still. It is the sort of poem that makes possible such stanzas as the following:

There's a great text in Galatians,
  Once you trip on it, entails
Twenty-nine distinct damnations,
  One sure, if another fails:
If I trip him just a-dying,
  Sure of Heaven as sure can be,
Spin him round and send him flying
  Off to Hell, a Manichee?

In his love poetry Browning not only resembles the novelists, but resembles them when at their least trammelled. The inhibitions forced on nineteenth-century novelists were not so strictly forced on poets. Readers did not so much object to outspokenness in verse. They felt poets to be privileged as novelists are not, that poetry is 'only' poetry after all, and that in poetry any baser matter is less offensive by being mixed up with roses and sunsets. Browning's love poetry showed up Tennyson as unnecessarily squeamish. He spoke out where Tennyson hinted, he criticized where Tennyson accepted. Tennyson did hint more frankly later on, particularly in 'Vivien' (1859) and 'Lucretius' (1869), the second written at a time when what he called the 'poisoned honey stolen from France' was being insinuated into the poems of Swinburne. But Browning had been outspoken from the forties. The result is that a much more complete and close account of sexual love is provided in his poems than in the poems and novels of his contemporaries. Other poets did not take advantage of their opportunities, or not so fully as he. Rossetti—in *The House of Life*—and Swinburne were to be as daring, but not so complete in range. Thackeray, George Eliot, and Meredith could only hint the completeness that interested them. What we miss in their novels we find in Browning.

He is entirely content to be human. Look at the

following poem, ironically called 'Poetics', which should
be read slowly, so as not to overlook the punctuation:

'So say the foolish!' say the foolish so, Love?
'Flower she is, my rose'—or else 'My very swan is she'—
Or perhaps 'You maid-moon, blessing earth below, Love,
That art thou!'—to them belike: no such vain words from
  me.

'Hush, rose, blush! no balm like breath,' I chide it:
'Bend thy neck its best, swan—hers the whiter curve!'
Be the moon the moon: my Love I place beside it:
What is she? Her human self,—no lower word will serve.

So much for the critics who think Browning was
interested in love only as the source of problems. In *In
Memoriam* Tennyson looks forward to man's 'working
out the beast', and to the dying in him of the ape and tiger.
Browning would have thought twice before applauding.
Much as he admired the intellect and the social aspirations
of man, he admired equally the animal in him. He saw
that intellect had usually, perhaps always, to wait on the
body and the body's attainment of satisfaction. In 'the
Last Ride Together' he writes:

    Then we began to ride. My soul
    Smoothed itself out, a long-cramped scroll
    Freshening and fluttering in the wind.

And the thinking arrived at by the lover in that poem is
partly the product of the bodily pleasures of riding. In
'Bishop Blougram's Apology' comes the devastating
suggestion that a vision of truth depends on bodily
condition:

    ... don't you know,
    I promised, if you'd watch a dinner out,
    We'd see truth dawn together?—truth that peeps
    Over the glass's edge when dinner's done,
    And body gets its sop and holds its noise
    And leaves soul free a little ...

Browning would have greeted with a delighted guffaw the suggestion that his optimism had its origin in his own physical well-being. In one of the best of the *Parleyings* he rounds on the critic-biographer who reported, falsely as Browning asserts, that Francis Furini, the Italian artist, arranged in his will for the burning of his many paintings of the nude. His retort has been shown to have been made partly in the interests of Pen Browning, his son, to whose paintings certain critics were raising objections. What he said in the 'Parleying', however, he might have said at any time:

> I trust
> Rather, Furini, dying breath had vent
> In some fine fervour of thanksgiving just
> For this—that soul and body's power you spent—
> Agonized to adumbrate, trace in dust
> That marvel which we dream the firmament
> Copies in star-device when fancies stray
> Outlining, orb by orb, Andromeda—
> God's best of beauteous and magnificent
> Revealed to earth—the naked female form.

To speak fairly, Browning sometimes thought that physical love when it engaged the whole man, mind, body, and spirit, was enough in itself, and sometimes that it led man to see a 'widening glory' beyond itself.

Browning acknowledges frankly that love exists much more widely than in marriage. He wrote of lovers who are in love, whether or not their love is legalized:

> Then a mile of warm sea-scented beach;
> Three fields to cross till a farm appears;
> A tap at the pane, the quick sharp scratch
> And the blue spurt of a lighted match,
> And a voice less loud, thro' its joys and fears,
> Than the two hearts beating each to each!

When illicit love had been treated in poetry it had usually been in poetry that condemned or deplored it; but in this

poem Browning celebrates, between the lines, the happiness of the stolen encounter, which has 'joys' as well as
'fears'. So also in 'Confessions':

> What is he buzzing in my ears?
>   'Now that I come to die,
> Do I view the world as a vale of tears?'
>   Ah, reverend sir, not I!
>
> What I viewed there once, what I view again
>   Where the physic bottles stand
> On the table's edge,—is a suburb lane,
>   With a wall to my bedside hand ...
>
> At a terrace, somewhere near the stopper,
>   There watched for me, one June,
> A girl: I know, sir, it's improper,
>   My poor mind's out of tune.
>       .  .  .  .  .  .
>   As she left the attic there,
> By the rim of the bottle labelled 'Ether',
>   And stole from stair to stair,
>
> And stood by the rose-wreathed gate. Alas,
>   We loved, sir—used to meet:
> How sad and bad and mad it was—
>   But then, how it was sweet!

He sees it as all so much gained that people are in love. In
'De Gustibus' his blessing falls on

> ... those two in the hazel coppice—
> A boy and a girl ...
> Making love, say,—
> The happier they!

(That was in 1855, by which time 'respectability' was
growing very stuffy: but twenty years earlier, when at
least a little more frankness was allowed, Tennyson had
gone out of his way to legalize a similar country couple:

Or when the moon was overhead,
Came two young lovers lately wed …)

One of Browning's poems is called 'Respectability', a title which, being his, must always have been read as a challenge. The scene is laid in Paris. The argument runs something like this:

If the world had happened to bless our plighted but unwedded love, how long we should have been before we really understood the world's true character and 'what it fears'. How long we should have lived among respectable folks before we had dared to act our love truly and, ignoring wind and rain, wandered in the Paris night, watching the city waken up to its real life.

Yes, the world does not actually forbid love; it allows it if it remains a matter of superficial blandishments. What lengths men have gone to have its good word! At the newly founded Institute the radical Montalembert is being received by the royalist Guizot. Would you believe it! Come on down this alley way, and let's get away from the mockery.

Feeling respectability to be unclean, they feel what every couple feels when their love is 'true'. Illicit love of the right sort is preferable to wedded love of the wrong sort. The point of 'The Statue and the Bust' is that a loving adultery is better than a loveless marriage. It is equally obvious to Browning that marriage is the thing for lovers to aim at, if only because it brings them into the world that men and women inhabit by daylight. 'By the Fireside' records a reminiscence prompted by the presence of children playing about his chair. Marriage is obviously convenient, but that is all he can say in its favour: that love should be true, is enough for him. And in *The Ring and the Book* he makes amply clear what a loveless marriage is like. Pompilia is speaking:

… Guido—who stood eyeing him,
As eyes the butcher the cast panting ox
That feels his fate is come, nor struggles more,—

While Paul looked archly on, pricked brow at whiles
With the pen-point as to punish triumph there,—And said
'Count Guido, take your lawful wife
'Until death part you!'

                    All since is one blank,
Over and ended; a terrific dream.
It is the good of dreams—so soon they go!
Wake in a horror of heart-beats you may—
Cry 'The dread thing will never from my thoughts!'
Still, a few daylight doses of plain life,
Cock-crow and sparrow-chirp, or bleat and bell
Of goats that trot by, tinkling, to be milked:
And when you rub your eyes awake and wide,
Where is the harm o' the horror? Gone! So here . . .
        . . . By special grace perhaps,
Between that first calm and this last, four years
Vanish,—one quarter of my life, you know.

The fiction that marriage is a happy-ever-after is less interesting than fact. In some of his greatest poems he achieves the profundities of, say, 'Any Wife to Any Husband' and 'Adam, Lilith and Eve'.

Browning's soundness on the subject of love was attested beforehand by Dr. Johnson, who allowed that while there might be advantages for adult people in retiring into the life of monks and nuns, this retirement should be forbidden to youngsters, who lack knowledge of their natures, which is the point Fra Lippi makes, and the justification, no doubt, for the bishop's ordering his tomb—he gloats over the sexual life he has achieved despite his vows, which achievement makes the jealousy of Gandolf all the sweeter. For Browning the bishop is not entirely a rogue. Trollope saw that love made men into poets—poets of the Byronic sort.[1] Browning saw that it also made them into clowns. In 'A Lovers' Quarrel'

[1] See p. 259.

the reason why a hasty word cannot be accepted as final is
that their love has been of the right sort:

> Teach me to flirt a fan
> As the Spanish ladies can,
>   Or I tint your lip
>   With a burnt stick's tip
> And you turn into such a man!

Trollope must have half envied the daringly truthful
Browning, who, being as he claimed 'free of [language's]
four corners', was free of love's also, and did not shrink
from showing how silly lovers are, which might have
offended the readers of novels.

No wonder Henry James wrote: 'If Browning had
spoken for us in no other way, he ought to have been
made sure of, tamed and chained as a classic, on account
of the extraordinary beauty of his treatment of the special
relation between man and woman.'[1]


Some of the people, then, that Browning writes of are
as ordinary as the people in novels of Thackeray and
Trollope. Unlike Thackeray, however, and like Dickens
and even Trollope, Browning knew that ordinary people
like to read of the sensational. The mid-century was
expressly the age of the 'sensation novel', the principle of
which is partly an affirmation of the literary ideal of
Thackerayan truth, and partly a denial of it. The matters
serving sensation writings may be combined variously.
Mrs. Radcliffe had thrilled her readers with Gothic horrors encountered in foreign parts, and was intent on
accounting for the horrors in practical terms. She was
interested in truth, therefore, but preferred it both horrifying and foreign, and drawn from the past or the
present. Collins and Reade wanted the thrills to be

[1] 'Browning in Westminster Abbey' (1890); collected in *English Hours*
(1905).

English and up to date, but were not so much concerned with verisimilitude. When we read their thrilling stories we raise objections as stolid human beings, even if they are overborne. We know from our own experience that the person for whom a conversation was vital would not be likely to overhear it by chance from behind a gravestone, that a particular mode of escape from a burning windmill would not be physically possible. To read their novels is to be delighted with the actuality of gravestone and windmill, and to know that thrills are possible in St. John's Wood or Sheffield—but also to be ashamed of ourselves as adult readers reading on through the falsity of such coincidences and feats as are a condition of the thrills and progress of the story. Browning's relation to these novelists could easily be plotted. He preferred to contrive his sensations abroad, whether past or present—those of *The Inn Album* are exceptional in happening in Wales. But he did not outrage our sense of the verisimilitude of events. When the reviewer of *The Ring and the Book* said that to read it was like reading a newspaper he spoke accurately; in his day newspapers reported criminal cases in full. Browning's 'sensations' are credible; indeed it was from newspapers and law-reports that he had borrowed them. Browning's love of sensation was equalled by his love of fact—a favourite word of his, as of Reade's.

Instances of his sensational people and events have already been mentioned. Several of those people are mildly sensational in being eccentrics. Even in his jingles he indulged eccentricity, as Dickens indulged it. The flask of claret in the pond might well have conjured up for Dickens the sensational foreign corpse it conjured up for Browning. As a boy he had had the run of his father's eccentric library of old books, and made the most of the freedom, celebrating it *in extenso* in the late *Parleyings with Certain People of Importance in Their Day*. The matter of *The Ring and the Book* is gutter-press matter. A sub-title in

*Bells and Pomegranates*, III, is 'Madhouse Cells', and covers two poems later given the titles 'Johannes Agricola in Meditation' and 'Porphyria's Lover'. But how many of the people in his poems could have inhabited those cells! The Duke of Ferrara would certainly qualify for inclusion under the sub-title. The very opening of the poem raises our suspicions:

> That's my last Duchess painted on the wall,
> Looking as if she were alive; I call
> That piece of wonder, now: Fra Pandolf's hands
> Worked busily a day, and there she stands.

'Last', besides being unfeeling, suggests a string of wives. Then, again, the picture is a fresco, and we assume the date to be that when frescoes were popular in Italy. Browning was among the pioneers in the study of the Italian Renaissance, and in that age a work of representative art was judged by its literal accuracy as representation. To say that the portrait of a woman looked 'as if she were alive' was, therefore, the highest praise. The Duke we see as an up-to-date *cognoscente*, and his fresco is evidently first-rate. To speak so of one's dead wife, however, merely as an art critic would, is to add to the callousness already suggested by 'last'. It is only later that we piece together the evidence that the portrait's subject might still be alive in fact, had it not been for the Duke's arrangements. Directly or indirectly, he has murdered his Duchess, and placed her as an object on a par with her portrait, just as he has placed the duchess for whom he is now in treaty on a par with another noteworthy *objet d'art*:

> ... We'll meet
> The company below, then. I repeat,
> The Count your master's known munificence
> Is ample warrant that no just pretence
> Of mine for dowry will be disallowed;
> Though his fair daughter's self, as I avowed

> At starting, is my object. Nay, we'll go
> Together down, sir. Notice Neptune, though,
> Taming a sea-horse, thought a rarity,
> Which Claus of Innsbruck cast in bronze for me!

As the poem has proceeded the Duke has revealed himself as a monster.

It is to people as interesting as the Duke that Browning gives 'dramatic monologues'. The human matter he put into them, though often eccentric, implies something about everybody, whether eccentric or not. Browning must be credited with the discovery that, from the point of view of the individual, at least some of the acts he is blamed for seem to himself, if not innocent, at least less guilty than they seem to others. This may be merely one more instance of self-deception: it was Newman who discovered that we cannot be too suspicious of ourselves. What matters is that here is an apologia poured out by a human being called on to take stock of himself. Most of us would be appalled by the challenge. What is plain, however, is that whatever the honesty or dishonesty of the confession, the matter is human at its ripest and profoundest. That is why this particular literary form attracted Browning, and attracted him to expand it as he did for *The Ring and the Book*. He may almost be said to have invented it, perhaps helped by the appearance in 1824 of James Hogg's *Confessions of a Justified Sinner*. Introducing a reprint of this classic in 1947 André Gide compared it to the speech Browning gives to Johannes Agricola, the founder of the sect of Antinomians. The reader of such outpourings yields his sympathy or not as he judges the evidence, but the fame of Browning's poems of this kind is a proof that their interest is universal. Another thing in their favour is that though they are 'dramatic' monologues, and so not about Browning, the reader forms a picture of their writer as he reads them.

Altogether, the open-mindedness and breadth of sympathy attested by them in all their variety and numerosity—there are nine of them in *The Ring and the Book*—remove Browning out of the novels of Dickens into those of George Eliot. As we listen to what is being said we forget that Browning is listening to what he himself has created. He cannot acquit Guido of his murders, but he listens to him for the length of some 20,000 lines before he is sentenced, and to some 2,500 more after, surely an unparalleled feat of creative patience over a malefactor. And Browning allows so much in palliation. He gives full weight to Guido's education and the morality of his class:

> Weigh well that all this trouble has come on me
> Through my persistent treading in the paths
> Where I was trained to go ...

Furthermore, Browning is prepared to allow for his ill luck. When it was touch and go, the wrong person opened the door for him:

> Then was I rapt away by the impulse, one
> Immeasurable everlasting wave of a need
> To abolish that detested life. 'Twas done:
> You know the rest and how the folds o' the thing,
> Twisting for help, involved the other two
> More or less serpent-like: how I was mad,
> Blind, stamped on all, the earth-worms with the asp,
> And ended so.

He goes even further and deeper, giving Guido the devastating lines:

> What shall I say to God?
> 'I am one huge and sheer mistake,—whose fault?
> Not mine at least, who did not make myself!'

Browning cannot bear to think that this is the end; and already, in the preceding book the Pope has seen beyond it. Guido has appealed to him, and is condemned to death—the only hope for him lying in the very 'suddenness of fate', the momentary vision of the truth:

So may the truth be flashed out by one blow,
And Guido see, one instant, and be saved.
Else I avert my face, nor follow him
Into that sad obscure sequestered state
Where God unmakes but to remake the soul
He else made first in vain; which must not be.

The mid-century was a time for sensations of the mind in unprecedented abundance. They flowed in from geology, physics, and biology, all of which disturbed the long-established authority of the Bible and Christianity. Browning, like Tennyson, was much concerned with these mental sensations. As thinkers the two poets were of similar stature. We have no right to ask a poet to be a thinker as Hume was a thinker. It is enough if he has hunches. He may try to draw his intuitions into a system, but usually it amounts to little more than giving them repeated and varied expression. What we demand of him is poetry, whether or not he is providing would-be-great thinking in it. Browning did not forget this desideratum. Even in *La Saisiaz*, which his phrase, 'mere grey argument', might seem to describe, there is poetry—feeling and music and imagery. He chose for it the vigorous if 'falling' metre of 'Locksley Hall', and gave the thinking a fully described occasion. He records all that is relevant of an actual experience. He had planned an ascent of Mount Salève near Geneva with his friend Miss Anne Egerton Smith, who, a few hours before the start was planned for, suddenly died. Under the impact of this sensational death, Browning represents in the poem a record of what may well have taken place, even if not so promptly—his climbing the mountain alone after the funeral, five days later:

Five short days, sufficient hardly to entice, from out its den
Splintered in the slab, this pink perfection of the cyclamen;

Scarce enough to heal and coat with amber gum the
    sloe-tree's gash,
Bronze the clustered wilding apple, redden ripe the
    mountain ash:
Yet of might to place between us—Oh the barrier! Yon
    Profound
Shrinks beside it, proves a pin-point: barrier this, without a
    bound!
Boundless though it be, I reach you; somehow seem to
    have you here
—Who are there. Yes, there you dwell now, plain the four
    low walls appear;
Those are vineyards they enclose from; and the little spire
    which points
—That's Collonge, henceforth your dwelling. All the same,
    howe'er disjoints
Past from present, no less certain you are here, not there:
    have dared,
Done the feat of mountain-climbing,—five days since, we
    both prepared.

The thinking in the poem is presented as being done during that day on the mountain, as the thinking of the pupils about their grammarian is presented as being done while they carry the body to its mountain burial-place. Leslie Stephen took *La Saisiaz* as an instance of Browning's parochialism as a thinker: Browning, he alleged, did not seem to know that the thoughts he was thinking were old.[1] It was the familiar complaint against poets adventuring into the field of more professional thinkers—Dr. Johnson had charged it against the author of *An Essay on Man*. But he also allowed Pope poetical merit, and this must also be allowed Browning, who drops such lines and phrases as 'the city's congregated peace of homes and pomp of spires', 'truth—Thunderpealed by God to

---

[1] 'He repeats the most familiar of all arguments ... as if they had never occurred to anyone before' ('Browning's Casuistry', *National Review*, 1902, p. 541).

Nature', and 'Roughness of the long rock-clamber lead not to the last of cliff'.

Here and elsewhere Browning shows men concerned with a matter of much importance in his day, the religion of the various churches. Whole books have been written about the usefulness of his poems to Christians and others, and especially to Christians of the wilder kind who do their thinking under the Nonconformist umbrella. More than that of Carlyle, Clough, and Arnold, Browning's thinking about religion has a Christian colouring as well as a theistic. Though in *Christmas Eve and Easter Day* he represents himself as finding what finally he most admires in a back-street chapel, his imagination was much taken up with the churches he found in Italy, and the way of life of the Roman clergy. There was more to keep the eye busy in the elaborate Italian churches. He shared the interest, also, of the new historians of religion, and in 'Caliban upon Setebos' made a contribution to 'natural theology' as well as to great poetry. There is much about the more recent history of religion in 'Bishop Blougram's Apology', where Browning was speaking some of his own best thoughts, and not simply providing an interesting ecclesiastic with an explanation for his tenure of a dazzling social position. He might have denied it. In 'House' he insists that the whole front of a dwelling must come down before the complete being of the occupant stands confessed: he ends by quoting from Wordsworth's sonnet on the sonnet 'With this same key / Shakespeare unlocked his heart', adding sceptically:

Did Shakespeare? If so, the less Shakespeare he!

For Browning the dramatic poet is the greatest among poets, and he himself was more a dramatic than a lyric poet. The ideas he put into his poems are, then, the less likely to be his own. Certainly we are not warranted in making out that he was 'sincere' in them in the sense that, say, Newman was in the *Apologia*—or, for that matter, Kingsley in his attack on Newman. But we can perhaps distinguish between what Browning says about people who might have existed as they do for him in any age, and his treatment of those who, whether of his own age or not, are represented as thinking about matters of much urgency in his own age. What Browning said in his poems about religion, therefore, is likely to be not 'apologetic' and explicatory, but the best general thinking Browning himself could do on the topic. The matter in itself is mainly of historical importance—we today are free to read the religious poems irrespective of whether what is said in them was originally 'sincere' or not. Browning's first readers took what was being said about burning issues as what the writer himself thought, using all his powers to achieve truth irrespective of person.

Where 'Bishop Blougram's Apology' is concerned the question is the more literary because of the unusual form that poem takes. The body of it consists of what the bishop said to a certain journalist, but to that is added an appendix in which the poet takes over from the bishop, to this effect:

> For Blougram, he believed, say, half he spoke.
> The other portion, as he shaped it thus
> For argumentatory purposes,
> He felt his foe was foolish to dispute.
> Some arbitrary accidental thoughts
> That crossed his mind, amusing because new,
> He chose to represent as fixtures there,
> Invariable convictions (such they seemed
> Beside his interlocutor's loose cards
> Flung daily down, and not the same way twice)
> While certain hell-deep instincts, man's weak tongue
> Is never bold to utter in their truth
> Because styled hell-deep ('tis an old mistake
> To place hell at the bottom of the earth)

He ignored these,—not having in readiness
Their nomenclature and philosophy:
He said true things, but called them by wrong names.

The appendix is brilliant, but may be read as evidence
that, having written his poem, Browning felt its argument would be found intolerable. The opposite view has
been taken recently, ascribing to the bishop a tongue
which, for the occasion, waggles in the cheek. For me,
then, the bishop's arguments are Browning's, and so
any man's, if men had the courage to admit as much. In
other words great weight must be allowed to this superb
passage:

      And now what are we? unbelievers both,
      Calm and complete, determinately fixed
      To-day, to-morrow, and for ever, pray?
      You'll guarantee me that? Not so, I think,
      In no-wise! all we've gained is, that belief,
      As unbelief before, shakes us by fits,
      Confounds us like its predecessor. Where's
      The gain? how can we guard our unbelief,
      Make it bear fruit to us?—the problem here.
      Just when we are safest, there's a sunset-touch,
      A fancy from a flower-bell, some one's death,
      A chorus-ending from Euripides,—
      And that's enough for fifty hopes and fears
      As old and new at once as Nature's self,
      To rap and knock and enter in our soul,
      Take hands and dance there, a fantastic ring,
      Round the ancient idol, on his base again,—
      The grand Perhaps! we look on helplessly,—
      There the old misgivings, crooked questions are—
      This good God,—what he could do, if he would,
      Would, if he could—then must have done long since:
      If so, when, where, and how? some way must be,—
      Once feel about, and soon or late you hit
      Some sense, in which it might be, after all.
      Why not, 'The Way, the Truth, the Life?'

Weight is claimed for this passage by the very magnificence of its poetry. It is saying that the rationalist and the materialist have themselves moments when experience points out two ways to walk along. If the Christian, or more generally the supernaturalist, chooses the one along which the materialist cannot follow him because of the weight he gives to other experiences, had not the materialist better let the Christian be, and not claim his own path to be the only one? The argument continues unflaggingly almost throughout the remaining 700 lines. The poem is not a *tour de force* on the part of a bishop worldly in part, but the thinking of Browning himself, who, because of his fear that it would offend, affected in his appendix half to withdraw it.

Browning's love of thinking is the special reason why he gave lovers so big a place in his poems. He was interested in what engages their intellects. Love provides so many reasons for thinking. If they are doing nothing beyond feeling, they engage him only for a moment—like the two in the coppice, 'making love, say,— / The happier they!': to which he adds:

> Draw yourself up from the light of the moon,
> And let them pass, as they will too soon,
>   With the beanflowers' boon,
>   And the blackbird's tune,
>   And May, and June!

Let them pass, he is saying, till they mature into the complicated creatures I prefer to put into my poems. Interested in men and women, he honoured their complexities, opening them up for special study more persistently than any poet had ever done before. What Virginia Woolf praised in *Middlemarch* ('one of the few English novels written for grown-up people') can be transferred to Browning's poems—they treat of matters that engage all human beings who have survived a score or so of years, whatever the quality of the intellect that is available to deal with them. 'By the Fireside' analyses all that prompted the decision of the moment when the lovers bound themselves in marriage—with the strange discovery that the vital push was administered by the forest the two happened, as it were, to be in the midst of:

> ... we were mixed at last
> In spite of the mortal screen.
>
> The forests had done it ...

Many of Browning's people are interested in the idea which, in many forms, occupied the nineteenth century—that of change, decay, growth, development. Paracelsus has a remarkable excursus on the divine creation, in his last speech:

> and God renews
> His ancient rapture! Thus He dwells in all,
> From life's minute beginnings, up at last
> To man—the consummation of this scheme
> Of being, the completion of this sphere
> Of life: whose attributes had here and there
> Been scattered o'er the visible world before,
> Asking to be combined. ...

And Cleon, one of the 'men and women', exists to argue the inevitability of progress from the minds of one age to those of the next, and of a life on earth to a better one after it. Browning liked the sort of thinking prompted by times of transition—a word that in the nineteenth century came to denote 'the passage from an earlier to a later stage of development or formation'. In 'An Epistle Containing the Strange Medical Experience of Karshish, the Arab Physician', as also in 'Cleon', he showed the addition made by Christianity to Jewish and Greek thought. For the purposes of suggesting the former process he enlarged 'Saul', originally a *Bells and Pomegranates* poem, for inclusion in *Men and Women*.

In the individual Browning saw transition as often happening suddenly, which was how the scientists were coming to see it. The well-known phrase in the dedicatory letter of 1865 to the revised text of the bewildering *Sordello* attested as much: Browning noted what it ought not to have been necessary to state, that 'my stress lay on the incidents in the development of a soul: little else is worth study'. His dramatic monologues are the monuments to moments of this importance.

Like Tennyson, Browning grounds his belief that the soul is immortal in the process he sees active in the entire universe. He almost welcomes man's imperfections because of the pleasure to be taken in improving. In the 'Grammarian's Funeral' he gives the idea its most vigorous expression:

> Oh, if we draw a circle premature,
>   Heedless of far gain,
> Greedy for quick returns of profit, sure,
>   Bad is our bargain!
> Was it not great? did not he throw on God,
>   (He loves the burthen)—
> God's task to make the heavenly period
>   Perfect the earthen?

And its most stately expression in 'Abt Vogler': the musician has been extemporizing,

> Well, it is gone at last, the palace of music I reared ...
> Never to be again! But many more of the kind
>   As good, nay, better perchance: is this your comfort to
>     me?
> To me, who must be saved because I cling with my mind
>   To the same, same self, same love, same God: ay, what
>     was, shall be.

> Therefore to whom turn I but to Thee, the ineffable
>   Name?
> Builder and maker, Thou, of houses not made with
>   hands!

What, have fear of change from Thee who art ever the
    same?
Doubt that Thy power can fill the heart that Thy power
    expands?
There shall never be one lost good! What was, shall live as
    before;
The evil is null, is nought, is silence implying sound;
What was good, shall be good, with, for evil, so much
    good more;
On the earth the broken arcs; in the heaven, a perfect
    round.

Browning's thinking includes thought individual and
general. Some of it could have been done only by an
individual who nevertheless could be scarcely other than
typical of a group, large or small. The rest was that of
Everyman. It is seldom that we get this universal thinking from the novelists he otherwise so much resembled.

They do not generalize so freely into passages such as
Blougram's about man's voyage across life, or into things
like:

Ah, but a man's reach should exceed his grasp,
Or what's a heaven for?

Browning's 'Nationality in Drinks' reminds us how
much attention was being given to the characterization of
the nations, especially those of Europe and America. All
told there is probably as much about nations as about
external nature in nineteenth-century literature. In one
field Browning was among the pioneers. His bringing in
Spaniards was unusual—Richard Ford's epoch-making
*Handbook* did not appear till 1845, which was three years
after the 'Soliloquy in a Spanish Cloister', and the year
following 'Garden Fancies'—and his brief excursions
into Hungary and Russia were also surprising at that date.
Again, he pioneered the exploration of Renaissance Italy,
and Ruskin's praise of the St. Praxed's poem was all the
more solid for that poem's being what was surely the

very first study of that period—he said of it in *Modern Painters*, IV (1856):

I know no other piece of modern English, prose or poetry, in which there is so much told, as in these lines, of the Renaissance spirit,—its worldliness, inconsistency, pride, hypocrisy, ignorance of itself, love of art, of luxury, and of good Latin. It is nearly all that I said of the central Renaissance in thirty pages of the *Stones of Venice* put into as many lines, Browning's being also the antecedent work.

Swinburne in his attack on Browning in 'The Chaotic School'[1] allowed that 'He has an admirable capacity for compressing as with a vice or screw into the limit of some small monodrame or monologue the representative quality or spiritual essence of a period ...'

Browning was also up to the minute in his interest in Greek (and his neglect of Latin). There was 'Artemis Prologizes' in No. III of *Bells and Pomegranates* (so near and yet so far from the Tennysonian) and 'Cleon' in *Men and Women*, and then, splendidly, *Balaustion's Adventure, including a Transcript from Euripides* (1871), the 'product', as DeVane notes, 'of a life-long interest in Greek drama, and especially in Euripides'—Euripides the psychologist who, as Mrs. Browning said, was to be valued for 'his touchings of things common'.

Modern Italy, however, was his field of special study, much of it being done at first hand, to what effect such poems as 'De Gustibus' and 'Up at a Villa—Down in the City (As Distinguished by an Italian Person of Quality)' exist to show, the ninth of the ten paragraphs of the latter giving something Louis MacNeice might have written:

Ere opening your eyes in the city, the blessed church-bells
    begin:
No sooner the bells leave off, than the diligence rattles in:
You get the pick of the news, and it costs you never a pin.

[1] See p. 9 above.

By and by there's the travelling doctor gives pills, lets blood,
    draws teeth;
Or the Pulcinello-trumpet breaks up the market beneath.
At the post-office such a scene-picture—the new play, piping
    hot!
And a notice how, only this morning, three liberal thieves
    were shot.
Above it, behold the archbishop's most fatherly of rebukes,
And beneath, with his crown and his lion, some little new law
    of the Duke's!
Or a sonnet with flowery marge . . .
Noon strikes,—here sweeps the procession! our Lady borne
    smiling and smart
With a pink gauze gown all spangles, and seven swords stuck
    in her heart!
*Bang, whang, whang,* goes the drum, *tootle-te-tootle* the fife;
No keeping one's haunches still: it's the greatest pleasure in
    life.

Browning was one of the first to see, as Carlyle put it, that the world was rapidly becoming 'one village'. Though he longed to be in England in the spring, he was also happy not to be. He realized the ambition that was already that of the wealthy New Englander—to be thoroughly cosmopolitan, and learned in the European past.

Another topic included in the developing interests of his time found Browning knowledgeable—the topic of music as it exists for executants and theorists. Not many of our poets since the seventeenth century have understood music as a thing made. Browning did, and had all the passionate love of it along with the technical understanding. He recalled how as a child he stole out of bed to hear his mother playing, and when she stopped flung himself into her arms, sobbing 'Play, play'. But he was unusual among poets also because of his skill as an executant and of his knowledge of the principles of harmony—as a youth he planned to compose an opera—and of the history of music. He also recalled that 'I was studying the grammar of music when most children are learning the multiplication table, and I know what I am talking about when I speak of music'. He saw that each age has its own sort of music—in music, he said, 'the Beau Ideal changes every thirty years'. If he had written music as well as he played and listened to it, it would have conformed to the new music of Schumann, Brahms, and Wagner, all of whom he honours in his verse.

Browning's technical interest is exhibited whenever music crops up, as is his aesthetic interest: in 'Master Hughes of Saxe-Gotha' fugues receive the Homeric epithet 'mountainous'; in 'A Toccata of Galuppi's' there is a reading of what is dark to many people:

What? Those lesser thirds so plaintive, sixths diminished,
    sigh on sigh,
Told them something? Those suspensions, those
    solutions—'Must we die?'
Those commiserating sevenths—'Life might last! we can
    but try!'

and one of Browning's supreme moments comes when Abt Vogler speaks of 'the C Major of this life'. Much of his creator exists in that learned phrase[1]—his sanity, his power of making connections, and his knowledge of what music amounts to.

His emotional response was so strong that he came to believe that music, as well as love, held the key to the mysteries of the universe, as his Abt Vogler claimed. The body in love may find further reaches of truth, and the body listening to music also. The scientists were claiming as knowledge only what came in through the senses. Browning would agree but with this difference—that the senses are most helpful when, because of a rise in the rate of the pulse, the mind is least purely an intellect and most

[1] Leslie Stephen complained, 'I don't know what a C Major is' ('Browning's Casuistry', 548).

fully exercising its power to feel. He saw the philosopher
as best employed when, as Newman would say, 'the
whole man moves', the whole man when he was most
alive:

> ... nor soul helps flesh more ... than flesh helps soul.

It may well have been his experiences when sexually
active, and when listening to music, that led him to
denounce the implications of Darwin's theory. As a
young man he had warmed to vague ideas about
development. He loved things on the move, and to see
man; as Herbert Spencer did, progressing quickly along
the endless but muscle-toning road to perfection.

I have noted his contribution to the topic of that æon-
long development that interested Darwin. Because of his
respect for matter he might have been expected to have
responded happily to Darwin's theory. What stood in the
way was his theology. He had accepted the idea of God
the 'all-loving', and had found no difficulty in reconciling
that idea to the presence of evil in the world. He agreed
with what was implied in Blougram's ironic and brilliant
conclusion:

> And that's what all the blessed Evil's for.

Evil existed to allow man to grow by struggling with it.
God, he saw, was cruel so as to be kind. He could accept
everything Darwin advanced, except the absence of God
from his scheme. Browning's God was not even present
obscurely in it—he was 'extinguished'. And so, in one of
the 'Parleyings', he made Furini break out against the
'Evolutionists', on the ground that, as Mrs. Orr succinctly put it:

The Scientist acknowledges no mind beyond that of man; he
seeks the impulse to life within itself, and can therefore only
track it through the descending scale of being into the region of
inorganic atoms and blind force. The *believer* refers that
impulse to a conscious external First Cause, and is content to

live surrounded by its mystery, entrenched within the facts of
his own existence, guided (i.e. drawn upwards) by the progressive revelations which these convey to him.

Henry James beautifully summed up Browning's
claims on the score of his matter:

. . . the great value of Browning is that at bottom, in all the deep
spiritual and human essentials, he is unmistakably in the great
tradition—is, with all his Italianisms and cosmopolitanisms,
all his victimization by societies organized to talk about him, a
magnificent example of the best and least dilettantish English
spirit. . . . He was indeed a wonderful mixture of the universal
and the alembicated. But he played with the curious and the
special, they never submerged him, and it was a sign of his
robustness that he could play to the end. His voice sounds
loudest, and also clearest, for the things that, as a race, we like
best—the fascination of faith, the acceptance of life, the respect
for its mysteries, the endurance of its charges, the vitality of the
will, the validity of character, the beauty of action, the seriousness, above all, of the great human passion.[1]

Equally notable are the words just preceding these,
words in which James notes a deficiency on a score other
than matter: Browning is great, he says, 'in spite of a
surface unsuggestive of marble and a reckless individual-
ism of form'.

The problems raised by Browning's technique are
more complex than James's summary suggests. They
may be said to be posed by my having used, on the one
hand, the word 'classical' and, on the other, the words
'verbosity', 'carelessness', and 'cloudy'. How find the
coin that has these two things for faces? Let me grant at
once that, as to verbosity, Browning did often write at
too great length. Bishop Blougram goes on too long, *The
Ring and the Book*, which is twice as long as *Paradise Lost*,
could have been briefer without loss, and therefore with

[1] 'Browning in Westminster Abbey'.

gain. Even some of the shorter poems could have been
cut. In 'By the Fireside' there is description of place at its
most felicitous:

> A turn, and we stand in the heart of things;
> The woods are round us, heaped and dim,
> From slab to slab how it slips and springs,
> The thread of water single and slim,
> Thro' the ravage some torrent brings!

That is stanza 8. Stanza 9 consists of as felicitous a description of the vast scene spread out before them with a lake
below, and on a level Alps meeting Heaven in snow.
Stanza 10 tells of the way the path proceeds:

> By boulder-stones where lichens mock
> The marks on a moth, and small ferns fit
> Their teeth to the polished block.

Equally felicitous! Then something about the yellow
mountain-flowers, with a spill-over into stanza 12, which
brings in the autumn colouring: 'These early November
hours'

> ... crimson the creeper's leaf across
> Like a splash of blood, intense, abrupt,
> O'er a shield else gold from rim to boss,
> And lay it for show on the fairy-cupped
> Elf-needled mat of moss.

After 'moss' comes a comma in the original that leads to a
description of the mushrooms next the moss ... and so on
until stanza 21. All the stanzas, admittedly, have their
felicities, and the sharp outlines original to Browning,
but there are too many of them on several counts. One
count is according to the general law that meant much for
Dr. Johnson—that a reader welcomes variety. Browning
does pile up variety, but only of things, and so does not
achieve any variety of category. Another count is according to psychological truth: the speaker of the poem is
represented as recalling an 'incident in the development

of a soul'. A certain amount of cataloguing, then, was psychologically necessary—part of the point of the argument is that place can help lovers to turn a corner in their relationship. An excess of it, however, suggests that the lover's temperature is lower than it should be, that his mind is wandering. Stopford Brooke noted Browning's readiness to be led on by the easy pleasure of accumulating details from the 'world's multitudinousness':

There is a fine picture of the passing of a hurricane in *Paracelsus* ... which illustrates this inability to stop when he has done all he needs. Paracelsus speaks:

> The hurricane is spent,
> And the good boat speeds through the brightening
>     weather;
> But is it earth or sea that heaves below?
> The gulf rolls like a meadow-swell, o'erstrewn
> With ravaged boughs and remnants of the shore;
> And now, some islet, loosened from the land,
> Swims past with all its trees, sailing to ocean;
> *And now the air is full of uptorn canes,*
> *Light strippings from the fan-trees, tamarisks*
> *Uprooted, with their birds still clinging to them,*
> *All high in the wind.* Even so my varied life
> Drifts by me.

I think that the lines I have italicised should have been left out. They weaken what he has well done.[1]

Sometimes the length is excessive because of Browning's readiness to accept thought that offers most conveniently. Dryden, who was also given to length, confessed that a rhyme sometimes led him to a thought, and that confession suggests one of the things wrong with *Sordello* which, like Keats's *Endymion*, used the same seductively loose version of the heroic couplet. In some of his poems the great architectural structure helps to keep the detail in its place. We always know where we are

[1] *The Poetry of Robert Browning* (1902), p. 98.

on the vast map of *The Ring and the Book*, or in *Pippa Passes*. But in other works, including later works such as *Fifine at the Fair* and *The Inn Album*, following the main path is embarrassed by undergrowth. We wish that Browning had recalled more often the maxim of Pope:

> But how severely with themselves proceed
> The men who write such verse as we can read!

In the 'Parleying' with Avison, the Newcastle musician of the preceding century, Browning made a virtue of his liking for wandering thought. He tells us at length how he came to think of Avison at all—'first of all, the little fact / Which led my fancy forth'—and so achieves an early instance of the use of casual associations as important matter for literature.

Browning's being 'cloudy' is not altogether a disadvantage. It is not so in 'How it Strikes a Contemporary', the purport of which is the relation of the poet both to the 'man in the street' and to God. The poet is represented as an old-fashioned aristocrat, standing apart from the other men in the street, though observing them closely. What the man in the street sees of the poet is, though strange, clear enough. It is what he is up to when at home that is the mystery. From that address he is thought to write letters to 'our Lord the King', letters that account for what makes the town's news:

> Had he to do with A's surprising fate?
> When altogether old B. disappeared
> And young C. got his mistress,—was't our friend,
> His letters to the King, that did it all?

Whether or not the puzzled man in the street is right about that, he is certainly wrong when he pictures the rest of the poet's domestic life:

> I found no truth in one report at least—
> That if you tracked him to his home, down lanes
> Beyond the Jewry, and as clean to pace,

You found he ate his supper in a room
Blazing with lights, four Titians on the wall,
And twenty naked girls to change his plate!
Poor man, he lived another kind of life
In that new stuccoed third house by the bridge,
Fresh-painted, rather smart than otherwise!
The whole street might o'erlook him as he sat,
Leg crossing leg, one foot on the dog's back,
Playing a decent cribbage with his maid
(Jacynth, you're sure her name was) o'er the cheese
And fruit, three red halves of starved winter-pears,
Or treat of radishes in April. Nine,
Ten, struck the church clock, straight to bed went he.

Such is the gist of the explicit thought in the poem. What it is saying implicitly—and we feel it is saying something—is anybody's guess. Perhaps its Carlylean message is that the poet is a judge, that there is something godlike in his understanding of his fellows. The poem, clear as any poem ever was in so much of what it says, works otherwise through suggestion rather than statement. His method is one alternating patches of clarity with patches of varying obscurity, the former conferring clarity on the latter prospectively and retrospectively. In other words, Browning's methods of expressing the course of his sense resembles his account of the piebald experience of religious faith, in 'Bishop Blougram's Apology':

... That way
Over the mountain, which who stands upon
Is apt to doubt if it's indeed a road;
While if he views it from the waste itself,
Up goes the line there, plain from base to brow,
Not vague, mistakeable! What's a break or two
Seen from the unbroken desert either side?

That method pursues its way against odds. His poems make unusual, sometimes exorbitant demands on the reader. These demands pertain to their matter in the first place, but also to their manner, since the reader's likely ignorance could have been enlightened if the matter had been expressed in a more explanatory way. Browning discussed his manner in 1855 in answer to a complaint from Ruskin:

For your bewilderment more especially noted—how shall I help *that*? We don't read poetry the same way, by the same law; it is too clear. I cannot begin writing poetry till my imaginary reader has conceded licences to me which you demur at altogether. I *know* that I don't make out my conception by my language; all poetry being a putting the infinite within the finite. You would have me paint it all plain out, which can't be; but by various artifices I try to make shift with touches and bits of outlines which *succeed* if they bear the conception from me to you. You ought, I think, to keep pace with the thought tripping from ledge to ledge of my 'glaciers,' as you call them; not stand poking your alpenstock into the holes, and demonstrating that no foot could have stood there;—suppose it sprang over there? In *prose* you may criticise so—because that is the absolute representation of portions of truth, what chronicling is to history—but in asking for more *ultimates* you must accept less *mediates*, nor expect that a Druid stone-circle will be traced for you with as few breaks to the eye as the North Crescent and South Crescent that go together so cleverly in many a suburb.[1]

The brilliant images are as clear as they are original. It is their application to the major term that is disturbing. Browning suggests that his expression is a druid's circle that does duty for thought that exists for him as complete as a Crescent. We are surely entitled to doubt that existence, simply on grounds of what human beings, including poets, are like; simply because anybody who has come by complete thought is proudly aware of its preciousness, and so unwilling to maim it by incompleteness of wording. There is a further ground for

[1] W. G. Collingwood, *The Life and Work of John Ruskin* (1893), I. 199–202. [For Ruskin's letter see 'Ruskin and the Brownings: Twenty-five unpublished letters', ed. D. J. Delaura, *Bulletin of the John Rylands Library*, spring 1972. *Ed.*]

doubt, Browning so often achieving full and clear
expression of thought. The quotations in this chapter are
instances of that. When he is cloudy in expression, we
suspect, then, that he is cloudy of thought. And yet
cloudiness in places is not altogether a disadvantage in
practice. What he said of the progress up the mountain's
side, whether it suits the Christian faith or not, suits the
reader of Browning's poems. Looking at them from a
distance, we see the path run up from base to brow. When
we are actually reading, we lose the path here and there,
but find it again as we proceed. This experience keeps the
brain active. Browning thinks the reader likes a scrap of
puzzle now and again.

Some of his puzzles are puzzles only to those lacking
the information that can be found in a reference library.
They begin in his titles, from *Bells and Pomegranates*
onwards. That promoted phrase (as Browning vouchsafed when pestered) denotes in 'Rabbinical (and Pat-
ristic) acceptations' an 'alternation, or mixture, of music
with discoursing, sound with sense, poetry with
thought'! In this instance, it is not that the symbols were
invented by Browning, but that he chose them from
places rarely frequented—though the two words occur
together at Exodus 28: 33–4, and so were more available
in the mid-nineteenth century than in the mid-twentieth.
His poems loudly call for the annotation he did not care to
provide. Without special knowledge, there are patches
from which we cannot get more than a blurred meaning.
And even when we have the knowledge we need to be so
sure of the context as to give even an occasional run of
simple words the particular meaning Browning requires
of it on this occasion. Take 'Respectability', already
cited.[1] Its last stanza is:

> I know! the world proscribes not love;
>> Allows my finger to caress
>>> Your lips' contour and downiness,

[1] See p. 349.

Provided it supply a glove.
The world's good word!—the Institute!
Guizot receives Montalembert!
Eh? down the court three lampions flare—
Put forward your best foot!

Reading this, we are confused by the exclamation invoking the Institute, and by the named Frenchmen, and only
when we remember that Guizot is a royalist and Montalembert a radical do we get the sense clearly. But that
rocky stretch of the mountain-path could have been
roughly inferred if we had been alert enough to allow
'The world's good word!' an active meaning in our mind,
allowing it to govern the sense of what follows—and so
to see the Institute as the sign of worldly approval, to see
Guizot bestowing that approval, and Montalembert for-
feiting his principles to receive it. Browning expects a
great deal from his readers. That he sometimes expects
too much was a risk he was evidently prepared to take.

His plain justification lay in the multitude of readers
who have insisted on adventuring over his sense. Some
have been like Mrs. Orr, working almost alone, and one
Berdoe in 1891 brought out a Browning *Encyclopaedia*.
Others have sought help widely. T. J. Wise, in his preface
to the reprint of the first five *Bells and Pomegranates* in
1896, happens to mention that 'some twenty or more
Societies have been for the past sixteen years engaged in
studying Browning's works'. To which it is only necessary to add that New England was particularly intent on
the study, which had an effect on T. S. Eliot, whose own
poetry is obscure for the same reasons as Browning's, as
is that of all the many poets who have written in his wake.
Whereas Tennyson asks of the connoisseur of expression
a mainly aesthetic response—that of admiring and wondering at expression perfect at all points (efficiency in
conveying the sense, aesthetic things like music and
verbal colouring)—Browning asks him to participate in a
process of perfecting expression which, already metrical

and alive with his moth-brown colours (so different from Tennyson's rainbow, so much less radiantly sensuous) is not yet wholly complete in point of efficiency. Browning's poems have the advantage that all obscure poetry hopes to reap—that the aesthetic pleasure the reader gets from it is accompanied by a sort of moral pleasure at having passed examinations in intelligence and divination.

And so, at last, to the other, the unimpeachable side of the coin. There is little room for argument about Browning's aesthetic principles in general. He requires us to read attentively, and to attend to several things together. Take, for instance, the poem that Swinburne thought the best, 'Women and Roses':

> I dream of a red-rose tree.
> And which of its roses three
> Is the dearest rose to me?

> Round and round, like a dance of snow
> In a dazzling drift, as its guardians, go
> Floating the women faded for ages,
> Sculptured in stone, on the poet's pages.
> Then follow the women fresh and gay,
> Living and loving and loved to-day.
> Last, in the rear, flee the multitude of maidens,
> Beauties unborn. And all, to one cadence,
> They circle their rose on my rose tree.

To each in turn he offers his love, but in vain—the dancers circle unheeding.

The idea in the poem is the sort that can stand repeated expression, and Browning expressed it succinctly as the conclusion of 'Two in the Campagna':

> Infinite passion and the pain
> Of finite hearts that yearn.

Other ideas, also implicit, are present, or suggestions for ideas. But much is present beside ideas. There is a whole

ballet to look at, and the elaborate stanza scheme. Like
Tennyson, he sometimes fixes into a recurrent pattern
irregularities that in other poets would be merely accidental. The first and alternate stanzas consist of three lines
each, each line having three stresses and the same
rhyme-words, while the stanzas alternating with them
have four-stress lines that conform to a pattern of masculine and feminine rhymes, the last line repeating as a
refrain. The upshot is that the poem is rather about a state
of the male mind than an idea. Browning takes advantage
of what he was to express in *The Ring and the Book*:

> ... Art may tell a truth
> Obliquely, do the thing shall breed the thought

—another instance of his achievement of the lucid expression that argues lucidity of thought.

There is always, furthermore, the maximum of surprise because of Browning's principle of avoiding—to
express it negatively—the traditional forms. (His only
sonnet is very early: the uncollected 'Eyes, calm beside
thee ...') Not only did he avoid traditional forms, he
avoided the traditional music. I have said that if he had
composed 'actual' music it would have been up to the
minute in newness, and new music by a good composer is
always strange to ears schooled to older. It took young
poets to see his greatness: even when we allow for Rossetti's interest in Italian themes, we have to account for
his making a bible out of *Sordello*. I have also said that
Browning avoided beautiful things, and among them
were beautiful lines, lines such as Tennyson could
scarcely avoid writing. Browning preferred hammer-
and-tongs scrunches to flutes that float and hover. The
power to admire this avoidance Hopkins learned from
him, and it accorded with that deep feeling in the age that
literature should not smell of the lamp, should not stand
too far above the sort of prose people write who have no
more consciousness of their employing a medium than

had the uninstructed M. Jourdain. Browning went even further, favouring verse that was more like conversation even than the prose reeled off in a hastily scribbled letter. Rossetti found much to imitate in his rugged metre, and it is obvious that Hopkins owed him much on the metrical score as on the syntactical.

If this informality was Browning's first principle, one would have expected him to write always in blank verse. He did so write on many occasions, and with results that would warrant much scrutiny. Evidence of an unusual sort comes in a *Primer of English Verse* (1892) by a Cornell professor, Hiram Corson:

[The] blank verse [of *The Ring and the Book*], while having a most complex variety of character, is the most dramatic blank verse since the Elizabethan era. Having read the poem aloud to classes every year for several years, I feel prepared to speak of the transcendent merits of the verse. One reads it without a sense almost of there being anything artificial in the construction of the language; and by artificial I mean *put consciously into a certain shape*. Of course it was put consciously into shape; but one gets the impression that the poet thought and felt spontaneously in blank verse. And it is always *verse*—though the reader has but a minimum of metre consciousness. And the *method* of the thought is always poetic. That is saying much, but not too much. All moods of the mind are in the poem, expressed in Protean verse.

In that vast poem he has given each speaker a style of his or her own. An individual style was given to Blougram, who shows a preference for polysyllables (sometimes two to a line), and to Caliban, whose primitiveness is suggested by his odd syntax. Browning has much energy in his rhythms, except for occasional patches of fumbling, and is to verse what Carlyle is to prose. When his verse is blank, it is seen as his partly because it runs into a striking pattern. A single page of Book III of *The Ring and the Book* has these four lines scattered over it:

We want no name and fame—having our own ...
Prepared to pant in time and tune with ours ...
Scintillant, rutilant, fraternal fire ...
A wife worth Guido's house and hand and heart.

Browning's love of patterning, even when writing blank verse, explains why he uses stanzas so often. Occasionally the same (more or less elaborate) stanza form is used for more than one poem, but Browning preferred to give each new poem a new stanza form, as he preferred to give it a new general structure, or its own type of rhyme: 'Pacchiarotto' employs feminine rhymes throughout its long length, some of them trisyllabic. At the base of his poetry is this double wish to be informal and formal, conversational and patterned. Admittedly, his technique cannot sustain the standard set by his felicities. But these felicities are frequent, and there is a pleasure for the reader in the sheer inventiveness that offsets the intermittent failure to sustain competence. One feels that a breeze blows through his workshop, and that a breeze is better than stuffiness, even if here and there a thing is fluttered out of straight.

His love of elaboration is seen in the architecture as well as in the individual bricks and stones of his poem. The reader can receive a poem only as word succeeds word, but he is sometimes aware in reading Browning that words are building up, over and above their immediate function in particular contexts, something both elaborate and on the grand scale. In their bold elaboration of design, *Pippa Passes* and *The Ring and the Book* may be said to have set up new genres. These grand structures provide aesthetic satisfaction. They also contribute to the expression of the sense. *Pippa Passes* is a recommendation of the universe in that, unknown to herself (or himself) a good person can have an effect on others. The architecture of *The Ring and the Book*, simply by existing as a design, demonstrates the complexity of things that from one angle may seem simple, the difficulty of any one person's knowing the ins and outs of events, the shadow of guilt that can be cast on innocence, the many excuses that the guilty can proffer, so hard to be weighed justly. Again, in the 'Grammarian's Funeral' there are four courses, perhaps five, along which the poem progresses simultaneously—the men are climbing a hill, the night is passing into day, the coffin that is being carried contains the body of a man whose life-story, which they are chanting, combines the two movements of bodily decay and of mental growth proceeding from strength to strength—even though the matter for thought is becoming more and more concentrated on details. In that same poem, as it happens, Browning describes the *modus operandi* he himself must have adopted:

> Image the whole, then execute the parts.

(And the stanza proceeds with jubilant extravagance:

> Fancy the fabric
> Quite, ere you build, ere steel strike fire from quartz,
> Ere mortar dab brick!

That final exclamation mark is in part a confession of unrepentant high spirits.) If in the execution of the parts there is some fumbling, we must acknowledge the well fancying of the fabric, the building as a whole.

One of the reasons why Browning elaborated his verse was the opportunities it offered for sharpening his picture of human eccentricity. The 'Soliloquy of the Spanish Cloister' owes part of its sharpness to the exacting metre—exacting because of its demand for feminine rhymes which Browning makes of the difficult sort:

> Whew! We'll have our platter burnished,
> Laid with care on our own shelf!
> With a fire-new spoon we've furnished,
> And a goblet for ourself,

> Rinsed like something sacrificial
> Ere 'tis fit to touch our chaps—
> Marked with L. for our initial!
> (He-he! there his lily snaps!)

Other grotesque rhymes are abhorrence / Lawrence, scarcely / parsley, horsehairs / corsair's. After such fireworks the transition to quiet metres has unusual significance, enforcing the transition to quieter matter. In Browning the most frequent transition is from the elaborate to the simple—to such slippered couplets as those of 'My Last Duchess' or the half-flexible blank verse of the 'Bishop orders his Tomb'. In such poems the metre is enough of itself to proclaim that the lines will be more nearly like the prose we speak, the aim now being to present a person to our deeper, more Shakespearian enjoyment.

The final thing to say about his technique is that not only is it as far away from singing as possible, and as near to speech as possible, but that its speech is rather to be heard than read. To treat it simply as writing is to mistreat it. Browning restored literature to its origins as a thing recited. His verse begs to be heard; and many things in it that look like defects do not sound like them. His early attraction to the stage and persistent liking for dramatic form strike deep; it is as if he continued to write parts for actors—not only his fifty and more men and women, but himself. We know the sound of their voices.

# APPENDIX:
# THACKERAY'S *ESMOND*

Admirers of *Henry Esmond* are open to an obvious challenge.
Prospective readers may point with apprehension at the full
title of the novel: *The History of Henry Esmond, Esq., A Colonel
in the Service of Her Majesty Q. Anne. Written by Himself*, a title
that is followed by a quotation from Horace[1] which, when we
have read the book, turns out to be witty. That complete title
may well suggest difficulties, and admirers of *Esmond* have to
admit them. The line of defence, however, is plain—before
anything else *Esmond* is a novel. What may well be its finest
scene is that in which Beatrix tells Esmond why they cannot
marry,[2] a scene which shows Thackeray as one of our most
perceptive psychologists, and on a perennially interesting
topic not much favoured in the mid-nineteenth century—the
topic of incompatibility as a marriage runs its course. Plainly
the man who could imagine that discussion was not going to
allow anything merely historical to get in the way of its
producing its strongest effect. And we can put it more positively, for *Esmond* is a novel that is a better novel because it is a
historical novel. The history in *Esmond* is an asset. Its action is
set in 'the great world of England and Europe' as it existed in
the latter years of the seventeenth and early years of the
eighteenth century, and Thackeray chose that setting for it
because he found in it a literary inspiration. He saw that it was a
function of his peculiar genius to recreate the past, which may
lie hopelessly dead in history books, but which does not lie
dead for those who read books of memoirs. Such books are the
work of the men who made the times. (*Esmond*, fictitious as it
is, can stand as a handy sample of them.) The past is not dead

---

[1] 'Servetur ad imum / Qualis ab incepto processerit, et sibi constet' (*Ars
Poetica*, 126).
[2] Bk. III, Ch. iv (cf. Ch. vii).

when we read of it in memoirs because memoirs are full of people. Thackeray is so much aware of the peopled past that he goes so far as to say that in the making of history people count more than political principles: 'in my mature years, I own that I think Addison's politics were in the right, and were my time to come over again, I would be a Whig in England and not a Tory; but with people that take a side in politics, 'tis men rather than principles that commonly bind them'.[1] And on another occasion he omits an account of certain 'battles and sieges', riding off on this excuse: 'Go, find them in the proper books; this is only the story of your grand-father and his family.'[2] The excuse is an exaggeration, for Book II of *Esmond* 'Contains Mr. Esmond's military life' in some detail. But it is valid nevertheless. *Esmond* is memoirs, which, being fictitious, make it a novel. The story is one of human beings though it is embroidered on a web of history, or to be more exact, though what those human beings do makes a piece of what we call history. And the people that are Thackeray's subject-matter are of all sizes from 'the d——d psalm-singing cobbler' who is a member of the mob that insult the Esmond family with its cries of 'No Popery!',[3] from Nancy Sievewright, the black-smith's daughter, 'a bouncing, fresh-looking lass, whose face was as red as the holly-hocks over the pales of the garden behind the inn',[4] from the French soldiers who fled 'even ... without their soup-kettles'[5]—from all such upwards through-out the many ranks until we confront Louis XIV and Queen Anne. And though Thackeray's main interest is in the high and mighty, his grandees are seen complete, and not simply from the 'official' angle that flatters them. *Esmond* is a novel by a writer who had a theory that history consists in more than gets into books of dynastic and constitutional history: he makes Esmond

wonder shall History ever pull off her periwig and cease to be court-ridden? Shall we see something of France and England besides Versailles and Windsor? I saw Queen Anne at the latter place tearing down the Park slopes after her stag-hounds, and driving her one-

[1] Bk. II, Ch. xii.   [2] Bk. III, Ch. v.
[3] Bk. I, Ch. iv.    [4] Bk. I, Ch. viii.
[5] Bk. II, Ch. xii.

horse chaise—a hot, red-faced woman, not in the least resembling that statue of her which turns its stone back upon St. Paul's, and faces the coaches struggling up Ludgate Hill. She was neither better bred nor wiser than you and me, though we knelt to hand her a letter or a wash-hand basin. Why shall History go on kneeling to the end of time?[1]

And in accordance with that theory this is how a sudden intrusion finds the son of James II:

Would you know how a prince, heroic from misfortunes, and descended from a line of kings, whose race seemed to be doomed like the Atridae of old—would you know how he was employed, when the envoy who came to him through danger and difficulty beheld him for the first time? The young king, in a flannel jacket, was at tennis with the gentlemen of his suite, crying out after the balls, and swearing like the meanest of his subjects. The next time Mr. Esmond saw him, 'twas when Monsieur Simon took a packet of laces to Miss Oglethorpe: the Prince's ante-chamber in those days, at which ignoble men were forced to knock for admission to his Majesty. The admission was given, the envoy found the King and the mistress together: the pair were at cards, and his Majesty was in liquor. He cared more for three honours than three kingdoms; and a half-dozen glasses of ratafia made him forget all his woes and his losses, his father's crown, and his grandfather's head.[2]

And Thackeray claims his theory as a first historical principle. He shows history—as history is dynastic and con- stitutional—turning its course because the people who count most at a crisis are people and nothing more. According to *Esmond* the reason why the Hanoverians followed Queen Anne was that the son of James II was a weakling and a profligate, who at a pinch was less interested in being King of England than in certain other things. Part of the interest of *Esmond* is that a score of great people we have read about in history books, and also in textbooks of literary history—for Thackeray does not forget the great writers of the time—are presented as intimately as Jane Eyre and David Copperfield, though much more briefly.

And there was a further reason why Thackeray was attracted to the time of Queen Anne. He saw in it an

[1] Bk. I (opening).     [2] Bk. III, Ch. viii.

opportunity to endow his novel with an aesthetic value—with a darkness and melancholy against which the scattered patches of sunshine and candlelight show, as in a Cruikshank etching, all the more tenderly. He found in that age something like what Mozart and Beethoven found in the key of C minor. He saw it as coloured with cloud and tempest, an age of close physical danger, of choices which might prove fatal, of 'dark intrigues' and apprehensions, culminating in 'that momentous game ... of which the noblest crown in the world was the stake'.[1] The main actors of the novel are Tories when to be a Tory might mean being a Jacobite, one who gave his first and unalterable allegiance to 'a Papist family [James II's] that had sold us to France',[2] but which having once been royal was royal still by divine right. It is interesting to follow Esmond's meditations on this allegiance and on the things that conflict with it, and to note the place given at a later date to the impatience of the American colonies—'ere long we shall care as little about King George here [in Virginia] and peers temporal and peers spiritual, as we do for King Canute or the Druids'.[3] Such times were the last of the heroic ages because they brought death so near—Jacobitism was treasonable. That age brought death near in other ways—smallpox (almost obsolete by the mid-nineteenth century) turns the course of the story, as does duelling (also obsolete). That death is so near is a great gain for the novel when the novelist can rise, as Thackeray can, to its special opportunities.

All these historical things are a gain to Thackeray's novel because it is a novelist who sees them and uses them. But just because *Esmond* is a novel much of it is outside time. The story is bathed in human feeling—feeling about the jealous love of the sexes and the family—love both glorious and seamy— about human goodness and the lack of it, about costly loyalty and heroism, and about the painful course of time. The passing of time and the constant awareness of what it means to men, and perhaps especially to women, are never touched by Thackeray without his showing himself to be a poet. For *Esmond* is a poetical novel, written in an archaic style that shines with grace.

[1] Bk. III, Chs. x, xii.    [2] Bk. III, Ch. viii.
[3] Bk. III, Ch. v.

Among the things that transcend time is the psychological truth that is the heart of *Esmond*, recurring wherever men and women live together. We cannot speak about its central triumph—the relationship of Esmond with Rachel and Beatrix—without robbing the reader of the pleasure sprung by the great surprise of the book. That surprise has been the source of much comment, but is the sort of surprise that Johnson analysed when he spoke of 'the sublime'—'that comprehension and expanse of thought which at once fills the whole mind, and of which the first effect is sudden astonishment and the second rational admiration'. One of the pleasures of rereading *Esmond* comes from being endowed with the foreknowledge that shows many a quiet remark to be a stroke of irony. During a first reading these strokes of irony are either quite innocent of suggestion or no more than faintly suggestive. They are at most straws in a gentle wind. But when we read a second time we see how brilliant, multitudinous, stealthy, and various are the indications that a surprise is on the way.

*Esmond* has very little of the satiric comedy that is a prime characteristic of Thackeray's genius. But it has everything else.

# INDEX